G r e e n l a n d

Reykjavik

W9-BUG-845

WITHDRAWN

Baffin

Bay

Sirmilik
National Park

Baffin

Island

Auyuittuq
National Park

Davis

Arctic Circle

Melville
Peninsula

Foxe

Basin

Southampton
Island

Iqaluit

Hudson Strait

Strait

Labrador Sea

ATLANTIC

Peninsule
d'Ungava

Hudson Bay

L a b r a d o r

OCEAN

P e n i n s u l a

New

**NEWFOUNDLAND
AND LABRADOR**

& Labrador

ny

Labrador
City

THE EAST

St
ohn's

Natashquan

QUÉBEC

Newfoundland

Sept-Îles

Anticosti I.

CENTRAL CANADA

Chicoutimi

**PRINCE EDWARD
ISLAND**

Channel-Port-
aux-Basques

Ontario

skasing

ONTARIO

Val-d'Or

Timmins

Québec City

Sydney

P.E.I.

New

NOVA SCOTIA

Lake Superior

Sault
Ste Marie

Sudbury

Trois-Rivières

Montréal

Sherbrooke

**NEW
BRUNSWICK**

Scotia

Halifax

Lake Huron

Ottawa

St Lawrence R.

Lake Michigan

Kingston

Oshawa

MONTRÉAL

rtland

N.H.

Wisconsin

Michigan

Toronto

Hamilton

L. Ontario

New
York

Boston

Mass.

London

Niag

acuse

Milwaukee

Detroit

TORONTO

L. Erie

Pennsylvania

New
York

Canada

0   500 km

0   500 miles

N

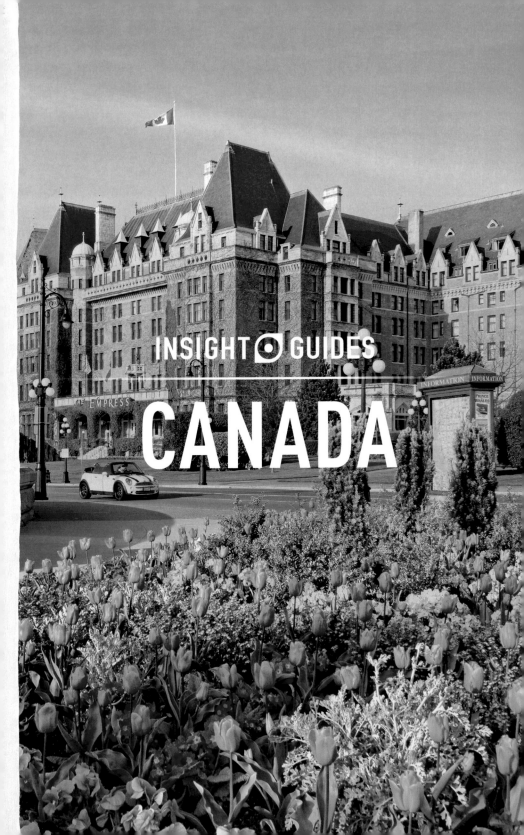

INSIGHT ⊙ GUIDES

CANADA

PLAN & BOOK
YOUR TAILOR-MADE TRIP

BRAZIL CHILE ECUADOR

TAILOR-MADE TRIPS & UNIQUE EXPERIENCES CREATED BY LOCAL TRAVEL EXPERTS AT INSIGHTGUIDES.COM/HOLIDAYS

Insight Guides has been inspiring travellers with high-quality travel content for over 45 years. As well as our popular guidebooks, we now offer the opportunity to book tailor-made private trips completely personalised to your needs and interests. By connecting with one of our local experts, you will directly benefit from their expertise and local know-how, helping you create memories that will last a lifetime.

HOW INSIGHTGUIDES.COM/HOLIDAYS WORKS

STEP 1

Pick your dream destination and submit an inquiry, or modify an existing itinerary if you prefer.

STEP 2

Fill in a short form, sharing details of your travel plans and preferences with a local expert.

STEP 3

Your local expert will create your personalised itinerary, which you can amend until you are completely satisfied.

STEP 4

Book securely online. Pack your bags and enjoy your holiday! Your local expert will be available to answer questions during your trip.

BENEFITS OF PLANNING & BOOKING AT INSIGHTGUIDES.COM/HOLIDAYS

PLANNED BY LOCAL EXPERTS

The Insight Guides local experts are hand-picked, based on their experience in the travel industry and their impeccable standards of customer service.

SAVE TIME & MONEY

When a local expert plans your trip, you save time and money when you book, even during high season. You won't be charged for using a credit card either.

TAILOR-MADE TRIPS

Book with Insight Guides, and you will be in complete control of the planning process, from the initial selections to amending your final itinerary.

BOOK & TRAVEL STRESS-FREE

Enjoy stress-free travel when you use the Insight Guides secure online booking platform. All bookings come with a money-back guarantee.

WHAT OTHER TRAVELLERS THINK ABOUT TRIPS BOOKED AT INSIGHTGUIDES.COM/HOLIDAYS

Trip to Portugal

Every step of the planning process and the trip itself was effortless and exceptional. Our special interests, preferences and requests were accommodated resulting in a trip that exceeded our expectations.

Corinne, USA ★★★★★

Trip to Vietnam

The organization was superb, the drivers professional, and accommodation quite comfortable. I was well taken care of! My thanks to your colleagues who helped make my trip to Vietnam such a great experience. My only regret is that I couldn't spend more time in the country.

Heather ★★★★★

DON'T MISS OUT BOOK NOW AT
INSIGHTGUIDES.COM/HOLIDAYS

CONTENTS

Travel tips

TRANSPORTATION

A – Z

LANGUAGE

FURTHER READING

Maps
Inside front cover Canada
Inside back cover Ottawa; Montreal Metro;
    Toronto Subway and Rapid Transit System

LEGEND
🔎 Insight on
📷 Photo story

THE BEST OF CANADA: TOP ATTRACTIONS

△ **Niagara Falls, Ontario**. It really is spectacular – and there is no charge for the excellent view from Table Rock of the raging waters crashing down over both Canada's Horseshoe Falls and the American Falls. See page 155.

△ **Québec City**. More French than Montréal, this small city is a captivating slice of Europe in North America. Wander round the Old Town and soak up Québec City's unique atmosphere. See page 193.

▽ **Polar Bear Capital**. Churchill, Manitoba, is a very popular attraction as scores of polar bears arrive each fall until the ice on Hudson Bay is solid enough for them to continue their journey. See page 310.

△ **Québec City Winter Carnival**. A celebration of winter, with activities ranging from winter sports competitions to ice-sculpture contests. See page 351.

△ **T. Rex Discovery Centre.** Fossil-hunting is an interesting option in Eastend, Saskatchewan, where one of the world's most complete T. Rex skeletons is on display. See page 302.

△ **The Cabot Trail**. A spectacular 187km (303-mile) drive around Cape Breton, Nova Scotia, that weaves around hairpin bends and tiny fishing villages, from cliff tops to sea level. See page 230.

▷ **Stanley Park**. Vancouver's jewel, a 400-hectare (1,000-acre) evergreen oasis, full of majestic cedar, hemlock, and firs – rimmed by breathtaking views from the 10km (6-mile) seawall that locals jog, in-line skate, cycle, and amble around. See page 257.

◁ **The Aurora Borealis**. Even if you understand the aurora borealis, you will never tire of the magic. Best seen north of 60° latitude, these dancing lights will mesmerize you in any of Canada's three territories. See page 328.

▷ **Calgary Stampede (July)**. One of the biggest rodeo events in the world, with chuckwagon races and every sort of rodeo event imaginable, all surrounded by a midway, cotton candy, and fireworks every night. See page 348.

△ **Signal Hill, St John's, Newfoundland**. The site of the first transatlantic wireless message Marconi received also affords magnificent views over the Atlantic, the harbor, and the city – well worth the half-hour hike. See page 249.

THE BEST OF CANADA: EDITOR'S CHOICE

Lake Brome in fall.

BEST WINTER SPORT DESTINATIONS

Lake Louise. A diverse ski/snowboard area offers infinite and varied terrain in the heart of Banff National Park. See page 292.

Fernie Mountain Resort. In B.C., renowned for its legendary powder and limitless terrain.

Whistler-Blackcomb. Consistently ranked as the top ski resort in North America, with more than 200 trails, three glaciers, 16 alpine bowls, and unlimited backcountry. See page 264.

Mont-Tremblant. The highest peak in Québec's Laurentians, with 95 runs and over 7 hectares (18 acres) of ramps, rails, and jumps, as well as an Olympic-caliber superpipe. See page 191.

Le Massif. In Québec's Charlevoix region, Le Massif has the highest vertical drop in Eastern Canada, and is renowned for its snowfall, averaging almost 7 meters (22ft) per season.

The Largest Skating Rink in the World. In Ottawa, the 7.8km (4.8-mile) Rideau Canal Skateway winds through the capital city, attracting more than 1 million skaters each winter. See page 145.

Skiing in British Columbia.

BEST MARKETS

Byward Market, Ottawa. A traditional farmers' market that still sells all manner of foods, flowers, plants and produce.

Saint John City Market. A lively market full of New Brunswick fare including fiddleheads and dulse. See page 213.

Atwater Market, Montréal. Capturing the spirit of Montréal's French heritage, Atwater offers an enormous selection of fruit and vegetables, cheeses, meats, breads, and pastries.

St Lawrence Market, Toronto. Selling everything from fish and freshly baked bread to Ontario cheese and all sorts of organic edibles. See page 131.

Granville Island Market, Vancouver. An island in the city that combines a food market with theaters, restaurants, and artisans – a place with something for every taste. See page 262.

Granville market in Vancouver.

TOP VIEWS

Cape Enrage, New Brunswick. Just east of Fundy National Park, this view is of rugged, remote beauty above the pounding sea. See page 215.

Terrasse Dufferin, Québec City. For its panoramic views from the base of the imposing Château Frontenac – over the St Lawrence river to the south shore and the distant mountains beyond. See page 194.

CN Tower, Toronto. A favorite icon, including the famous glass floor, where kids can jump up and down 342 meters (1,112ft) above mere mortals below. See page 130.

The Banff Gondola. On Sulphur Mountain, this provides a bird's-eye view of Banff and the Rockies; a great starting point for a mountain hike. See page 291.

Grouse Mountain, North Vancouver. For its stunning views over the city, and as far as the San Juan Islands on a clear day. See page 263.

The CN Tower, Toronto.

Dog sleds in the Yukon.

BEST MUSEUMS

Pier 21, Halifax. More than 1 million immigrants first arrived here from 1928 to 1971, including World War II British "guest" children, post-1945 war brides and thousands of refugees. Their hopes, fears, and tears are captured brilliantly. See page 222.

Museum of Anthropology, Vancouver. The city's most important museum, focusing on the art and culture of British Columbia's First Nations. With a spectacular collection of Haida carvings and totem poles. See page 258.

Royal Ontario Museum, Toronto. Already Canada's foremost museum, when the ROM opened its new glittering, crystal-shaped extension designed by Daniel Libeskind in 2007, it added amazing architecture to its fabulous collections. See page 136.

Musée d'archéologie et d'histoire de Montréal. Hi-tech presentations and archeological finds bring the old city amazingly to life. See page 175.

National Gallery of Canada, Ottawa. If pressed for time, skip everything but the indigenous gallery, which houses both art of the first peoples of Canada, and aboriginal art from other parts of the world. See page 147.

An exhibit from the Museum of Anthropology in Vancouver.

BEST BEACHES

Long Beach. On Vancouver Island's west coast, this is a glorious stretch of golden sand between Ucluelet and Tofino, and a particular challenge to experienced surfers. See page 277.

Sauble Beach. Gracing the Lake Huron shoreline in Ontario, this is a pristine stretch of sand cradled by the shallow warmth of the lake. See page 162.

Sandbanks Provincial Park. Home to three of Ontario's sandiest beaches, each of them great for swimming, windsurfing, sailing, and boating. See page 150.

A beach on Canada's west coast.

British Columbia Legislature,
Vancouver Island.

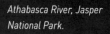
Athabasca River, Jasper
National Park.

Fruit-picking in the Laurentians, Québec.

Mount Seymour Provincial Park.

HOPE AND PROMISE

Charles Dickens once described Canada as a land of "hope and promise." Today it is that and more: a land of exuberant cities, breathtaking scenery, and diverse cultures.

A black bear in Ontario.

The writer George Woodcock said, more than 40 years ago, "The national voice of Canada is muted," and it remains true. Canadians are among the last people to sing the praises of their exceptionally fine land, and proclaiming its attractions has usually been left to foreigners.

"I saw a great and wonderful country; a land containing in its soil everything that a man desires; a proper land, fit for proper men to live in and to prosper exceedingly," observed British Field Marshal Lord Montgomery in 1946.

More than 100 years earlier, another traveler from Great Britain, Charles Dickens, was equally enthusiastic: "Few Englishmen are prepared to find out what it is. Advancing quietly; old differences settling down, and being fast forgotten; public feeling and private enterprise alike in a sound and wholesome state; nothing of flush or fever in its system, but health and vigour throbbing in its steady pulse; it is full of hope and promise."

Squamish Nation annual Pow Wow celebrations.

Nowhere is this hope and promise better demonstrated than in the cosmopolitan cities near Canada's 5,500km (3,400-mile) border with the United States – from Montréal, with its old-world charm and new-age outlook with massive modern and postmodern skyscrapers alongside gracious red-brick mansions; to Toronto, teeming with street energy, theaters, and ethnic restaurants; to Vancouver, on the far west coast, where individuality is a valued trait, and the pioneer spirit of a young culture pervades every aspect of life.

In between, and north of the big cities, lies some of the most beautiful landscape in the world. At last count, there were 46 national parks, home to wild birds and grizzly bears, four national marine conservation areas, and 42 rivers totaling more than 10,000km (6,250 miles) in the Canadian Heritage Rivers System. Over half the countryside is forest, and trees soaring to a height of more than 60 meters (200ft) are not uncommon.

Theaters, art, restaurants, breathtaking scenery. It's time to put all modesty aside, because Canada has a great deal to shout about.

SEARCHING FOR AN IDENTITY

With the history of its peoples spanning thousands of years and a multitude of cultures, a national identity for Canadians is proving elusive.

For the native peoples, the Canadian identity stretches thousands of years into the past – their search is a struggle to retain elements of their ancient culture. Unlike the far more tangible character of the United States, Canada's identity is more reclusive and subtle.

The sense of antiquity and elusiveness in Canadian culture is perhaps the product of its unusual history. As the late Northrop Frye, a noted Canadian intellectual, once observed, the vast majority of early Canadians (with the exception of its aboriginals) were people who did not wish to be in Canada.

The French, abandoned by France after 1763, were left "high and dry" in Québec; the Scottish and Irish were pushed off their lands through the Highland clearances in the 16th, 17th, and 18th centuries and were shipped to Canada; thousands of Loyalists fled the American Revolution and journeyed to Canada in support of British sovereignty; others found their way to Canada because of poverty and persecution.

In short, many of the initial immigrants were fugitives, clinging to their culture and traditional customs, in the hope that they might be able to reproduce in Canada what they had possessed at home. In Canada one experiences echoes of different pasts, all harmonized into a Canadian score.

MULTICULTURALISM

This is not to say that Canada has not had its own particular effect on its inhabitants. The cold, the hostile environment, the bounty of food, the availability of land – all combined to make Canada both a haven and a hell for its first immigrants. Songs, poems and paintings of early Canada celebrate its compassion and callousness. Yet underlying these themes of survival is the notion of multiculturalism.

Playing on Canada's enormous coastline.

From coast to coast, there is no one thing that will mark a person as Canadian except perhaps for the ubiquitous "eh?" everyone seems to use without reservation, as in "It's cold outside, eh?" or "The prime minister's not talking any sense these days, eh?"

In 1971, multiculturalism became an official government policy in Canada (and became an act of law

Within each region there are definite qualities that demarcate Prairie folks from Maritimers, Ontarians from Québécois. The Canadian identity is an odd mixture of assertive regionalism and resigned nationalism.

in 1988). The policy was designed to reflect one of the original principles of Confederation: that Canada become a system of coordination among different but equal parts. As a result there is a certain tolerance of ethnic and religious plurality (the growing numbers of Sikhs, Hindus, Buddhists, Muslims, and Jews attest to this). Canada's international image is promoted as a "mosaic" not a "melting pot."

As a national ideology, the notion of a mosaic neatly fulfils Champlain's original wishes in the 17th century to found Canada on principles of justice and compassion. As an implemented

refugee from Hong Kong who came to Canada with her parents in 1942, held this high-profile post from 1999 to 2005. Michaëlle Jean, an immigrant from Haiti, was Canada's third female, and first black, governor general, serving from 2005 to 2010. Slowly, more and more groups are being represented in positions of power and influence. As with many Western countries a populist movement has been growing in strength in recent years. However, as of 2011, an estimated 20 percent of the Canadian population spoke a language other than English or French in their

An Acadian lighthouse in Grande-Anse, New Brunswick.

Young Inuit girl, Nunavut.

process, however, it falls short of success. John Porter, in his classic *The Vertical Mosaic*, harshly denounced the Canadian mosaic as a highly differentiated, hierarchical structure that forced certain ethnic groups into occupational ghettos. Some critics have claimed that the cultural mosaic has only served to obscure the fact that Canada remains a rigidly class-divided society.

While statistics indicate that the financial, political, and cultural interests in Canada are controlled by a group of just 2,000 people, mostly white males of European descent, this group is changing. Until recently, none was a woman, a member of a First Nation or an Inuit. However, since 1999, two of the country's governors general have been women. Adrienne Clarkson, a

homes, so one can reasonably expect this trend towards multiculturalism to continue.

NATIVE PEOPLES

Perhaps as long as 20,000 years ago, Canada's first inhabitants crossed the Bering Strait to settle the frozen regions of the north. For many millennia, aboriginal life flourished in Canada. This, however, was drastically altered when European explorers, greedy for the riches of Asia, stumbled across the New World and began to colonize North America. Disease, death by gunfire, and forced settlement severely reduced the number of Canada's first populations.

Comprising a little under 4 percent of the total population, Canada's First Nation, Inuit, and Métis peoples continue to struggle against policies that discriminate against them either implicitly or explicitly. Communities that have been forced to live on reserves find themselves in semi-colonial territories where government handouts, "white" schools, and running water are supposed to be accepted as improvements over the old way of life.

Visitors to Canada will frequently encounter a certain tragic pathos in the native peoples here. Reserves are often places of substandard living conditions, severe poverty, neglect, and a deathly lethargy; cheap hotels and broken-down

from the First Nations, land claims and treaty negotiations are identifying ways to correct some of the wrongs of the early settlers and their European rulers. The Canadian First Nations, Inuit, and Métis have emerged as a force to be reckoned with.

FRENCH CANADIANS

When Jacques Cartier established a settlement along the St Lawrence river at the sites of Hochelaga (modern Montréal) and Stadacona (Québec City), little did he know that his fledgling community would become Canada's

Fort Henry Guard musicians, Kingston.

bars frequently house the inner-city aboriginal alcoholic or drug addict.

Responding to a renewal of sorts, since the 1970s, colorful ceremonies and festivals have taken a larger part of First Nations communities, as preservation of culture and the establishment of equality form the focus of their leaders. In those parts of the country where land was simply taken

> *For the French Canadians biculturalism is a matter of being recognized as a founding partner of the nation, and having their children grow up in a French culture.*

"black sheep of the family." Abandoned early on by France and reluctantly adopted by Britain, French Canada continues to embody a fierce ethnic pride, a distinct cultural identity, and a tenacious traditionalism, especially in rural Québec.

A British-dominated Canada often treated the Québécois demands for cultural autonomy as the cries of a spoilt child. But, like dousing an already well-lit bonfire with gasoline, nothing would aggravate French Canadians more than trivializing the issue of French ethnicity in Canada. As a result, French Canadian attitudes towards *les Anglais* (which was just about everybody else) would range from stern disapproval to outright hatred. Many English Canadians were capable of showing the same range.

While there are still, perhaps, some places in Québec and the rest of Canada where a few words in the other's language will get stony and silent stares, bicultural relations are steadily improving. Despite the naysayers, by the beginning of the 21st century, a countrywide French immersion program has more than 2 million English-speaking students studying French as a subject in school, and nearly 30 percent of the population of young people in the country, aged between 18 and 29, are, if not bilingual, at least able to communicate in both official languages. What with these statistics and the

The Scots in particular are proud of the Macdonald, Mackenzie, and other families who provided the first prime ministers, and dominated banking and railway management, as well as the fur and timber trades.

immigrants who traveled directly from England, Canada received many of its British inhabitants via the United States. Loyalist "Yankees" flee-

Aboriginal dancer performing in traditional colorful costume.

downfall of the separatist Parti Québécois (PQ) in Québec's 2003 election, it would appear that there are many more people in Québec and the rest of Canada who are attempting to understand and respect each other's differences.

ENGLISH, SCOTTISH, AND IRISH

Canada was once a predominantly "British" nation. The pomp and ceremony of public events, the ubiquitous portraits of the royal family in hallways and antechambers, the presence of a parliamentary government – all are suggestive of an English ancestry.

The history of Anglo-Saxons in Canada is much more piebald in nature than British traditions might acknowledge. In addition to those

ing the American War of Independence entered Canada in droves during the latter part of the 18th century and tipped the scales in favor of an Anglo-dominated population.

English immigrants were joined by Irish refugees (many of whom were victims of the potato famine) who had come across the Atlantic in search of food and employment. Similarly, Scottish immigrants, pushed off their lands to make room for sheep farms, ventured to Canada. The combination of Irish Catholics and Protestant Scots was rarely harmonious, and riots, usually occurring during one of the annual parades, were common in the19th century.

Today, cultural images of the Irish, English, and Scottish are almost everywhere in Canada, whether it be in the opening session of parliament or in a neighborhood pub. Highland games, Irish folk festivals, and political ceremonies are common sights in each of the provinces.

A glance across a map of Canada will also reveal that many of the towns and cities have been named after a favorite spot or person in the British Isles: Prince Edward Island, Victoria, New Glasgow, Oxford, Windsor, Caledonia, Liverpool.

GERMANS AND SCANDINAVIANS

Next to the French and British, peoples of Germanic stock were among the earliest European

UKRAINIANS

The late 19th century saw the influx of thousands of Ukrainians – "the people of sheepskin coats" as popular journalism of the time named them. Attracted by free farms in the west and undaunted by prairie fields, the first wave of Ukrainian immigrants settled in Saskatchewan, Manitoba, and Alberta. They were later joined by Polish, Czech, Slovak, and Serbo-Croatian immigrants. Canada has the world's third-largest Ukrainian population after Ukraine and Russia.

Brazilian soccer fans celebrate in Montréal.

settlers. Germans came to Nova Scotia as early as 1750 and founded the town of Lunenburg in 1753. This tiny metropolis eventually became a thriving center of Maritime shipbuilding. German Loyalists also immigrated to Upper Canada and established a (still-existing) community in a town they named Berlin, which was later changed to Kitchener during World War I, owing to fear of anti-German sentiments.

Swedes, Norwegians, and Finns have also established settlements in the west that have retained their original ethnic flavor. A group of Icelanders fostered the prairie town of Gimli, "a hallway of heaven," and have managed to thrive on the successful commercial production of two Canadian delicacies: goldeye and whitefish.

THE ASIANS

Abandoning the exhausted goldfields of California, the Chinese first came to British Columbia as miners. Others arrived in the 1880s and were recruited to work in the railway gangs that built the Canadian Pacific. Laboring under duress and in dangerous conditions, many Chinese died in the service of a country that considered them

Next to French Canadians, Ukrainians have, perhaps, the most vocal and assertive sense of a national identity, and pursue recognition of their ethnic heritage energetically.

to be less than human. They were soon joined by Japanese, whose sheer endurance and a knack for frugality enabled them to prosper in the face of racist government policies. Then in 1903 the first Sikhs established a large community.

Jealousy of the Chinese success in developing lucrative commercial enterprises led to the Chinese Immigration Act of 1923, which effectively barred the immigration of Asians to Canada until the 1960s, when immigration policies were relaxed. Hundreds of thousands of immigrants from Asia, including India, Pakistan, Hong Kong,

Taiwan, Vietnam and, more recently, China, came to Canada with dreams of a land of opportunity. Many arrived in Canada under an immigrant investor program, bringing with them money to invest in a business. These more affluent groups have had a huge impact on Canadian society, bringing exciting cultural and social variety to the country and making Canadian cities much more cosmopolitan than many of their neighbors to the south. As their numbers grow, these proud new Canadians are politically active and interested in having a strong voice in their country.

A whale-based business in Victoria.

☉ BLACK CANADIANS

Black slavery was first introduced here by the French through a royal mandate issued by Louis XIV in 1689 that permitted Canadians fully to own African slaves.

By 1783, slavery was well established in Lower Canada, when around 3,500 black Loyalists, who had fought for Britain during the American Revolution in return for freedom, fled to what is now Nova Scotia and New Brunswick. Despite the promises, however, blacks continued to be denied equal status. Farther west, John Graves Simcoe, Upper Canada's first lieutenant-governor, proposed a bill in 1793 that led to the eventual abolition of slavery in Canada. This made Canada an attractive destination for many. As news filtered down to the southern states,

refugee slaves began the often dangerous trek via the Underground Railroad, which brought thousands of fugitives to Canada. When slaves were legally emancipated throughout the British Empire by the Emancipation Act in 1834, the majority of slaves in British North America had already obtained their legal freedom.

By 1960, blacks accounted for approximately 0.2 percent of Canada's population. With immigration policy reforms in the 1960s, the doors opened to increasing numbers of blacks from the Caribbean and Africa. By the 2011 Census, 945,665 Canadians identified themselves as black, around 2.9 percent of the entire population.

Engraving by Edward Finden, from John Franklin's 'Narrative of a Journey to the Shores of the Polar Sea', 1823.

DECISIVE DATES

THE FIRST CANADIANS

70,000 BC–c.AD 1000

First arrivals are proto-Mongolian peoples, followed by several Indian cultures c.8,000 BC, the Inuit in c.6,000 BC, and Icelandic Vikings, who establish coastal settlements in Newfoundland and Labrador c.AD 1000.

EUROPEAN EXPLORERS

1497

John Cabot arrives on Canada's east coast, believing it to be the northeast coast of Asia.

1534

Explorer Jacques Cartier claims Canada for France.

NEW FRANCE

1608

Samuel de Champlain founds Québec, capital of the colony of New France, and establishes a network of trading routes across the interior.

1642

Montréal is founded.

1670

The Hudson's Bay Company, the world's largest fur-trading company, is founded. England begins competing with France in North America.

Immigrants arrive from Europe, 1903.

ENGLISH DOMINATION

1713

England conquers Newfoundland, New Brunswick, and Nova Scotia.

1759

Battle for Québec on the Plains of Abraham. New France becomes a British colony.

1775–83

American Revolution results in United Empire Loyalists moving to Québec, Ontario, Nova Scotia, and New Brunswick.

1791

The colony is divided in two: Upper Canada (later Ontario) and Lower Canada (Québec).

1812

The United States begins a decade of skirmishes with Indians, French, and British in Canada, ending in a stalemate.

1840

The Act of Union combines Upper and Lower Canada.

1857

After gold is discovered along the Fraser river, Britain declares British Columbia a colony.

CONFEDERATION

1867

The British North America Act establishes the Confederation of Canada. Ontario, Québec, Nova Scotia, and New Brunswick collectively form the Dominion of Canada.

1870

Hudson's Bay Company sells Rupert's Land to Canada, sparking an uprising by the Métis. Manitoba, created from parts of Rupert's Land, joins the Confederation. The Northwest Territories are formed.

1871

British Columbia joins the Confederation conditional upon forging a permanent rail link to the West Coast.

1873

Prince Edward Island joins the Confederation.

1881–6

The Canadian Pacific Railroad is built, spearheading countrywide settlement.

1905

Alberta and Saskatchewan are created from the Northwest Territories and join the Confederation.

WARTIME CONFLICTS

1914–18

Canadian troops support Britain, with the taking of Vimy Ridge considered a decisive moment in defining the Canadian identity, notwithstanding more than 10,000 casualties.

World War II poster.

1939–45
World War ll; Canadians suffer heavy losses at Dieppe and invade Juno Beach on D-Day.

POSTWAR GROWTH
After 1945
A new wave of immigration arrives, as does economic prosperity.

1949
Newfoundland joins the Confederation.

1959–62
Two new transport routes stimulate Canada's economy: the St Lawrence Seaway and the Trans-Canada Highway. Toronto emerges as the country's most important industrial center.

CAMPAIGN FOR SEPARATISM
1960
Québec's separation crisis begins with the "Quiet Revolution." The Parti Québécois calls for independence from Canada.

1980
In a first referendum, the majority of Québécois decide to remain part of Canada.

1982–92
Canada Act ends British control and the country receives a new constitution.

1989
Free Trade Agreement between Canada and the USA (NAFTA) leads to increased trade between the two countries.

1995
In a controversial referendum, Québécois vote by a 1 percent margin to remain within Canada.

1999
On April 1, the Northwest Territories are divided, creating Nunavut, a self-governing homeland for the Inuit.

2005
Paul Martin's Liberal government is ousted, ending more than 12 years of Liberal rule.

2006
Stephen Harper leads the recently formed Conservative Party to victory with a minority government.

2008
Québec City celebrates its 400th anniversary.

2011
The Conservative Party wins a majority and undertakes dismantling of much of the Liberal "social safety net" in the hope of reducing budget deficits without increasing taxes.

2012
The Prince of Wales and the Duchess of Cornwall visit Canada as part of the Queen's Diamond Jubilee celebrations.

2015
The Liberal Party wins the November elections; Justin Trudeau becomes PM.

2016
Canada signs milestone Canada-Ukraine Free Trade Agreement (CUFTA).

2017
Wildfires in British Columbia cause the evacuation of 39,000 people.

2018
Doug Ford and the Progressive Conservative Party wins the regional election in Canada's most populous province, Ontario; Canada legalizes recreational marijuana

2019
The XXVII Canada Games will be held in Red Deer, Alberta.

2026
Canada, along with Mexico and the United States, will host the FIFA World Cup.

Québec citizens lobbying for independence in the 1990s.

On Stone by J. Brandard, from the original Drawing by Captain Ross.

SHULANINA.   TULLUACHIU.   TIRIKSHIU.

A NATION IN THE MAKING

The steady population of Canada began around 20,000 years ago with the arrival of Indian tribes and later the Inuit.

The first settlers to arrive in Canada, long before the Europeans, were nomadic bands wandering from Siberia across the Bering Strait. These robust and courageous souls sought a new life in the frozen wilds of northern Alaska and Yukon. They are thought to have arrived some 5,000 to 10,000 years ago. Their reception was not a warm one. Facing bitter temperatures and hostile winds, it is a wonder that they survived in such an unfriendly climate. These first "Canadians" developed a remarkable subsistence technology suited to the brutal environment, and traces of their ancient culture linger. They have come to be known as the Inuit.

THE INUIT PEOPLES

The ancestors of contemporary Inuit needed both intelligence and imagination to thrive in their new continent. If one word can describe the theme of life in their culture, it is survival.

Chief Duck and the Blackfoot family.

> The Inuit spoke Inuktitut, a language with no word for chief or ruler – authority resided within the group. Today, more than 35,000 Canadians claim it as their first language.

The Arctic Inuit are noted because of the simplicity of their hunting and cooking utensils. Bows and arrows made with tips of flint, ivory, or bone were the main means of catching the family dinner. They also created special tools to accommodate the seasonal needs of hunting – and many of these practices remain today.

Archeologists celebrate the Inuit for their ingenious winter ice-spears. The spears have tiny feathers or hairs attached to one end, which the hunter holds over a hole in the ice waiting for movement that would indicate the presence of an animal. This often involves sitting over a hole in the freezing cold for several hours at a time.

Food was a major obsession and they hunted seals, walruses, whales, and caribou. Blubber, meat, and fish were staples and always eaten raw (when they are most nutritious). Partially digested lichen found in a caribou's stomach was considered a delicacy and sometimes created a little diversity in a meal.

Inuit are often associated with dome-like snow huts or igloos. Without trees (and therefore timber) the prospects of constructing even a simple hut were poor – and snow was a readily

> *When natural food supplies ran out, families would move to another area, usually on sleds made of frozen fish or hides – these could be eaten if necessary.*

available resource. Igloos, dwelling structures that are still constructed on occasion by contemporary Inuit, are made of snow blocks – the result looks much like a ski toque. The house

Existing in a harsh and rugged world, Inuit needed "luck" to exist in a world full of malevolent spirits – when a person died, their "luck" had run out. The Inuit philosophy, then and now, can be summed up in a simple sentence: "If you knew of the dangers I live through each day, you would understand why I am so fond of laughter."

WEST COAST TRIBES

As people traveled to other parts of Canada and spread into the plains and woodlands, many distinct languages and cultures flourished.

Champlain's men defeat an Iroquois war party on Lake Champlain, 1609.

consists of one or two interconnecting rooms. Inside, a platform for sleeping or working stands across from the entrance way; an area for animal carcasses and a heating lamp completes the layout.

Early Inuit had no word for chief or ruler. Theirs was a different understanding of authority. In these nomadic bands the underlying theme was a principle of harmony within a family group.

About AD 1250 the Inuit encountered medieval Norse Viking hunters in areas around present-day Newfoundland. From 1570 to the 1850s several European expeditions looking for the Northwest Passage also encountered these resourceful people. The Inuit greatly valued the iron they acquired for harpoon points and knife blades.

Throughout Canada today, one finds evidence of a remarkably rich and varied aboriginal history – a cultural heritage that was greatly disturbed through the process of colonization. The West Coast supported several populations; among these were the Kwakiutl, Bella Coola, Nootka, Haidas, Tsimshian, Coast Salish, and Tlingit Indians. These groups found the Pacific Coast to be extremely abundant in natural resources. The sea provided salmon, halibut, and edible kelp and the forests yielded deer, beaver, and bear.

Unlike the Inuit, the inhabitants of the Northwest Coast were able to make extensive use of timber: the red cedar tree was – and still is – the source of woven bark capes and hats, baskets, wooden implements, and totem poles. They are also known for their huge dugout canoes, often stretching to 20 meters (66ft) in length, and their 80-meter (270ft) long wooden clan houses. The ancestral fishing grounds that still lie along the rugged Pacific Coast were the sites of much activity and often a few weeks of hard work yielded enough food for the year.

Given the bounty of food and building materials, Northwest Coast cultures were able to devote ample time to the creation of objects. Many of their styles and techniques remain in use today, and travelers to the museums and

considered to be a strong interest in "private property and material wealth."

Travelers to this area of Canada will undoubtedly hear of the famous potlatches. These were exchange ceremonies given by a chief and his local group to another chief and his followers. During the ceremony, huge quantities of gifts were given to each guest to assure that they bore witness to all the changes formalized during the ceremonies. Much feasting was followed by lengthy speeches. These celebrations marked a change in the status of a member of the hosting group such as

A 19th century Inuit family in front of their "snow home."

craft reserves note the omnipresence of animals, mythical creatures with protruding canines, and strangely painted human forms. Found on totem poles, houses, canoes, and bowls, these beings, depicted like European crests, became associated with particular family lineages and came to represent rank, wealth, and status.

The material wealth and artistic skills of the Northern Coastal cultures engendered a lively system of trade among tribes – this network was later to become very important to the fur trade in Canada. Nootkas specialized in whale products, while the Haidas mass manufactured ceremonial canoes. The result was a fairly sophisticated practice of interchange. Colonial officials in the late 19th century were disturbed by what they

the movement of an inheritor into an inheritance. Frequently, if two men were eligible to inherit one position, a series of rival potlatches were held. These often involved the destruction of valued property by burning or demolition – sometimes the slaying of a slave was a part of the procedure. The potlatches continued until one contester was "broken" financially and relinquished his claim.

PLAINS TRIBES

Inhabiting yet another area in Canada's broad geographical milieu were the Plains tribes: the Blackfoot, Cree, Ojibwa, Sarcee, and Assiniboine tribes. Each group possessed a distinctive language so incomprehensible to the others that sign language was used to facilitate trade.

The Blackfoot tribe used to be the great hunters of the Rockies' foothills and prairies. Buffalo then satisfied all their needs – for food, clothing, and shelter.

Yet each tribe was bound to the others through their dependency on the buffalo. The buffalo was the nucleus of life. From the buffalo came pemmican (a protein-concentrated and later eaten. Dependency on the buffalo made the Plains peoples nomadic.

Such mobility demanded a transportable house; it is from this that the origin of the teepee can be traced. A conical-shaped hut with an aperture at the tip for smoke, the teepee was not only practical but sacred. The floor represented the earth of mortal life, and the peak the sky of the gods. The roundness of the tent symbolized the sacred circle of life.

Until the coming of the "White Man" and firearms, Plains people remained fairly loosely

'Indian Encampment', oil on canvas by Paul Kane, 1845.

preserved meat that could be easily transported), skins that were used as blankets, clothes, and tent coverings; and hair that was dried and either woven into rope or used to stuff moccasins.

Before the arrival of the horse in the late 18th century, buffalo were hunted on foot, often by stampeding the beasts into a compound. This procedure, referred to as "buffalo jumping," involved every member of the group – a herd was chased toward an enclosure erected around a pit. One person covered himself with a buffalo hide and imitated the animal's movements in the hope of drawing the herd toward the pit. Once inside the enclosure the buffalo toppled into the pit, and was then shot with arrows, butchered,

organized. Originally the political unit of the band was a leader; when several of these bands united, a council was formed of all the leaders. During trading ventures, wars, and celebrations the council acted as a guiding body.

One of the most famous festivals associated with the Plains people was their Sun Dance. A sacred pole was erected to the Great Spirit and offerings tied to it. The bands danced around the stake, recited war deeds, and prayed for guidance in their hunt of the buffalo. Plains youths would perform acts of self-mutilation, one of which involved piercing the chest with skewers tied to the pole with leather thongs, the idea being that self-inflicted torture would arouse the compassion of the Great Spirit.

WOODLAND TRIBES

Perhaps the best known, next to the Inuit, of Canada's native peoples are the aboriginals who lived in the eastern woodlands. As early as 1,000 BC eastern Canada began to be settled by semi-nomadic tribes. It is here that one discovers the contrasting lifestyles and values of the peaceful Huron, the fierce Iroquois Confederacy, and the entrepreneurial Algonquin.

Like the rest of Canada's aboriginals, the people of this area made maximum use of their environment. Distinctive features of their culture were longhouses within palisaded villages, widespread use of fired pottery, clay smoking pipes, and bundling the bones of the dead for burial. They also cultivated the land and sub-

> *While violence was a staple in Iroquois society, the Huron were considered far more peaceful, and the Algonquin embraced a more entrepreneurial approach to life.*

sisted on staples of squash, beans, sunflower seeds, and maize.

It was the Huron who first met and baffled French missionaries to Canada. The French discovered a people who demonstrated a partial equality between the sexes and a form of consensus rather than authoritarian government.

Walking through the woods of lower Ontario, it is easy to speculate where buried Huron and Iroquois sites might lie. They chose locations for their villages on the basis of four criteria: access to water, nearness to forests for timber, nearness to rich soil for cultivation, and strategic placement for defense.

By way of contrast to the Huron, the Iroquois were a fiercer group of people who were more inclined to warfare, and developed a reputation as brutal warriors who would torture and sacrifice their captives. They were the only aboriginals of Canada to believe in two Great Spirits, one good and the other evil. In Iroquois religion, the two deities were constantly at odds with one another, and their myths are most frequently incidents of clashes between the good and evil gods. Before the arrival of the Europeans the Iroquois had sown the seeds of a great empire:

they had developed a unified system of currency (wampum) that regulated trade, and they had organized the confederacy for warfare against enemy tribes. Although the history of Canada is in part a history of burgeoning European society, for the native people it is a tale of exploitation, strife, and partial extinction.

Such is the stage setting, so to speak, for the arrival of the first Europeans: a vast land inhabited by highly differentiated groups, each adapted to a particular lifestyle.

"Miss One Spot."

⊘ LIVING CONDITIONS

The Jesuits and other explorers vividly describe their horror at the living conditions within the palisaded compounds. Samuel de Champlain, aghast at what he perceived to be filth and disorder, wrote of the longhouses in which two or three dozen people lived. "The smoke from each fire in the house," he wrote, "circulates at will, causing much eye trouble, to which the natives are so subject that many become blind in their old age." Despite notions of communal sharing and sanitation that offended the Europeans, it was only when the indigenous peoples became exposed to European viruses that they suddenly began to die of disease in huge numbers.

The Vikings reached Canada from Iceland around AD 1000.

VOYAGES OF DISCOVERY

The early explorers dreamed of finding gold and gemstones; instead they found timber, and waters teeming with fish.

The first visitors to encounter Canada after the crossing of the nomadic hunters were the Vikings, whose ancestors had traveled from Norway to Iceland. From Iceland, the Vikings moved westward when Eric the Red discovered and settled Greenland. A fierce and hardy people, the Vikings were great sailors and often took to the seas in search of food and adventure. On one such voyage a seaman, Bjarne Herjolfsen, caught sight of North America and returned home to tell of the unknown land. Around AD 1000, Eric the Red's son, Leif, set out to find the new continent.

The Viking sagas tell of Leif's strange adventures and his discoveries of Helluland (Baffin Island), Markland (Labrador), and Vinland. In 1961 an archeologist, Helge Ingstad, stumbled upon the remains of a Norse settlement in L'Anse-aux-Meadows and decided that Vinland was probably Newfoundland. One year after the expedition, Leif's brother Thorvald returned to North America hoping to make contact with Vinland's natives. Legends tell of how "Skraelings" attacked Thorvald and his crew with bows and arrows. In other tales the illegitimate daughter of Eric the Red, Freydis the Brave and Cruel, defends the Vikings by rushing towards the Skraelings and frightening them with her wild eyes and gnashing teeth.

Who were the Skraelings? The Viking sagas describe them as dark-skinned people who wore their hair in a strange fashion. Historical anthropologists have speculated that they may have been Algonquins or early Inuit people. Whoever they were, they prevented the Vikings from establishing permanent settlements on the mainland. It is possible that the Vikings returned to northern Canada. The tall, blond

Martin Frobisher, the 16th-century explorer, set out in search of the Northwest Passage.

"Copper Eskimos," so named by the explorer Vilhjalmur Stefansson in 1910, have led some to suggest that these may be the offspring of early Norse people and the Inuit of Baffin Island.

CABOT AND CARTIER

The dream of discovering a route across the Atlantic to the spices, jewels, and silks of the Orient became an obsession with kings and merchants. As improvements in shipbuilding occurred, the dream became a possibility. John Cabot is the first explorer to have "officially" discovered Canada and claimed it for a king. An Italian navigator, Cabot was known for his imaginative flights of fancy and adventure-some spirit. In 1496 he persuaded Henry VII to give him leave to find a route to the Indies and claim it for England. On May 2, 1497, Cabot boarded the *Matthew* with 18 men and set sail for the Americas. After 52 weary days at sea, the *Matthew* sighted land – historians are uncertain whether it was Newfoundland, Labrador, Cape Breton, or even Prince Edward Island – where Cabot landed on June 24. Cabot claimed the country to be under the sovereignty of Henry VII. But where was all the gold?

The early settlement of Québec.

Cabot soon discovered that the soil was extremely fertile and the climate warm and friendly. He was convinced that he had found the northeast coast of Asia; further investigation would surely lead him to the precious silks and gems of which he had so often dreamed. Cabot found neither, but he did report banks of teeming fish and a great abundance of timber.

Upon Cabot's return, Henry VII, who had wanted gold, was singularly unimpressed with the explorer's tales of fish and paid him £10 for his efforts. Still, in 1498 Cabot was given permission to make a second voyage. He set off from Bristol with five ships manned by 300 crew, never to be heard from again. Many explorers

set out after Cabot but were not successful until Jacques Cartier, who was sent by Francis I of France, ventured to North America in 1534. His expedition marks the origin of French and British competition for its control.

> *The West Coast of Canada was yet another site of interest for the ever-curious Europeans attempting to find an easy northern ocean passage to Europe.*

On his first trip, Cartier traveled inland until he found the Gulf of St Lawrence. Assured that the river was a water route to the Orient, Cartier sailed up the St Lawrence until he came to the Iroquois villages of Hochelaga and Stadacona (the sites of modern Montréal and Québec City respectively). Francis I was disappointed that gold had not been found, but Cartier mollified the king by telling him a cross had been erected in his name on Gaspé Peninsula, and that the country had been named New France.

THE ARCTIC EXPEDITIONS

While the early explorers devoted their time to discovering a new route to the Orient, 50 years after Cartier others became obsessed with the Northwest Passage. One such man was Martin Frobisher. With a reputation as a daredevil, in 1576 Frobisher was sent by Elizabeth I to find an ice-free route to the Americas. Despite Frobisher's inability to produce anything of consequence for British history, he still remains something of a folk hero. More than 300 years after Frobisher's voyages, the explorer Charles Francis Hall discovered the relics of a structure Frobisher's crew had built. Hall wrote that in 1861, the native peoples spoke of Frobisher as if he had just visited them.

Henry Hudson was another man drawn to the excitement of exploration. Hoping to open a passage to China, Hudson made several trips to North America, his last one ending tragically. In 1609 the *Discovery* froze in the ice of James Bay. After a long, tense winter, Hudson quarreled with a member of his crew, John Greene, who later led his shipmates into mutiny. Hudson was set adrift in the bay with his son and seven others loyal to him, and was never heard of again.

Following on Hudson's heels in 1631 was Thomas James – after whom James Bay is named – who wrote vividly of his excursions in an account titled *Strange and Dangerous Voyage*. The writings of his log later became the material upon which Coleridge based his poem *The Rime of the Ancient Mariner*. After James, William Edward Parry, a British naval officer, pushed through the northern icebergs to reach

journey. Franklin, only a few miles from success, had died of exhaustion and exposure.

From 1903–6, Norwegian explorer Roald Amundsen became the first person successfully to traverse the fabled and ever-frozen Northwest Passage in a single ship. After 1909, discouraged by the news of Robert Peary's successful foray to the North Pole, Amundsen turned his attention to Antarctica.

TRAVELERS TO THE WEST

In 1778 Captain James Cook landed on Can-

Explorers traveled up the West Coast rivers of Canada in search of furs.

In 1778 Captain James Cook explored the Pacific Coast in search of a river route through the continent.

Melville Island in 1819 – he had come the farthest yet.

Perhaps the most heart-wrenching story of all the explorers is that of John Franklin, a British rear admiral and explorer. In 1819 Franklin was put in charge of an exploration that was to mark out a route from Hudson Bay to the Arctic Ocean. He made a second trip in 1825 after the success of his first voyage and returned to North America a third time in 1845. On his last expedition, Franklin was sure he would find the Northwest Passage. His ships, *Erebus* and *Terror*, were last seen on July 26, 1845. Years later a rescue mission discovered their skeletal remains and a diary of the last days of the

ada's West Coast in the course of his Pacific explorations. Cook volunteered to find a waterway through North America originating in the west but finally had to conclude that it did not exist. George Vancouver followed in 1791–5 and discovered the outlet of the Bella Coola river. Seven weeks later, Alexander Mackenzie, traveling overland, ended up at the same spot.

Such is the early history of Canada. For the Europeans, it yielded neither gold nor gems and was a disappointment. With resignation, the rulers of France and England began to make plans for the colonization of the New World.

Trading pelts for export to meet the demands of European fashion (1758).

THE RISE AND FALL OF NEW FRANCE

The 17th century witnessed the development of a flourishing fur trade, continuing exploration, and bitter differences between settlers and tribes.

Colonizing the New World was no easy task for the rulers of Europe in the 17th century. Cold, barren, and unexplored, Canada held little appeal for the people of England, France, and Spain. Those, however, who did venture to Canada encountered a burgeoning system of trade between the Europeans and the aboriginal peoples and soon realized the economic potential of settling in Canada.

THE FUR TRADE

Curious and for the most part friendly, the tribes that met French and British settlers in Canada became enamored of European metalware, which, for them, represented a massive technological improvement over their crude stone and wooden utensils. As a result, they developed a dependency on the Europeans – a dependency that was to change their lives.

Samuel de Champlain, one of Canada's many progenitors.

Although they never quite understood the "white man's" infatuation with the beaver, First Nations hunters became the main suppliers to the fur merchants, trading European-manufactured wares for their pelts.

Initially, aboriginal peoples had little to offer in return for the highly valued knives and axes, and the Europeans complained bitterly of the relative uselessness of their handcrafted canoes and snowshoes. By the late 1600s, however, the fur trade had begun. When the milliners of Europe obtained beaver pelts from Canada, they created a rage for beaver hats, which were touted as the warmest and most durable in the world. This established an immense and ongoing market for furs in the new colony. Although they never quite understood the "white man's" infatuation with the beaver, First Nations hunters became the main suppliers to the fur merchants. By the early 1700s the fur trade in Canada was booming and competition for the monopoly of the fur market in North America had begun.

FATHER OF CANADA

The man who was in many ways responsible for expanding the fur trade in Canada was the French explorer Samuel de Champlain. An idealist with a passion for exploration, Champlain is probably the most frequently cited "Father" of Canada and is often honored because of his wish to found Canada upon principles of justice and compassion.

Acting on behalf of the French monarchy, in 1604 Champlain established the first French colony in North America in Acadia (Nova Scotia). After Acadia, Champlain continued his explorations into the interior of Canada and on July 3, 1608, on the site of an old Indian settlement called Stadacona, Champlain founded Québec. Though momentous for Canada's history as a whole, the founding of Québec for him was quite un-extraordinary and, as he indicated in his diary, a location he chose more for convenience than historical importance: "When I arrived there [Québec] on July 3 I looked about for a suitable place for our buildings, but I could not find any more convenient or better situated than the point of Québec, so called by the savages, which is filled with nuts and trees... near this is a pleasant river, where formerly Jacques Cartier passed this winter." The "pleasant river" turned out to be the mighty Gulf of St Lawrence, which later became an important passageway for the export of furs to Europe.

THE HURONS

One year after Champlain's settlement of Québec, a group of traders came down from the northwest to exchange their pelts with the French. Upon their arrival the Frenchmen were astonished by the appearance of their half-shaven heads and the tufts of hair that grew perpendicularly to their scalps. Likening their hair to the bristles on the back of an enraged boar (la hure), the French called them the Hurons. Thus began a long and tragic relationship.

One of Champlain's main objectives while in Canada was to control the flourishing fur trade and to establish stricter management of the aboriginals. Already allied with the Hurons, Champlain failed to see that the fur trade was exacerbating existing hostilities among Indian tribes. Animosities of a ritualistic nature had always existed between the Hurons and the Iroquois Confederation. With the fur trade the disputes acquired a mercenary element. When Champlain established an alliance between the French and the Hurons, he immediately became the Iroquois' enemy.

While Champlain was organizing settlements and repelling hostile Iroquois, other colonists, mostly men from France, began to appear.

Samuel de Champlain's infamous Ticonderoga expedition resulted in the massacre of 300 Iroquois – an event that inspired a deep and lasting hatred of the French.

THE PIONEERS

These early settlers, who became known as the *coureurs de bois*, or woodsmen, looked to New France as an escape from a life of drudgery –

Smallpox threatens a shipload of immigrants.

many had exchanged prison sentences for emigration papers. The *coureurs de bois* became the backbone of Canada's trading system.

Trapping animals for a living – a precarious existence in the bush that involved fighting off hostile natives – these early immigrants were the intrepid entrepreneurs of Canada's early days. By the 1750s Canada had become an economically prosperous investment for France, and Britain began to take a closer look at a country she had virtually ignored for almost half a century.

When Samuel de Champlain and other explorers ventured to Canada in the early 17th century, their plans for the settlement of the new colony, although the dreams of imaginative men, were essentially expressions of the grandiose visions of European monarchs. For them, Canada was merely an addition to the ever-expanding empires of England and France. Canada was a valuable piece of property on the "Monopoly board" that the superpowers of the 17th and 18th centuries ruthlessly fought to claim.

But for the others who journeyed to Canada – the farmers and fishermen, the women and children, the missionaries, and even the reckless *coureurs de bois* – Canada was much more than just a geographical acquisition. It was a very real place, empty and enormous. And at times, life was very hard.

Franciscans who enthusiastically plunged into the bush in search of the "heathen savages." The Récollets patiently began to work on saving their souls – but with little success. Not long after, the Jesuits were invited to join the Canadian missions, and in 1625 Fathers de Brébeuf and de Noué left France to begin converting the Iroquois and Huron.

The Jesuits, like most Europeans, failed to understand the native way of life. Communally oriented, lacking hierarchical structures and methods of authority, openly polytheistic, and

Jean de Brébeuf, a Jesuit priest who worked among the Huron, is tortured to death by the Iroquois.

On claiming Canada for France, Samuel de Champlain's first task was to regularize the fur trade. His second task was to set about converting the native population to Christianity so that the continent could truly become a land made for "the glory and praise of God and France."

The years 1632 to 1652 are often referred to as the "golden years" for the missions in Canada – a somewhat misleading phrase because, although it captures a sense of intense religious activity in Canada during this time, it fails to express the low success rate (in terms of conversions).

THE MISSIONARIES ARRIVE

The first missionaries brought to Canada by Champlain were four Récollets, strict

possessing different concepts of diet and sanitation, they seemed to the Jesuits "barbaric."

Needless to say, the Jesuits were not always welcome and many of them, given the name of "black robes" by the Iroquois, became symbols of evil and misfortune. Despite their ethnocentric attitudes, some of the Jesuit missionaries were men of great courage. Many suffered horrible deaths and became the first martyrs of Canada. Such is the story of Father Jean de Brébeuf, a Jesuit who worked among the horticultural Huron.

Brébeuf's martyrdom on March 16 1649 was recorded by a contemporary, Christophe Regnault, in *Jesuit Relations*: "The Iroquois came ... took our village and seized Father Brébeuf and his companion; and set fire to all the huts. They proceeded to vent their rage on these two fathers, for they took them both and stripped them naked and fastened them each to a post. They tied both their hands and feet together. They beat them with a shower of blows from cudgels ... there being no part of their body which did not endure this torment."

After Brébeuf's slow and painful death, the Iroquois were so impressed by his fortitude that they ate his heart, believing that by so doing they would become as brave as Brébeuf.

demanded arduous labor, crops were slow to start growing, and a year's food could be ruined instantly by bad weather. Wild beasts and hostile natives were also constant worries.

Early homes in New France were wooden huts crudely built of rough logs; in winter, water for the household had to be drawn from a hole in the ice. Soon, however, the wooden shelters gave way to houses built of stone, with steep roofs and large fireplaces. As the forests were cleared, as settlements became towns, and as farmers prospered on their strips of land (called

Cornelius Krieghoff's portrait of the life of a French-Canadian family in the 19th century.

FIRST FRENCH CANADIANS

In the early annals of Canadian history, there were two types of settlers who traveled to the New World: the *coureur de bois* and the *habitant*, the French colonist who settled on the fertile shores of the St Lawrence river and cultivated the land. From the very beginning these two lifestyles were radically different. To the *habitant* the fur traders were as treacherous and vengeful as the despised Iroquois, while the farmer frightened away their game and pushed the *coureur de bois* farther into the wilderness. Although the *coureurs de bois* are often portrayed as the more robust of the two, life for the *habitants* was also very difficult. Clearing the heavily forested lands of the St Lawrence shores

seigneuries), some families of New France eventually enjoyed higher standards of living than their European counterparts.

For the farmer of early Canada, tenant dues and church tithes were low, no taxes were paid, fertile land was available for the asking, food was bountiful, and everyone possessed the right to hunt and fish. By the 1630s the little settlements of Québec and Montréal had burgeoned into bustling centers of commerce and become bastions of French sovereignty. The French clergy, so unsuccessful among the natives, had founded schools, hospitals, and even a university (Jesuit College in Québec City was founded in 1636, one year before Harvard). An elaborate system of courts and litigation procedures was implemented.

In 1640 New France had 240 inhabitants – by 1685 the population had swelled to more than 10,000. Montréal and Québec had become lively and popular colonial capitals. The artist Cornelius Krieghoff, one of the most insightful chroniclers of early Québécois culture, portrays the French Canadians as hardworking but cheerful people.

Extremely fond of their children, the French Canadians socialized mainly through family gatherings, card playing, dancing, and drinking parties. (By 1749 drunken horse-driving had become so serious in Québec that a strict law fining inebriated drivers six *livres* – about six dollars – came into effect.) The only ominous presence seems to have been the clergy, who sternly disapproved of dancing, cards, jewelry, and even hair ribbons. In 1700 Bishop Laval furiously chastised Québécois women for their elaborate coiffures and scandalous wardrobes.

SETTLEMENTS AND SKIRMISHES

While the Jesuits continued to promulgate Catholicism, and French colonists resolutely

A favorite pastime of the inhabitants, card playing, was strictly forbidden by the Catholic Church.

⊙ ACADIA AND ACADIANS

Acadia's tiny villages set in the Maritimes became the subject of folktales and poems. Champlain's Acadian village of Grand Pré was immortalized in Henry Wadsworth Longfellow's epic poem *Evangeline*. Of Acadia and Acadians, Longfellow wrote:

Thus dwelt together in love these simple Acadian farmers...

Neither lock had they to their doors, nor bars to their windows;

But their dwellings were as open as day and the hearts of the owners;

There the richest was poor and the poorest lived in abundance.

set down roots, Samuel de Champlain and other French officials were faced with the problem of maintaining control over the new colony. Several skirmishes with other governments over territory had already occurred.

In 1627 the notorious Kirke brothers, English adventurers who supported the Huguenot effort in France, blockaded the St Lawrence river for three years and wrested the fur trade from France's charter: The Hundred Associates. At the same time Acadia (Nova Scotia) was claimed for James VI of Scotland by Sir William Alexander. Various disputes ensued until 1632 when Canada and Acadia were restored to France under the Treaty of Saint-Germain-en-Laye.

> By the 1630s the settlements of Québec and Montréal had become bustling commercial centers, although still dependent upon the fur resources of Northern Québec and Ontario.

GOVERNMENT IN NEW FRANCE

Bitter complaints about New France were constantly arising from the colonists – one of which was the lack of a central, authoritative govern-

consisted of a governor general, an intendant (royal civil servant) and a superior council. The Bishop of New France was made a member of the council but was more often than not engaged in bitter argument with the reigning governor.

One of New France's more colorful governors was the Comte de Frontenac, a man of great personal charm who was also extravagant and unscrupulous. From the beginning of his career, Frontenac set himself in opposition to the most influential clergymen in Canada. He complained that the Jesuits exerted unreasonable control

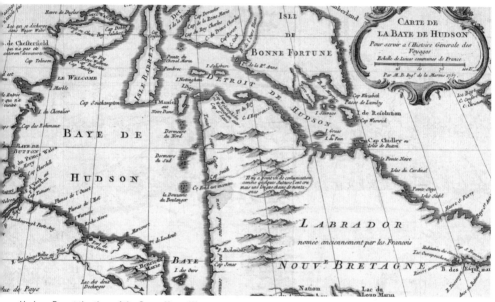

Hudson Bay at the time of the Seven Years War.

ment. As a result, in 1647, a council consisting of a governor, the religious superior of the Jesuits, and the of Montréal was instituted. Although the council's role was to monitor economic activities in the colony, this model proved inefficient. Consequently New France was officially made a ward of the Crown (under Louis XIV) in 1663.

Two men in particular were instrumental in bringing a strong, centralized government to French Canada. The first was Jean Baptiste Colbert, an ambitious finance minister, who endeavored to recast French colonial policy by establishing a new administrative system. Colbert sought to make New France a province with a government similar to that of France. To this end he implemented a new structure, which

over the colonists. Scandalizing New France by his disrespectful attitude toward them, Frontenac also overlooked the aggressive presence of the British Hudson's Bay Company in the west and underestimated its importance in Canada's future.

Jean Colbert's reorganization of the colony gave New France a firmly centralized government that could efficiently deal with day-to-day problems. Jean Talon, the first intendant of Colbert's model, quickly set about reorganizing the settlement and was able to bring in thousands of new colonists, including women. Most of the population flocked to three towns: Montréal, Québec, and Trois-Rivières. Colbert and Talon hoped that settlers would establish

Colbert's neglect of the western regions, together with the formation of the monopolistic Hudson's Bay Company, enabled the British to gain a firmer hold on the New World.

permanency along the St Lawrence, but many traveled inland.

The transient nature of the population was a major obstacle in the settling of New France

New England and were escorted to Britain. In London Groseilliers and Radisson persuaded a group of London merchants to assume control over the fur trade in the middle of Canada by forming the Hudson's Bay Company: the company claimed exclusive trading rights in all territories draining into Hudson Bay, a massive stretch of land.

New France suddenly found herself in an awkward position: to the south were the Dutch- and British-supported Iroquois and to the north was the expanding Hudson's Bay Company. Fearful

Hudson Bay Trading Store, 1888.

– Colbert, feeling that mobility was deleterious to French interests, subsequently forbade colonists to leave the central settlement and confined the fur trade to the areas of Montréal, Trois-Rivières, and Tadoussac. Colbert's neglect of the western regions enabled the British to gain an even firmer foothold in the New World.

ANGLO-FRENCH RIVALRY

In the 1660s two malcontent trappers, Médard des Groseilliers and Pierre Radisson, decided they were going to do something about the high costs of hauling furs back to Québec (as ordered by the colonial government) and the exorbitant taxes they were paying on fur pelts. They fled to

of losing their new colony, New France's militia began to launch expeditions to keep the British from expanding their reach.

By the start of the 18th century, hostilities had increased, especially in the east, where New England farmers began to covet Acadia. For several years New France was kept active by repelling new settlers and engaging its armies in ruthless, devastating raids.

Agreement, however, was reached in 1713 when the Peace Treaty of Utrecht was signed and North America was carved up among the European powers. The French gave up much of their land. Acadia and Hudson Bay were ceded to the British and Article 15 of the treaty recognized British sovereignty over the

After 150 years of struggle against the harsh wilderness, New France was abandoned, the old country displaying a cruel lack of enthusiasm for what Voltaire dismissed as quelques arpents de neige – "a few acres of snow."

Iroquois people and permitted them to trade with the other tribes in traditionally French domains.

The death of General Wolfe at the siege of Québec (1759).

Despite France's reluctance to honor the treaty, three decades of peace reigned. Canada began to prosper – the fur trade flourished; the population increased from 19,000 in 1713 to 48,000 by 1739; agriculture and fishing blossomed; and lumbering began to develop.

British imperialist economic aspirations, however, soon emerged and fighting broke out between the colonial powers again in 1744. A series of small battles followed until in 1756 a war was finally declared between France and Britain, which was to prove decisive.

France, characteristically nonchalant in her attitude toward the new colony, sent the Marquis de Montcalm with meager reinforcements to Québec. Lack of soldiers and food supplies made defeat seem almost inevitable. In addition, France did not wish to risk sending her fleets to North America since it would leave the mother country in a vulnerable position. New France's frontier was long and lightly guarded – how could Montcalm hope to defend it?

THE FALL OF NEW FRANCE

Québec seemed (to both nations) to be the deciding factor in the war. In 1759 a force under General James Wolfe began an advance. Montcalm,

Competing for trade.

relying upon the strategic position of the city atop formidable precipices, let the invaders come to him. After several unsuccessful frontal attacks, one of Wolfe's men suggested that he should try a flank attack. On the night of September 12, Wolfe and his troops crossed the St Lawrence River under the cover of darkness and scaled the cliffs. Unprepared, the French repelled the British but panicked and hastily retreated (not knowing that their attackers, too, had panicked and were about to retreat). Wolfe was killed in the exchange and Montcalm was mortally wounded.

After the fall of Québec it was only a matter of time before the rest of New France fell to the British. By 1763, under the Treaty of Paris, France lost her lands in Canada to Britain.

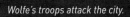
Wolfe's troops attack the city.

British troops scale the Heights of Abraham, ready to attack Québec.

ARRIVAL OF THE BRITISH

While Britain established control over the country, its attempts to anglicize 70,000 French Canadians proved somewhat overambitious.

When Canada was ceded to the British, few tears were shed in France. New France had become a gnawing irritation for French officials, and its removal from France's empire was met more with relief than with regret. Britain's victory in Canada began to produce major changes; one such was the shift in control of the fur trade from French hands to British ones. Although glowing from its recent economic advancement in Canada, Britain was still faced with one serious problem: the vast majority of its newly acquired colony were people of foreign descent.

From the first, Britain planned to extirpate French culture from its colony. British colonial officers hoped that American settlers would eventually move into the region and outnumber the nearly 70,000 French Canadians. For the French *habitants* the prospect of cultural defeat only added further to their already traumatized condition – they felt themselves abandoned by France and, although not cruelly treated by Britain, in the hands of an insensitive and arrogant administration.

Acutely aware of the rebellious rumblings to the south, Carleton urged Britain to negotiate with the French, else it might find itself faced with continental insurrection.

Britain's attempts to anglicize Québec proved futile. More than 99 percent of the white population in Canada were French, and it soon became clear that a compromise with the French was necessary and could be advantageous.

Toe-tapping amusement in 1840.

Governor Sir Guy Carleton was one of the administrators who recognized the importance of securing the fidelity of the French Canadians. Under his guidance, the Québec Act 1774, which granted the Québécois cultural, political, and economic protection, was passed. Under the Act, British criminal law was retained but French civil law restored; the Catholic Church retained the right to levy tithes and prosecute the recalcitrant; and Franco-Catholics were no longer excluded from public office.

THE AMERICAN REVOLUTION

Carleton proved to be perspicacious in his treatment of the Québécois for, as American disenchantment with Britain climaxed, it became apparent that French settlers might favor British interests. Carleton's Québec Act, however, only served to accommodate the interests of the *habitants* and consequently alienated and angered British subjects. These tensions were brought to the surface with the advent of the American Revolution. The rebellion itself was, to some extent, engendered by the Québec Act – irritated by the extensions of French-protected trapping regions (which encroached upon traditionally American

Benedict Arnold's attack on the British in Québec in 1775.

lands), the American Continental Congress instituted a plot of revenge against the British in 1775. The first act of the Congress was not to declare independence from Britain but to invade Canada.

In British North America (formerly New France) sentiments about the war were mixed. The intervention of France on the American side briefly raised hopes among the Québécois. British merchants continued to sulk over what they perceived to be a betrayal of their government. The arrival of British regulars, however, in 1776, seemed to convince French and British dissenters alike that to side with Britain would be the most prudent course.

The American Revolution served to cement British rule in Canada in several ways. The relative weakness of the invaders convinced British businessmen that it was in their economic interests to support the imperial struggle.

In Nova Scotia the experience of the American Revolution had a more distressing dimension. Settlers here identified themselves with New England and found themselves caught between conflicting loyalties. In the end the war strengthened ties between Britain and Nova Scotia, again for economic reasons.

Another significant effect of the American Revolution was the influx into Canada of 60,000 United Empire Loyalists, men and women who did not support American grievances. The Loyalists radically altered the composition of Canada's population; their presence created a cultural dualism that contained all the pronounced differences existing between the French and British peoples.

UPPER AND LOWER CANADA

The aftermath of the American Revolution brought with it a renewed bitterness among the British over what they perceived to be pro-French policies in the colony. The Loyalists wanted a representative government (something denied by the Québec Act). Carleton, newly named Lord Dorchester, returned to Québec to rectify what was becoming "a delicate situation," the result being the Constitutional Act of 1791.

Under its directives the colony was to have an elected assembly that would exercise legislative authority in conjunction with a legislative council appointed by the king. Most importantly the Constitutional Act divided the St Lawrence Valley into two colonies: one named Upper Canada and the other Lower Canada. This development marked a new dawn in the emergence of Anglo-French rivalries and ushered in another act in the drama of British North America.

After the Revolution, hostilities between the British and Americans flared up in 1812 when American rebels attempted to invade Canada. They were finally routed during the Battle of Queenston Heights. Although Britain lost some of its territories to the fledgling nation, the War of 1812 formalized British North America's right to remain part of the British Empire.

Eng.ᵈ by A.H. Ritchie.

Guy Carleton

The radical William Lyon Mackenzie, who campaigned for "Responsible Government" in Upper Canada.

CONFEDERATION CANADA

Disenchantment with British rule and rebellions calling for an elected assembly led to the emergence of a unified Dominion of Canada.

The aftermath of the War of 1812 brought with it a new sense of vigor and self-determination among Canadians. As the economy flourished, Upper Canada settlers began to evaluate the political and economic role of Britain in the colonies. In Lower Canada, similar questions were being raised, although for different reasons: widespread unemployment and growing poverty engendered bitter criticism of the British among French Canadians.

Canadian settlers were mainly disenchanted with the political structure of their colony. Although the Assembly was an elected body, a council appointed by the King of England held executive powers and frequently overruled resolutions passed in the elected legislature. Frustrated by patronage, corruption, and privilege, Canadians began to call for Responsible Government, in particular an elected council.

REBELLION AGAINST BRITISH RULE

In Québec, the Council, an elite group of wealthy merchant families called the *Château Clique* received the brunt of its criticisms from the acerbic Louis-Joseph Papineau, the founder of the Patriote Party. The *patriotes* drew up a list of 92 resolutions and demanded the elimination of the appointed Council.

Britain refused to accommodate their wishes. Eventually pushed beyond the point of polite discussion, the *patriotes* took to the streets in October 1837 and clashed with British soldiers. After several deaths, the uprising was quelled and the party was left without a leader when Papineau fled to the United States.

In Upper Canada, the fight for Responsible Government was spearheaded by William Lyon Mackenzie, a fiery Scotsman who was the publisher/editor of a local newspaper. Mackenzie, known for

Sir George Simpson establishes a council to administer British Columbia (1835).

his lacerating attacks against the Family Compact (the name for the appointed council in Upper Canada), had been elected to the Assembly in 1828 but expelled from it in 1831 for libel.

In 1837 Mackenzie rallied several hundred angry protestors in Montgomery's Tavern on Toronto's Yonge Street. After a few shots of whiskey, discontent began to turn into active dissent and the group of rebels marched toward the government buildings. They were met by a group of 27 armed militiamen. When a colonel shot at the rebel blockade, he was killed by return fire. The mishap so flustered the protestors that they fled in panic, Mackenzie going to the United States.

Britain adopted a severe stance against the rebellions, although many Canadians shared the sentiments of the insurgents. When two leaders of the Upper Canada rebellion were hanged, vexation with the British way of governing heightened.

John Ryerson said of the execution: "Very few persons present except the military and rufscruf of the city. The general feeling is total opposition to the execution of these men."

Britain did recognize the need to reform the colony's outmoded constitution. A royal com-

through the unification of the colonies into a single province.

Durham also believed that such a union would relieve the tension between the English and French settlers by drawing the latter into mainstream British culture. French culture (which Durham privately thought was essentially backward), the report explained, had been retarded by French colonial policies.

Despite the glaring ethnocentrism of the report, it did recommend that all citizens be granted Responsible Government. Adopting, but

Scottish-born John A. Macdonald, the dominion's first prime minister.

Macdonald's wife, Baroness Macdonald.

mission was established to investigate the problems. The man chosen to direct the inquiry was a politician from one of the wealthiest families in England, Lord Durham, nicknamed "Radical Jack" by his colleagues. A man of dour intensity and a violent temper, Durham was appointed governor general.

Following six short months of investigation, Durham returned to England to prepare his report on the "Canada Issue." In the document, Durham complained that the five colonies were stagnating and that in order to exist alongside the dynamic and aggressive United States, Canada would have to develop a viable economy. Such an economy, he believed, could be realized

modifying, some of Durham's suggestions, Britain united Canada West and Canada East and awarded each sector equal representation in a new joint legislature. In 1849 the new legislature formed an administration for the Province of Canada (Upper and Lower Canada).

THE BEGINNINGS OF CONFEDERATION

The feeling that American or British domination would always threaten Canada while the colonies remained separate geographic units pervaded political thought in the 1850s and early 1860s. Confederation, a notion that had been discussed for nearly a century, suddenly reappeared as a viable possibility.

After self-government was achieved, politics became sectional in Upper and Lower Canada. Issues such as the importance of developing an intercolonial railway and the need to acquire new territories were neglected because of conflicting party interests.

Political deadlock finally contrived in 1864 to bring together a coalition of rival parties united on the one issue of Confederation. At the same time similar discussions were also taking place in the Maritime provinces. A conference of provincial ministers was held, and in 1867 the British North America Act was passed by Parliament in England, creating a confederated Canada comprising Ontario and Québec (formerly Upper and Lower Canada), New Brunswick, and Nova Scotia under the title "Dominion of Canada."

The unlikely midwife of a unified Canada was Sir John A. Macdonald, a man who had originally opposed the concept of Confederation when the Liberal newspaper magnate George Brown had proposed it, but who was to become the dominion's first prime minister. Born in Scotland, in the year of Napoleon's Waterloo, and brought to Kingston, Ontario, when still a small boy, Macdonald was perhaps the most improbable person in public life to nurture a fledgling Canadian territory.

Macdonald, a tall, gangly figure with a careless but stinging sense of humor, didn't seem to fit the mold of a Canadian prime minister. An audacious alcoholic and a bit of a dandy, he lacked the prim reserve of a British politician. But what he lacked in demeanor and appearance, he compensated for through his sharp intelligence and keen powers of insight.

THE MÉTIS REBELLION

Confederation, once approved by London, was not distinguished by a smooth transition. One of the first omens of trouble to come was the acquisition of Rupert's Land from the Hudson's Bay Company for £300,000.

Unwisely, the government regarded the territory as the sole property of the company and neglected to take into account the indigenous population living there, namely the Métis of the Red River Colony. Trouble soon followed. The Métis, who spoke French and practiced Catholicism, were homesteaders who had long thought of themselves as a sovereign but autonomous nation of neither European nor aboriginal extraction, but

one of both. When Rupert's Land was acquired without their consultation, the Métis organized under the leadership of Louis Riel, a man of charismatic eloquence. They seized Fort Garry, a British outpost, and set up a provisional government. No blood was shed during the insurrection.

Supported by an American fifth column of infantrymen, the Métis were in a strong position and the Macdonald government knew it. Negotiations had commenced and all might have ended peacefully if a young upstart, Thomas Scott (who had been captured by the Métis),

Métis rebels on the march.

⊙ JOHN A. MACDONALD

Macdonald introduced to Canadians crucial qualifications for a prime minister: wit, articulate attack, and rebuttal. Despite his polished exterior, Macdonald's life was tragically fraught with misfortune. He had married his cousin Isabella Clark, but soon afterwards her health failed. Macdonald's first years as a politician fluctuated between attending heated arguments in the Assembly and returning home at night to watch his wife slowly die. Nine years after Isabella's death, Macdonald married Susan Agnes Bernard. Their daughter Margaret Mary was born with brain damage. Macdonald doted on his daughter, but was scarred by the event for the rest of his life.

had not tried to throttle Louis Riel. Riel had the prisoner court-martialed and shot. Much to Macdonald's dismay, Scott had been a citizen of Ontario; worse, he was a Protestant murdered by a Catholic. Predictably the affair became politically "delicate." It was finally settled when the colony entered the Confederation as the province of Manitoba. Riel fled to the United States. Despite its promises, the Canadian government did not respect the integrity of the Métis community and, more than a decade after the first rebellion, Riel returned to begin a second one,

The coming of the railways was – despite this storybook representation – fraught with hardship and scandal, which led to the prime minister's resignation.

this time in Saskatchewan. Eventually captured by British troops, Riel was put on trial for treason. Perhaps the blackest stain on Macdonald's otherwise illustrious career was his decision to have Louis Riel hanged. Responding to indignant French cries of opposition, the prime minister remarked: "He shall hang though every dog in Québec should bark in his favor." Riel's death only served to entrench the old, bitter hatred between the French and the English.

THE RAILWAY SCANDAL

A second slight on Macdonald's political record occurred through the Pacific Railway scandal.

By the time a second election was due in Canada, Prince Edward Island, the Prairies, and the Pacific Coast had been added to the Confederation. The problem of connecting the provinces became a major issue in the elections of 1872. A national railway stretching from coast to coast seemed to be the natural solution.

The Canadian Pacific Railway was a project proposed by Macdonald's party and was organized by Sir Hugh Allan, a prominent Montréal shipping magnate. The railway was backed by large American and Scottish investments, and Macdonald bluntly told Allan that foreign capital must be eliminated from the project. Allan agreed, but deceived Macdonald by retaining his American partners and keeping them in the background.

Six weeks before the election day, Macdonald found himself desperate for campaign funds; he asked Hugh Allan for support. Mysteriously, $60,000 appeared; another $35,000 soon followed. In a moment of fatal foolhardiness Macdonald wired Allan for a final amount: "I must have another ten thousand. Will be the last time of calling. Do not fail me."

Macdonald's ticket won the election. At the moment of his relief, however, others were planning his demise. The offices of Sir Hugh Allan's solicitor were ransacked, and stolen documents were sold to ministers of Macdonald's rival party, the Liberals, for the sum of $5,000.

The Liberals exposed the scandal: it seemed that Prime Minister Macdonald had given Hugh Allan the Canadian Pacific Railway project in exchange for election funds. Eventually forced to resign, Macdonald left office in disgrace. The railway was later completed, but it would always lack the luster of accomplishment of which Macdonald had dreamed.

THE CLOSE OF A CENTURY

When Macdonald left office, the task of shaping Canada's future was taken up by Alexander Mackenzie. Macdonald later returned as prime minister, then others followed: Sir John Abbott, Sir John Thompson, Sir Mackenzie Bowell, Sir Charles Tupper. By 1900 Canada was well on its way as a nation.

Continually facing new challenges and reconciling divergent interests, Canada saw the advent of the 20th century as the beginning of a future of golden promise.

THE DOMINION OF CANADA IS BORN

Throughout the early 1800s the idea of uniting the five British colonies in North America was discussed on both sides of the Atlantic.

Unification, it was argued, would not only strengthen the economy, it would provide a solid force against any future aggression by the United States. A joint legislative assembly for Upper and Lower Canada had been established in Ottawa in 1849. But rather than tackling major issues, activity centered on petty political bickering. Governments lasted a few months, then a few weeks, until in 1864 political deadlock emerged.

With the American Civil War raging to the south, Canadians were chilled by the prospect of renewed Anglo-American conflict. Confederation seemed to be a timely way to get the colonies going again. In the same year as the deadlock, a coalition of rival parties (the Blues led by George Étienne Cartier, the Conservatives headed by John A. Macdonald, and the Liberals by the powerful newspaper magnate George Brown) was formed. Their union was based upon a platform of Confederation.

In the Maritimes a similar discussion of uniting the coastal provinces had surfaced. The provinces had called for a conference to draw up a strategy for Confederation, when the governments of Upper and Lower Canada heard of their plans. A delegation consisting of John A. Macdonald, George Brown, and six other ministers decided to "crash" the conference and push for their own proposals.

The *Queen Victoria* was chartered in Québec City and, loaded with $13,000-worth of champagne, set sail for Prince Edward Island. Although somewhat disconcerted by the fact that they were met by only one official in an oyster boat, the delegation was able to persuade the Maritime governments that Confederation should include Upper and Lower Canada. The rough terms of Confederation were drawn up at "the great intercolonial drunk" (as one disgusted New Brunswick editorial described it) and received ratification a few weeks later at the Québec Conference.

At the London Conference in London in 1866, final discussions were held with the Colonial Office (Prince Edward Island and Newfoundland had withdrawn from the talks at the last minute), leading directly to the most important statute in Canadian constitutional history.

On July 1, 1867, Confederated Canada became a reality when the British North America Act divided the British Province of Canada into Ontario and Québec (formerly Upper and Lower Canada) and united them with New Brunswick and Nova Scotia. The new nation was called the Dominion of Canada. An extract from the Act read as follows:

The fathers of Confederation in debate.

"*Whereas the provinces of Canada, Nova Scotia and New Brunswick have expressed their Desire to be federally united into One Dominion under the Crown of the United Kingdom of Great Britain and Ireland, with a Constitution similar in Principle to that of the United Kingdom;*

And whereas such a Union would conduce to the Welfare of the Provinces and Promote the interests of the British Empire;

And whereas on the Establishment of the Union by Authority of Parliament, it is expedient, not only that the Constitution of the Legislative Authority in the Dominion be prepared for, but also that the Nature of the Executive Government therein be declared;

And whereas it is expedient that Provision be made for the eventual Admission into the Union of other parts of British North America."

Celebrating progress and prosperity.

TORONTO'S

GRAND SUMMER

CARNIVAL

INDUSTRY INTELLIGENCE INT

JARVIS S.T PROMENADE

30th JUNE
1st 2nd 3rd

SETTLEMENT AND WAR

The first half of the 20th century was a period of increased settlement and development, albeit one punctuated by the trauma of two world wars and the lingering effects of the Depression.

A tentative prosperity and progress ushered Canada into the 20th century. Under Prime Minister Wilfrid Laurier's government, railway construction continued apace, and by 1914 the Canadian-Pacific extended from one coast to the other. Although diplomatic relations began to be forged with the rest of the world, most international ties were organized through Britain, and Canadians began to grumble about being ruled by a tiny island thousands of miles away. Further resentment erupted over the "Alaska Boundary Fiasco."

To settle a dispute between the US and Canada over the Alaska/Yukon boundary, a commission of three Americans, three Canadians, and one British minister was formed. The Americans issued a proposal that was overwhelmingly in their own favor. Lord Alvertone, for Britain, voted with the US, which was seen by Canada as a betrayal of their interests and further evidence of British duplicity.

A poster encourages British families to emigrate.

To attract immigrants to the country's unpopulated West, advertisements reading "The Last Best West; Homes For Millions; 160-Acre Farms In Western Canada; Free," were distributed throughout Europe.

Britain was also contributing to the burgeoning influx of Europeans. Canada's immigration policy favored Anglo-Saxon migrants, but the influx was not enough and the west, in particular, loomed large and empty.

Laurier's Minister of the Interior, Clifford Sifton, initiated a widespread advertising scheme designed to attract other European settlers to the prairies. The result was the mass migration of Ukrainians, Czechs, Slovaks, Poles, Hungarians, and Serbs to Alberta and Saskatchewan (provinces created in 1905).

Like the French *habitants*, prairie homesteaders faced difficult beginnings. The tough prairie scrub had to be cleared, and soil, dried for thousands of years under a blazing sun, had to be plowed. Winter temperatures, so cold they could freeze human flesh within five seconds, and torrid summers were difficulties offset only by successful harvests. Canada's unique brand of democratic socialism was born of the rugged lives of prairie farmers struggling to survive in the early 20th century. It is in this era that one discovers the roots of populist, radical, and progressive movements in Canadian politics.

Women had a voice, too. Nellie McClung and Emily Murphy led a movement in the famous "Persons Case." The frontier women objected to the chauvinistic interpretation of the "persons clause" in the British North America Act, which specified that "persons" could be nominated to the Senate. The Canadian parliament understood this to mean men only. McClung's and Murphy's petition was turned down by the Supreme Court but an executive committee in London overruled its decision. As a result, the Senate was opened to both sexes in 1929.

Registering immigrants.

THE RISE OF INDUSTRIALISM

With the development of new businesses and industries, many Canadians experienced radical changes in their lifestyles: for the entrepreneur, commercial development meant assured affluence, but for many others it meant a life of drudgery and exploitation.

In the east, the factory became the oppressive environment of the urban immigrant. Twelve-hour days, six-day weeks, and low wages were standard practices. The hiring of women and children at lower rates of pay was also common.

When questioned by a Labor Commission in 1910 about the appropriateness of brutally whipping six-year-old girls in his textile factory, one Montréal merchant replied that just as training

a dog required strict forms of punishment, so, too, did the hiring of children necessitate rigorous discipline. Five years earlier, David Kissam Young, a writer for the *Industrial Banner*, had described the Canadian factory owners' creed as: "Suffer little children to come unto me; for they pay a bigger profit than men you see." This led to the rise of trade unions and labor organizations. In 1908 Ontario passed the first child-labor law in Canada – the minimum age at which a child could work was 14 years.

WORLD WAR I

The 1914–18 war in Europe had profound consequences for Canada. Still considered a loyal subject of the British Empire, Canada felt duty-bound to enter the war in support of Britain. The decision was not without its own advantages. When Russian wheat exports were hindered by fighting, Canada became the main agricultural supplier of Britain and its allies. Canadian munitions industries sprang up overnight and fortunes were made. But these economic benefits were gained at the expense of many lives.

Robert Borden was prime minister of Canada for the duration of World War I. His main task was to ensure that Canada found the 500,000 men it had promised in support of Britain.

Efforts actively to support the war in Europe began to pervade Canadian society. Appeals to civic pride were made by political leaders, ministers preached of Christian duty, army officials advertised the glamour of wearing complete highland regalia, and women wore badges reading "Knit or Fight."

Unmoved by loyalty to either France or Britain, French Canadians were reluctant to join the war effort, and Québec inhabitants responded cynically to the government's patriotic propaganda. Tensions eventually led to anti-conscription riots in 1918. In one skirmish, soldiers from Toronto opened fire on crowds in Québec and killed four civilians. Ottawa warned that future rioters would be conscripted on the spot.

On August 18, 1918, Canadian and Australian troops broke through a German battalion near Amiens. The German soldiers were pushed farther back until the final day at Mons on November 11 when the German army was defeated. By the time the war was over, Canada had lost 60,611 lives – thousands of others returned home severely and permanently mutilated, both physically and mentally.

THE PURRING TWENTIES

If the 1920s roared in the United States, they at least purred in Canada. In the States, a modern equivalent of the Inquisition, the Big Red Scare, swept across the country and sought to purge America of any "suspected or real communists." The movement never made any serious headway in Canada. Radical parties in the prairies, union organizers, and the handful of self-avowed com-

bolstered a small-town conservative attitude – an attitude given a literary form in Stephen Leacock's *Sunshine Sketches* (1914).

There were new Canadian directions to be taken as well, early in the century. In the arts, the Group of Seven created a stunning but scandalously different visual image of the Canadian landscape. Using the techniques of Cézanne, the Impressionists, and Art Nouveau, Lawren Harris, A.Y. Jackson, Arthur Lismer, Frederick Varley, J.E.H. MacDonald, Franklin Carmichael, and Frank Johnston re-explored

Around 105,000 Canadian soldiers lost their lives in World Wars I and II.

munists experienced mild to severe harassment, but Canada lacked the fanatic allegiance to "democracy" of the US.

To mirror glamorous silent film stars, women shed several pounds of clothing, cut their hair, and fought for new gender identities.

Like Americans, Canadians were thrilled by the glamorous Toronto-born Mary Pickford and flocked to see Douglas Fairbanks and Rudolph Valentino in their latest silent films: but Canada was still a land of small towns. As such, it

Canada as bold iconoclasts – their works distinguished Canada internationally and had a lingering effect on the country's visual arts for many decades.

GRAIN DRAIN

When the Depression hit Canada in 1929, it hit hard, exacerbated by the collapse of the world grain market – a wheat glut had made it more economical for Canada's clients to buy from Argentina, Australia or the Soviet Union.

R.B. Bennett's Conservative government quickly rallied to address the problems of a faltering economy. Relief programs and social services (which became expert at detecting "fraud and waste") were swiftly established. Callous in their lack of understanding of the hardship the Depression caused, politicians claimed that "jobs were there to be found," and they created work camps in British Columbia for single men. Hundreds of workers either froze to death on the trains or were murdered on their way to find work. Those who made it to the camps were paid 20 cents a day. In Toronto, a team of men would shovel snow from the driveway of a wealthy Rosedale family for seven hours, only to be paid 5 cents. These were the lucky ones. Widespread unemployment sent men and women into the

to become Canada's socialist party, the NDP (New Democratic Party).

As the Depression deepened throughout Canada, radio sets became the main means of escape and, in what the government claimed was an attempt to allay the misery of millions, the Canadian Radio Broadcasting Commission was set up. Sports events, radio dramas, the lively commentaries of Gordon Sinclair, and reporting of events such as the Dionne quintuplets born in Calendar, Ontario, served as diversions for many Canadians. When the Depression

Settlers travel west on the Canadian-Pacific (1915).

streets, and nowhere was destitution greater than on the prairies. Out west it seemed as if the forces of nature had collaborated with the vagaries of the economy to make life as miserable as possible. In 1931 raging winds swept away the fertile topsoil; in 1932 a plague of grasshoppers devoured the crops; and 1933 marked the beginning of a series of droughts, hailstorms, and early frosts. Even Newfoundland, barely surviving itself, sent prairie families dried cod cakes. Not sure what to make of the cod, some westerners used it to plug up holes in their roofs.

Prairie hardship influenced the development of the Cooperative Commonwealth Federation (CCF), a farmers' labor movement that was later

ended, a decade of hardship had produced a thrifty generation.

WORLD WAR II

Just days before Britain declared war on Germany, the pervading mood throughout Canadian society was a belief that the war would just go away. But on September 3, 1939, Canadians had their heads pulled out of the sand. Newspaper headlines this time read: "British Empire At War – His Majesty Calls To Britons At Home And Overseas."

Canada's involvement was complicated by the fact that in 1931 the Statute of Westminster had made it an autonomous community within the British Empire. Legally Canada could remain out of the war – but morally there seemed to be no alternative but to enter it.

In French Canada the politician Maurice Duplessis challenged the government's right to speak for *all* of the people of Canada. Québec, Duplessis argued, ought to remain independent of any European struggles. Then, in the spring of 1940, when the German *blitzkrieg* began, Duplessis's calls for neutrality were lost amid the scrambling of French Canadians to register for overseas service.

Prime Minister Mackenzie King maintained support for the war by promising that conscrip-

The Québécois in French Canada voted against conscription and a fierce nationalist movement rose up to resist the draft.

Trudeau, later to become one of Canada's most popular prime ministers. Fortunately for King, it was not necessary to conscript soldiers until the final months of the war. In 1942 in Dieppe it was mostly Canadian men who suffered the huge losses of that debacle and on D-Day, under

The Depression, compounded by freak weather conditions, almost destroyed life on the prairie homesteads in the 1930s.

tion would never be thrust upon them. Soon the country was spending $12 million a day on the war effort; by 1943, 1.5 million were employed to work in munitions factories.

When Japan attacked Pearl Harbor in 1941, Canada, in recognition of the growing bonds being forged between itself and the US, promptly declared war on Japan.

As the war raged on, Britain began to experience severe manpower problems. King decided to see if the Canadian people would agree to conscription, through a national plebiscite. The majority of voters agreed, but the vast majority of Québécois voted against conscription and a fierce nationalist movement rose up to resist the draft; in its ranks was the young Pierre Elliott

the banner of "Allies," it was the Canadians who landed at Juno Beach. By the time the fighting was over, Canada had lost 45,000 lives.

The troops had fought bravely and had played a vital role in the war's deciding battles. But like other nations, Canada's record was not unblemished. Using the pretext that angry neighbors might harm Japanese Canadians, the government had interned 15,000 in camps and had auctioned off their property. Under Minister of Justice Ernest Lapointe, Canada refused to admit all but a few Jewish refugees, both during and after the war. With these blots to its copybook, and with a returning army of displaced and tired soldiers, the Canadian nation set about the task of building a new future.

Brush fires clear land for Vancouver's spreading suburbs in British Columbia.

GROWING PAINS

The conclusion of World War II left Canada in a position of relative strength and its standard of living soared.

World War II, along with integrating Canada's investment and trading systems into the North American grid, had brought to new levels of success the old "National Policy" of Sir John A. Macdonald. Central Canada's industrial wealth was promoted, through federal policy, by harnessing the resources of the country's regions. The result was a spectacular continent-wide prosperity. And in 1949, Canada welcomed its tenth province into the Confederation: Newfoundland.

At the same time, the federal government's power increased to historic highs. Armed with taxing and spending powers gained from the provinces during the crisis of the war, the Liberal government of Mackenzie King laid the foundations of the Canadian welfare state. Old-age pensions were increased, unemployment insurance was expanded, and federal-provincial welfare programs grew rapidly.

Throughout the 1950s, with a population of just over 14 million, the basics of Canadian public life remained stable. A seemingly permanent Liberal government in Ottawa, now under the stewardship of Québec's Louis St-Laurent, continued to win elections with a coalition anchored in Québec and the west. US investment combined with Canadian enterprise to expand industry and resource sectors rapidly. Future Prime Minister Lester Pearson levered Canada's international status to give it a voice in international bodies such as the United Nations. His proposal for the first use of UN peacekeeping troops – the now familiar "blue helmets" of the world's hotspots – in the 1956 Suez Crisis, won him the Nobel Peace Prize.

Powerful forces were reshaping Canadian society. The population increased by 50 percent between 1946 and 1961, to 18 million people, with 2 million coming in the greatest immigration in the nation's history. The face of urban Canada began to

Pierre Trudeau addressing the press.

change, as Mediterraneans and Eastern Europeans transformed dull cities. The country became one of the world's most urbanized nations, with 77 percent of Canadians living in towns by 1961. Television and other mass communications, massmerchandising, and suburbanization were accelerating social and cultural mobility, and women's roles were changing, with an increase in female participation in the workforce.

The political and cultural upheavals of the 1960s were prefigured by the upset victory of John Diefenbaker's Progressive Conservatives in 1957. His minority-government election, based on eroding Liberal support in urban Ontario and the west, became a majority triumph a year later, when Québec's right-wing provincial government

The face of Canada began to change as its population grew by 50 percent between 1946 and 1961, transforming bland cities into multicultural mosaics.

delivered the province to Diefenbaker, creating a national landslide. Although Diefenbaker's period in office, which lasted until 1963, was unable to reorder the political dynamics of Canada, it was a harbinger of an accelerating transformation.

to the provincial government, and promoted the development of a French-speaking state sector as a competitor to the Anglo business establishment. The social energies released by the Quiet Revolution ran in two opposing directions, both with deep roots in Québec's political tradition. Some sought to parlay Québec's self-assertion into a greater role in national politics, to bring "French Power" to the federal government in order to secure for Québec all of the benefits of modern Canada rising around it. Montréal intellectual Pierre Trudeau, who abhorred what he

Trudeau's wife, Margaret, dancing in Studio 54.

THE QUIET REVOLUTION

In 1960, a pivotal provincial election in Québec brought to power a new Liberal government with a new vision of the province.

For decades, Québec's political development had followed its own path, in many respects separate from the currents of change afoot throughout the Western world. The pillars of Québec society – a parochial government, a powerful Catholic Church, and a dominant Anglo-Saxon business elite – were to be dramatically transformed in what became known as *la révolution tranquille*. With the slogan *"maîtres chez nous"* (masters in our own house), the government of Jean Lesage transferred responsibility for the health and education systems from the Church

saw as the inward-looking character of Québec nationalism, would become the exemplar of this current. Others saw Canadian federalism as incapable of responding to Québec's unique imperatives of cultural survival, and sought to fulfill Québec's aspirations through the growth of a separate nation-state.

THE SEPARATIST MOVEMENT

The separatist movement began among radical intellectuals and traditionalist folk singers, but gained credibility as more powerful adherents joined, most notably René Lévesque, who had a been a minister in the Lesage government and would become the first separatist premier of Québec from 1976 to 1983. This crystallization of the federalist and separatist tendencies in Québec politics dominates the life of the province to this day.

The growing assertiveness of Québec clashed with the increasing activism of the federal government, Liberal once again under Lester Pearson from 1963 to 1968 and ambitious to continue building the welfare state through such initiatives as a national medicare system. Perhaps the greatest boon to Canadian prosperity came in 1965, when Canada and the US signed the Auto Pact allowing free trade in automobiles and parts.

Québec's social ferment was probably more

Mitchell, Leonard Cohen, and Neil Young; not as loud as their contemporaries in the US – Jimi Hendrix or Janis Joplin, for example – but certainly more reflective.

As elsewhere, the ferment culminated in tragedy when radical separatists, the *Front de la* Libération du Québec *(the "FLQ")*, kidnapped a British diplomat, James Cross, and Québec's Minister of Labor, Pierre Laporte, in October, 1970. The federal government responded swiftly, at the request of Québec's provincial government, by imposing the War Measures Act – a

Prime Minister Lester Pearson in 1956.

politicized than that of the rest of Canada during the early 1960s. Through much of the decade, English-speaking Canada – along with the United States – reveled in sustained prosperity and a growing sense of sophisticated modernity. This culminated in two events: 1967's World's Fair in Montréal, at which a 100-year-old Canada played host to an approving world; and, in 1968, the election as prime minister of the urbane, even hip, Montréal intellectual Pierre Trudeau. Simultaneously, the current of philosophical discontent found fertile ground in Canada – from student radicalism to the sexual revolution, easier divorce, and the awakening of feminism.

The key popular-music figures of the period in Canada were singer-songwriters such as Joni

move widely supported at the time and seemingly vindicated when Laporte was found murdered, but since believed by many to have been a panicked overreaction. The episode concluded with the release of Cross in exchange for safe passage of the kidnappers to Cuba. Throughout Canada there was a genuine sense of innocence lost as the legacy of the "October Crisis."

In the 1970s the rising oil- and gas-rich western provinces began to challenge the federal government's national policies and its preference for central Canadian industry.

THE CRACKS WIDEN

The 1970s were a pivotal decade for Canada. Backdropped by "stagflation" (low growth, high inflation, and unemployment), politicians and pundits argued such topics as "the limits of growth" and the "revolution of rising expectations".

Three crucial events shaped and echoed this sense of dislocation, cracking the basic pattern of Canada's national life and threatening her very existence. The first was the oil shock of 1973, and the end of the "Long Boom" that had transformed the country and the world in the postwar fundamentally altered the nation's politics. Oil- and gas-rich western provinces began to join with a still more assertive Québec in a drive to transfer powers to the provincial governments.

The third key event was the election in 1976 of a separatist Parti Québécois (PQ) government in Québec under René Lévesque. While the PQ was elected on a good government platform that downplayed separatism, Lévesque pressed ahead with a province-wide referendum in May 1980. The result seemed conclusive: 41 percent of voters cast a *Oui* ballot and 50 percent said

René Lévesque, premier-elect, 1976.

years. The Canadian economy slowed through the 1970s, distorted by double-digit inflation. Chronic unemployment began. Taxes continued to rise, as did spending, but a gap began to appear between the government's revenues and expenditures, which continued to widen until the 1990s. Paul Martin, as Minister of Finance, introduced cost-cutting policies to eliminate the country's chronic budget deficit. In time, federal-provincial politics became a contest over who could most convincingly shift the blame for declining service levels and chronic budgetary deficits.

The second critical development came in the form of political and economic rebalancing stemming from the oil shock. The rise of western Canada, for generations an economic hinterland, *Non* to the government's request for a mandate to negotiate separatism.

Prime Minister Trudeau campaigned actively in the referendum contest. His promise took the form of a crusade to "repatriate" the Canadian Constitution so that it could be amended without British consent, and to add to it a Charter of Rights and Freedoms. This proposal carried considerable support, and Trudeau used it to fashion a Constitution Act that was proclaimed in 1982, over the angry protests of Québec.

On his resignation in 1984, despite some important achievements in his 16 years of power, Trudeau's desired legacy of a strong federal government with a united country seemed further away than ever. Federal-provincial relations were rancorous, westerners increasingly alienated from national affairs, and Québec sullen over its exclusion from the constitutional deal. Moreover, the Canadian economy had stagnated badly.

PROSPERITY AND PROVINCIALISM

The disastrous financial performance of the last Trudeau government was largely due to the recession that rocked the Canadian economy in 1981 and 1982. With unemployment reaching 11 percent and interest rates topping 20 percent, Canadians saw their financial security disappear, and abandoned

now growing insecure with Mulroney's Québec policy. His promise to amend the constitution had been, it seemed, fulfilled in the April 1987 Constitutional Accord signed at Meech Lake in Québec.

At Meech Lake, all 10 premiers and the federal government had agreed to amend the constitution to meet five specific demands of Québec, including legal recognition of the province as a "distinct society." But trouble arose because women feared their rights would be compromised. First Nations, finally beginning to have a voice in Canadian politics, complained that their constitutional issues

Bourassa and Lévesque cast their votes.

the Liberals to give the Progressive Conservatives and their new leader, Brian Mulroney, a chance. The result was the greatest federal election victory in Canadian history, with 211 out of 295 seats in the House of Commons going Conservative.

For most of the country, the classic images of the 1980s were luxury cars, chic restaurants and soaring property values. But for many Canadians the boom never really happened. Unemployment remained considerable, rural and Atlantic Canada stayed in decline, and in the cities, homeless people became a feature of urban life.

Optimism was sufficient, however, for the Mulroney government to win re-election on a platform of free trade with the US. Although it never became a campaign issue in 1988, many Canadians were

had been ignored. Recent immigrants worried that their rights would be undermined. Then, in 1989, Premier Bourassa – whose Liberal Party had ousted the PQ in Québec in 1985 – bowed to separatist pressures in Québec and introduced a law banning the use of English on signs. This assertion of French as the language of Québec resulted in widespread opposition to the Accord.

A NEW DEAL FOR THE NINETIES

If the brinkmanship and backroom deals of the Meech Lake process soured the national mood, the economic events of 1990 curdled it. A recession longer and deeper than any since the Great Depression engulfed the country's economy. Unemployment soared, property values tumbled, and businesses folded. In this troubled context, Québec reacted angrily to the failure of the Meech Lake Accord. Premier Bourassa embarked on a two-year review of Québec's political options, including separation. Slowly, however, the elements of a new deal emerged, to include: replacing the appointed Senate with an elected body, modifying five of Québec's Meech Lake demands, reconfirming the rights of immigrants and women, and self-government for First Nations. This ambitious project culminated in a second Accord, in August of 1992 at

In 1995, the separatist provincial government of Québec held a referendum that shocked Canadians with its result: the proposal to secede from Canada was defeated by a very slim margin of 1.12 percent.

Federally, the Liberal Party remained in power until 2006. Between 2003 and 2006, the right wing gained momentum, as the Canadian Alliance merged with the moribund Progressive Conservatives to become the Conservative Party of Canada. The Liberals were defeated in 2006 and their slow demise continued through

Spanish animal activists protest against the slaughter of seals.

Charlottetown, P.E.I. To pass, the Accord needed majority support in a national referendum from all provinces. Six provinces passed it; four, including Québec, rejected it. In the wake of the defeat, all talk of constitutional amendment was abandoned, and Brian Mulroney resigned. At the next election, the Progressive Conservatives suffered the worst loss suffered by a ruling party.

The Liberals, under Jean Chrétien, took power. The Bloc Québécois, without running any candidates outside Québec, won enough seats to become the official Opposition, operating on a clear separatist agenda. The result boosted the fortunes of Lucien Bouchard, a former Progressive Conservative minister who had quit over the failure of Meech Lake and founded the Bloc Québécois.

⊘ SOCIAL ISSUES

Canada has managed to remain reasonably steadfast in its liberal approach to social issues. Those who are terminally or chronically ill have been allowed to use medical marijuana since 2001. In July 2005, the Civil Marriage Act, which legitimized same-sex marriages countrywide, was introduced by Paul Martin's Liberal government, and passed. And in June 2008, Stephen Harper apologized in the House of Commons to former students of native residential schools for the wrongful policy of assimilation that had been run by a federally financed program – one that had a deeply damaging impact on First Nations, Métis, and Inuit peoples – until as recently as 1996.

several leaders, each unable to generate enthusiasm for the middle road.

In 2006, the Conservative Party, led by Stephen Harper, won with a minority government that included significant gains in Québec. A 2008 election returned Harper with another minority government. A third election in 2011 gave Harper a majority, but the big surprise was the surge of the New Democratic Party under its dynamic leader, Jack Layton (he died in 2011). This left-of-center party had never held more than 37 seats (in a house of 308, in 2008) and suddenly found itself as

and pushing for greater gender equality. However, following the election of US President Trump, tensions have risen between the two neighbours with fights over trade and policy becoming the norm.

DIVIDED WE STAND

If there is a cause for optimism in assessing Canada's political and economic prospects, it probably lies in the country's historic ability to muddle through. As one commentator pointed out, the 1995 vote in Québec was in its way a vindication of the country's strong democracy since, in 90 per-

Prime Minister Justin Trudeau with Prince William and the Duchess of Cambridge during a royal visit to Canada in 2016.

the official Opposition, with more than 100 seats. The Liberal Party was left in a shambles, as was the Bloc Québecois, the latter serving as a signal that Quebeckers, English and French alike, were generally more interested in the social agenda of the Bloc than its stance on separatism.

In October 2015, however, the Liberal Party returned in style, decisively winning the federal election, with the party's leader Justin Trudeau becoming the new prime minister. Trudeau has politics in his blood – his father was Pierre Trudeau, one of the most influential Canadian politicians in history. Trudeau Junior has introduced many reforms in the country's domestic policy, among them resettling up to 50,000 Syrian refugees to Canada, withdrawing Canadian fighter jets from Iraq and Syria,

cent of the world's countries, the leaders of such a forceful secessionist movement would have ended up in jail. Moreover, the last three recessions have taught Canadians some painful lessons about taking prosperity for granted. Those who wish the country to remain together in the future have at their disposal some powerful economic arguments. For the rest of the world, the drama seems baffling. Why should Canadians be putting at risk what is an enviable prosperity? But the forces that tug at Canada's unity are, after all, part of the nation's heritage. Building a thriving, humane society on the unpromising ground once described by Voltaire as *quelques arpents de neige* ("a few acres of snow") was a formidable achievement, and one that won't lightly be discarded.

📷 NEW ARCHITECTURAL HEIGHTS

Today, Canada stands at the forefront of modern architecture and its architects are sought after the world over for their flair and expertise.

From the log cabins of the frontiersmen to the vibrant skyline of modern Toronto, Canada has an eclectic array of architectural styles. In the early days of colonization, settlers simply built replicas of their home-country buildings. The French, for instance, erected the simple stone houses they had been familiar with in Normandy, while the Ukrainians constructed onion-domed churches across Manitoba.

Architects – sometimes military engineers – drew on their own design heritage and by the late 19th century a form of building etiquette had evolved: parliament buildings and churches tended to be designed in the Gothic style, banks and train stations were Classical, legislative buildings looked to the Renaissance, the French chateau style was reserved for hotels, while houses, particularly in the Atlantic provinces, drew on English Georgian influences.

FUTURISTIC DESIGN

As the 20th century progressed, Canadian design began to take on its own distinct identity. Montréal's Expo '67, with Moshe Safdie's "Habitat" of stacked dwellings, and the 1976 Montréal Olympics, characterized by Roger Taillibert's circular stadium, attracted international recognition.

Since then the country hasn't been afraid to commission buildings on a large scale, and a number of influential architects have emerged, including Moshe Safdie (National Gallery of Canada, Ottawa), Douglas Cardinal (Musée Canadien des Civilisations, Gatineau, Québec), Patricia and John Patkau (Canadian Clay and Glass Gallery, Kitchener, Ontario), while in the Maritime provinces Brian MacKay-Lyons is making an impact with his designs for urban living.

The neo-Classical City Hall in Kingston.

The Musée Canadien des Civilisations in Gatineau, Québec.

The Edmundston-Madawaska steel bridge, in New Brunswick, connects Canada with Maine in the US.

Habitat '67, a set of futuristic condominiums designed by Canadian architect (of Israeli origin) Moshe Safdie.

Style Maker of the Museums

For an architect who was asked to withdraw from his architectural studies at the University of British Columbia, partly because his designs were thought too radical, Douglas Cardinal has not done too badly. He now ranks among the world's top practitioners.

After graduating with honors from the University of Texas in the 1960s, Cardinal practiced in his hometown of Red Deer, Alberta, and then in Edmonton, pioneering the use of the computer in structural calculations with his award-winning St Mary's Church, and gradually gaining recognition for his distinctive approach influenced, in part, by his aborginal heritage.

In 1983 he won the prestigious commission to build the Musée Canadien des Civilisations in Gatineau, Québec to house the nation's collection of native artifacts.

Drawing both on nature and technology, the museum's curving shape, according to Cardinal, symbolizes the emergence of a continent sculpted by winds, rivers, and glaciers.

Following on from the success of this project, Douglas Cardinal Architects went on to design the Smithsonian's National Museum of the American Indian, in the heart of Washington DC.

Sculpture at the Simon Fraser University, Vancouver.

The Esplanade Riel is a pedestrianized bridge spanning the Red River in Winnipeg. Have lunch at Mon Ami Louis restaurant, located on the bridge.

A traditional hunting and fishing lodge on Tagish Lake, British Columbia.

Salon Rouge, home to the
National Assembly in the
Parliament Building, Québec City

A street with French-style architecture in Québec City, with Château Frontenac in the background.

THE FRENCH AND THE ENGLISH

Historically, the relationship between the French- and English-speaking peoples has been uneasy, if not explosive. But bridges are being built across the cultural divide.

Eight hundred kilometers (500 miles) separate Québec City from Toronto. Situated between these two cities are cosmopolitan Montréal and Loyalist Kingston; in between these two cultural focal points lie 400 years of Canadian history, tradition, and circumstance. Québec City is archetypically French, politically resistant, insular, its visual splendor and old worldliness reminding one of Europe, of the ancient towns in Normandy or along the Rhine. Toronto is both typically English Canadian and North American. The city serves as an economic center for the entire country. Everything from its skyline, waterfront, and endless suburban sprawl to its professional baseball team places Toronto squarely in the model of a North American urban center. These two cities share in common a vast country called Canada. But what else do they share? One city communicates in French, the other in English. One city looks to France for its cultural heritage and for much of its music, film, and literature. The other city combines the vestiges of British custom with strong leanings toward American popular culture.

The Confederation of Canada in 1867 did not guarantee that these two worlds would unite. Economically, Québec and English Canada do communicate on a regular basis. The St Lawrence Seaway, the Trans-Canada Highway, the tourist charms of Montréal and Québec City serve to maintain a steady flow of traffic between the two communities. Economic ties, along with political commitments (through the federal government in Ottawa), remain strong. Canada is a country – a viable and functioning nation noted for its size and natural wealth. Yet a fragmentation exists. Once beyond economic and political considerations, the ties between

Traffic sign in French and English, Québec City.

the French and English grow more tenuous, more problematic. Eventually a difficult question must be asked; culturally, spiritually, what do these two worlds have in common?

THE WEIGHT OF HISTORY

Any understanding of French–English relations today must begin deep in North America's past. The weight of history was upon the New World from its inception. North America was a battleground for the English and French to wage imperial war. In Canada, the French arrivals tended to settle along the banks of the St Lawrence, in the area now known as Québec, with the English establishing themselves farther inland, initially in the Great Lakes region. By the

1750s, less than 100 years after the first influx of population, the lines were already drawn between French and English areas. With the rapid growth of the English community to the south, which was soon to be called the United States of America, the French were in a very real way already isolated.

The population of New France was less than a tenth of that of the English colonies. What consolation they found in their weaker position derived largely from the "safety net" of mother France, watching over their interests. After

1759, however, this too disappeared. The subsequent English military possession of Québec virtually ruled out hope of reconciliation between the two communities.

What Confederation gave Québec was a political framework for change – the provincial government. The decentralized nature of the agreement, allotting considerable power to each province, should have provided the Québécois with a means to reassert themselves. For many reasons this did not really happen for almost 100 years. The seeds were planted, however, the very same day the country was born.

ENGLISH BOSSES

The first half of the 20th century saw little overt change in the situation. English Canada expanded, solidified its borders, with Ontario coming quickly to dominate the economic scene. Naturally the markets of Montréal and Québec City were worth preserving. Statistic after statistic from this period suggests basic problems: companies located in Québec with an entirely French-speaking work staff but entirely English-speaking management; blatant instances of discrimination against French-Canadians; English-Canadian businessmen earning huge profits from the province without reinvesting it in the economy.

Toronto looks, in many ways, like an American city.

Provincial politicians – especially the looming figure of Maurice Duplessis – found themselves supporting English hierarchies to maintain their political lives, seeking outside investment, inadvertently suppressing the aspirations of the Québécois to strengthen the province's financial status.

In English Canada the French were seen as backward, remote, a society of Catholic farmers and blue-collar workers with little to offer the rest of the country except the brilliant hockey players of the Montréal Canadiens. English was simply not spoken in most parts of the province. Even in Montréal, where the anglophone community ignored the Québécois culture around it, the majority of the inhabitants were unable to function in the economic and political language of Canada. Ottawa and Toronto controlled the lives of most Québécois, dictated their social and economic position, yet had relatively little to do with their day-to-day existence.

In 1945 Montréal writer Hugh MacLennan published his novel *Two Solitudes*, a bleak if

⊘ THE DECISIVE BATTLE

After the battle on the Plains of Abraham, the British were the conquerors, the Québécois the defeated. Consequently, the French settlers were abandoned by their country and left to fend for themselves on an English continent. A pattern emerged in 1759: a largely English-speaking government dictating to a largely French-speaking population. By 1867, a fairly rigid socio-economic relationship had developed. The English-speakers in Québec were the bankers, the power brokers; the French were the workers who created and sustained a rich folk-culture. So the English continued to play the role of victors and to reap the spoils.

honest account of relations between the two communities. MacLennan portrayed both English and French Canada as inward-looking, defensive, unwilling to take the necessary step to end the "solitude" in which each existed.

This phrase, "two solitudes," has come to be an important part of the Canadian vocabulary. To some extent the term is as applicable today as it was 50 years ago. Yet the period between 1955 and 1980 saw a remarkable change in the fabric of both groups. In particular, the cultural and political awakening in Québec shifted the dynamics of the relationship. The tremendous upheaval this awakening wrought on society put the Canadian experiment to a trial by fire.

A QUIET REVOLUTION

In the late 1950s a group of artists, journalists, and political figures – future prime minister Pierre Trudeau among them – began to assert the cause of Québec. Known in retrospect as the *révolution tranquille*, this movement sought to create an autonomy entirely known as Québec, by strengthening the cultural fabric of the society. Songwriters, poets, playwrights, painters, filmmakers, historians all rallied around the concept, which also involved a rejection of the traditional power vested in the Catholic Church. That the *révolution tranquille*, which evolved into the separatist movement of the 1970s, had its root in cultural change is important. These artists were demanding that the Québécois take pride in their culture, their language, themselves. Québec was something quite different from the rest of Canada; it needed to be vigilant and protective of its identity.

THE OCTOBER CRISIS

From the enlightened leadership of premiers Jean Lesage and Daniel Johnson, to the rise of René Lévesque and the Parti Québécois (PQ), the movement's political wing grew in prominence. A dark manifestation of this impulse, the terrorist group Front de Libération du Québec (FLQ), gained much attention in the English-Canadian press. While Albertans or Torontonians were oblivious to the cultural excitement in Québec, to the music of Gilles Vigneault, the writing of Hubert Aquin or Jacques Godbout, they were acutely aware of the bombings in Montréal. They interpreted Québec's struggle

for its identity as a denunciation of the English and rejection of the entire country, fueled by terrorist groups running amok. This distortion and misunderstanding was disastrous to the cause of improving French–English relations.

The so-called "October Crisis" of 1970, when British diplomat James Cross and Québec politician Pierre Laporte were kidnapped, brought Québec's self-assertion to the forefront across the country. Prime Minister Pierre Trudeau declared a state of emergency, shocking English and French alike. Suddenly all the news reports

Newspaper headlines the day after the referendum.

were filled with images of soldiers, of house-to-house searches, and of army checkpoints, not in some war-torn country on the other side of the world, but at home in Québec, Canada. For a few days Canadians witnessed with horror a brief and extremely exaggerated period of social unrest. The crisis took Québec into the next phase of its quest for an independent identity.

Québec's growing pains forced people to examine their priorities and their sense of self. What if Québec separated? Would Canada manage to survive the split?

THE PROUD PROVINCE

The remainder of the decade saw the strengthening of the PQ, their assumption of power in 1976, and the referendum on sovereignty-association of 1980. By the summer of that year, Québec, while apparently unwilling to sever its ties with the rest of Canada, had emerged as a force to be reckoned with. Assertive, self-possessed, the province now had a mind of its own and, because of the nature of provincial governments, a mandate within the Confederation to exert considerable control over its internal

Byward Market in Ottawa, one of Canada's most bilingual cities.

affairs. In a sense the gauntlet had been thrown at the feet of English Canada.

In the meantime, immigration to urban centers, in particular Toronto and Vancouver, had altered the social make-up. The "WASP" (White Anglo-Saxon Protestant) dominance of commerce in central Canada, while still unquestionable, was being flavored by new influences, new faces. Just as Montréal was no longer simply English-controlled and French-populated, so was Toronto no longer simply a city of English money, and Anglo-Saxon temperament. Québec's growing pains greatly affected the economics of Canada. They also forced people to examine their priorities, their sense of self. Québec's struggle

had initiated a kind of collective debate across Canada on the nature of its national being.

After the close-run referendum of 1995, Québec remains a partner in the Confederation. At times, difficult economic conditions have relegated questions of independence to a secondary position, but the issue still simmers on the back burner. To some extent the Québécois' point has been made; ownership of business is again largely internally (or US-) controlled, French is the language of commerce and politics, and the cultural life of the province continues to thrive.

The exodus from Montréal of many English-language businesses offered – for the media, anyway – graphic representation of the isolation of the communities. Legislation brought in by the PQ, especially the controversial Language Bill 101, left a bitter taste in the mouths of non-French-speakers in Québec, along with frequent charges of discrimination by the government. Indeed many of the policies had the effect of further entrenching the country's "two solitudes." In its bid to fortify, Québec seemingly added bricks to the considerable wall that already existed between itself and English Canada.

What then is to be said of Canada's bilingual experiment? While there are still those who ask why someone in Calgary should be expected to learn French, or why Manitoba should have its laws written in French as well as in English, many more people are realizing that, in today's world, speaking only one language poses a considerable disadvantage.

The federal government felt sufficiently strongly about the need for ongoing support for bilingualism to announce, in March 2003, that it would invest more than $750 million over the next five years on boosting bilingualism in schools, community programs, and the federal civil service. And surveys repeatedly show there is support for two official languages. The support is strongest among young Canadians, to whom the value of knowing and using both English and French is increasingly obvious, from a global as well as a patriotic perspective.

Québécois' willingness to give federalism another chance was resoundingly demonstrated in the April 2003 provincial election. Jean Charest (a former Progressive Conservative cabinet minister under Prime Minister Brian Mulroney) led the province's Liberals to victory, taking 76 of the 125 seats. Charest won again, with a minority government, in 2007, but was returned with his third mandate and a majority government on December 8, 2008. His party's success may have been partly due to the lead-up to the federal election held in October of that year. Stephen Harper and his Conservatives went to great lengths to curry favor with Québec, but once word got out that his government planned to cut $45 million from the budget for arts funding – something very close to the heart of the most Québécois – support for the federal Conservative party evaporated, leading to yet another minority government in Ottawa. How Trudeau's government handles tariff

> *While English Canada can no longer patronize Québec, it can no longer complain of inequality. Both are equal, siblings in a challenging experiment in nationhood.*

negotiations, involving the Quebec dairy industry, may go a long way in determining relations going forward.

Historically, English Canada had almost no exposure to the wealth of literature, film, and visual art that was flourishing throughout Québec. But with the success of wunderkind Robert Lepage from Québec City, Cirque du Soleil's reinvention of the circus, Michel Tremblay's widely translated and acclaimed plays, La Bottine Souriante's wild folk music, and the films of Denys Arcand, to name but a few, Québec is making its mark around the world and by extension on the rest of Canada. There is no longer any question of Québec being viewed by English Canada as impoverished and backward.

OTTAWA, THE BILINGUAL CITY

The city of Ottawa is regal, stately, in the image of an old English town. Home to the country's Parliament, Ottawa was once the quintessence of English Canada. Now, however, it is one of the most bilingual cities in Canada and has a strong and vocal Franco-Ontarian population. On any street, in any store, French is as likely to be spoken as English.

Five bridges cross the Ottawa River, linking Ottawa – which, in 2001, amalgamated with 10 other municipalities to become a much larger city – with what, until 2002, was known as Hull. It, too, was merged with other municipalities, to form the city of Gatineau. It used to be that Hull, with its late-night cafes and bars, was a lively night out for the citizens of Ottawa. But changes were made on both sides of the border around the turn of the 21st century. After years of battling seedy bars and clubs, Hull City Council decreed that their bars should close at 2am (a new proposal

La Bottine Souriante, a Canadian folk band famous for performing traditional Québecois music.

to keep bars open until 3am may be back in the near future). At the same time, Ontario changed its law to allow bars to stay open until 2am. While Gatineau still has a lively nightlife, Ottawa's visitors and residents have no special reason to cross a bridge to party. Indeed, the clubs around Ottawa's Byward Market or along Elgin Street are packed most nights of the week.

There was a time when Ottawa and Hull represented the reality of Canada's "two solitudes." Today, so many people who live in Ottawa work in Québec, and vice versa, that is no longer the case. Contact between the communities has transformed from infrequent and ill at ease to frequent and perfectly comfortable.

Inuit woman in traditional caribou clothing, Nunavut.

THE INUIT

For 5,000 years the Inuit and their predecessors have inhabited the Arctic region. Only now are their culture and way of life earning the respect they deserve.

The Inuit are among the least well understood aboriginal peoples in the world. Their rich culture evolved in a land both inhospitable and isolated, independent of outside influences. As the north becomes more accessible and Inuit travel south, the richness of the culture and history are being revealed and documented.

The Arctic environment has not always been static; it has undergone both warming and freezing trends, with a variety of life living in the region at different periods. The north's nomadic inhabitants have had to adapt accordingly.

The first group to live in the north migrated across the Bering Strait during a relatively warm period. This nomadic group, known as the pre-Dorset, spread north into the Arctic Archipelago and east to Greenland. These people hunted seals and fished the waters of the Arctic Ocean.

Around 1,500 BC a cooling trend began in the north that forced them to move south onto the mainland. It was during this period that the pre-Dorset culture evolved into the indigenous Dorset culture. These people now stalked the caribou herds instead of hunting on the sea ice. Their cultural links with their cousins west of the Bering Strait were broken.

Yet the Dorset are not the direct ancestors of the Inuit. Starting in AD 900 another warming trend began that heralded the migration of the Thule from Alaska. The Thule hunted sea mammals. With the retreat of the permanent ice pack on the mainland, the whales, seals, and walruses swam through the Bering Strait and into the Beaufort Sea. The Thule were quick to follow.

Ancient Thule site near Resolute Bay.

The Thule differed from the Dorset in several respects: one was that they lived in fairly large settlements along the coastline, unlike the Dorset, who lived in small family groups. Secondly, the Thule were technically more sophisticated hunters. Ironically, about AD 1500, the Thule found themselves in a position similar to that of the Dorset 3,000 years earlier: yet another mini-ice age had set in. This period saw the ice pack grow so large that the number of sea mammals passing through the Bering Strait to the Arctic Ocean decreased and the migration patterns of the caribou shifted southward. The Thule broke into smaller groups and became more nomadic. It is these people who are called the Inuit.

> *With the growth of the ice pack, the Thule adapted; breaking into smaller nomadic groups, they depended less on the huge bowhead whale, more on belugas, narwhals, seals, and caribou.*

ARCTIC HOME

The Inuit chose to make the Arctic their home, in spite of the adversity they encountered. Their history, culture, and language are unlike those brought with them, they still frequently encounter tremendous emotional upheaval in adjusting to the isolation of northern climes. The Inuit do not have that sense of isolation; for them the wind, the snow, the seasons of light and darkness are a part of life.

EUROPEAN CONTACT

In 1576 Martin Frobisher, an Elizabethan explorer and privateer, sailed into a large bay on Baffin Island in search of gold and the Northwest Passage to India. He was met by Inuit who

A spear-hunting expedition.

of the ancestors of today's First Nations of Canada and American Indians, who moved south soon after crossing the Bering Strait.

In that harsh, unforgiving land the Inuit perfected the building of igloos and airtight kayaks; they became experts in tracking polar bear and seal on the Arctic ice. Although they suffered from famines and exposure, the Inuit stayed.

Forged with their innate ability for innovation was a humility that made the Inuit a tolerant, stoic society, who accepted their limitations in a land where darkness reigns for six months of the year. The fact the Inuit have endured for centuries becomes even more remarkable when one considers that despite the technological sophistication that Euro-Canadians have

circled his vessel in their kayaks. In a bid to coax them closer he rang a bell, the sound of which had probably never been heard in the Arctic before.

One curious Inuit was close enough to reach for the bell. Frobisher, with both hands, pulled the man and kayak up and into the ship and stowed him away, like booty, in the hold. After the search for gold and the passage both proved fruitless, Frobisher returned to England and, in the habit of the day, brought the Inuit man as evidence of the peoples he had encountered. On a second voyage, he captured three more Inuit (a man, a woman and a baby, but not from the same community), using them as "proof" of the strange places he had visited. All died in captivity.

Apart from Frobisher's expedition, the Inuit of the high Arctic seldom had contact with any Europeans until 1818, when whaling vessels started arriving in the eastern Arctic Ocean. These whalers risked navigating through the treacherous iceberg-laden Davis Strait in search of the bowhead whale. In the 1830s there was a series of whaling disasters, with vessels becoming trapped by the Arctic ice.

A solution to these problems was to establish whaling stations. In the 1840s William Penny,

Unfortunately, because the whaling had proven so successful, by the 1880s the bowhead whale population in the Arctic was greatly reduced. In spite of this decline in the whaling industry, the contact with the southerners, or *Kabloonat*, continued because of the growing presence throughout the Arctic of the Hudson's Bay Company, Canada's largest fur-trading company. Although the Inuit maintained their semi-nomadic life, they began to rely on trapping and trading to provide for themselves.

Captured on film beside the Great Whale River (c.1920).

a typically shrewd Scottish whaling captain, began to employ local Inuit at his station on Baffin Island. He found that they were exceptional whalers, hardly surprising when you consider that the Inuit had been whaling for centuries. Soon Penny and other astute whalers began to adopt the warm clothing, harpoons, and other paraphernalia of Inuit technology.

William Penny noted on his arrival in Baffin Island in the 1840s that there were 1,000 Inuit. By 1858 there were only 350 due to the prevalence of tuberculosis and influenza.

This shift away from living off the land to a barter, and then cash-based, economy provided the Inuit with guns, cooking utensils, and foodstuffs from the south. For some, the Hudson's Bay stores became a base or second home.

However, this arrangement changed abruptly when the price of furs fell dramatically in the 1840s. On Baffin Island, two-thirds of the Hudson's Bay stores closed their doors. The Inuit could no longer purchase ammunition or the other goods they had come to depend upon.

A long period of starvation and deprivation began. While the Inuit economy was collapsing, missionaries were filing reports to medical authorities that tuberculosis (TB) and influenza epidemics were annihilating the people. One anthropologist studying at Coronation Gulf found in the 1920s that 30 percent of the Inuit population had died from influenza over a 14-year period. Similarly, in Coppermine in 1931, 19 cases of TB among a population of 100 were found.

THE GOVERNMENT INTERVENES

For the most part, until the late 1940s the Canadian government ignored the Inuit. However, after prodding from the churches, it began to take action. In 1950 medical authorities ordered

nomadic life and move into government-built permanent settlements. These artificial communities provided housing, medical facilities, churches, and schools.

However well-intentioned policy-makers were, they failed to understand that the Arctic tundra and ocean is home for the Inuit. From the beginning of this resettlement period the Inuit struggled to retain their identity. The first step was made in 1959; in that year the Cape Dorset Artists Co-op was formed on Baffin Island.

Inuit artist carving a narwal tusk.

Inuit items carved from leather, bone, ivory, and stone.

1,600 Inuit, or 14 percent of their population, to sanatoriums in Edmonton and Montréal. This action, though necessary in the absence of hospitals in the Arctic, was devastating for the Inuit, the vast majority of whom had never left the north. As well as treating tuberculosis, the health authorities were startled by the high rate of infant mortality. In 1958 infant mortality was at 257 per 1,000 live births. By 1970 it had dropped to 100 per 1,000, and in 2016 it was still almost 18 per 1,000 – still 3 times the Canadian average.

The federal government introduced more than a medical plan for the Inuit; they created a set of policies designed to rocket the Inuit into Canadian society. The central tenet of all these policies was to encourage them to abandon their

A SENSE OF COMMUNITY

Over the centuries the Inuit have worked with ivory, stone, bones, and skins to make clothing, utensils, hunting tools, toys, and amulets. Often intricate designs were patterned onto these objects. When whalers arrived, trading began to take place, with the resourceful Inuit even manufacturing ivory cribbage boards for trade. It was in the 1950s that southerners began to discover the Inuit's remarkable skill in carving and other traditional crafts, and funding was made available to develop these skills.

As a result the Inuit co-ops have flourished, receiving international recognition for their work in several mediums, including stone-cut prints, stencil, sculpture, and carving.

The co-op system has evolved to become more than enclaves for artists. In many communities it manages hunting expeditions, municipal services, and trading posts. The philosophy behind the co-ops reflects the Inuit concept of community and what Western thinking might call egalitarianism. For this reason, Inuit town meetings tend to be excruciatingly long for outsiders and are filled with lengthy meditative silences. Generally, the Inuit will not leave a local meeting before a well-thought-out consensus has been forged.

were equally puzzled when they attempted to unravel whose children belonged to whom.

Within the Inuit community there is clearly a different set of values operating from those in the south. The pursuit of personal wealth is for the most part played down. The respect one can earn in the eyes of the community is important. For men this respect has traditionally been earned through becoming a good hunter or trapper, although this is now changing. Carving, despite its lucrative nature, has not been regarded as such a worthy occupation. The Inuit do under-

An Inuit woman and her child in the Northwest Territories.

THE NEXT GENERATION

In a society where the line between nuclear family, extended family, and community is blurred, the importance of children cannot be overestimated. Traditionally, Inuit women are encouraged to have many children; many start from puberty and still bear children into their mid-forties. If, for whatever reason, the parents of a child are unable to support it, the child will be adopted by the grandparents or by some other member of the family. Illegitimacy is less of an issue here than in other societies, which is partly attributable to a sense of communal responsibility for children. In the 1960s the Inuit were baffled when social workers first attempted to formalize adoption procedures. Social workers

stand that protecting language and culture are critical to their survival, and Inuktitut is one of three official languages in Nunavut. Their relationship with the land has made the Inuit, particularly the older generation, ambivalent toward higher education and the learning of "southern skills." Mandatory school attendance was seen as a method of either forcing them to follow their children into government-built communities, or separating them from their children by sending them away to school. Many Inuit questioned the relevance and importance of their children learning subjects like English, science, and math.

The federal government has attempted to integrate the educational system into the community. However, a program to recruit and train

Inuit to become teachers failed in part because few Inuit were willing to leave their community for eight months at a time to train.

The young adult Inuit population has been dramatically affected by the complications of living in a world with two divergent cultures. These Inuit are the children of the "baby boom" that swept across the Arctic in the 1950s and 1960s, in part created by the lowering of infant mortality and generally improved health.

The question that faces this group of people is how they will support themselves and build a

...it, Nunavut Territory.

future. As part of government policy many children were sent away to attend regional high schools. That isolation had a disorienting effect. They failed to learn, as their parents had, how to live off the land, how to keep warm while out in the cold, how to build a temporary snow shelter if the weather changed. Knowledge of survival techniques forms a keystone of Inuit culture. Yet, if the young are not familiar with traditional skills and their implicit philosophy, they also have not acquired the skills necessary to compete for management positions in government or in industry.

The continuity in passing down the knowledge and communal values from one generation to another has been broken. The resulting problems have manifested themselves in alcoholism, vandalism, and suicide. Inuit youth suicide is 11 times the national average.

ADOPTING NEW TECHNOLOGY

In many ways, technology has brought about a safer and more comfortable life for the Inuit. They ride on snowmobiles, watch satellite TV and hunt with high-powered rifles. They have running water. They no longer live in snow houses. The question that many would ask is: has technology made the Inuit more or less Inuit?

The Inuit have traditionally been eager to adopt new technology. In their environment they had to be great innovators. It is what the technology represents that bothers the Inuit. The challenge for the Inuit is to make technology their own; then they will be rulers in their own land. In adopting this technology, the Inuit must look to their knowledge of how they lived in the past if they are to avoid becoming strangers in their own land.

For more than 5,000 years the Inuit and their predecessors have politically, aesthetically, and socially been building and rebuilding a society that has allowed them to live independently in an environment where others could not bear the physical and psychological pressure.

It is their unique culture that has allowed them to make the north their home. If the young are not permitted to capture that spirit, if they are overwhelmed and bullied by Western society, then they will no longer be Inuit. And Canadian society will lose a unique and valuable fragment of its colorful mosaic.

⊘ EXPORTING INUIT CULTURE

In addition to Inuit carvers and printmakers, Inuit artists from other genres are making their mark on the world stage. Inuit throat singing is a competition between two women, who stand facing each other. One begins by voicing a series of rhythmic sounds, including sounds made in the throat by inhaling and exhaling. She then repeats the series, leaving small silent gaps. The other singer must fill in the gaps with another rhythmic pattern. Throat singing continues until one of the women runs out of breath or can't keep up. She generally starts laughing, thus losing the game. A typical session can last two or three minutes.

Inuit man building an igloo on Baker Island.

Canadian Celine Dion sings in both English and French.

ART AND PERFORMANCE

Canadians have worked with great determination to
create a vibrant artistic, dramatic, and literary scene
that reflects the talents of its multicultural population.

Although artistically Canada is a young nation,
its contribution to the arts world is impressive. It
has renowned writers, respected literary events
and drama festivals, and boasts much-admired
theater and dance. In the world of music, it has
leaders on all fronts, having spawned exceptional
classical performers, along with mainstream
and alternative composers and performers. Its
French-language films consistently win international accolades, and Toronto and Vancouver vie
for the title of Hollywood North, having initially
gotten the chance to compete as locations in
the filmmaking world thanks to a low Canadian
dollar. Now, the fluctuation of the dollar is less
a consideration than the ready supply of skilled
professionals and the great locations that can
replicate big American cities or, in the case of
Vancouver's local quarry, backdrops that suit science fiction and futuristic films.

Given that most Canadians live within 240km
(150 miles) of the US border and are permanently
exposed to North American cable television,
newspapers, books and magazines, fast food,
and shopping malls, the influence of American
culture and lifestyle has always been strong. A
quick browse through the daily papers makes
one wonder what constitutes Canadian culture.

Since World War II, artists' efforts to develop
a sense of identity have been backed by government protection of "cultural industries" in its
negotiations with the US.

In spite of this intervention, after the war
many serious Canadian artists went abroad, to
England, France, and America. That changed
in the 1960s, in part thanks to Canada's anti-
American sentiment amplified by the Vietnam
War, when Canada was identified with the distinctive voices of Leonard Cohen, Joni Mitchell,

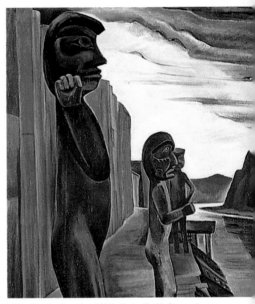

'Blunden Harbour', c.1928–30, by Emily Carr, who
painted in British Columbia.

and Neil Young. Government grants at that time
made it possible for the next generation of artists to have more successful careers at home,
or at least to promote themselves as Canadians
and be recognized as talented.

REGIONAL STRENGTHS

The search for a cultural identity is also an
attempt to unify a vast land. Canada's most
popular authors and artists are often identified
with specific regions.

In literature, Québec is historically associated
with Mordecai Richler, Michel Tremblay, and
Gabrielle Roy; Nova Scotia with Hugh MacLennan
and Antonine Maillet; Manitoba with Margaret

Laurence; the Yukon with Pierre Burton; and rural Ontario with Stephen Leacock and Alice Munro.

Early Canadian society, with its long winters and agricultural industrial base, presented many limitations. Nineteenth-century artists in a sparsely populated country were isolated and without an audience. In the colonial period, Canadians turned to France, Britain, and the US for inspiration and approval. This trend continued in the 20th century. In a country suspicious of the arts, Canadians found fuller expression of their talent, and public recognition, abroad.

The physically demanding industries such as mining, forestry, and fishing ("rocks, logs, and fish," as the poets say) and hardships of the pioneers left them little time for artistic creativity. Pioneering writers such as Susannah Moodie considered that escape was to be found only in the grave. Even today many writers and artists continue to explore subject matter provided by their ancestral pasts, their immigrant backgrounds, and the pioneering days of their forebears.

Nowhere is the difference of experience more defined than between the English-speakers

'To Prince Edward Island', the disturbingly realistic art of Alex Colville.

⊘ CREATIVE CANADIANS

Creative Canadians have had to struggle to be heard for the simple reason that they are outnumbered by their American and British counterparts. The world media is also controlled elsewhere, so making a name in many artistic endeavors means leaving home. When a humorous commentator once explained that Canada's fourth-largest city is Los Angeles, the statistician in the crowd wonders if that might not be true. It has long been recognized that to succeed financially, an artist has to leave Canada, and Los Angeles has obvious attractions, particularly for those wanting to get into the movies.

and the French-speakers of Québec, the "two solitudes," as the novelist Hugh MacLennan described it. The constant tension between the two communities has given a demanding dynamic to the country, which is reflected in the arts.

Such 19th-century movements as the Canada First movement and the Confederation Poets (or Maple Leaf school) drew inspiration from the landscape. Lucy Maud Montgomery's (1874–1942) still popular *Anne of Green Gables* novels and Mazo de la Roche's 16 impossibly romantic *Jalna* (1927) novels would sell millions of copies around the world. The short stories of Morley Callaghan; the pioneer novels of Frederick Philip Grove; the struggle of pioneering artists in the poems of E.J. Pratt; tales of shipwrecks and seal hunts, and epics of rail building and missionaries – all of these were serious efforts at coming to terms with the Canadian experience.

ARTS FUNDING

When Prime Minister Lester Pearson gave the country a flag in the early 1960s, it was a time of optimism for Canada's creative class. The Centennial in 1967, and the famed Expo fair in Montréal the same year (which lived on as the "Man and His World" exhibition until 1981) generated

THEATER

Ceremonials and ritual drama are central to aboriginal and Inuit social and religious activities, which use masks, costumes, and properties to enhance dialogue. Great ritual drama, like the Kwakiutl, takes five months to perform. Most Canadians are not familiar with these traditions. Native theater and dance companies and a Native Writing School are now restoring traditions that were almost lost in the 20th century.

Since the mushrooming of theaters in the 1970s, Canadian audiences have had a choice of

A 1976 production of 'Anne of Green Gables: The Musical' at the Confederation Centre of the Arts, Charlottetown, Prince Edward Island.

a new-found nationalism, stimulating a cultural revolution, supported by direct funding through the Canada Council.

When the economy is good, Canada Council funding increases. The other side of this coin is that, as soon as there is a downturn in the economy, funding is stripped out of the government's budget. The result is that artists live with uncertainty which occasionally sparks amazing prolific spurts of creativity, occasionally sends them out of the country, and occasionally forces them to abandon their dreams altogether. The lack of stability has had a huge impact on the development of a sustainable artistic underpinning to the Canadian identity.

regional theaters and the summer festivals that take place across the country. The most prominent of these events is the Stratford Shakespeare Festival in Stratford, Ontario, founded in 1953. With a budget of close to $60 million, and attendance of a half a million people, it presents a six-month season of Shakespeare's plays, a variety of musicals, and contemporary classics in four separate theaters. It is fair to say that Stratford is in large part responsible for the other summer Shakespeare festivals that have sprung up in virtually every province across the country. As a training ground for performers, directors, and stage technicians, Stratford sets the standards that other companies aspire to, or sometimes react against.

The Stratford Shakespeare Festival in Ontario attracts an audience of 500,000 to its annual six-month season. Popular summer Shakespeare festivals include those held in St John's, Halifax, Saskatoon, Calgary, and Vancouver.

Next in prominence is the Shaw Festival, at Niagara-on-the-Lake, founded in 1962 to showcase the plays of George Bernard Shaw. Char-

has always been to attract an audience with a relative unknown playwright, particularly when the material being addressed was often controversial. But more and more Canadian plays are being written and performed, including noteworthy work by First Nations playwrights Tomson Highway (*The Rez Sisters* and *Dry Lips Oughta Move to Kapuskasing*) and Drew Hayden Taylor (*Toronto at Dreamer's Rock* and *Only Drunks and Children Tell the Truth*).

A major challenge to the nearly 90 smaller theaters in Toronto during the 1990s was the suc-

Karen Kain in a production of 'Carmen'.

lottetown, on Prince Edward Island, is home of the longest-running Canadian musical, *Anne of Green Gables*, first performed in 1965. In the west, Vancouver's Bard on the Beach delivers excellent Shakespeare all summer in two large tents in an idyllic setting. The back of the main stage is extended with its open view of the mountains. There is always at least one crowd-pleasing comedy, a tragedy, and one of the lesser-known Shakespeare plays.

It has taken time for Canadian plays to emerge. In the 1960s and 1970s some small alternative theaters opened, including Vancouver's Savage God; Toronto's Theatre Passe Muraille, Factory Theater, Tarragon Theater; and Halifax's Neptune Theater. The challenge

cess of the blockbuster international musicals, such as *Les Misérables* and *Phantom of the Opera*. The Princess of Wales Theater in Toronto was built especially for *Miss Saigon*. Now, however, the long-running shows have closed or moved on, to be replaced by more touring productions.

In financially difficult times, special-interest theaters have grown. Fringe festivals have evolved in most major cities to a world-class level. Toronto's comedy club acts are broadcast worldwide, and have nurtured such talents as Dan Aykroyd, Jim Carrey, and Martin Short.

DANCE

The Canadian Ballet Festival movement, launched in Winnipeg in 1948 to give dancers a sense of what their colleagues were doing elsewhere in Canada, soon developed into a strong regional ballet movement across the country. Four years later the first experimental dance company, Les Grands Ballets Canadiens, was established in Montréal, while Celia Franca established Toronto's National Ballet of Canada, developing international ballet stars such as Karen Kain and Veronica Tenant.

With freedom to create non-literal and abstract dance, modern dance experiment companies – such as the Paula Ross Company

PAINTING AND SCULPTURE

Prior to Confederation, documentary tradition dominated Canadian painting. Painters were usually inspired by European trends. But landscape painting changed immeasurably in Canada in 1920 with the first exhibition of the modernist Group of Seven (1920–33). The painting tended to post-Impressionist mannerisms, with great dabs of mysticism. It caught the public interest, and the artists' claim to be Canada's national painters aroused furious debate among critics. An associate of the group, Tom Thom-

Admiring 'Tribute to Diabolic Robert' by Canadian painter Jean Paul Riopelle.

and Anna Wyman Dance Theatre of Vancouver, the Toronto Dance Theatre, Robert Desrosiers of Montréal, as well as dozens of independent choreographers – challenged the classics of the larger companies and, by the 1980s, classical ballet and modern dance companies were eager to learn from each other.

According to Canadian arts advocate Max Wyman, Canada's professional dance scene today reflects the country's emergence as a modern nation. Whether working in classical or contemporary styles, their dance is enriched by the traditions of aboriginal people, influenced by European and American cultures and inspired by generations of immigrants who have come to Canada from around the world.

son, became romanticized after his mysterious drowning in 1917. His paintings of pine trees and lakes are among Canada's most famous images, and one even sold at auction for close to $3 million in 2010.

Most early 20th-century artists worked in isolation and were disregarded, experiencing success posthumously. Emily Carr (1871–1945), for example, worked on the west coast, painting forests, native villages, and totem poles with bold strokes and color. David Milne (1882–1953) introduced modernist techniques and he, too, found success only in his later years.

Montréal painters took a different path. Alfred Pellan, Paul Emile Borduas, and John Lyman returned from France inspired by the example

The work of Inuit artists has achieved the recognition it long deserved. In some villages, soapstone carving and printmaking are the most important sources of revenue for the community.

of modern European art, especially Cubism and Surrealism, and called themselves the Automatists, after their 1947 exhibition. The most prominent of the younger painters was Montréal-born

Nobel Prize-winning Canadian author Alice Munro.

⦿ MUSICAL MILESTONES

Among those who made their mark in music are Glenn Gould (whose interpretation of Bach's Goldberg Variations in 1955 and again just a year before his death in 1982 are still referred to as landmark recordings) and jazz wizard Oscar Peterson (whose 1962 *Hymn to Freedom* became a rallying song for the American civil rights movement and was played at the Obama inauguration in January 2009).

In the classical world, individual performers on the world stage today include pianists Angela Hewitt and Jon Kimura (Jackie) Parker, along with an astonishing number of singers: Nancy Argenta, Elizabeth Bayrakdarian, Russell Braun, Judith Forst, and Ben Heppner.

Jean-Paul Riopelle. Québec painting would soon show the new dynamics of color, abstract expressionism, and non-figurative forms.

The painter Borduas's 1948 manifesto *Refus Global* advocated spiritual and artistic freedom and attacked the repressive government and Church in Québec culture.

The manifesto effected change in all the artistic disciplines, including dance, music, theater, painting, and sculpture. Despite his own personal hardships, Borduas's paintings and manifesto represent one of the major achievements of Canadian art.

Toronto dominated artistic expression in the 1950s. Jack Bush, Harold Town, and William Ronald were the major painters of a group who took the name Painters Eleven and promoted the new American abstractions of the 1950s. In the west, Gordon Smith, John Koerner, and the late Jack Shadbolt experimented with a variety of styles and techniques. The late Toni Onley's distinctive and mystical representation of the beauty of the Pacific Northwest became synonymous with the landscape.

Painting is now being challenged as the leading edge of the visual arts by conceptual art, sculpture, video, performance, and the work of the First Nations people.

Since the mid-20th century the work of Inuit and West Coast native artists has earned the recognition it deserves, winning international acclaim, and becoming an important force in the country's culture. In the 1950s and 1960s, with the help of the Hudson's Bay Company and Canadian Handicrafts Guild, Inuit-owned co-operatives were set up in many Arctic communities, as much as a source of income for the people as to encourage local skills. Art galleries countrywide, including Québec's fine Canadian Museum of History, have devoted considerable space to First People's art.

MUSIC

From the classics to pop, the music scene in Canada has been consistently and extraordinarily varied. It has a strong lyric quality and is never afraid of breaking new ground. Outdoor concerts are an important part of the summer in every part of the country.

After the 1967 Centennial a remarkable flourishing of compositions explored new directions; chance music, electro-acoustic music, with R.

Murray Schafer and Harry Somers pre-eminent among the *avant-garde*.

Canada has more than 100 professional or community orchestras, although the classical orchestras face funding issues, as they do in many parts of the world. In its intensity and diversity, the country's music has assumed great proportions. Toronto has become a center for new and alternative music in North America and a leader in Caribbean-influenced pop.

In the summer, live rock concerts feature the best of national and international performers. Canadian hard-rock groups such as Nickelback, The Tragically Hip and Rush, and singers such as Bryan Adams, Céline Dion, Michael Bublé, Drake, The Weeknd, Shania Twain or Justin Bieber, stage sell-out concerts. Most towns in Canada have rock clubs and bars.

There is a long history of singer-songwriters who have found international fame since the 1960s, including Leonard Cohen, Paul Anka, Joni Mitchell, Neil Young, Alanis Morissette, k.d. lang, and Diana Krall. Perhaps the best example of this is David Foster: while most people are not aware that he is Canadian, he is the epitome of a Canadian performer – diverse, equally adept at writing, performing, arranging, and producing music. His extensive list of compositions includes *I Have Nothing*, sung by Whitney Houston in the film *The Bodyguard* and nominated for both a Grammy and an Academy Award.

The CRTC (Canadian Radio-Television and Telecommunications Commission) regulatory agency ensures at least 35 percent of music played (Monday – Friday) on the radio is Canadian and that 50 to 60 percent of broadcast television is of Canadian content – a policy that has helped to give many popular Canadian performers a start to their careers.

A national party station, MUCH-Music, takes popular music seriously, showcasing the political, social, and artistic side of contemporary performers from England, France, and multicultural Canada. Though jazz clubs have short histories in most Canadian cities, the summer jazz and blues festivals attract thousands across the country, as far north as Dawson City in the Yukon. Celtic-style music is also popular in the Atlantic provinces, with Cape Breton fiddlers Ashley MacIsaac, Jerry Holland, and Natalie

MacMaster finding fame, along with Newfoundland band, Great Big Sea.

MODERN WRITING

While prose and poetry have a long history in Canada, historically readership was small; most works were not published until accepted by a US or British company. Toronto's Harbourfront Reading Series, founded by poet Greg Gatenby in 1974, is pre-eminent in the world for its festival of national and international literary celebrities. In the 1960s, writing communities flour-

Drake performing at Coachella.

ished coast-to-coast. Writers' festivals provide Canadian authors with the opportunity to crisscross the country to promote their books and meet their readers. Canadian festivals attract international writers as well, whose publishers recognize that Canadians are avid readers and a good market for their stable of authors.

It is fair to say that events since the turn of the millennium wrought havoc on both the book publishing and magazine industries in Canada, but equally fair to say that many have simply embraced the internet as an opportunity to attract new readers. Major literary critics, such as George Woodcock, Marshall McLuhan, and Northrop Frye, set new standards for the appreciation of Canadian letters. Toronto is still

The list of important Canadian writers alive today is too long to enumerate, but a few worth exploring include first Canadian Nobel Prize in Literature winner Alice Munro (2013), Margaret Atwood, Joseph Boyden, Douglas Coupland, Rohinton Mistry, Yann Martel, Bev Sellars, and Michael Ondaatje.

important, but it is no longer the place for writers to make their mark. Indeed, the diversity of the

As filmmakers began to turn their interest from educational and informative films to the fiction feature film, Hollywood moved to protect its interest. Despite complex talks of quota systems, there was virtually no feature filmmaking in English Canada until the 1960s. However, Canada did command worldwide respect for work in short-film animation. Nearly all the films were produced by the NFB. Especially outstanding is the work of Norman McLaren, who dazzled millions around the world with such films as *Neighbours*, which won an Academy

Dan Aykroyd and Jim Belushi.

country supports their staying "home" and allowing their writing to reflect their place in the world.

FILM AND TELEVISION

English-speaking Canada is considered part of the American domestic film market, and Canadian films have limited opportunities to be shown in Canadian theaters and on television. World War II changed the Canadian film industry, with the formation of the National Film Board (NFB), which began to train and develop Canadian filmmakers. Internationally, the NFB is practically synonymous with quality documentary film. Beginning with documentary film needed for the war effort, the NFB expanded into areas of ethnic groups, Canadian art, and social problems.

Award (1952), and *Pas de Deux* (1969), with its haunting dance sequence developed with an optical printer.

The development of the 16mm camera and the influence of French "new wave" film-making led to a more personalized cinema. By 1970 such films as Don Shebib's *Goin' Down the Road* and Gordon Pinsent's *The Rowdyman* were commercial and artistic successes. An important figure was David Cronenberg, whose low-budget horror films created a cult following at home; he has since become a major international director with such films as *The Fly*, *M. Butterfly*, *Crash*, and *Spider*.

In the 1980s, there were notable successes by such filmmakers as Anne Wheeler, Philip Boros, Patricia Rozema, and Atom Egoyan, who

won the Grand Jury Prize at Cannes in 1997 for *The Sweet Hereafter*. The world-famous Toronto International Film Festival held each September is considered as important as Cannes. In fact, it has been ranked by the *Los Angeles Times* as number one in the world.

Québec filmmaking likewise has had its share of challenges, but it has produced some exceptional prize-winning films: Denys Arcand was twice nominated for an Academy Award for *Jesus of Montréal* and *The Decline and Fall of the American Empire*. Claude Jutra and Jean Beau-

bringing out the sharp differences between life in Toronto and Montréal.

If there have been hard times at home, actors have sought fame further afield. From the early days of Mary Pickford and Lorne Greene, through the era of television (where William Shatner dared to boldly go and Michael J. Fox was a Young Republican in *Family Ties*) and on to Pamela Anderson, Jim Carrey, Jason Priestley, the Ryans (Gosling and Reynolds), and Ellen Page, Canadian actors, producers, and writers have found success in Hollywood. Larger-than-life heroes

The director and one of the actors from 'Bon Cop, Bad Cop', a film about an English-speaking police officer from Toronto, and a French-speaking police officer from Québec. The film is half in English and half in French.

din made significant titles such as *Mon Oncle Antoine* and *J.A. Martin, Photographe*.

While the early 1990s saw the Québec film industry again in crisis, with less money and fewer productions, in the late 1990s there was a significant resurgence. On the international stage, Denys Arcand won the Best Foreign-Language Oscar for *The Barbarian Invasions* at the 2004 Academy Awards, and Jean-Marc Vallée's *C.R.A.Z.Y.* won Canada's own annual Genie Awards for best motion picture in 2006. A testimony to the courage and inventiveness of the Québec film industry is the 2006 comedy thriller buddy cop film *Bon Cop, Bad Cop*, a film that mixes French and English indiscriminately,

Superman, Ghostbusters, and Rambo originated from Canadian-born authors. Ottawa-born comedian Dan Aykroyd even made a tongue-in-cheek feature film about the Canadian plot to take over the Hollywood empire, while Ontario-born Mike Myers launched Austin Powers at the world. Such figures are recognized internationally, just as many of Canada's writers and musicians have made their names outside the country. Sometimes it is a surprise to discover that such well-known people are Canadian, and not American after all. But their roots are the same as those who have stayed at home, where local arts are still active day after day. There is no lack of opportunity for attending a performance.

📷 ANCIENT INUIT ART

Canada's galleries and museums now give full recognition to its rich heritage of native art dating back to the Dorset peoples of 600 BC.

Traditionally there was no word for "art" in the Inuktitut language. Early carvings tended to be functional – tools, weapons, and utensils – or they were used for spiritual purposes, such as amulets and masks. The sculptures of animals, birds, sea creatures, and human figures simply represented daily life.

The first people known to produce what is now recognized as "art" belonged to the Dorset culture (c.600 BC–AD 1000). They used ivory, bone, and wood and, like today's artists, kept as close as possible to the original shape of the material. The items were often small and remarkably smooth.

INUIT ANCESTORS

Thule people, the ancestors of today's Inuit, migrated east from northern Alaska around AD 1000 and replaced the Dorset inhabitants. Their art was more feminine and less ritualistic. It consisted of decorated everyday items such as combs, needlecases, pendants, and female figurines, harpoon toggles, and gaming pieces. In the 16th and 17th centuries a colder climate led to the demise of the Thule culture. European exploration was beginning, and the Inuit started to barter their carvings with the traders and explorers who made their way across the north.

In the 1940s, the federal government began to encourage the development of Inuit art as a means to bring much-needed income to the isolated communities. With the help of the Hudson's Bay Company and the Canadian Handicrafts Guild, Inuit-owned co-operatives were set up across the Arctic.

Contemporary Inuit art has achieved international status, and museums and galleries across Canada devote considerable space to its exhibition.

A finger mask used by women during dance entertainments, representing the moon spirit.

In 2005 the Musée National des Beaux-Arts du Québec acquired the extraordinary Raymond Brousseau collection of Inuit art, consisting of over 2,500 works (mostly sculptures) throughout the Canadian Arctic.

Animals, birds, and fish are often the subject of Inuit sculptures. This small carving (8cm/3in tall) of two polar bears wrestling was made in the 19th century on the northwest coast.

A mask symbolizing a shaman's spirit flight; the face in the center represents the shaman's soul.

Contemporary Artists at Work

Inuit art comprises a great number of regional styles determined by tradition, available materials, and the artists themselves.

Many of today's artists have experienced life away from their communities, and combine the various cultural influences in their work. David Ruben Piqtoukun, whose sculptures have been exhibited widely, was born in 1950 north of the Mackenzie river delta. His father was a hunter and trapper. At the age of five, Piqtoukun, like so many of his generation, was sent away to school and forced to come to terms with an English culture. His work has a strong spiritual element on the one hand, while also exploring the impact of outside influences on his culture. He lives outside Toronto and regularly returns to his home community of Paulatuk.

Ovilu Tunnillie also experienced life in an alien world, which is reflected in her carving. She was born on Baffin Island in 1949. As a child she contracted tuberculosis and spent three years in hospitals in Manitoba. On her return she had to relearn both her language and her way of life. Taught by her father, Tunnillie began carving in 1972. Her sculptures are exhibited worldwide. She died in 2014.

Inuit stone sculpture, found near Frobisher Bay, Nunavut.

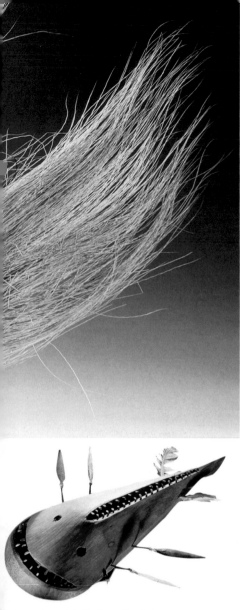

A shaman's mask in the form of a whale.

An inukshuk (stone landmark) stands guard over Whistler Mountain, British Columbia.

Skiing in the Coast Mountains, British Columbia.

CANADIANS AND THEIR LANDSCAPE

A well-educated population and the realities of geography and language make for both work and leisure activities that are as diverse as the country itself.

How Canadians juggle work and play is as varied as Canada's geography, in part because of that geography and in part because of its sparse population. The country's total population is about 10 percent less than that of California, mostly located along a thin strip to the north of its 6,400km (4,000-mile) border with the United States. Its people are generally well-educated, but how do they earn a living and what do they do when they are not working? How has this changed over the more than 400 years since the first French explorers set up a permanent settlement and established the fur trade?

Historically, Canadians were thought of – and thought of themselves – as hewers of wood and drawers of water. The evolution of Canadian industry followed a path determined by explorers and entrepreneurs who were more interested in either adventure or personal fortune than creating a vision for the country. As explorers opened up the country, through contact with First Nations people, they learned what riches each corner had to offer and determined whether these were useful for the purposes of trading or for sending back to Europe.

The resources that found favor progressed beyond the fur trade through gold, silver, forestry, coal, and oil. Each of these industries needed large numbers of unskilled or semi-skilled workers, willing to perform hard physical labor. After the initial flush of the gold rush faded, and there were no more nuggets to be harvested by panning the creeks and rivers, gold mines were required. The daily grind of earning a living wage by digging and blasting away the rock that encased a vein of gold held little appeal for those who craved excitement and adventure. They moved on, to chase the next dream. New immigrants arrived, willing to take on this brutal work to get a foothold in a new country and save enough money to send for their families.

Climbing an oil rig in Alberta.

LAND DIVISION

In 1870, the Hudson's Bay Company (which was granted initial right to most of what is now Canada by Charles II of England in 1670) ceded its interest in the territory between Ontario and British Columbia to the newly created Canada.

The land was divided in square mile (2.6 sq km) sections. One section was made up of 640 acres (close to 260 hectares). Similar to the American plan to attract settlers, much of this land was made available to immigrants to "homestead." That is, in exchange for the promise that they would build a house and cultivate a small portion of the land, they were granted a quarter-section of land (160 acres/65 hectares). The program triggered mass immigrations from Britain, in particular Scotland

and Ireland, where the poor saw an opportunity for a better life. Numerous other nationalities followed suit, which explains varied pockets of Ukrainian, Danish, Swedish, and Dutch Mennonites (who came to Canada via the area of the Russian empire that is now the Ukraine) across Manitoba, Saskatchewan, and Alberta.

Oil is the main resource that provides jobs for Canadians. In Alberta, massive tar sands are "mined" – bitumen-rich ore is extracted by open-pit mining, crushed, and processed, ultimately creating synthetic crude oil.

The legacy of that settlement and images of the vast prairie wheat fields create a misleading picture of Canada as an agricultural economy. While more than 30 percent of the population lived on farms in 1931, statistics for 2011 show that around 2 percent of the Canadian population is involved in farming, with those that are farming getting older and older. As farmers retire, their children are simply not interested in carrying on a business that is barely sustainable, so larger agri-businesses purchase the land and mechanize operations, achieving economies of scale, but often reducing diversity and sacrificing quality.

INDUSTRY AND STATE

Today, oil is the main resource that provides jobs for Canadians. Off the coasts of Nova Scotia and Newfoundland, offshore drilling attracts the adventurers of today, who are willing to work under intense and risky conditions for a few years, often hoping that the money they accumulate (there isn't a lot of opportunity to spend money on an oil rig) will give them a nice nest egg for their future. The shale oil and gas revolution, much of which occurred in the US and damaged the Canadian oil industry, is expected to reach Canada next, as it sits on a grouping of supposedly massive shale fields.

As the prices for gold and other metals soar, mining is seeing a resurgence, although it is frequently in the form of reprocessing by sifting through long-abandoned tailings, activities that require more technological innovation than manpower. Another less publicized industry is diamond mining – while the Northwest Territories

has the first diamond mines in North America, it appears that there are other locations in northern Ontario, Québec, and Nunavut that have commercially viable quantities of diamonds. Like the tar sands developed for oil mining, massive capital investment is required to set up the initial facilities (when De Beers set up its Snap Lake mine, the cost came close to one billion dollars).

Primary industries such as mining and forestry employ only a small percentage of Canadians. Beginning early in the 20th century, the government, looking to build a stable and independent

Saint Romuald oil refinery, Québec City.

economy, recognized that Canada did not have sufficient economies of scale to survive. In the absence of a large investment class, government stepped in and helped create industry. When two other rail lines became insolvent after World War I, the government created CN Rail, focused on maintaining a supply line for prairie wheat to export markets.

Often, the approach was for the government simply to create an entity, like the airline Air Canada in 1937. The 1975 creation of the state-owned oil company Petro-Canada was part of a national energy policy, ultimately sold off in 2009. Once created, these companies (or "crown corporations" as they were generally called) operated as businesses, with an important exception: if they were not profitable, the government stepped in

The 1989 free trade agreement with the United States had a major impact on Canadian industries and the subsidies and tariffs that had governed their operation.

to cover the shortfall. While these operations helped achieve national political and economic objectives, their shareholders rarely demanded the same rate of return as private companies.

minimum wage in a coffee shop. Taxes in Canada are high, in part to maintain a universal health-care system and a comprehensive welfare system, including legislation providing for extended maternity leave (partially subsidized by the mandatory unemployment insurance program). Educated youth are looking at their career options and asking how they will ever be able to afford the lifestyle their parents took for granted. They are often forced to remain at home long into their twenties, a reality that is changing family dynamics and often frustrating all concerned.

White-water rafting.

Public policy was designed to compensate for the country's shortfalls in population and expertise. Industries that benefited included the shoe and clothing industries in Québec and the steel and automotive industries in Ontario. Subsidies disappeared at the same time as offshore production of these same goods soared in the "global economy." The result: Canadians looking for work were increasingly limited to service-sector jobs. In fact, three out of four Canadians work in the service sector.

Today, whether in the service sector or primary industries, Canadians face the same challenges as other Western countries: an aging demographic expects generous pensions for their years of service while younger generations are wondering how they will ever get ahead earning

LANDSCAPE AND LEISURE

It's not all about work, however. Geography and the seasons play a big role in how Canadians enjoy their free time. The landscape is magnificent, whether it's the rocky coast of Newfoundland, the boreal forest of the north or the mountains in both east and west. It is logical

Bombardier, the world's rail equipment manufacturing and servicing industry, now has manufacturing facilities in close to 30 countries, but still maintains a significant part of its workforce in Canadian plants.

More than 40 national parks cover more than 300,000 sq km (115,800 sq miles), with each province having its own park system. All the provincial parks in British Columbia combined are about the size of England.

that Canadians associate leisure time with time outdoors.

"Summer vacation" is typically defined as two to

the blades as there are fewer backyard outdoor rinks lovingly created by dads imaging their son as the next great Canadian hockey player. When the weather gets really nasty, Canadians are terrific travelers, hopping on planes for Mexico, the Caribbean, or southern US for a quick winter break to recharge their batteries.

Regardless of the weather, Canadians get outside. They simply don't see sub-zero temperatures as an obstacle. In the fall, snow tires go on the car, while storm windows replace the screens that have been keeping the mosquitoes at bay. In

Ice skating on Rideau Canal, Ottawa.

three weeks in July or August, spent in some outdoor activity, whether it's time at the family cottage in Muskoka, or a road trip and camping. Generally fitter and more active than their American neighbors, Canadians embrace hiking, cycling and water sports that range from swimming to sailing and fishing. In summer, the farther north you travel, the longer the days, but even in the cities along the US border, 16-hour days lure most people outside.

In winter, activities and venues change. The 2010 Winter Olympics in Vancouver and Whistler showcased one of the many outdoor playgrounds Canadians take for granted. On the West Coast, residents are smug about being able to ski and sail on the same day. Skating is seen as a national pastime, although, in fairness, fewer people now don

Canadians embrace winter. In Ottawa, the citizens anxiously wait for the Rideau Canal to be frozen solid so they can pull out skates and glide from the Parliament Buildings down to Dows Lake, a 7.8km (4.8-mile) journey that makes the canal the largest skating rink in the world.

spring, the reverse activity is accompanied by the planting of vegetable plots in the back yard. The only debate is which weekend will ensure the seedlings that have been carefully nurtured on windowsills will not freeze overnight.

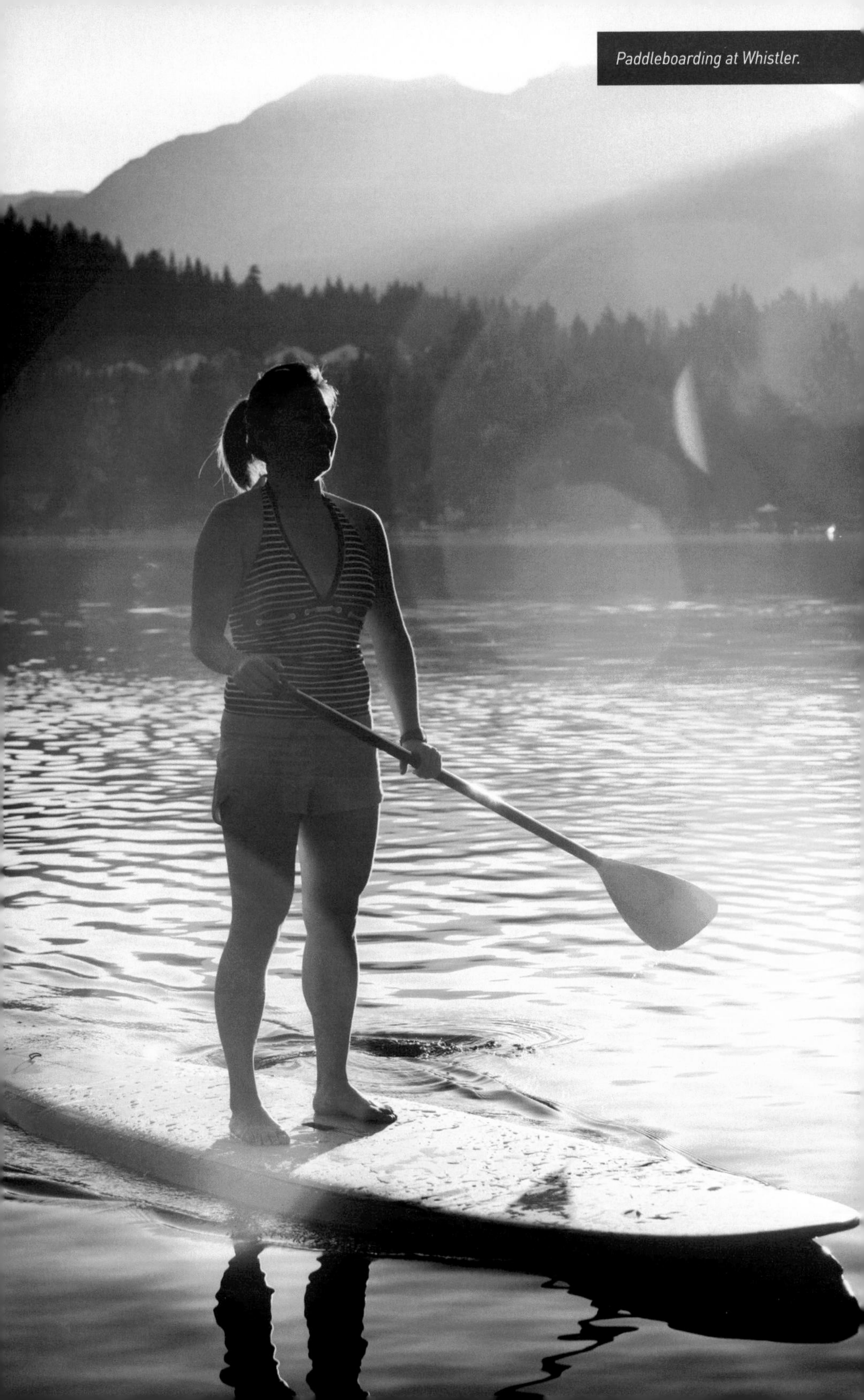

Paddleboarding at Whistler.

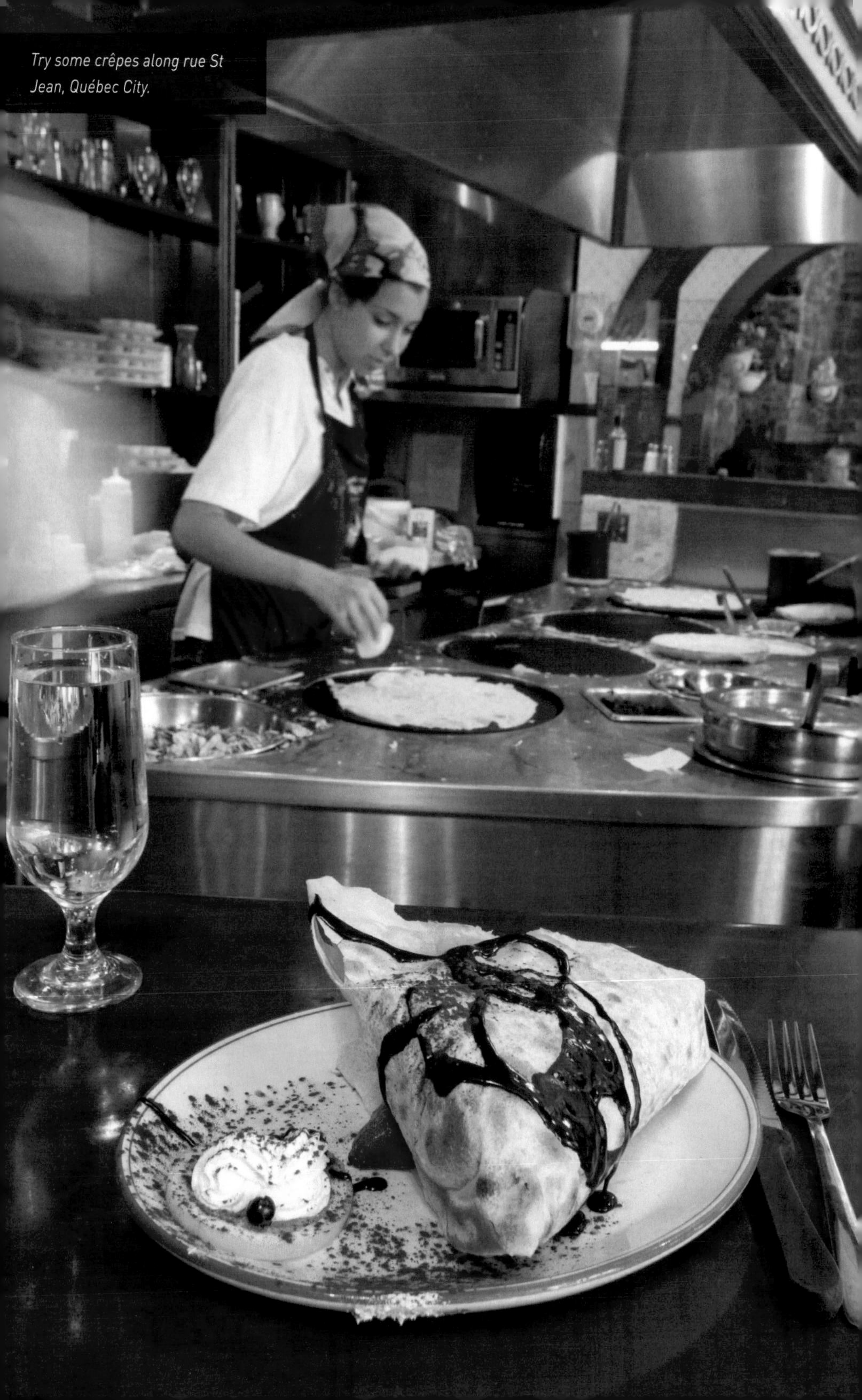
Try some crêpes along rue St Jean, Québec City.

FOOD AND DRINK

Canadian cuisine is a combination of influences from the native peoples to recent immigrants, using the country's own abundant food resources.

Early settlers faced many challenges, and the first Canadian cuisine consisted of eating what you could hunt, fish, and forage – most of it learned from the native peoples, saving many a fur trader and explorer from certain starvation.

As a result, there is no single cuisine that defines Canada but rather one made up of several components. There are more than 80 cultural communities, and some 5,000 restaurants at any given time in a city such as Toronto, where the Italian population rivals a mid-size Italian city and Chinatown is one of the busiest in North America. If a food or ingredient exists, it's probably available somewhere in Canada, and definitely in the larger cities.

Over the past 400 years, successive streams of immigrants have brought their recipes and ideas with them, each contributing to Canada's food culture.

Foreign visitors can be forgiven for thinking that mainstream Canadian food is interchangeable with American. Hamburgers and French fries are standard fare at any Canadian shopping mall, just as in any American city. But a closer look reveals Japanese sushi, Korean *bulkokee*, Chinese stir fry, Ukranian and Polish *pierogies*, and Greek *souvlaki*. Canadians are used to combining foods from four or five cultures on the same plate and see nothing unusual about this approach to eating.

THE 100-MILE DIET

The various trends and obsessions with fresh and organic are at home in Canada. First

Fresh pickles and blue carrots in Saskatchewan.

Nations cultures all across the country evolved diets and favorite foods that were directly related to what was available and what could be stored for the winter. As a country of abundant game, fish, corn, squash, beans, berries, and greens, the cuisine was varied in summer, but very limited during the long winters. Much of the food eaten by settlers and colonials was an attempt to recreate food from the countries they had left behind; this not being practical, they began to adapt to the land and learn a new way of eating.

Now, modern technology has helped farmers cultivate more exotic foods in Canada profitably, so the bounty that can come out of a local Canadian garden is truly astonishing.

FOOD FOR ALL TASTES

The ethnic diversity of immigrants brought with it all manner of food styles and tastes. The country is almost pathologically receptive to whatever is happening on the international food scene, so what you can expect in Canada is a cuisine that's like an orchestra, with native and colonial strands and a plethora of richly varied imports. *Churrasco*-style (Portuguese) barbecued chicken can coexist with Jamaican ginger beer, as can Armenian *lahmajoon* (flatbread spread with ground

There are few exclusively Canadian foods. However, butter tarts are so prevalent in Canada that they deserve special mention. The doyenne of Canadian cuisine, Elizabeth Baird, in confirming their unique position, even recommends them as a great treat for Canada Day (July 1). Their origin is unclear but one theory claims they are an adaptation of the southern US pecan pie. These little pastry shells, filled with a sticky mixture of butter, brown sugar, corn or maple syrup, and sometimes raisins or pecan nuts, are the subject of endless debates: should they be

Fiddleheads at the market.

Canadian maple pies.

lamb) with Thai salad and real ale from a microbrewery. The idea of melding all these cuisines into one distinct Canadian school of cookery has largely failed: simply put, Canadian cuisine focuses on the best of all its constituent cultures.

Of course there are the regional specialties that the whole country enjoys and that people use as a shorthand to define a region and its culture. In the Maritimes, for example, it's lobster, mussels, oysters, and fiddlehead greens (ostrich fern), along with Prince Edward Island's famous potatoes; in Québec, maple-sugar pie, Oka cheese, and old-style bagels; in Alberta, possibly the best beef on the continent; and in British Columbia, cedar plank salmon.

⊘ PICK OF THE WINES

Ontario and British Columbia wines consistently win major international awards. The quality assurance program VQA (Vintner's Quality Assurance) ensures that labeled wines come from specified lands as well as pass sensory tests to confirm varietal characteristics. Every winery has something special to offer, but here are a few of the highlights:

In British Columbia: Black Hills Estate Winery, Lake Breeze Vineyards, Quails' Gate Winery, Sumac Ridge Estate Winery, the Vibrant Vine and Tinhorn Creek Vineyards.

In Ontario: Cave Spring Cellars, Château des Charmes, Malivoire, Thirty Bench Wines, and Peller Estates.

runny or chewy, is sugar or syrup or both the best, and where are the best butter tarts in the country?

CREATING A CANADIAN CUISINE

Today Canada is home to some of the finest chefs in the world, many of whom create "market-inspired" cuisine, relying on the excellence and abundance of local ingredients to craft inspired dishes with blueberries, fiddlehead greens, wild rice, maple syrup, bison, and seafood. One well-known Canadian chef, Michael

In the Atlantic Provinces, the first French settlers have left a lasting and treasured legacy. Although most of those settlers, the Acadians, were forcibly removed by the British in the 18th century (transported south to Louisiana, becoming the forefathers of today's Cajuns), many managed to return. Their influence is apparent in Nova Scotia and New Brunswick cuisine, in *galettes* (oatmeal and molasses cookies), *fayots au lard* (pork and beans), and *poutines* (delectable fruit pastries, not to be confused with the *poutine* of Québec, French fries topped with

That finishing touch makes all the difference.

Stadtlander, abandoned Toronto to move operation to a farm in the country, where he could switch to the 5-mile (8km) diet for his patrons.

Canadians are keenly aware of their country's gastronomic resources, and are using more homegrown foods and produce. Indeed, menus have become longer, not because there are more items, but because the descriptions include the provenance of the main ingredients. In Vancouver, the duck will be Polderside, the pork Sloping Hill Berkshire, the oysters Fanny Bay, and the lamb from Salt Spring Island. While the descriptions may seem pretentious, they aren't – people here genuinely care about their food and are interested in knowing everything about it, not least its provenance.

gravy and cheese curd). Halifax became the center of British social life, German farmers settled in Lunenburg, and the Loyalists brought with them the flavors of New England and the South. In the 19th century, Irish and Scottish immigrants introduced oatcakes and shortbread, along with traditional stews.

Some of North America's oldest culinary traditions are found in Newfoundland, settled by Irish and English fishermen. Salt cod, salt beef, pork, molasses, and root vegetables are still staples today, although many of the recipes have been updated.

Most of Québec's early settlers came from northeastern France, some from the Charente-Maritime region north of Bordeaux. Today, its cuisine draws gourmands from all over the continent, both with its traditional fare, such as *tourtière* – a meat pie with ingredients that vary according to region – and contemporary French cuisine, using local products including foie gras, cassis, and shockingly good cheeses.

Long before the first European settlers arrived in southern Ontario, the Huron and Iroquois nations were cultivating corn, pumpkins, and beans. The United Empire Loyalists who came north after the American Revolution were mostly of British stock. The province's culinary

British Columbia enjoys the flavors of Asian cuisines as well as the initial British penchant for joints of meat and hearty stews. Vancouver enjoys a restaurant scene that is hard to beat: its environmentally aware populace have supported sustainable programs, including Green Table, whose member restaurants commit to reduced waste and more recycling, more eco-friendly practices, and more products that benefit the local economy.

The gourmet influence extends to the Yukon, the Northwest Territories, and Nunavut, at least as far

A fine selection of freshly baked bread.

Wine for sale at Blasted Church Vineyards.

contribution today rests on its agricultural produce, its wines from Niagara vineyards, and Toronto's unbelievable array of ethnic cuisines.

Manitoba, Saskatchewan, and Alberta have come a long way since immigrant Scottish crofters to the prairies survived on little more than oatmeal, and the Métis cooked according to the traditions of their Indian and French-Canadian heritage. Mennonites, Scandinavians from the Dakotas, and American ranchers moved north, and cowboys lived on steak, beans, flapjacks, and raisin pies. Ukrainians, Eastern Europeans, Icelanders, European Jews, and Chinese, with their own culinary traditions, contributed to shifting the emphasis from a heavily British one to a brave new multicultural world.

as serving tourists is concerned. After decades of canned and packaged foods, people are slowly refocusing on the bounty of the land, including caribou, moose, arctic char, and wildfowl.

DRINKS

Wine and beer are mentioned in separate panels – suffice to add that there are impressive selections of both. Aside from beer and wine, Canadians like their share of spirits. Globalization has had its influence on the bar scene in cities across the country, so vodka rules, but more as a statement of identity. Downtown bars in Toronto and Vancouver frequently boast selections of single malt whiskies to rival anything in Edinburgh.

Whether it's a classically Canadian Caesar with its clam and tomato (Clamato) juice, tabasco and Worcestershire or an espresso Martini (equal parts of chilled espresso coffee, vanilla-infused vodka, Kahlua, and Frangelico), Canadians like to make statements with their choice of drink. Canada, despite high taxes on alcohol, boasts some of the most ardent supporters of the highest quality products. For visitors, it's a great opportunity to taste magnificent wines from all over the world.

On the non-alcoholic front, the European-style cafe, complete with croissants and *pains au chocolat*, was once to be found only in Montréal, but now cafes are readily found in all cities and many smaller towns. While Starbucks outlets abound, there are plenty of independents offering a quality personalized experience as well. Even the Canadian doughnut chain Tim Hortons has developed its version with its iced cappuccino (not something that would appeal to a die-hard Italian coffee-lover, but a step up from drip coffee with a scoop of ice cream...).

Canada has a long brewing tradition.

⊘ A QUICK GUIDE TO CANADIAN BEERS

Part of the Canadian stereotype is beer, along with back bacon, hockey, and winter. While the rest may be questionable, the beer part has a ring of truth. Canada has a long brewing tradition, initially dominated by Molson and Labatt's. There were some smaller regional breweries, but nothing really exciting until microbreweries took off in the mid-1980s. Microbreweries focus on offering natural beers of distinction and taste, and brew-pubs across the entire country now produce an array of specialty beers, from ales and lagers to bitters and stouts.

The big breweries have formed alliances with (or been bought outright by) international consortiums, so the quest for a truly "Canadian beer" leads the discerning

drinker to the craft breweries. Passionate beer devotees now make the discovery of each town's best beer an exciting adventure as important as any museum, park or historic site. Forget the multinational brands: choose the local beverages and compare across the regions. Here are a few producers and noteworthy beers to watch for:

Beau's - Lug Tread
Broadhead Brewing Company - Blueberry Blonde
Phillips Brewing Company – Blue Buck Ale
Picaroons Traditional Ales – Winter Warmer
Propeller Brewing Company - Propeller IPA
Yellowhead – Yellowhead Premium Lager
Yukon Brewing Company – Espresso Stout Midnight Ale

Moraine Lake, Banff, Alberta.

Québec Old City.

Charlevoix, St Irénée, Québec.

Fall colors at Algonquin Provincial Park, Ontario.

INTRODUCTION

Planning a visit to Canada that includes more than one destination is bound to seem intimidating, as the distances are so enormous. But the journey itself becomes a large part of the adventure, as you cross the wide open spaces separating one city from another.

A grizzly bear in the mountains around British Columbia.

Canada is the second-largest country in the world, stretching over 5,500km (3,400 miles) from the Atlantic Ocean to the Pacific and over 4,600km (2,900 miles) from the northern tip of Ellesmere Island to the United States border.

With a little more than 35 million people this sprawling country is not, of course, fully inhabited: 89 percent of the land has no permanent population. Nearly 82 percent of Canadians live in large urban centers located within a few hours' drive of the southern border, mostly in Ontario, Québec, or British Columbia.

The country is dominated by its three principal cities: Toronto, Montréal, and Vancouver – places that have elicited comment for centuries. Toronto, for instance, invited the observation by Charles Mackay in 1859 that "there is a Yankee look about the place... a pushing, thrusting, business-like smart appearance." Montréal, on the other hand, "conveys the idea of a substantial, handsomely built European town, with modern improvements of half-French, half-English architecture." Vancouver is a different kind of place altogether, looking neither to America nor to Europe for its inspiration.

Rural Canada is divided into 10 provinces and three territories. Newfoundland and Labrador is the most easterly province, in the North Atlantic; Prince Edward Island is the smallest; Nova Scotia is a peninsula; New Brunswick is nearly rectangular with two coastlines; Québec's and Ontario's cities and high-octane profiles make them the

Downtown architecture, Toronto.

best known – although Alberta is fast catching up; in the Prairies, Saskatchewan's reputation for innovation is beginning to match the splendor of its landscapes, although Manitoba is somewhat less exuberant.

Rudyard Kipling was particularly pleased with British Columbia's clean air and pioneering spirit, observing in 1908 that "such a land is good for an energetic man. It is also not so bad for the loafer." Time is needed for exploring Canada's three territories: the Yukon, the Northwest Territories, and Nunavut, but you can loaf here, too. Or anywhere in Canada, for that matter.

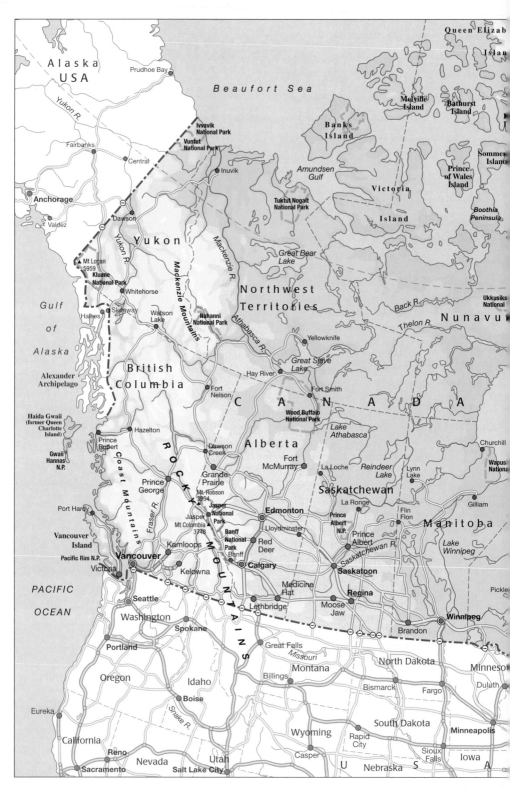

ICELAND

Reykjavik

Greenland

Arctic Circle

Baffin

Bay

Sirmilik
National Park

Davis

Baffin

Island   Auyuittuq
National Park

Strait

Melville
Peninsula

Foxe

Basin

Labrador Sea

Iqaluit

ATLANTIC

Southampton
Island

Hudson   Strait

OCEAN

Peninsule
d'Ungava

Labrador

Hudson Bay

Peninsula

Newfoundland

Red Bay   St Anthony

& Labrador

Labrador City   Gros Morne
National Park

Québec   Natashquan   Newfoundland   St John's

Sept-Îles   Anticosti I.

Channel-Port-
aux-Basques

Albany R.   Gaspé

Chibougamau   Prince
Ontario   Edward   P.E.I.   Sydney
Geraldton   Kapuskasing   Chicoutimi   Rimouski Island   Charlottetown
                                                   New
Thunder Bay   Timmins   Val d'Or   Québec City Brunswick   Nova
                                                              Scotia
Lake Superior Sault   Sudbury   Trois-Rivières Maine   Saint   Halifax
             Ste Marie   Montréal   John
                            St Lawrence R. Sherbrooke

                                      Ottawa

Wisconsin   Michigan   Kingston   Vt   N.H.   Portland
             Oshawa   New
             Toronto   L. Ontario York Mass.   Boston
Milwaukee   Hamilton   Niagara   Syracuse   Providence
Lake Michigan London   Falls
             Niagara   Buffalo
Lake Huron   Falls
             Detroit   L. Erie   Pennsylvania   New York

Canada

0   500 km
0   500 miles

N

CENTRAL CANADA

Heartland of Canada's colonial history, Ontario and Québec offer a wealth of different experiences for the traveler.

Fresh berries in a Montréal market.

For the last century or so, Québec and Ontario have housed not only Canada's most prosperous cities, but also nearly 60 percent of its population. While the West – specifically British Columbia and Alberta – is catching up fast in the prosperity stakes, Québec and Ontario pull rank when it comes to their cultural traditions. These provinces represent the origins of colonial Canada, including the historic tension between their British and French forebears.

They also have the most tourists – almost 57 percent of all Canada's international visitors, who generate 54 percent of the country's tourism revenues. Toronto, with its lakeside setting and bubbling nightlife, is an obvious starting point. The nation's capital, Ottawa, is on the eastern edge of Ontario, which extends north and west to the Arctic.

Often overlooked, northern Ontario is a vast but accessible region of pristine lakes and quiet townships. The chapter on the province is designed to give a feel for every nook and cranny. Ottawa is highlighted, as well as gems such as Stratford, Elora, Kingston, Picton, and Algonquin Park.

Kingston boating docks.

Québec is the other historical center of Canada. Here the emphasis is on Québec's uniquely French nature, its cultural institutions, its festivals, and the efforts of the province's inhabitants to retain their heritage. A detailed account of everything Montréal has to offer is followed by a visit to Québec City, and a scenic trip up the St Lawrence River, ending at the Gaspé Peninsula in the St Lawrence estuary.

The Toronto skyline viewed from Toronto Island.

TORONTO

The multicultural city of Toronto has a dazzling assortment of ethnic neighborhoods, a vibrant waterfront, theaters, concert halls, clubs, galleries, and some of the best shopping in North America.

The largest city in the second-largest country in the world is best approached by car and at night. Toronto is cradled within small hills that roll down gently to the calm north shore of Lake Ontario. A sheltered Great Lakes port, it has a magnificent downtown skyline when viewed from the highways that hug the lake shore. In the dark, the glowing office buildings and the trademark CN Tower have an alien beauty.

A MEETING PLACE

From around 1,000 BC, natives gathered here to trade, socialize, and relax. In fact the name Toronto comes from a Huron Indian word meaning "place of meeting." In 1615 an explorer called Etienne Brûlé discovered an Iroquois village here on the Humber river, and later a fur-trading post was established by the French in 1720. The British became the ruling power after the defeat of the French on the Plains of Abraham in 1759, and in 1787 they purchased the land Toronto now stands on from local Mississauga Indians – who by then had replaced the Iroquois. Gradually a settlement grew around the natural harbor.

In 1793 Toronto, renamed York, became the new capital of Upper Canada (today's southern Ontario). Throughout the War of 1812, York remained loyal to Britain, although in 1813 it was briefly occupied twice by the Americans.

A street performer at Buskerfest.

After incorporation in 1834, the city was renamed Toronto. From the early 1800s, waves of British immigrants arrived, and later 40,000 Irish immigrants, as a result of the potato famine in 1847. The first Jewish immigrants arrived from Europe in the 1830s, and another wave came in the 1880s.

LOYAL ROYAL SUBJECTS

Until the end of the 19th century, British immigrants were the largest group by far, and their loyalty to Queen Victoria and to everything the British Empire

◎ Main attractions
Rogers Centre
CN Tower
Hockey Hall of Fame
St Lawrence Market
Distillery District
Harbourfront Centre
Toronto Islands
Art Gallery of Ontario
Royal Ontario Museum

Map on page 128

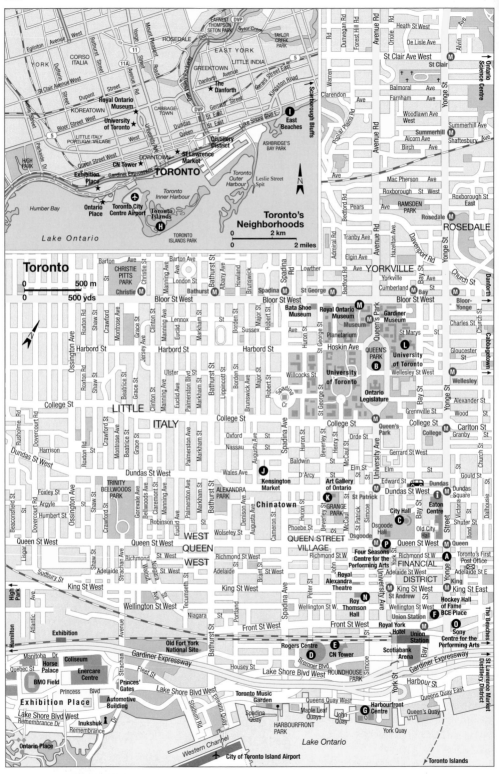

Toronto's Neighborhoods

0 ___ 2 km
0 ___ 2 miles

Toronto

0 ___ 500 m
0 ___ 500 yds

stood for meant that Toronto life was firmly shackled by a code of rigid moral values, including draconian Lord's Day legislation that prohibited most working, sporting, and entertainment activities on the Sabbath.

This did not, however, deter immigration. Following World War II, Toronto's population swelled with the arrival of refugees from Europe. In the 1970s, as a result of relaxed federal immigration laws, fresh waves came from Asia, Latin America, Africa, and the Caribbean. By the 1990s, Toronto's population of 3.8 million included hundreds of thousands of Caribbeans, Chinese, Italians, Greeks, and South Asian immigrants and their descendants, along with substantial groupings from most other parts of the world. According to a recent survey, some 51.5 percent of Toronto's residents belong to a 'visible minority group'. Today more than 140 languages are spoken by the city's 90 (and counting) different ethnic groups. One result of this vibrant mixture, layered over the solid British underlay, is that Toronto became, de facto, the political, cultural, and financial juggernaut of Canadian accomplishment.

SUBWAYS, STREETCARS, AND BUSES

Among Toronto's attributes are four subway lines, with all-night buses taking over after the trains stop rolling around 1.30am, 11 streetcar routes, and about 150 bus routes. Despite the system's convenience and safety, Torontonians have been switching to automobile use over recent years. Efforts by the Toronto Transit Commission to lure them back to the trains sometimes result in commuters being jolted out of their early morning reverie by droll quips from a conductor over the PA system. Controversies over how best to develop (and fund) new Light Rail Transit (LRT) or subway lines continue to plague municipal politics.

TORONTO'S LONGEST STREET

Yonge Street divides the east and west sides of the city. It is commonly said to stretch 1,896km (1,178 miles) northwest from the lake shore in Toronto to Rainy River on the Ontario/Minnesota border, but in reality, is actually consider to stretch a "mere" 56km (35 miles). Up until 1999, the Guinness Book of World Records repeated this misunderstanding. Regardless, the underside of Toronto's thriving economy becomes apparent as you walk along the **Yonge Street Strip** Ⓐ, between King and Bloor streets, but it's worth investigating – not least because the bizarre mix of restaurants and stores offers some excellent bargains. Far more leafy surrounds, trendy restaurants, and smart boutiques are to be found if you walk up Yonge, north from Bloor.

POWER PLAY

Usually a peaceful haven in the heart of Toronto, **Queen's Park** Ⓑ is home to the Ontario Legislature Buildings. Built between 1886 and 1892, the imposing sandstone building – which officially

You can eat a range of cuisines in Toronto.

Queen's Park.

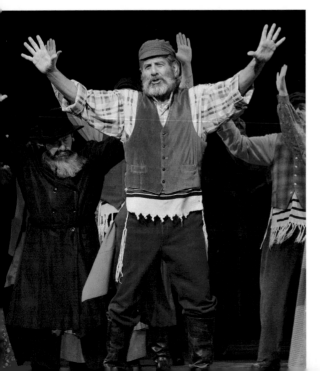

Topol performs 'Fiddler on the Roof'.

opened in 1893 - has a historic Legislative Chamber and an impressive collection of 19th century and early 20th-century Canadian art. After the landslide victory of the Progressive Conservative Party in the 1995 provincial election, and its re-election in 1999, legislation with far-ranging consequences for Ontario's social and municipal infrastructures – which reflected the party's so-called "Common Sense Revolution" – was pushed through the legislature. Conservative rule came to an end in 2003, with a sweeping victory for the more moderate Liberals. Under Premier Dalton McGuinty, the Liberals won a second majority in October 2007 – although they have been tenuously holding on to a minority government since October 2011. In 2013, another Liberal Kathleen Wynne replaced McGuinty as Ontario's premier, becoming the first female premier of Ontario and the first openly gay head of government in Canada. In 2018, Doug Ford's Progressive Conservatives won enough to form a majority government.

DYNAMIC DOWNTOWN

What distinguishes Toronto from most North American cities is the vibrancy of its downtown. Running through its center is **Bay Street**, the main artery of the country's financial capital. Most Canadian head offices and a huge stock exchange are on or close to it.

At the corner of Queen and Bay streets, Toronto's newest **City Hall** Ⓒ, which was designed by the Finnish architect Viljo Revell in 1965, is striking. Its vast rotunda and two curved towers, which flank the central dome, lord it over Nathan Phillips Square, where visitors can admire the sculptures. Henry Moore's sculpture *The Artist* was a controversial addition in the square's early years.

Minutes away are sizeable clusters of residential housing, from exclusive condominiums to government-funded co-operative housing, the **Entertainment District** (Toronto claims to have the world's third-largest live theater industry, after London and New York) with its attendant restaurants and clubs, and some of the city's most famous attractions.

Toronto's downtown is also the destination for thousands of sports fans. The Toronto Blue Jays play baseball at the 53,500-seat **Rogers Centre** Ⓓ formerly the SkyDome . The world's first retractable domed stadium squats besides another record-breaking building. A couple of blocks east, the **Air Canada Centre** is home to the Toronto Maple Leafs hockey team, the Toronto Raptors basketball team, and the Toronto Rock lacrosse team. BMO Field, a few kilometres west, hosts the football teams FC Toronto and the Toronto Argonauts. The type of "football" you will watch will vary greatly so do check if you'd prefer Major League Soccer or Canadian Football. The **CN Tower** Ⓔ (daily 8.30am–11pm; www.cntower.ca) is, at 553 meters (1,815ft), the tallest freestanding structure in the western hemisphere (the Burj Khalifa in Dubai is the tallest freestanding structure in the world), the 9th tallest in the world, and an ever-present exclamation above the city. There are eateries cheek by jowl in this part of town, from the lofty **360** revolving restaurant at the top of the tower to cheerful Italian at **Kit Kat** on King Street West. A few blocks east, in BCE Place, at the corner of Front and Yonge streets, is the **Hockey Hall of Fame** ❻ (Daily 10am–5pm; www.hhof.com). It's a mecca for hockey buffs, with its collection dedicated to the history of Canada's national game; grown men have even been known to weep in front of the hallowed Stanley Cup sometimes considered the greatest trophy in professional sports.

At the intersection of Front East and Jarvis Street is the **St Lawrence Market** (Tue–Sat), where the tradition of shopping goes back to 1803, although not in the same building. Torontonians still come in droves every Saturday. The site was also home to Toronto's first two city halls. In this historically preserved neighborhood, old warehouses have been transformed into offices, studios, and restaurants. Between Parliament and Cherry streets, the Gooderham and Worts Distillery has become a cultural hotbed.

The Distillery District (55 Mill Street; tel: +1 416-364-1177; daily; www.thedistillerydistrict.com) occupies what was once the largest distillery in the British Empire. Founded in 1832, the 44 buildings of this site comprise the best-preserved collection of Victorian industrial architecture in North America. The business closed in 1990, and a little over 10 years later, a local development company acquired the entire complex and proceeded to turn it into Toronto's newest arts center. Today it houses art and dance studios, galleries, performance spaces, boutiques, restaurants, cafes, and even a microbrewery.

DOWN ON THE WATERFRONT

Summers are special on Queen's Quay at **Harbourfront Centre** ❼ (daily, check hours of individual venues online; www.harbourfrontcentre.com; many events free). The former warehouse has been converted into specialty stores, restaurants, and a theater. Patios overlook the lake, where sailboats, dinner

Looking down on the Distillery District.

Shopping in Chinatown, Toronto.

cruises circling Toronto Islands, and the occasional tall ship grace the waterfront. World-class dance companies perform in the Fleck Dance Theatre, and in nearby York Quay Centre a dynamic range of cultural ventures takes place year-round, including the International Festival of Authors – a 11-day celebration of the world's best-known writers of fiction, poetry, drama, and biography. Waterfront development continues to revitalize the space.

Toronto Islands ⊕ are actually a 5km (3-mile) strip of sandbar with several names, jutting out into the city's harbor. The island community is a unique aspect of Toronto, with a group of residents intent on preserving their simple way of life. In summer the choice land swarms with picnickers and, on occasion, youths with ghetto blasters, while the bitter winters bring winds that sweep mercilessly across Lake Ontario. Food and other supplies have to be ferried across or delivered to the airport at the island's west end. It's not what you'd call easy living, though most islanders wouldn't change it for the world. However, the

controversial launch of Porter Airlines in 2006, a small but growing airline that uses the Toronto Islands' airport as its base, continues to be viewed as a threat to their way of life, with the federal government in 2015 refusing to support the airports expansion – and one that was further aggravated by the more recent addition of Air Canada flights, mainly to Montréal.

It's a lovely haven in summer, and only about 10 minutes away by leisurely ferry. Once there, the 600-acre (243-hectare) park offers secluded beaches, meandering bicycle trails, the village community, and an amusement park. You can transport a bike across or rent one there for some of the nicest riding in the city. The **Rectory Cafe** is a hidden gem on the southside boardwalk of Ward's Island, although it's difficult to beat the tranquility of an evening picnic amid the trees bordering the north shoreline, watching the sun set over the city.

PARKS AND BOARDWALKS

Toronto's waterfront has become increasingly accessible to walkers,

cyclists, and in-line skaters, as lakeside trails are extended and widened. They stretch from **Scarborough Bluffs** in the east to the **Humber Bay Park** in the west, with its butterfly habitat and stunning memorial to the victims of the Air India crash. Well worth a detour is **High Park**, the city's largest park and home to a rare stand of black oak savannah and unusual plants such as blazing star and the sassafras tree. One of the most imaginative arrivals on the waterfront, the **Toronto Music Garden** (479 Queens Quay West; daily) was conceived by internationally renowned cellist Yo-Yo Ma and is based on Johann Sebastian Bach's Suite No. 1 for Unaccompanied Cello. Each of the six dance movements within the suite corresponds to a different section in the garden.

The **East Beaches** ❶ are a favorite haunt on Toronto's east side. The best time to stroll along the boardwalk is on weekdays and evenings. Sailboats and seagulls skim the waves of Lake Ontario on one side, while joggers and strollers enjoy wooded parkland on the other. You can cut up to Queen Street, where an assortment of cafes, restaurants, and pubs caters to most palates and budgets. Among them are **The Beacher Cafe**, a Queen East mainstay, where you can sample eggs Benjamyn (eggs Benedict with smoked salmon), and the **Remarkable Bean**, which serves limited-edition coffees at chessboard tables.

EXPLORING TORONTO'S "VILLAGES"

Toronto's neighborhoods reflect the city's vibrant history, from the early Anglo-Saxon, pro-monarchist immigrants to the Afro-Caribbeans, Italians, Greeks, Chinese, Portuguese, Ukrainians, Poles, Indians, and Irish – among many others – who have all come to the city, each group carving out a neighborhood or two for its own.

You'll find Greeks on the Danforth, Italians and Portuguese on College Street and St Clair Avenue, the Chinese on Dundas Street, East Indians on Gerrard Street, Jamaicans on Bathurst Street, and Eastern Europeans on Roncesvalles Avenue or in Bloor West Village.

KENSINGTON MARKET, CHINATOWN, AND LITTLE ITALY

Kensington Market ❶, with its old-world boisterousness and scruffy charm, has witnessed much of this, since it began with Jewish immigrants in the 1920s and 1930s, who were later supplanted by Portuguese, Chinese, and West Indians.

The main thoroughfares are Augusta and Kensington Avenues, and their connecting streets, Baldwin and Oxford. Here you'll encounter frail, elderly Chinese ladies haggling with the Portuguese women who sell fruit and do incredible mental arithmetic in lieu of a cash register; leisurely Rastafarian merchants hawking spicy beef patties and sharp ginger beer; and black-clad Italian widows carrying home several tonnes of fresh fruit or vegetables on one arm. Drop by **Amadeu's**, a popular Portuguese eatery that specializes in seafood and

Toronto's harbourfront.

⊘ WORTH THE WAIT

For three years, visitors to the Art Gallery of Ontario made do with a much-reduced gallery amidst massive reconstruction. Their patience was amply rewarded with its reopening in November 2008. Reaction to the innovative design of celebrated architect Frank Gehry – particularly to the Douglas fir-clad curving staircase rising from the Walker Court and to the Galleria Italia, a powerful, soaring space that fronts AGO's north-facing facade – has been ecstatic. Although Gehry was born in Toronto, this was his first work in Canada.

Close to half of the permanent collection of some 73,000 works of art documents Canada's art heritage from pre-Confederation to the present, with pivotal works by Cornelius Krieghoff, James Wilson Morrice, Tom Thomson, the Group of Seven, David Milne, and Emily Carr, and an impressive collection of Inuit work.

Of these, 2,000 came from Ken Thomson's (Lord Thomson of Fleet, Canadian art collector) extraordinary collection; among them, an important group of First Nations objects spans two millennia, from around 200 BC to the late 19th century, greatly enriching the gallery's holdings of historical First Nations art. One highlight is Rubens's masterpiece *The Massacre of the Innocents* – purchased by Lord Thomson for a record $117 million in 2002.

Portuguese wines at reasonably modest prices, at the south end of Augusta.

At Augusta and Dundas Street West, **Chinatown** and Kensington Market meet. With the massive growth of its Chinese population, the greater area of Toronto now has seven distinct Chinatowns. This one is the biggest, and bustles with shoppers and hawkers all day and long into the night. Sprawling along Dundas and north up Spadina are overflowing fruit and vegetable stands, Chinese herbalists, and grocery stores. Mouthwatering smells wafting through open doors may well prompt you to search out some of the city's best Chinese restaurants – with places like Asian Legend.

Presiding on the threshold of Chinatown is the **Art Gallery of Ontario ⓚ** (Tue, Thu, Sat-Sun 10.30am–5pm; Wed and Fri until 9pm). The AGO commenced a three-year, $500 million expansion in 2005. The doors to the transformed art gallery reopened in 2008, with more than 68,000 visitors streaming through in its opening week, eager to visit the new glass-fronted galleries with their additional 10,000 works of art. The AGO has the world's largest public collection of Henry Moore sculptures, most of them a direct gift from the sculptor, and an impressive collection of Inuit work. The permanent collection ranges from 15th-century European paintings to international contemporary works of art.

The Italian community is the city's largest non-Anglo ethnic group, numbering considerably more than 420,000 people (close to 10 percent of the city's population). Long popular with students and artists, **Little Italy** is one of the earlier communities, centered on College Street between Grace and Ossington Streets.

A perfect evening begins at **Grappa**, for its cheerful atmosphere and excellent food; and ends at the **Sicilian Ice Cream Company** for *gelati* and cappuccino.

South of Little Italy, in the city's West End, two up-and-coming neighborhoods are grabbing attention. **West Queen West** was once a down-at-heel extension of Queen Street West, but inexpensive rents have led to an influx of art galleries, eclectic boutiques, and trendy eateries and bars. The flavor of the area is concentrated on the blocks between Bathurst and Ossington, where the people on the street are an interesting mix. The alternative set and students hang out at cafes, funky clothing stores, and run-down bicycle repair shops; city professionals shop for designer goods that could be from the pages of glossy magazines, while down-and-outs break into fights outside cheap bars.

THE UNIVERSITY DISTRICT AND AROUND

Northeast of Chinatown, close to the **University of Toronto ⓛ**, the Annex is a well-established bohemian neighbourhood, stretching along Bloor Street West from Spadina Avenue to Bathurst Street. To the north, gracious buildings on shady streets are either student fraternity houses or the elegant (and pricey) homes of professionals and artists. Housing south of Bloor is usually of a more modest scale, built

The Green Iguana Glassworks, Mirvish Village.

THE CN TOWER

Torontonians are inclined to be blasé about the CN Tower but it nevertheless remains a powerful symbol of the city and civic pride.

A trip to the top of Canada's tallest self-supported tower, gracefully rising 553 meters (1,815ft) above the city, is pretty much a requirement of a visit to Toronto, regardless of the relatively high cost and crush of tourists standing in line to share the experience. From the adrenaline rush of the high-speed, glass-fronted lifts to the vertigo-inducing stand on the glass floor and the panoramic views from the Sky Pod, it really is a terrific thing to do. Choose a clear day, buy tickets in advance if you can, and either get there early in the day or arrive just before sunset to see the view then watch the city light up.

Despite numerous attractions and shopping opportunities at the foot of the tower, most visitors are anxious to get in line for one of the six elevators. The ride quickly exposes those who suffer from vertigo – they are the ones at the back with their eyes closed – while their fellow passengers are glued to the sight of the city disappearing below at a speed of 22kph (15mph). After 58 seconds, the lift deposits you at the **Look Out Level**, 346 meters (1,136ft) above ground, with glass windows all around and the terrifying glass floor, where you can stand and look past your feet at the ground below.

This level of the Tower has become even more exciting since 2011, with the introduction of EdgeWalk. Visitors can walk in groups of six, hands-free, around the world's highest full circle. Worry not, you are attached to an overhead safety rail via a trolley and harness system for the 30-minute out-door walk. Trained EdgeWalk guides encourage participants to push their personal limits, leaning back over Toronto with nothing but air and breathtaking views of Lake Ontario beneath them. Those less enamoured by these dizzying heights can watch on internal monitors.

Back inside, an internal lift whisks you up through the core of the tower to the **Sky Pod**, at 447 meters (1,151ft), for the ultimate high-rise experience and incredible views. Be prepared for the encircling glass curving in at the bottom, which can be a little unnerving. Up here you can see for 120km (75 miles) on a clear day, maybe even as far as the spray rising from Niagara Falls.

Many people forget that the CN Tower was built primarily not as a tourist attraction but to improve telecommunications in the city, after a spate of 1960s skyscraper construction had disrupted radio and TV waves. Torontonians had some of the worst TV reception in the whole of North America. Now, not surprisingly, it has some of the best, with all major broadcast, AM, FM, and DAB radio stations – as well as wireless service providers – using the CN Tower for transmission.

Started in 1973, the tower took 40 months to complete and cost $63 million. The highly regarded (and highly priced) **360 Restaurant** (tel: +1 416-362-5411 for reservations), which revolves once every 70 minutes or so, was added in 1995, and a further $40 million has been spent since then on improved security and visitor amenities.

The CN Tower.

A busy Woodbine Beach.

to accommodate the waves of Jewish, Chinese, Italian, and Portuguese newcomers as they arrived in Toronto.

Inexpensive eateries offering an enticing variety of ethnic cuisines are an integral part of the Annex. Two popular longtime fixtures are **By The Way Café** for its Middle Eastern-inspired dishes, and **Pauper's**, a pub housed in a former bank, with a lively piano bar downstairs and a romantic sundown rooftop patio above.

Three remarkable museums border the Annex. The **Bata Shoe Museum** (daily 10am–5pm, Thu until 8pm, Sun noon–5pm; www.batashoemuseum.ca), at Bloor and St George streets, houses an extraordinarily comprehensive collection of shoes and related artifacts in a dramatic "shoebox" structure designed by renowned architect Raymond Moriyama. Spanning some 4,500 years, its collection explores the extent to which shoes reflect the living habits, culture, and customs of the people who wore them.

A few minutes' walk away, on University Avenue, is the **Royal Ontario Museum** Ⓜ (daily 10am–5.30pm, Fri until 8.30pm; www.rom.on.ca). Known locally as ROM,

Royal Ontario Museum.

the museum is one of the world's few multidiscipline museums and its exhibits range from science to art to archeology. ROM's East Asian collection is world-renowned, and includes an impressive collection of temple art. A stunning crystal annex composed of five interlocking prismatic structures and housing seven additional galleries, designed by Daniel Libeskind, opened in 2007.

On the other side of University Avenue is the **Gardiner Museum** (daily 10am–6pm, Fri until 9pm, Sat–Sun until 5pm; www.gardinermuseum.on.ca). It's another one-of-a-kind in North America, with a spectacular collection of pottery and porcelain treasures spanning some 3,000 years.

Abutting the Annex is **Yorkville**, a couple of fashionable blocks delineated by Cumberland Street and Yorkville Avenue, where – in red-brick, Victorian houses – Yorkville's designer boutiques and trendy art galleries are all the rage. The neighboring streets of Hazelton and Scollard are fertile territory for collectors of North American Native Indian artifacts and Inuit sculpture and prints.

Amid the glitz is **Buca Osteria and Bar**, an Italian restaurant that dishes up marvelous pizzas, pastas and seafood.

The Anglo-Saxon roots of Toronto still hold dominion in one neighborhood. **Rosedale**, northeast of Yorkville is where the reticent, affluent people who run the financial and legal district centered on Bay Street continue to live – often with a BMW or two in their garage. The tour buses detour here from time to time for a quick, wish-it-were-me-living-here gawk.

OUTER VILLAGES

Farther north, another of the city's livelier neighborhoods is **The Danforth**. For about 10 blocks, from Broadview to Coxwell, the Greeks have taken over the main east–west artery of the city, Danforth Avenue. Even the street signs are bilingual, while every other restaurant is a taverna. At the long-established **Asteria Souvlaki Place** patrons enjoy bouzoukis and souvlakis on the outside patio in summer, while a highly touted, more elegant alternative is **Pan on The Danforth**.

One of the oldest of Toronto's residential areas, on the east side of town, is Cabbagetown, which is noted for its fine Victorian houses, lovely parks, and Toronto's oldest cemetery, the Necropolis. The curious name stems from the simple fact that its early residents, Irish settlers who came to escape the Great Famine at home, grew vegetables in their front gardens. It was a working-class area that later transformed into a desirable neighborhood, with a number of notable residents – their homes are marked by blue plaques in some of the well-tended front gardens (no cabbages in sight these days). Flags bearing the cabbage symbol denote buildings of particular architectural interest.

In **Roncesvalles Village**, out to the west, Polish newcomers took over from the original very British community after World War II. In no time, they had established their own shops and their own church. Another influx of Polish immigrants fleeing communist Poland arrived in the 1980s. Today its Old World ambience has become more edgy, with the liveliest stretch encompassing a 10-block stretch from Galley Avenue to Howard Park Avenue in the north. Jazz and cabaret-style clubs and pubs, as well as several acclaimed restaurants, sit amongst the fruit and veggie markets, and the Polish butchers, bakers, and delis.

WHEN NIGHT FALLS

For decades, it seemed, Torontonians were accustomed to their city being disparagingly referred to as "Toronto the Good" by other Canadians. Indeed, Toronto nightlife used to be plagued by a Victorian carry-over, enforcing tight restrictions on the city's bars. Today's legislation permits them to stay open until 2am with the city's music industry continually pushing for a later time.

The live-music scene is eclectic and very good, offering jazz, rock, funk, folk, or almost anything else you might be into. Toronto has a good underground of amateur bands and it's a habitual

⊙ **Tip**

Toronto has the largest population of gays and lesbians in Canada. Daily Xtra is an online LGBTQ-focused magazine that outlines events in the city.

Dancing in downtown Toronto.

Fancy footwear at the Bata Shoe Museum.

stop on most music tours, especially for European bands. Prices and quality vary hugely from place to place so it's best to consult the advertisements in *Now* entertainment weekly.

Multiculturalism, naturally, has an imprint on Toronto entertainment. Each October, in Little India, Diwali – or the Festival of Lights – is the largest festival celebrated in the city's South Asian community, while Caribana, the annual Caribbean festival, is an exuberant affair that's one of the city's biggest summertime draws.

On a more sophisticated note, the Toronto Symphony Orchestra, the Canadian Opera Company, and the National Ballet of Canada are all world-class outfits based in Toronto, with extensive fall and winter seasons. Those able to meet the pecuniary demands of the box offices of the **Roy Thomson Hall N**, **Sony Centre for the Performing Arts O**, and the sparkling **Four Seasons Centre for the Performing Arts P**, will undoubtedly be suitably impressed by the performances at these venues. Built in 1894,

the legendary and acoustically splendid Massey Hall manages to hold its own, despite competition from the more modern "newcomers."

A CULTURED CITY

Toronto is one of the world's greatest theater cities, with almost 200 professional theater and dance companies. Since 2007, local, national, and international artists take to Toronto's stages, streets, and public spaces for 10 days each June, offering theater, dance, classical and contemporary music, film, literature, and visual arts during Luminato. On the literary scene alone, with its annual International Festival of Authors and year-round Harbourfront Reading Series, Toronto has been compared with Paris in the 1920s. Toronto writers and filmmakers are recognized as international trendsetters.

And yet Toronto manages to retain, with its varied population, both a small-town aura and healthy dollops of European charm. With enough of whatever it takes to make a great city, it's something of a joy to visit.

⊙ A FILM LOVER'S DREAM

Most cinema aficionados in Toronto agree that the TIFF Bell Lightbox is the jewel in the crown of the city's Entertainment District. Built to house the long-established annual Toronto International Film Festival, the largely glass, five-story podium presides at the corner of King and John streets. Fronted by a super-scaled Douglas fir canopy, the Bell Lightbox appears as boxes within boxes, encompassing five cinemas, a bistro, a cafe, a bar, and two galleries, topped by an outdoor rooftop terrace and – this being downtown Toronto – a towering condo. In addition to the 10-day Toronto International Film Festival, year-round activities include TIFF Kids International Film Festival, TIFF Next Wave Festival, a carefully curated program of Canadian and international cinema, TIFF Nexus (a program designed to help Ontario storytellers successfully navigate the rapidly evolving digital media landscape), and much, much more. There's no question that glitz and glamour take over during the September film festival. However, since this welcoming complex is part movie theatre, part cultural center, part educational center, and part social hub for the rest of the year, it's well on the way to answering the hopes of Piers Handling, TIFF's CEO, to wit: "I want every film lover to feel like TIFF Bell Lightbox is theirs."

COMEDY CLUBS

People aren't kidding when they say Canadians are funny – comedians such as Mike Myers, Jim Carrey, John Candy, Dan Aykroyd, Eugene Levy and Martin Short have long dominated the humor industry on both sides of the US-Canadian border. More recent comedy stars, such as Seth Rogan, Katherine Ryan, and Samantha Bee continue the tradition.

Many of these comedians got their start doing stand-up and sketches in Toronto clubs such as Second City or Yuk Yuk's. Just why Canadians are so funny is often debated. Toronto-born Lorne Michaels, the legendary producer of the long-running hit comedy TV show *Saturday Night Live*, says he thinks his Canadian baby-boomer generation has a talent for comedy partly because it grew up on a diet of British humor, such as *Monty Python* and the *Carry On* films.

Eugene Levy and Martin Short agree there's more irony and humor in Canada than in the US, possibly because of the polite nature of Canadians and the country's clearly defined social rules – they create the perfect foil for comedy, which thrives on opposition and contrast. And being in the shadow of the all-powerful US of A for more than two centuries has finely honed the country's talent for self-deprecation.

Whatever the explanation, going to a comedy club in Toronto is a great – and inexpensive – way to spend an evening. Here are three of the best.

THE SECOND CITY

Dan Aykroyd and Gilda Radner helped kick off the Toronto branch of this Chicago-based club in 1973. Since then it has spawned at least a dozen big-name comedians, and the hugely popular TV series *SCTV*, starring Eugene Levy, John Candy, and Martin Short. The club has moved several times, but has kept its tradition of presenting fast-paced sketch comedy with top-notch talent. A cast of six present rapid-fire skits that skewer politicians, Canadian and American

culture, relationships, even lizards, with some improv thrown in at the end of the evening. 51 Mercer St; tel: +1 416-343 0011; www.secondcity.com; daily.

YUK YUK'S

This brick-walled basement feels meaner and tougher than many comedy clubs, and it is – comics and patrons here aren't afraid of taking a chance with risky humor. This is Toronto's oldest stand-up comedy club (now a national chain) and some of the biggest names in comedy have appeared here, including Jay Leno and Jim Carrey. Shows feature several comics and an MC. 224 Richmond Street West; tel: +1 416-967-6431; www.yukyuks.com/toronto.

THE COMEDY BAR

One of the more recent additions to Toronto's comedy scene, this basement venue prides itself on being different from most other clubs, promoting itself as a sketch and improv theater rather than simply stand-up comedy. Part of its mission is to provide a place for Toronto's many alternative acts, and its belief in encouraging local talent led to the inauguration of an annual Festival of New Formats each January – a fine way to forget the winter blues. 945 Bloor Street W; tel: +1 416-551-6540; www.comedybar.ca.

The Comedy Bar

The Governor General's Foot Guards during Changing of the Guard on Parliament Hill in downtown Ottawa.

ONTARIO

Ontario is one of the world's most urbanized regions, with towns standing like high-tech sandcastles by the Great Lakes. Venture north, however, and you'll discover a wilderness of water and forests.

Thrust down into the industrial heartland of the United States, Ontario is a highly modernized region, but it is also a wilderness with 90 percent of its area under forest.

But it is a land, a country, a home. Underlying the exotic diversity of Ontario's population is a common love of place, whether that place be a Gothic Revival farmhouse at Punkeydoodles Corners or a New Age zucchini plot on Toronto's Markham Street. In 1844 J.R. Godley, a traveler from Great Britain, described Upper Canada as a place where "everybody is a foreigner and home in their mouths invariably means another country." Today Ontario is still a land of many peoples, but its residents have found their home.

THE VOYAGEURS' HEARTLANDS

Although home to First Nations people for millennia, and a corridor for the fur trade, the living essence of modern Ontario isn't found in the longhouse or canoe portage, but in the limestone homes of the United Empire Loyalists that stretch along the St Lawrence River.

More than any other region of Ontario, **eastern Ontario** remains devoted to the Loyalist traditions of "peace, order, and good government." The stolid farmhouses, regal

courthouses, and towering Anglican spires proclaim that no matter what the "democrats and levelers" in western Ontario may do, the East will be faithful to the province's motto: "Loyal she began, loyal she remains."

There's no more historically resonant place to begin a tour of Ontario than in the counties of **Prescott-Russell** and **Glengarry**, wedged between the Ottawa and St Lawrence rivers. The lower Ottawa countryside appears more Québécois than Upper Canadian. Barns boldly decked out in orange

Main attractions

Ottawa
Sandbanks Provincial Park
Niagara Falls
Niagara-on-the-Lake
Point Pelee National Park
Algonquin Provincial Park

Maps on pages 142, 146

A blue jay in Ontario.

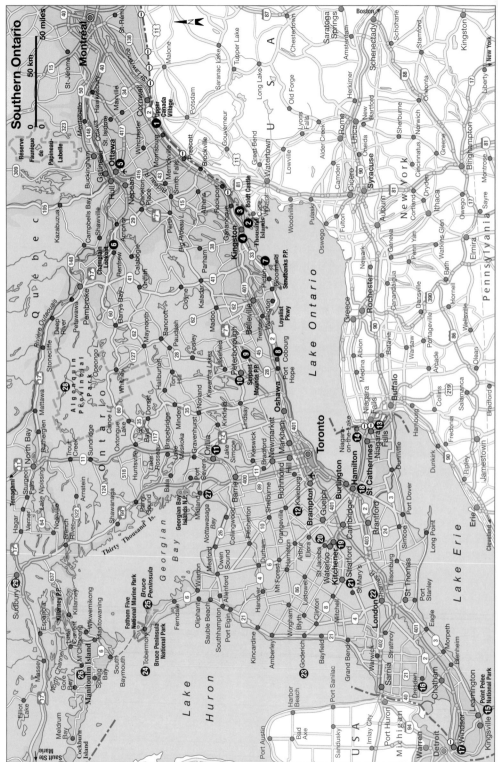

Southern Ontario

and green, silvery "ski-jump" roofs, and towns centered on massive parish churches reveal a distinct French-Canadian character.

But this is Ontario, not Québec. Surveyed by British army engineers, all of southern Ontario is rationally divided into little blocks (lots) within big blocks (townships) dissected by concession roads that irrationally ignore such non-Euclidian features as rocks, boulders, hills, lakes, and swamps.

Driving southwest from the Ottawa River, the French place names give way to towns named Dunvegan, Lochiel, Maxville, and Alexandria, tell-tale signs that this is now Glengarry County. Glengarry was the first of the hundreds of Scottish settlements in Ontario.

Beginning with the arrival of the Loyalist Royal Highland Emigrant Regiment in 1783, the hill country north of the St Lawrence became the destination of thousands of emigrant Scots. Entire parishes from Glengarry, Scotland, emigrated for the promise of free land and the chance to escape the oppression of their landlords.

RIVER OF EMPIRE

At **Cornwall**, Ontario's easternmost city, the **Robert Saunders St Lawrence Generating Station** stretches across the river to harness the thrust of the Great Lakes as they are funneled toward the Atlantic. Appropriately, an abstract mural by the artist Harold Town adorns the observation tower. For this is a triumph of the modern technological age over the defiant, age-old barrier of the Long Sault and International Rapids. With the opening of the **St Lawrence Seaway** in 1959, the interior of the continent was made accessible to the ocean-going giants and the St Lawrence superseded the Rhine as the world's foremost river of commerce.

It is a river of empire. The French and English struggled for 150 years to determine control of the Great Lakes waterway, and when they were done the Canadians and Americans took up the cudgels. Indeed, it is a ripe irony typical of Canada that in order to remain British, the American Loyalists emigrated to share this river with the

> **⊙ Fact**
>
> At Dunvegan, near Maxville, one of Glengarry Museum's prize exhibits is a cooking pot used by Bonnie Prince Charlie at Glengarry, Scotland, 1746.

A bagpipe band performs at the annual Glengarry Highland Games in Maxville.

ancient enemy of the British Empire: *Les Canadiens*.

At **Morrisburg**, upriver from Cornwall, **Upper Canada Village** ❶ (early May to early Sept daily 9.30am–5pm; www.uppercanadavillage.com) presents a historical re-creation of what life was like for these loyalist immigrants. Early log cabins are juxtaposed with spacious American Classical Revival houses, illustrating the changing fortunes of the first political refugees to find a Canadian haven. Wagon rides and a miniature train ride are available for families to enjoy.

Iroquois legend tells of two potent spirits, one good, the other evil, who battled for control of the mighty St Lawrence. In their titanic struggle, huge boulders were tossed across the river in a great cannonade, many to fall short into the narrows leading into Lake Ontario. With the triumph of the good spirit, a magical blessing fell upon the land, bringing rich forests of yellow birch, red and white trillium, silver maple, and winged sumac to life upon the countless granite chunks scattered about the river. Today they are called the **Thousand Islands** ❷.

Brockville, 85km (53 miles) southwest of Cornwall, a stately Loyalist city with early architectural treasures along Courthouse Avenue, serves as the eastern gateway to the islands. Cruises around the numberless islands leave from nearby **Rockport** and **Gananoque** ("gan-an-ock-wee"), a more rambunctious resort town 53km (33 miles) closer to Kingston. The Thousand Islands have long been a playground for the very rich who, no matter how bad their taste in architecture, always seem to have an eye for the world's most extraordinary real estate. The most famous of the millionaire "cottages" is an unfinished one named **Boldt Castle** ❸ (early May to mid-Oct daily from 10am; www.boldt-castle.com), which broods over Heart Island. As it is on American soil, visitors who are not American must bring proper identification, generally a passport.

Begun in 1898 by George Boldt, king of the Waldorf Astoria, it was never completed due to his grief over his wife's death. Today it stands open to the elements and to the curious, and a major ongoing restoration continues on this piece of island history. A more lasting monument to Boldt is the Thousand Islands salad dressing that his chef concocted in honor of the region.

KINGSTON AND THE RIDEAU CANAL

Briefly the capital of the United Provinces of Canada (1841–3), the city of **Kingston** ❹ has never quite recovered from Queen Victoria's folly in naming Ottawa the new capital of the Dominion of Canada in 1857. Kingston certainly meets all the requirements of a capital city: a venerable history stretching back to 1673 and Fort Frontenac; a quiet dignity redolent in the weathered stone houses that line its streets; and

The Power House of Boldt Castle in Thousand Islands.

a grandiose, neo-Classical **City Hall**, erected in 1843 in expectation of Kingston's greater destiny. The Martello towers strategically placed around the town's harbor and the great limestone bulwark of **Fort Henry** (mid-May to mid-Sept daily 10am–5pm; www.forthenry.com) are testimony to the enduring fear of invasion that the war of 1812 engendered.

Apparently, the spirit of 1812 lives on at **Queen's University**, the pride of Kingston, founded as a Presbyterian seminary in 1841. In 1956 the student body invaded the nearby town of Watertown, New York, under cloak of night, replacing the "Stars and Stripes" flying at public buildings with Union flags.

The memory of Sir John A. Macdonald, the first prime minister of Canada, is as permanent a fixture in Kingston as any fort or college. **Bellevue House** (Canada Day–Labor Day daily 10am–5pm, Victoria Day–Canada Day and Labor Day–Thanksgiving Thu–Mon 10am–5pm), an Italianate villa occupied by Macdonald in the late 1840s, is now a museum filled with memorabilia of the Old Chieftain. More importantly, Macdonald's unofficial political headquarters, the **Grimason House** (now the **Royal Tavern**), is still standing and open for business in the city center.

Just to the east of Kingston, between the harbor and old Fort Henry, lies the southern entrance of the **Rideau Canal** or **Rideau Waterway**. Built between 1826 and 1832, the canal follows the path of the **Rideau river** route northeast through 47 locks, numerous lakes, and excavated channels until it emerges beside Parliament Hill (located in Ottawa) on the Ottawa River. Today the canal region is a pleasure-boat captain's delight. Sleek-lined yachts and flat-bottomed cabin cruisers play snakes and ladders with the great stone locks, many of which are as they were over 150 years ago.

To the thousands of Irish laborers brought to Canada to construct the canal, the route was a foul, mosquito-ridden wilderness and their British Army taskmasters nothing less than Pharaoh's satraps. Rapids were

Ice skating on Rideau Canal, Ottawa.

The Rideau Canal waterway and Parliament, Ottawa.

dammed, boulders blasted, and huge stone blocks hauled through roadless forests. The cost in human life was terrible. During construction in the 30km (18-mile) long Cranberry marsh, 1,000 workers succumbed to yellow fever.

The purpose of the canal was military, not economic. The British Army wanted a second, more secure route connecting Upper and Lower Canada in the event of an American seizure of the St Lawrence. The military character of the canal is evident at **Merrickville**, 48km (30 miles) southwest of Ottawa, where the largest of the 22 blockhouses that were built to protect the route still looms over the river.

Many of the canal's laborers settled in the region. A bevy of Scottish master stonemasons, lured across the water to build the locks, stayed on to build the town of **Perth** on the Tay River, 41km (25 miles) west of Merrickville. Perth today is a feast of exquisite Georgian, Adamesque-Federalist, Regency, and Gothic residences – one of the most photogenic towns in Ontario.

OTTAWA

Queen Victoria's choice of **Bytown**, then newly renamed **Ottawa ❺**, as her capital in the Canadas was greeted with shock by her trusting subjects. Today's equivalent would be commanding all the capital's administrators, pollsters, and politicos to pack up their bags and begin working in Tuktoyaktuk in the Northwest Territories.

The indignity wasn't limited to just moving to a backwater; in the mid-1800s Bytown was also the most notorious work camp in North America. Lumber was king of the region and Bytown was its capital. Rival shantymen gangs the size of regiments set up shack towns here. Worked like machines, ill-fed, isolated, and racially divided, the lumbermen spent their recreational hours in drunken bouts of kick fights and eye gouging. It was in these muddy, dangerous streets that the **Parliament Buildings Ⓐ** (daily; tours, free; https://visit.parl.ca) were erected atop Parliament Hill (or just the Hill) between 1859 and 1865, rather like the proverbial pearl in a pigsty.

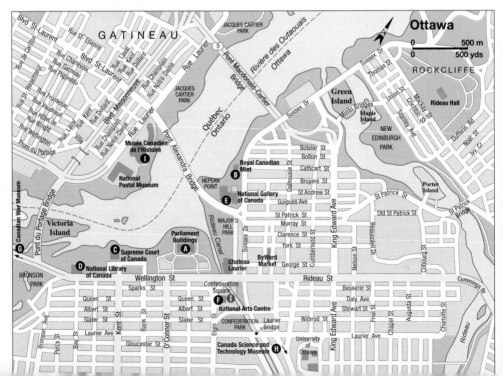

The contrast between these savage shantymen and their descendants – well-ordered, conformist civil servants – is wonderfully absurd. It is the contrast between settlement and wilderness, between convention and epic adventure that runs through Canadian history. The contrast has not quite vanished from Ottawa today. In the **Gatineau Hills** (located in Québec) that rise up behind Ottawa to the east, wolf packs still gather to howl. And at the **Royal Canadian Mint** Ⓑ (daily 8am–8pm; www.mint.ca), Canada's moneymakers still churn out coins depicting wild birds, moose, and beavers.

For Ottawa will never be a capital city in the style of Washington or Brasilia, fashioned around a grandiose design that reorders the world along geometric lines. Initiated in 1937, the Capital Region Plan of designer Jacques Greber emphasizes the area's natural beauty and molds the city around it. Consequently, pleasure craft wend their way through the downtown center's parks in summer,

while winter turns the Rideau Canal into an ice-skating promenade. The annual gift of thousands of tulips by the Netherlands, in gratitude for Canada's wartime hospitality to the Dutch Royal Family, makes spring in the city a visual delight.

Because of its national stature, Ottawa is richly endowed with superb cultural resources, museums, and galleries. Besides the Parliament Buildings, the Art Deco **Supreme Court of Canada** Ⓒ (May–Aug daily 9am–5pm, guided tours; Labor Day–Apr Mon–Fri 9am–5pm, reservations required for guided tours; www.scc-csc.ca; free), the **National Library of Canada** Ⓓ, and the residences of prime ministers, governors general, and foreign ambassadors, Ottawa boasts the **National Gallery of Canada** Ⓔ (May–Sept daily 10am–5pm, Thu until 8pm, Oct–Apr Tue–Sun 10am–5pm, Thu until 8pm; www.gallery.ca), the country's foremost gallery, made primarily out of glass; the **National Arts Centre** Ⓕ, comprising opera house, theater, and studio, and home to the acclaimed National

Sculpture outside the National Gallery of Canada.

Arts Centre Orchestra; the **Canadian War Museum** ⑤ (daily 9.30am-5pm, Thu until 8pm; free Thu 5–8pm; www.warmuseum.ca), which traces Canada's wars or involvement in wars from the 17th century; and the recently re-opened **Canada Science and Technology Museum** ⑪ (daily 9am-5pm; https://ingeniumcanada.org/cstm), containing an impressive display of steam locomotives.

Across the river in Gatineau (formerly Hull), in the province of Québec, stands the outstanding **Musée Canadien de l'Histoire** ① (daily 9.30am-5pm, Thu until 8pm; free Thu 5–8pm; www.historymuseum.ca), which predominantly explores the history and society of Canada, and also the art and traditions of the native cultures and ethnic groups.

THE UNKNOWN RIVER

Author Hugh MacLennan, in *Seven Rivers of Canada*, describes the Ottawa as the "unknown" or "forgotten" river of Canada. As the St Lawrence super-seded it as the principal trade route,

the image of the Ottawa was dimmed and it took on the status of a short tributary linking the cities of Ottawa and Montréal. To the *voyageurs* and the lumbermen of early Canada, however, the Ottawa River was *la grande rivière*, the main route to the Upper Great Lakes and the western prairies beyond.

In the **Ottawa Valley**, running north of the capital to **Pembroke** and **Deep Rivers**, the character of the old Ottawa river comes alive. At the **Champlain Lookout** ⑥, high above the town of **Renfrew**, you can see the power of the river's current as it bursts over narrows, and understand why the journey either up or down the Ottawa was dreaded by the *voyageurs*. The Ottawa Valley is full of tall tales of the bigger-than-big lumberjacks like Joe Mufferaw, who waged war on the forest to provide the British Navy with white pine masts. These are best heard in the Valley dialect, which is a complex mix of Gaelic, Polish, French, and Indian idioms.

PRINCE EDWARD COUNTY

Hwy 33 leads south from Hwy 401 to Prince Edward County, which locals simply call "the County." A peninsula that juts into Lake Ontario, south of Belleville, it was settled by Loyalists in the 1780s. Though more and more people are discovering its charms, there is still an island-like sense of remoteness to this area. The highway becomes the Loyalist Parkway, the County's main east–west artery, with lovely vistas of New England-style clapboard houses, of brick homes with gingerbread trim, and of Wellington Bay.

In **Wellington**, many older homes have been converted into restaurants and bed-and-breakfast places. **The Wellington Heritage** Museum (mid-May to mid-Oct Wed–Sun 9.30am-4.30pm; donation) is housed in a former 1895 Quaker meeting house and focuses mainly on the area's Quaker history.

Ø CULTURAL GEMS

Ottawa's **National Gallery of Canada** and, across the river, Gatineau's **Musée Canadien de l'Histoire**, stand out both for their architecture and for their remarkable collections.

The airy glass-and-steel turreted National Gallery by architect Moshe Safdie (1988) houses Canadian painting from the 18th to the 20th centuries, including the Group of Seven; European and American works from Filippo Lippi to Francis Bacon; the reconstructed, fan-vaulted, Rideau Street Convent Chapel; and, since 2009, the Canadian Museum of Contemporary Photography's collection, dedicated to work by Canadian photographers.

The photographic collection covers the history of the art from William Henry Fox Talbot through Eugène Atger, Walker Evans, and August Sander to the contemporary work of Diane Arbus and Man Ray. It is worth spending at least half a day at the gallery.

Dedicated to the human history of Canada, the Musée Canadien de l'Histoire, designed by Douglas Cardinal (1989), features the world's largest collection of totem poles. All aspects of life in Canada, from the earliest native peoples to the arrival of Norsemen and successive waves of Europeans, are shown in eye-catching displays. Exhibitions of native art make this a museum not to be missed.

Antiques are big business along the main street of **Bloomfield**, as are gift and craft stores, artist galleries, and bed and breakfasts, mostly housed in historic buildings. The County is ideal for exploring by bike, which can be rented from the Bloomfield Bicycle Company on Main Street. Nearby, Slickers County Ice Cream offers all-natural ice cream that is made daily by hand, using fresh County products.

Picton ❼ is the county's main town, with several historic buildings, including the County Courthouse and Jail on Union Street, where Sir John A. Macdonald, Canada's first prime minister, began practicing law. **Prince Edward County Museum** (Victoria Day–Labor Day Wed–Sun 9.30am–4.30pm) is housed in the old St Mary Magdalene Church – part of the Macaulay Heritage Park complex – and provides an excellent overview of the County's bygone days, including a fascinating presentation on Sir John as well as some detailed exhibits on the town's Loyalist connection.

ARTS AND LEISURE AROUND PICTON

When the **Regent Theatre** opened in Picton in 1918, it was a rare example of an Edwardian opera house with a stage equal in size to that of Toronto's Royal Alexandra Theatre. Barely surviving the whims of the entertainment industry during the 20th century, it too has been restored as close to its original state as possible, and is now the County's center for the arts, with a year-round program of theater, first run movies, and alternative films, as well as festivals for chamber music and jazz.

The County has been attracting artists and artisans for years, drawn by its inspiring surroundings (and, perhaps, by the lower than big city prices). Studios of photographers and woodcarvers, weavers, sculptors, and painters are found down many a backroad. Every year Picton hosts **Art in the County** (June–July over a two week period), a juried art show and sale, the Prince Edward County Studio and Gallery Tour (end Sept) and the Maker's Hand (early Nov).

Cobourg lighthouse.

Sailboats at sunrise, Picton.

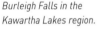
⊙ **Fact**

By the time boaters reach Lake Simcoe from Lake Ontario they will have negotiated 43 locks and ascended 180 meters (590ft).

One of its most popular attractions is **Sandbanks Provincial Park**. Formed by a vast freshwater sand dune system, it's a laid-back, family-orientated park, with giant sand dunes including the world's largest baymouth barrier dune, three wide golden sandy beaches, and shallow waters that are perfect for windsurfing, sailing, and canoeing, as well as swimming in warm weather. Every spring, birdwatchers arrive in droves. The County's sandy shoreline, limestone outcrops, lakes, forests, and wetlands attract over 300 species of birds.

Just east of Picton, there are over 20km (12 miles) of hiking trails in **Macaulay Mountain Conservation Area**, through both lowland and wooded escarpment. Birdwatchers come to see the likes of great crested flycatchers and winter wrens, others to see the quirky folk art of Macaulay's Birdhouse City, in which many of the 100 birdhouses are colorful reproductions of local historic buildings.

CENTRAL ONTARIO

There are no firm borders separating eastern from western Ontario, let alone the east from the middle. But when classical limestone gives way to red-brick Victorian, that nebulous line has been crossed. Firmly within the orbit of Toronto, whose fatted-calf suburbs have gobbled up rich farmland with alacrity, the hamlets and towns of the region struggle to maintain their own character and traditions.

The town of **Cobourg** ❽, 96km (60 miles) east of Toronto, is just far enough away to remain relatively unscarred by bedroom dormitory blight. It, like its neighbors **Port Hope** and **Colborne**, was once a bustling lake port in the age of Great Lake steamers. The harbors are filled with pleasure sails now, but these small lakeside ports are the best places to appreciate the vistas offered by Lake Ontario.

The center of Cobourg is dominated by the neo-Classical **Victoria Hall**. Completed in 1860, it contains a courtroom replica of London's Old Bailey, and is one of very few acoustically

Burleigh Falls in the Kawartha Lakes region.

perfect opera houses in North America. In its time it served as a marvelous statement of Canadian pretensions to cultural superiority over the rebel Yankees. Here, the colonial elite had something solid to point to in explaining why they chose to remain impoverished British North Americans while Uncle Sam boomed.

FINGER LAKES WITH BONES

To the immediate north of Cobourg, the long, thin **Kawartha Lakes** are strung like pegs on a clothesline tied to **Lake Simcoe** in the west. The Kawarthas have a pastoral appeal in contrast to the rugged beauty of the more northerly Canadian Shield Lakes. **Rice Lake**, the most southerly of the lakes, is especially beguiling. Framed by gently sloping drumlins bearing Holstein dairy farms on their elongated backs, Rice Lake is dotted with forested islands. Two thousand years ago, a little-known native civilization buried their dead by these shores in 96km (60-mile) long, snake-like ridges. **Serpent Mounds Provincial Park** ❾, 30km (19 miles) southeast of Peterborough, offers a cutaway viewing of the largest mound's bones and burial gifts; closed for a rebranding and revitalization project, this National Historic Site of Canada will be well worth visiting once it reopens.

The Kawartha Lakes form the basis of the **Trent-Severn Canal System**, which allows houseboats and cabin cruisers to sail uphill from **Trenton** on Lake Ontario to **Port Severn** on Lake Huron's Georgian Bay.

Peterborough ❿, the center of the Kawarthas region, is the star attraction along the canal. Here the **Peterborough Hydraulic Lift Lock**, the world-champion boat lifter since 1904, boosts a boat up with one hand while sinking a second vessel with the other. Settled later than the counties along Lake Ontario, the Peterborough district was reputed in the 1830s to have the "most polished and aristocratic society in Upper Canada." British army officers granted free land, and younger sons of the English gentry gave the backwoods of Peterborough and Lakefield a tone uncommon in earlier settlements.

Not that gentility made the hardships of pioneering any more bearable. Susannah Moodie, an early pioneer of Lakefield, and of Canadian literature, described in *Roughing It in the Bush* her feelings on being condemned to a life of horror in the New World, from which the only hope of escape was "through the portals of the grave." Today, Peterborough seems to have found a middle ground between aristocracy and poverty, for it is a favorite testing ground for the arbiters of middle-class taste – the consumer-marketing surveyors.

SUNSHINE SKETCHES OF EVERY TOWN

There isn't much of tourist interest in the town of **Orillia** ⓫, situated on the narrows between Lake Couchiching and Lake Simcoe, 96km (60 miles) north of Toronto – and that's what makes it so interesting. To be sure,

A "pioneer" makes maple syrup in the Kortright Centre for Conservation, Kleinburg.

there's a statue of Samuel de Champlain, noting the fact that he stopped nearby on his own Great Ontario Tour of 1615, but every town has a monument to someone or other.

No, the appeal of Orillia lies in the very ordinariness of the town: shady maples leaning over spacious side streets; wide front porches for socializing and spying; photographs of local hockey heroes in the barbershop-cum-agora. Stephen Leacock caught the flavor of the place – the flavor, for example, of Mr Golgotha Gingham, town undertaker who "instinctively assumes the professional air of hopeless melancholy" – in his book, *Sunshine Sketches of a Little Town*. A work of irony (one part affection, one part castigation), *Sunshine Sketches* won Leacock praise throughout the world when it was published in 1912. Everywhere, except Orillia. Now, Orillia has adopted the humorist as a favorite son and turned his home on Brewery Bay into a literary museum, the **Stephen Leacock Museum** (Mon–Fri 10am–4pm).

Harvesting tomatoes in Leamington.

South of Lake Simcoe, 40km (25 miles) north of downtown Toronto, lies another shrine to Canadian artists: the **McMichael Canadian Art Collection** (May–Oct daily 10am–5pm, Nov–Apr daily 10am–4pm) in the village of **Kleinburg** ⑫. Started as a private gallery, the collection has grown into the finest display of the Group of Seven's canvases in Canada, along with works by Tom Thomson, Group of Seven contemporaries, First Nations, Inuit, and other Canadian artists. Six members of the Group of Seven are even buried on the grounds. The McMichael Collection, with more than 13 exhibition galleries housed in log and stone buildings, is the perfect place to feast on their labors.

SOUTHERN ONTARIO

The excellent system of roads in southern Ontario is a sign of its long-accustomed prosperity. The Macdonald-Cartier Freeway, more widely known as the 401, spans the distance between Windsor in the west and the Québec border in the east. But it's on the country roads that travelers begin to encounter southern Ontario: the rolling fields of corn, wheat, or grazing livestock; the majestic elms and maples that line the town streets and shady farm lanes; the graceful houses, ranging from the earliest log and stone dwellings in "American vernacular" style to stately Victorian and Edwardian homes in red and yellow brick; and the rivers. It's difficult to drive anywhere in southern Ontario without crossing a creek, stream, or honest-to-God river.

West of Toronto lies some of the richest farmland anywhere, and strung along those smooth roads are towns that sometimes seem to have forgotten how they got there. But fast food and video rental outlets notwithstanding, the pioneer experience has made a deep impression. Almost every town and village blossoms annually with a fair or festival. Maple syrup festivals.

Apple cider festivals. Bean festivals. And everywhere are people who are determined to remember how they got there and what it was like before there were roads.

LOYALIST SETTLERS

With the capture of Fort Detroit in 1759, the British finally wrested control of the North American frontier from the French. But the settlement of the vast peninsula bounded by Lakes Ontario, Erie, and Huron lagged behind that of the booming colonies south of the Great Lakes. It wasn't until those colonies declared their independence from Britain in 1776 that the wilderness that would one day be Ontario became inviting to settlers. These were the Loyalists, whose impact on Eastern Ontario has already been noted. Their contribution to the western part of the province is even more fundamental. They gave up established homesteads to start all over again in the bush, simply because that bush remained under British law. Yet these people were Americans, and the egalitarian sentiments and pioneering spirit they brought with them helped to shape Ontario.

Southwestern Ontario was sculpted into its present shape by retreating glaciers at the end of the last Ice Age. In the late 18th century this rich soil lay under a different kind of sea: a green, rolling swell of dense forest. The French had not seriously attempted to settle the land. Clearing away the giant trees and draining the swamps would have driven back the beavers whose pelts were so lucrative to the fur traders. For a time the British adopted this attitude as well.

The American War of Independence changed all this. Thousands of settlers from the Thirteen Colonies who feared or distrusted the new regime poured across the Niagara River. John Butler, the son of a British army officer, led a group of Loyalists north to Niagara. In 1778 he recruited a band of guerrilla fighters, who became known as Butler's Rangers, and until the end of the war the group harassed the American communities in the area. Butler was

The Niagara Escarpment.

stationed at Fort Niagara and charged with keeping the Six Nations, whose territory was south of Lake Ontario, friendly to the British. At this he succeeded, even persuading the Seneca and Mohawks to engage in fighting the rebels.

The leader of the Mohawks was Joseph Brant, who had received an English education and was committed to the British tradition. When the former Six Nations' lands were ceded to the Americans in the 1783 treaty that ended the war, Brant appealed to the British for redress. He and his followers were given land beside the Grand River to an extent of 10km (6 miles) on either side. Part of that land took in Elora, where the Grand River has carved a canyon that has become one of the most popular retreats in southern Ontario. The only land that remains in the hands of the Six Nations of the Grand River is at Ohsweken, on the southeast outskirts of Brantford. Today it is one of Canada's largest native settlements and is currently engaged in a controversial claim over land in nearby Caledonia.

FAMOUS FALLS

The **Niagara Escarpment**, a rolling slope that falls away in a rocky bluff on its eastern face, is another legacy of the last Ice Age. It rises out of New York State near Rochester, follows the shore of Lake Ontario around to Hamilton, snakes overland to the Blue Mountain ridge south of Collingwood, divides Lake Huron from Georgian Bay as the Bruce Peninsula, dips underwater, resurfaces as Manitoulin Island, disappears to emerge again on the western shore of Lake Michigan, and finally peters out in Wisconsin. The first farmers in the Niagara region had no idea of the extent of this formation, but they and their heirs discovered that the soil between the escarpment and the lake was very fertile.

Perhaps the best way fully to appreciate the richness of the land is to follow the **Wine Route** (www.winecountryontario.ca). From Country Road

Niagara Falls.

24, some of the most glorious lake views are seen as the road descends into Vineland. The route eventually leads to St David's and Niagara-on-the Lake. Some of Canada's best wines are produced on the Niagara Peninsula, and the area's 65 wineries are easily accessed by following the Wine Route signs; most offer tours and tastings, and several have acclaimed restaurants.

The **Niagara Falls** ⓭, where Lake Erie overflows into Lake Ontario at the rate of 14 million liters (3.7 million gallons) of water per minute, have always been the most celebrated feature of the escarpment. Of his pilgrimage, Charles Dickens wrote: "We went everywhere at the falls, and saw them in every aspect... Nothing in Turner's finest watercolour drawings, done in his greatest days, is so ethereal, so imaginative, so gorgeous in colour as what I then beheld. I seemed to be lifted from the earth and to be looking into Heaven." Most would agree with Dickens and not with Oscar Wilde, who, noting the popularity of the Falls for honeymooners, remarked that "Niagara Falls must be the second major disappointment of American married life."

The Falls, or rather the crowds that swarm around them, have attracted a host of sideshows over the years. Until very recently, the greatest carnival draw was Blondin, the French daredevil who first crossed over the cataract on a tightrope in 1859. In 1901, Annie Edson Taylor became the first person to plunge over the Falls in a barrel and live. These and other "daredevils" are remembered in the **Niagara Daredevil Exhibition** within the Imax Theater (6170 Fallsview Boulevard; daily 9am–9pm; free). On June 15, 2012, Nik Wallenda earned worldwide acclaim by becoming the first to successfully cross near the base of the Falls, rather than downstream, from the US to the Canadian side.

The most popular way to approach the Falls is on a *Maid of the Mist* boat, which brings you to the very edge of the cascading wall of water. Wearing complimentary hooded raincoats for protection, visitors are boated up to the curve of the horseshoe close to the falls for a spectacular, if not intense, encounter with water. Journey Behind The Water is another attraction, reached on foot via an elevator through the rock from above, allowing you to emerge behind the falling water.

NIAGARA-ON-THE-LAKE

John Butler and his Rangers founded the town of Newark at the mouth of the Niagara River after the American revolutionary war. In 1792, when John Graves Simcoe arrived, the place was called "Niagara-on-the-Lake." It was the capital of Upper Canada, a province newly created out of the English-speaking portion of Québec. One of the first things Simcoe did was to choose a new capital, for Niagara-on-the-Lake was uncomfortably close to the US. He selected a site at a fork of the river,

> **◉ Tip**
>
> For a somewhat drier encounter with the Falls than aboard a boat, Konica Minolta Tower, 6732 Oakes Drive, and Skylon Tower, at 5200 Robinson, both have viewing platforms.

Tecumseh is killed by William Henry Harrison's forces at the Battle of the Thames, 1813.

Springtime at the Marsh Boardwalk, Point Pelee National Park.

which he named the Thames. The capital would be called London (naturally). But Dundas Street was no sooner hacked out of the bush than Simcoe moved the capital to Toronto – which he promptly renamed York. The Mohawk Chief Joseph Brant once remarked: "General Simcoe has done a great deal for this province, he has changed the name of every place in it."

Niagara-on-the-Lake  was blessed by its fall into political obscurity. It is one of the best-preserved colonial towns in North America. It's also home to the annual **Shaw Festival**, a major theatrical event featuring the plays of George Bernard Shaw as well as works by other writers.

THE WAR OF 1812

Canadian fears of American aggression were justified in June 1812 when the US took advantage of Britain's preoccupation with Napoleon to declare war. Many Americans thought Canada would be a pushover. Isaac Brock, the military commander of Upper Canada, wrote of his predicament: "My situation

is most critical, not from the disposition of the people... What a change an additional regiment would make in this part of the province! Most of the people have lost all confidence – I, however, speak loud and look big." He acted swiftly and decisively. His troops captured Fort Michilimackinac in northern Michigan and repulsed an attack at the Detroit River. These early victories won the native peoples in the area to the British cause and galvanized the settlers.

The Niagara region figured prominently in the war. The Americans attacked **Queenston**, just downriver from the Falls, in October 1812. Isaac Brock was killed in the Battle of Queenston Heights, though the town was successfully defended. The war dragged on, but without the example of Brock's boldness, the heavily outnumbered colony might not have held out at all.

The War of 1812 gave Canada a stronger sense of identity, though it did not end the political divisions between Tories and those calling for democratic

reform in the province. It also gave a signal to Britain that this colony was still too sparsely settled for its own security.

SOUTHWESTERN ONTARIO

The northern shore of Lake Erie is bordered by dairy farms and fishing villages, tobacco farms and beaches. West of St Thomas, the land becomes mixed-farming country. This, the westernmost tip of southern Ontario, is the southernmost part of Canada.

Point Pelee National Park ⑮ (daily), a peninsula jutting south of **Leamington**, 50km (30 miles) southeast of Windsor, is the southernmost part of mainland Canada. Lying at the same latitude as Rome and northern California, Point Pelee is home to plants and animals that are rarely seen in Canada. A trail through the woods and a boardwalk over the marshlands make it a living museum of natural history. The **Jack Miner Bird Sanctuary** at **Kingsville** (daily dawn–dusk; https://jackminer.ca; free), 10km (6 miles) west of the park, is one of the earliest and most

famous waterfowl pit stops in Canada. This haven is free to migrating birds, butterflies and humans alike. Jack Miner said: "In the name of God, let us have one place on earth where no money changes hands." The sanctuary is run by his family as a public trust.

THE UNDERGROUND RAILROAD

The southern border of Ontario played an unusual part in history: as one terminus of the "Underground Railroad." In the early 1800s, runaway slaves from the American South were sheltered by sympathizers along several routes that led to Canada.

Reverend Josiah Henson, a self-educated slave from Maryland, made the trip with his family in 1830. He settled in **Dresden** ⑯, 90km (56 miles) northeast of Windsor, and subsequently devoted himself to helping other fugitives. Henson was the prototype for "Uncle Tom" in Harriet Beecher Stowe's novel *Uncle Tom's Cabin*. His home in Dresden is part of **Uncle Tom's Cabin Historic Site** (mid-May to June,

The monarch butterfly migration in Point Pelee National Park.

Inside Dundurn Castle, Hamilton.

Sept–late Oct Tue–Sat 10am–4pm, Sun noon–4pm, July–Aug Mon–Sat 10am–4pm, Sun noon–4pm) that focuses on his life and works.

The city of **Windsor** N is the biggest urban center on Canada's border, a kind of half-sister to Detroit. Windsor is also an automobile industry town and has a pleasant downtown with extensive parks and gardens on the riverfront. It is noted for its casino.

LAKE ONTARIO

In the 1820s the growing towns and farms positioned along the western curve of Lake Ontario continued to nibble at the wilderness around them. **Ancaster**, **Dundas**, **Stoney Creek,** and **Burlington** all eventually lost their bids for supremacy at the lakehead to the town of **Hamilton** N, the "ambitious little city," 70km (43 miles) south around the lake from downtown Toronto.

The Niagara Escarpment, referred to locally as "the mountain," divides Hamilton into split levels. The city's steel mills and other heavy industries have given Hamilton a grim image in the minds of many. But the somewhat misleadingly named **Royal Botanical Gardens** incorporate a wildlife sanctuary called **Coote's Paradise**, with trails winding through 485 hectares (1,200 acres) of marsh and wooded ravines (indoor Mediterranean Garden daily 10am–8pm; outdoor gardens seasonal: daily 10am–dusk; www.rbg.ca).

Hamilton's architectural jewel is **Dundurn Castle** (Tue–Sun noon–4pm). Sir Allan Napier MacNab – landholder, financier, all-round Tory, and Hamilton's first resident lawyer – had it built in 1835 as a lavish tribute to himself. The finest home west of Montréal at the time and named for MacNab's ancestral homeland in Scotland, it is now restored as a museum to reflect the 1850s, when MacNab was premier of pre-Confederation Canada.

The first thing to note about nearby **Kitchener** N, 40km (25 miles) north of Brantford, and **Waterloo** is how prosperous they are. Kitchener is one of the fastest-growing municipalities in Canada. The second thing to note about the Twin Cities is how German

Celebrating the Oktoberfest at Kitchener.

⊘ ART, THE ENVIRONMENT, AND WAR

Long known as Steel City because of its steel industry, Hamilton is a place that few people, especially Torontonians, would have considered as a great day out. Today, however, this gritty steel town is transforming into a cultural hub – partly as cheaper rents and properties have attracted many Toronto-area artists.

Downtown, the **Art Gallery of Hamilton** is Ontario's second-largest art gallery. Within its striking gold-and-glass exterior, an exceptional collection of Canadian art can be viewed. The city has also overseen a massive environmental clean-up of its harbor and waterfront, to create a much-loved outdoor playground. A good way to explore is to follow the Hamilton Harbour Waterfront Trail from the nature sanctuary of Cootes Paradise, past the historic Desjardins Canal to the west harbor, a path shared by cyclists, runners and dog-walkers, night herons and mute swans. For a different experience of history, visit the **HMCS** *Haida*, a Tribal Class destroyer that saw active service during World War II and is now a National Historic Site of Canada. On the periphery of Hamilton International Airport, the **Canadian Warplane Heritage Museum** captures the magic of flight with displays on Canada's aviation history. One of its biggest attractions is the only operational Lancaster bomber in North America, and one of only two in the world.

they are. The original settlers in the area were members of the austere Mennonite sect transplanted from the German communities of Pennsylvania in the 1780s. The Mennonites soon had German neighbors of various creeds, and today Kitchener and Waterloo host North America's biggest **Oktoberfest** (9 days in mid-Oct). "Good cheer" is spelled *Gemütlichkeit* in this part of the country.

Ten kilometers (6 miles) north of Kitchener, the village of **St Jacobs** ⑳ was settled in the 1840s by German Mennonites. Many heritage buildings along Front Street have been converted into artisan studios and attractive stores. Among the casually attired shoppers, local Mennonites are solemnly dressed in black, the women in bonnets and the men sporting dark, broad-brimmed hats. They come here to sell their farm produce and handmade quilts, and are often seen bowling along the country roads in their horse-drawn buggies.

On King Street, **The Mennonite Story Visitor Centre** (Apr–Dec Mon–Sat 11am–5pm, Sun 1.30–5pm, Jan–Mar Sat 11am–4.30pm, Sun 2pm–4.30pm; donation) explains the history, culture, and religion of the Mennonite people. Founded in 1525 in Switzerland during the Reformation, they established the first "free Church" and introduced the now widely accepted principle of separation of Church from state. Considered revolutionaries, they were severely persecuted for several generations, before migrating first to Pennsylvania and then, after the American Revolution, to this corner of southern Ontario.

A few miles west of the village, **St Jacobs Farmers' Market** (year-round Thu and Sat 7am–3.30pm, mid-June to Aug also Tue 8am–3pm) is a huge farmers' market that attracts shoppers from as far away as Toronto. Besides stalls overflowing with fresh Ontario produce, it peddles all things maple – syrup, butter, fudge, even lollypops – and old country specialties such as homemade perogies, butter tarts, German apple cake, or raspberry apple cobbler. Somewhat incongruously, the

Market day in St Jacobs.

St Jacobs Outlet Mall across the street offers a 21st-century shopping experience, with more than 20 stores selling discounted top-name brands.

THE HURON ROAD

In the 1820s, the land between Lake Huron and the modern site of Kitchener was a piece of wilderness called the **Huron Tract**. The development of this, and other bits of Crown land, was the ambition of the Canada Company. The company's success can be attributed to its first superintendent of operations, the Scottish novelist and statesman John Galt, and to his chosen lieutenant, Dr William (Tiger) Dunlop. Galt's first task was founding a city on the edge of the wilderness. **Guelph**, 15km (9 miles) northeast of Kitchener, was inaugurated in April of 1827 and it is a striking collection of 19th-century architecture. The Roman Catholic church of **Our Lady of the Immaculate Conception** dominates the skyline with twin Gothic towers.

After surveying the Huron Tract, the exuberant Dunlop had

pronounced: "It is impossible to find 200 acres together which will make a bad farm." Galt wanted a road so that settlement could begin in earnest. In 1828, Dunlop directed the construction of that road, through swamps, dense forest, and tangled brush. Work was slow and fever plagued the work camps. It was a stupendous achievement that is not diminished by the many improvements the road has seen since. Now Highway 8, the Huron Road became the spine of settlement in the tract.

Eighteen kilometers (11 miles) into the bush, the first Huron Road curved at an attractive meadow by a river. Before long the settlement that sprang up there was called **Stratford ㉑**, and the river the **Avon**. The connection to Shakespeare was strengthened in the naming of wards and streets (Romeo, Hamlet, Falstaff), while Stratford boomed in the 1850s by virtue of being the county seat and at an intersection of railway lines.

In the years after World War II, Stratford native Tom Patterson was persistent, and finally successful, in peddling his dream of a Shakespearean theater for the city. On July 13, 1953, Alec Guinness stepped onto a stage in a riverside tent as Richard III, and the rest, as they say, is history. The tent-like (but permanent) **Festival Theatre** was opened in 1957, and its "thrust stage" has influenced a generation of theater-builders. The Stratford Festival now includes three other stages (the **Avon Theatre**, the Tom Patterson Theatre , and the **Studio Theatre**) and features music as well as plays. Over 500,000 people are attracted to the town annually.

Another road that helped to open up the Huron Tract is the one north from **London ㉒**, 60km (37 miles) south of Stratford. Or south to London, if you like, because all roads in southwestern Ontario eventually lead to London. Failing to become

A musical moment in Peterborough County.

the capital of Upper Canada, London stayed small until it became the district seat in 1826. British tradition and the American feeling of wide open spaces are in harmony here. On the street signs of London such names as Oxford and Piccadilly mix with names from Ontario's history like Simcoe, Talbot, and, of course, Dundas Street. Other names, like Wonderland Road and Storybook Gardens, may lead visitors into thinking that they have stumbled into a kind of Neverland. The impression will be reinforced by the squeaky cleanness, and greenness, of this relentlessly cheerful city. It isn't called "the forest city" for nothing; from any vantage point above the treetops, London visually disappears under a leafy blanket. The River Thames flows through the campus of the **University of Western Ontario**, a school whose presence is definitely felt in town. Also in London is the **Fanshawe Pioneer Village** (Victoria Day to Thanksgiving Tue–Sun 10am–4.30pm), a fascinating reconstruction of a pre-railway, 19th-century town, equipped with log cabins, a general store, a weaver's shop, and a carriage-maker's quarters.

WESTERN ONTARIO AND LAKE HURON

In Ontario Ministry of Tourism language, the Lake Huron shoreline is called Bluewater Country. It is a glorious lakefront with cottages, beaches, and places like **Bayfield**, 75km (46 miles) north of London. This village, with its intact 19th-century main street, shady beach, and fine marina, is a gem.

Lying 21km (13 miles) farther north is **Goderich 23**, Tiger Dunlop's town. Not merely planned, Goderich was designed; the **County Courthouse** sat on an octagonal plot (called The Square) from which streets radiated in all directions. Sadly, Goderich's claim to be "The Prettiest Town in Canada" was undermined by a devastating hurricane on August 21, 2011, when many of the old buildings and trees were severely damaged. Now the town has largely been

A red double-decker bus in London, Ontario.

A view in Tobermory.

Sainte-Marie, among the Hurons historic site.

restored and some of the most spectacular sunsets on earth can be seen from this spot. In fact, that goes for the whole of the Huron lake shore, including popular resort towns such as Southampton and Sauble Beach, whose wide sandy beaches have been attracting generation after generation of Ontario families.

When they saw how quickly the Huron Tract was being gobbled up, the British government threw open for settlement the First Nations territory immediately to the north of it. The Queen's Bush, as it was called, was not as fertile as land farther south, and some of the boom towns soon went bust. Those that remained on the stony soil turned to raising beef cattle. Several railroads snaked into Ontario between 1850 and 1900. Towns along the routes prospered, especially those where lines crossed. But as the rail lines fed city factories, industries in small towns declined and the smallest towns focused solely on the needs of the surrounding farming communities.

FROM GODERICH TO MANITOULIN

In the 1970s there was a swell of interest in the history and architecture of Ontario's small towns. A good illustration of this is the **Blyth Festival**. A community hall was built in 1920 in **Blyth**, 33km (20 miles) east of Goderich. Upstairs in the hall is a fine auditorium, with a sloping floor and stage, which lay unused from the 1930s until the mid-1970s when it was "discovered" and refurbished as the home for an annual summer festival dedicated to Canadian plays, most of them new, and most of them celebrating small-town and farming experiences. That the Blyth Festival has become a favorite with Canada's urban drama critics indicates both its theatrical quality and the potency of its subject matter, namely the history and people of rural Canada.

About 17km (11 miles) south of Blyth on the literary map lies **Clinton**, the home of writer Alice Munro, winner of the 2013 Nobel Prize in Literature. Her beautiful stories transcend regional

interest and "local color." There is no better introduction to the life of small-town Ontario.

This region has always been sparsely settled; the soil is thin, and navigation on the lake hereabouts can be treacherous. But many people make the effort to reach **Tobermory** ㉔, the fishing community at the tip of the 80km (50-mile) long **Bruce Peninsula** ㉕. The peninsula is bordered by Lake Huron's warmer and shallower waters to the west, while the Georgian Bay side is dominated by the Niagara Escarpment – a rugged wall of limestone that climbs to 100 meters (328ft) in places. On Colpoy's Bay, Wiarton is the gateway to the peninsula. Steep cliffs flank the harbor, providing a striking setting and sheltered waters for sailing and fishing. Across the peninsula are Oliphant and Red Bay, neighboring communities where families come for good beaches and safe waters. Farther north, 11km (7 miles) beyond Dyer's Bay, the **Cabot Head Lighthouse** (Victoria Day to Thanksgiving daily; donation) houses a small museum of local

history, while the adjacent Wingfield Basin Nature Reserve is frequented by 120 species of birds, ranging from the snowy owl to the great blue heron.

Bruce Peninsula National Park encompasses the northern tip. Its dense forest cover is a botanist's delight. Birders are also handsomely rewarded here, and the hiking is exceptional. Just off Tobermory lies **Fathom Five National Marine Park**. Established in 1987, and encompassing 19 islands and, at least, 22 shipwrecks, it is one of North America's premier diving sites.

Through the season, Tobermory is action-packed, especially when Little Tub Harbour is jammed with dive and cruise boats. Some visitors are heading north for **Manitoulin Island** ㉖, the largest freshwater island in the world, on board the giant ferry *Chicheemaun* (big canoe). Measuring 176km (110 miles) long with more than 80 inland lakes, Manitoulin is known for its tranquility and natural beauty. **Wikwemikong** is an unceded First Nations reserve that is known

Georgian Bay shore at Bruce Peninsula Provincial Park.

⊙ Tip

Entry to Algonquin Provincial Park is by permit (arrive early or book ahead, tel: +1 705-633-5572). Avoid peak vacation times if you plan to explore by canoe.

for hosting North America's largest Pow Wow each August and for its rich cultural heritage (a high number of internationally known First Nations artists hail from here, including Daphne Odjig, Leland Bell, and Jim Mishibinijima).

M'Chigeeng (formerly West Bay) is the second-largest native community on the island. Here, the **Ojibwe Cultural Foundation** (mid-June to mid-Oct Mon–Fri 8.30am–4pm, donation) showcases the work of many local artists along with the culture and traditions. Over the road, the **Immaculate Conception Church** is a striking circular building that blends traditional Christian and Native cultures. Little Current is the island's largest town and a popular port of call for Georgian Bay's extensive yachting community.

South of **Georgian Bay**, on the eastern ridge of the escarpment, a range of large hills provides the best ski-runs in Ontario. Ontarians call these the **Blue Mountains**, but not too loudly in the presence of anyone from western Canada.

⊙ AN UNUSUAL HERO

Countless Canadians of Chinese descent, and increasingly more visiting Chinese nationals, have been making a pilgrimage of sorts to the birthplace of a Canadian surgeon who died in China in 1939 while treating Mao Zedong's troops. The son of a Presbyterian minister, Norman Bethune was born in the Muskoka resort town of Gravenhurst. From these ordinary, middle-class beginnings, he trained in medicine, served as a stretcher-bearer in World War I, then declared allegiance to the Communist Party and developed the first mobile blood transfusion service while serving in Spain's Civil War. From there he headed to China and the second Sino-Japanese War. Before his death, he had built hospitals and medical schools while continuing to look after wounded soldiers. To this day he is revered in China, where innumerable memorials have been erected in his name, and every house in which he lived has been converted into a museum. In 1976 Parks Canada converted the Presbyterian manse into a Canadian memorial and in 2012, a new visitor center in his honor opened in Gravenhurst. Its intent is to educate the many Chinese visitors on his Canadian origins and others – including Canadians – on his pivotal role as a humanist and doctor in China. In 2017, a new World War I area opened next to the visitor centre.

STE MARIE AMONG THE HURONS

To visit the small peninsula poking out into Georgian Bay is to step a little farther back into history than most places in rural Ontario permit. This area is called **Huronia**, where 350 years ago French Jesuit missionaries traveled and preached among the Huron Indians.

When the lonely fortified mission of **Ste Marie Among the Hurons** was established in 1639, it was the only inland settlement of Europeans north of Mexico. It prospered for 10 years; but the Huron nation was eventually destroyed in wars with its enemies, the Iroquois, who also tortured and killed the Jesuits. Brian Moore's 1985 novel *Black Robe* (which was made into a movie in 1991) are set against this backdrop. Ste Marie was not attacked, but the fort was burned by retreating Jesuits to keep it out of Iroquois hands. After much research, the mission and its everyday life have been recreated on a site 5km (3 miles) east of **Midland** ㉗ (April - October 10am–5pm, daily; www.saintemarieamongthehurons.on.ca). It was in this area that Fathers Jean de Brébeuf and Gabriel Lalament were tortured and then brutally killed by the Iroquois in 1649. Their remains were housed across from the mission in the Martyrs' Shrine, a towering edifice that commands a spectacular vista over the surrounding country. Nearby is **Wye Marsh Wildlife Centre** (daily 9am–5pm; July–Aug Fri until 8pm; www.wyemarsh.com) with boardwalks extending over the marshlands. A visitors' center explains the ecology of the area and features guided tours.

The many thousands of lakes in Ontario and, particularly, those in the Canadian Shield region, just to the north, provide a cherished escape for city dwellers. The settlers' war of extermination against the trees has given way to a desire to preserve the woodlands and waters of the near north for recreational purposes.

However, the **Georgian Bay**, **Muskoka**, and **Haliburton** regions can no longer be described as forested wilds, dotted as they are by thousands and thousands of cottages. Ontario is one of the few places in the world where seemingly everyone, rich and not so rich, has a country estate even if it's only a humble cabin.

ALGONQUIN PROVINCIAL PARK

To the north of Haliburton and the northeast of Muskoka lies the last real expanse of wild land in southern Ontario – the 7,600-sq km (2,934-sq mile) **Algonquin Provincial Park** ㉘ (Visitor Center, see www.algonquinpark.on.ca for hours). Set aside as a provincial park in 1893, Algonquin preserves the primordial, aboriginal, and pioneer heritages of Ontario as a kind of natural museum.

Loons, the oldest-known birds, abound in the park's 2,500 or more lakes as they did 10,000 years ago after the last Ice Age. Algonquin Indian "vision pits" can be found in the northwest corner of the park. Here, in these rock-lined holes, a young Algonquin would fast for days waiting for the vision of a spiritual guardian who would draw the rite of passage to a close. In the park's interior, east of **Opeongo Lake**, lies the last stand of great white pines in Ontario. These few dozen ancient pines are all that is left of the huge forests cut to provide masts for the British Navy.

Algonquin should be seen by canoe. Heading north on **Canoe Lake** away from the access highway, it is only one or two portages before the motorboats and "beer with ghetto-blaster" campers are left behind. In the interior, porcupines, beaver, deer, wolves, bear, and moose can all be seen by canoeists. In August, park naturalists will even organize wolf howls, where campers head out en masse at night to try and raise the cry of the great canines. The loons, however, need no such encouragement. Their haunting cry, which the Cree believed was the sound of a warrior who had been refused entry to paradise, can be heard on every lake.

Each season brings its own character to Algonquin. Spring is the time of wild flowers, mating calls, white water, and blackflies as thick as night. Summer

A bird in Algonquin Provincial Park.

A canoe with a view in Algonquin Provincial Park.

brings brilliant thunderstorms, mosquitoes in place of blackflies, acres of blueberries, and water actually warm enough to swim in. In the fall, Algonquin turns into a Group of Seven canvas. The funeral for the forest's leaves is as triumphant and colorful as that of any New Orleans jazz singer. Uniform green gives way to a kaleidoscope of scarlet, auburn, yellow, and mauve, while in the winter, in total contrast to the rest of the seasons, the park falls deathly silent as it waits for the resurrection under a mantle of snow.

Algonquin, however, is not without its problems, problems typical of an urban society unable to control its effect upon the natural environment. Not only is 45 percent of Algonquin under license to logging interests, whose long-term effect on the ecosystem cannot be gauged; it is also being scarred by the ever-increasing effects of industrial pollution.

NORTHERN ONTARIO

A snowy forest in Temagami.

Highway maps of Ontario divide the province in two: one side showing southern Ontario, the other northern. **Sudbury** ㉙, 390km (242 miles) north of Toronto, is called "the gateway to the north" and it marks the boundary between the two. It is a city of 165,000, known for its copper and nickel mines, and its cultural focus points include **Science North** (daily, 10am–4pm, extended hours during summer season), an interactive museum and planetarium for families, and a lively summer music event, the **Northern Lights Festival Boréal**.

Most travelers never give the north of Ontario a look, never turn over the map. Myth has it that northern Ontario is an endless tract of conifers, lakes, bogs, mining camps, moose, and mosquitoes. Like all myths it's true in part, but only in part.

Just north of Algonquin Park is the Near North region of lakes and pristine wilderness areas, such as **Temagami**, toward the Québec border. Not far from North Bay, the region's largest center, is **Temagami Station**. Here, Grey Owl, the Englishman who successfully posed as a native environmentalist

writer in the 1930s in the UK and US, lived and wrote. In summer 2018, massive forest fires, caused by lightning, ravaged the area and brought on a state of emergency.

Cars taper off along northern highways, and settlements are farther apart. Every second vehicle is a logging truck. One of the most popular routes into the wilderness, which Canadians call "bush," is aboard the **Polar Bear Express**. It operates Monday through Friday, late June to late August, departing **Cochrane**, a place of fishing poles and down vests, at 9am and arriving, to the Arctic tidewater town of **Moosonee**, at 1.50pm. The adventurous bring their own canoes and paddle on to the isolated James Bay outposts.

Lying 296km (184 miles) west of Sudbury, **Sault Ste Marie** is a cultural and sporting center, whose attractions include the 183km (114-mile) Agawa Canyon train tour (end June to mid-Oct daily) and, for the angler, the largest fish hatchery in Ontario.

Located at the top of the Great Lakes, some 700km (435 miles) north of Sault Ste Marie, Thunder Bay's location is hard to beat. Surrounded by unspoiled wilderness – a constant source of inspiration to the city's many artists – it is backdropped by the Nor'Wester Mountains. On its doorstep, a string of islands entice kayakers, sailors, and hikers. The Sleeping Giant, a massive series of mesas at the tip of the Sibley Peninsula, forms an impressive guardian to Thunder Bay's harbor. With more than 80km (50 miles) of hiking trails, the Sleeping Giant Provincial Park's backcountry offers a world of peace and solitude.

Farther west still is the **Lake of the Woods** district and **Kenora**, a pulp and paper center, near the Manitoba border. This land rivals the Muskokas for resorts and bluewater camping. For those whose idea of Canada is a place where you contract a bush pilot and sea plane and fly in to an isolated cabin for a week or two, Lake of the Woods fits. "Fly-in" resorts are extremely popular, with loons, sunsets, a moose or two, and ads that read, "Ask for Don or Lynn." Now that's northern Ontario.

⊘ OLD FORT WILLIAM

In northwest Ontario, Thunder Bay's Fort William Historical Park brings early Canadian history to life, at the inland headquarters of the North West Company (NWC) and what was the world's largest fur trade post. The fort's *raison d'être* was beaver fur, which played a key role in forming the foundations of Canada. Here, in a good year, up to 90,000kg (200,000lbs) of fur (mainly, but not only, beaver) was shipped off to faraway lands to make top hats.

The fort on the Kaministiquia River has 42 historic buildings spread over a 10-hectare (25-acre) site, and is a faithful recreation of the original fort that was operated by the Nor'Westers from 1803 to 1821, with costumed interpreters bringing the early 1800s dramatically to life, whether they're working on the farm, in the apothecary or in the kitchen. A slice of pivotal Canadian history comes to life even more if you sign up to learn a heritage craft from some of Old Fort William's gifted artisans – whether it's the fort's modern-day tinsmith, fashioning items from hurricane lanterns to foot baths, butter churns, and measuring pots, or the cooper, crafting rawhide drums around wooden frames. Workshops such as these provide marvelous insight into life as it was 200 years ago.

MONTRÉAL

One of the five largest French cities in the world after Paris, Montréal has extraordinary personality. Worldly but romantic, perhaps a little extravagant, it is earnest in its aim to enjoy life.

The Québécois have a proud and often obsessive attitude toward their language and culture, and the 6.8 million French-speakers of the province are deeply aware of being surrounded by almost 300 million anglophones whose culture seems to impinge upon their own. But there is also a tinge of North American culture, with a refreshingly lively approach to both work and play, and a *joie de vivre* is evident on Montréal's rue St-Denis, rue Crescent, boulevard St-Laurent and avenue Mont-Royal.

Despite one of the city's most tenacious myths, **Mont-Royal** is not the result of a volcano, but in fact one of eight Monteregian hills, formed millions of years ago. At 233 meters (764ft) high, and with a park on its crest, its central location makes it Montréal's main landmark. From parking lots on rue Camilien Houde to the lookout with its splendid view of the city, it's still the ideal place to begin a visit to Montréal.

Surrounded by the waters of the St Lawrence, centering on the mountain, and penetrated by a maze of subterranean shopping plazas and passages, Montréal is an unusually three-dimensional city. Everyone refers to Mont-Royal as "the mountain" despite its being more of a hill. The surrounding terrain is so flat, however, that the view from the summit is excellent. In

the distance lie the other mountains of the Monteregian group. On a clear day, you can see as far as New York State's Adirondacks and the Green Mountains of Vermont.

The city spreads out down the mountainside to the St Lawrence. The view of the downtown core has changed rapidly over the last two decades, but the cruciform tower called **Place-Ville-Marie** on Boulevard Réne-Lévesque and, to the right, the slightly taller **Bank of Commerce** building, still dominates. Between them is the **Sun**

Main attractions
Musée des beaux-arts de Montréal
Place des Arts
Vieux-Montréal
Basilique de Notre-Dame
Le Vieux-Port
Oratoire St-Joseph
Biosphère
Jardin botanique de Montréal

Map on page 170

A young couple in Montréal's Latin Quarter.

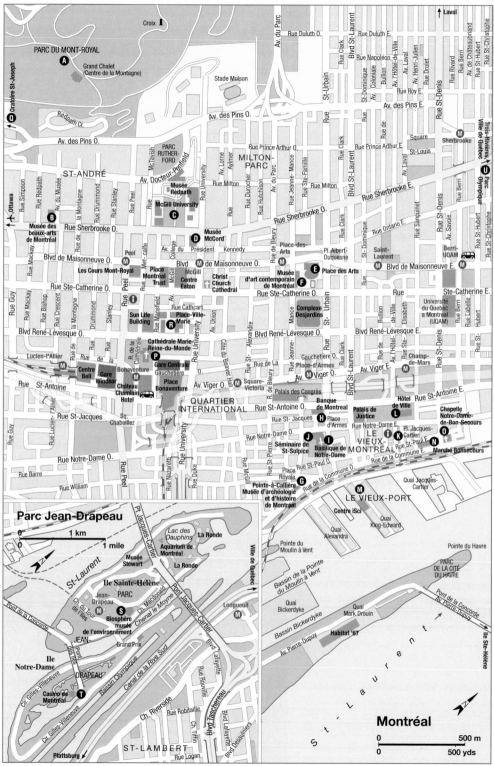

Montréal

Parc Jean-Drapeau

Life building, once the tallest building in the British Commonwealth.

FRENCH FIRST

French is the language of business as confidently as it is the language of road signs and storefronts, but visitors still find the city conveniently bilingual. Although, after the 1976 election of the separatist Parti Québécois, many English-speaking Montréalers left, many of their children, now adults, have since returned – eager to embrace the French language and a collegial relationship with the Québécois. Reciprocally, young French-Canadians are generally more comfortable speaking English than their parents, a pragmatic response to the realities of globalization.

DOWNTOWN MONTRÉAL

Côte des Neiges and rue Guy bring you down into the heart of the downtown shopping district. The finer grade of stores and hotels such as the **Ritz-Carlton** run along this section of rue Sherbrooke, being the lower limit of the Golden Square Mile, the old domain of the wealthiest anglos. In 1900, the district's 25,000 residents controlled a staggering 70 percent of Canada's wealth. Later the Square Mile suffered from the depredations of the modernizing wave of the 1960s, and many of its fine old homes were razed to make way for apartment towers that obscure the views of and from Mont-Royal.

Still, the area has an undeniable elegance, in spite of all the modern glitter, and even rue Sherbrooke retains some of its old dignity, despite the clusters of nondescript office towers that crowd its central stretch. Many of the greystone townhouses have been converted into boutiques, art galleries, and hotels, retaining their original grace, if not their purpose. The rich and powerful still meet for breakfast or pre-dinner drinks in the splendor of the Ritz-Carlton Hotel, where Elizabeth Taylor and Richard Burton celebrated one of their two weddings. Just down the street, Holt-Renfrew, Canada's own luxury department store, still sells furs and Armani gowns to an exclusive clientele.

One of rue Sherbrooke's major museums is the **Musée des beaux-arts de Montréal** ❸ (daily 10am–5pm, Wed until 9pm, closed Mon early Sept–May; www.mbam.qc.ca). Known for its exclusive exhibitions, it houses an extensive permanent collection of works by both Canadian and European masters. A few blocks east is **McGill University** ❸, former home of Ernest Rutherford, Stephen Leacock, and, many insist, Jack the Ripper. Its **Musée Redpath** (Mon–Fri 9am–5pm, Sat-Sun 11am–5pm; www.mcgill.ca/redpath; suggested donation) displays fossils, minerals, and zoological exhibits. Opposite the university stands the **Musée McCord** ❸ (late May–late Sept Mon, Tue, Fri 10am–6pm, Wed, Thu until 9pm, Sat-Sun until 5pm, late Sept–late May Tue, Thu, Fri 10am–6pm, Wed until 9pm,

⊙ Fact
The February Fête des Neiges is followed through the year by fireworks, jazz, comedy, gastronomy, film, and dance.

Modern art piece at the Musée d'art contemporain de Montréal.

PARC MONT-ROYAL

Mont-Royal – or, as Montréalers call it, *la montagne* (the mountain) – is more than a park; it's a cherished reminder of the city's rich and vibrant history.

The mountain embodies a kind of grandeur, a place where nature's sublime and wild moods play freely across a landscape blissfully untouched by the heavy hand of urban development. You can see it from just about anywhere in the city, whether you're buying a magazine at a newsstand, gazing idly out of a kitchen window, or taking the dog for its nightly walk. It looms up in the middle of the city like a natural obelisk proclaiming the city's presence.

Indeed it was here in 1535 that French explorer Jacques Cartier was led by the First Nations through wooded hills and up rocky crests all the

Cross-country skiing, Mont-Royal.

way to the summit. Today all kinds of modern Montréalers can be found sunning, sledding, strolling, folk-dancing, and picnicking on this mountain.

That Mont-Royal is not covered by a network of roads, walking trails, cafes, electric cable cars, and vast amphitheaters is largely due to the aesthetic sensibilities of Frederick Law Olmsted, the man who was hired by the City of Montréal in 1874 to design the park. Olmsted, who also designed Manhattan's Riverside Drive in New York as well as the elegant Morningside and Central parks, firmly believed that nature was a source of spiritual sustenance and that parks, properly designed, could provide urban dwellers with some relief from the oppressive routines of metropolitan life.

Olmsted urged Montréal to preserve its gracious mountain and warned off voracious developers and, so far, he has been heeded.

Most of Mont-Royal's pleasures can be enjoyed in any season: a stroll through its 200 hectares (495 acres) along winding trails, a walk to the summit for a look at the 30-meter (100ft) cross. Now illuminated by electric lights, the original cross was raised in 1643 by Paul de Chomedy, Sieur de Maisonneuve, when the fledgling colony of Ville Marie was saved from a flood.

Horse-drawn carriages *(calèches)* are a relaxing and romantic way to traverse the park and, in warmer months, nature walks – conducted in both French and English – start at Smith House, a stone cottage that also houses an exhibit on the park's history and a coffee shop. In winter, skaters take to Beaver Lake (an artificial pond) and cross-country skiers travel along tranquil tracks. Toboggan runs attract shoals of enthusiastic children.

On the park's northern boundary are two graveyards – the Catholic Notre-Dame-des-Neiges and the Protestant Mount Royal Cemetery. Together they cover more than half the mountain with elaborate monuments, lush vegetation, and hundreds of kilometers of sinuous trails. The cemeteries' permanent occupants are quite an eclectic lot, ranging from Calixa Lavalée, composer of Canada's national anthem, to Anna Leonowens, whose life was dramatized in the musical *The King and I.*

Sat–Sun until 5pm; http://www.musee -mccord.qc.ca/en) with its emphasis on the social history of Canada.

Rue Ste-Catherine, two blocks south, is livelier. It is lined with boutiques, cafes, department stores, fast-food joints (especially *croissanteries* and smoked-meat delis), and arcades. Intersecting this bustling artery is rue Crescent, one of the concentrations of bistros and restaurants that give Montréal its reputation for nightlife and table-hopping.

UNDERGROUND TRAVEL

Farther east, the largest department stores, and a nexus of multistory shopping centers – **Complexe Les Ailes**, **Place Montréal Trust**, **Les Cours Mont-Royal**, the **Montréal Eaton Centre** – are joined by underground passages to the Métro, Montréal's subway system. Trains on rubber wheels thread their way between "designer" stations, each having its own bold architecture. Opened in 1966, with its quiet, high-speed trains, it's still the most efficient and pleasant way to get around.

ARTS AND CULTURES

Still farther east are the **Complexe Desjardins**, another dramatically conceived shopping center, and the Quartier des Spectacles, a new range of indoor and open-air performance spaces including the **Place des Arts ❺**. This comprises six concert halls, housed on top of one another in the step-pyramid style building, including the **Salle Wilfred Pelletier**, with elegant, sweeping curves, and the **Maison symphonique de Montréal**, which opened in 2011 as the home of Montréal's orchestra, opera, and ballet.

L'Orchestre Symphonique de Montréal (OSM) has emerged as one of the world's great orchestras and is often called "the world's first and finest French orchestra," drawing rave reviews on tours and prizes for many of its recordings. Its home in the Place des Arts also houses Montréal's modern art museum, the **Musée d'art contemporain de Montréal ❻** (Tue 11am–6pm, Wed, Thu, Fri until 9pm, Sat–Sun 10am–6pm; www.macm.org).

Books and art prints for sale in Mile End.

Notre Dame de Bon Secours at night.

Beyond the Place des Arts on boulevard St-Laurent, affectionately known by locals as The Main (or Le Main), there emerges an eclectic jumble of small businesses representing the ethnic communities who have made this their neighborhood: Jewish, Italian, Portuguese, Greek.

Within this area lies another focus of Montréal's nightlife: **rue Prince Arthur**. Closed to motor traffic, Prince Arthur frequently fills up with hundreds of people lining up to eat at its popular Greek or Vietnamese restaurants. Most of Montréal's Greek restaurants allow patrons to bring their own wine, which makes an excellent dinner easy to afford. The crowds may appear daunting, but the lines move quickly.

Around the corner from Place St-Louis, the historic square at the east end of Prince Arthur, is rue St-Denis. One stretch of road here has been known for many years as the Quartier-Latin of Montréal: bohemian, a little ramshackle, politicized. Today it equals rue Crescent as the hub of Montréal's night time activity although it is more frequented by locals than visitors. The annual **International Jazz Festival** revolves around St-Denis and Place des Arts, but throughout the year St-Denis has a particularly Québécois vibrancy and charm. Shared by both Plateau Mont-Royal and Le Village (the vibrant heart of Montréal's gay community), Parc Lafontaine is a pretty 40-hectare (100-acre) park where mature trees and landscaped lawns enclose a waterfall, a fountain and two linked ponds where visitors can rent a pedal boat in summer and skate on the ice in winter. The park is also home to the Théâtre de Verdure, which stages open-air plays and concerts during the summer.

On the lower reaches of Le Main, below rue Ste-Catherine, is the Monument National. Built in 1893, it was an essential stop for such vaudeville greats as Edith Piaf and Emma Albani. The École Nationale de Théâtre now uses its beautifully restored theater to stage its student productions.

Place Jacques-Cartier and the Hotel-de-Ville.

VIEUX-MONTRÉAL

Although Jacques Cartier discovered an Indian settlement called Hochelaga (near the site of McGill University) when he landed in 1535, Montréal was not permanently settled until a century later. The founders' purpose was to save the pagan "savages" by converting them to Christianity. The project began when the Société de Notre-Dame de Montréal commissioned Paul de Chomedy, Sieur de Maisonneuve, to establish a settlement in this remote wilderness far from "civilization" – 70 recruits and young Jeanne Mance, a nurse, accompanied him.

The settlement of Ville-Marie in that year, 1642, was having a bad time defending itself against the brutal attacks of the Iroquois but, for whatever reason, the Iroquois ignored the new settlement. Once winter came, the settlers were able to erect a few huts and a log palisade.

The late 17th-century European vogue for hats made of beaver pelt gave Montréal a secondary purpose, the fur trade, which then became its primary object, with greater organization and profits. The accommodation of business and religion as twin forces in Montréal's history is visible everywhere, particularly in Vieux-Montréal. Archeological finds from the city are on display at the fascinating **Pointe-à-Callière Musée d'archéologie et d'histoire de Montréal**  (late June to early Sept Mon–Fri 10am–6pm, Sat–Sun 11am–6pm, early Sept to late June Tue–Fri 10am–5pm, Sat–Sun 11am–5pm; www.pacmusee.qc.ca) on Place Royale.

Horse and cart in Old Montréal.

Vieux-Montréal's longest square, Place d'Youville, is a long, narrow strip of grass that runs west for four blocks from the Old Customs House to rue McGill. Its main attraction is the **Centre d'histoire de Montréal** (Wed–Sun 10am–5pm, late June–early Sept also Tue), in what was formerly a stylish 1915 firehouse. The center's exhibits focus on the city's multiculturalism and the lives of ordinary Montréalers.

Place d'Youville was once the site of the parliament for both Upper and Lower Canada. The market building

Statues inside Notre-Dame Cathedral on Place d'Armes.

⊘ PLATEAU MONT-ROYAL

Plateau Mont-Royal has been labeled one of the coolest neighborhoods in North America. Predominantly francophone, the mix of artists, students, young families, and yuppie professionals live in the shadow of Mont-Royal, surrounded by the buzz of activity from boulevard St-Laurent, the designer boutiques of St-Denis, the "it" spots of avenue Mont-Royal, and the casual, bring-your-own-bottle eateries of rue Prince Arthur. Trendy stores share sidewalk space with butchers, bakeries, and delicatessens, yet the tranquility of Parc Lafontaine grounds them all. By night, people from near and far flock to the Plateau to catch the latest opening – theater or art – or to check out a Martini lounge or relax in the microbrew pub. For a compact neighborhood, the options are plentiful.

here, erected after the 1837 rebellion, lasted only a dozen years before rioters, protesting against an unpopular British bill, burned it down.

North up rue St-Pierre and east along rue Notre-Dame leads to the hub of Vieux-Montréal, **Place d'Armes Ⓗ**. Banks surround the square on three sides; it was once the heart of the Canadian financial establishment, dominated by anglo-Montréalers. On the south side stands the **Basilique de Notre-Dame Ⓘ**, the symbol *par excellence* of Québécois Roman Catholicism.

The facade of Notre-Dame is plain because stoneworkers were rare in Québec when the church was built around 1829. In stark contrast its interior is a magnificently ornate tribute to the importance of woodworking and decoration in Québécois tradition.

Everywhere there is paint laced with real gold leaf, and the reredos gleams in a vivid blue. Ironically, Montréal's finest church was designed by an Irish American, James O'Donnell, but the interior is the inspiration of a French Canadian, Victor Bourgeau.

St. Joseph's Oratory.

Neither ugly nor the epitome of subtle elegance, it is what it was meant to be: simply overwhelming.

The basilica is the closest thing the city of Montréal has to a state church, and anyone of note, from former prime ministers to hockey greats, has had their final rites celebrated within its walls. During former Prime Minister Pierre Elliott Trudeau's funeral in 2000, Cuban dictator Fidel Castro shared the front east pew with fellow honorary pallbearer, former US president Jimmy Carter. Canadian Mounties in striking red uniform jackets carried Trudeau's casket into the basilica for the ceremony. Four months earlier, a state funeral was held here for Maurice "Rocket" Richard, local hero and hockey great.

Adjacent to the west wall of the basilica stands Montréal's oldest building, the **Séminaire de St-Sulpice Ⓙ**, built in 1685. The Sulpicians became the seigneurs or landlords of all Montréal when they took over missionary responsibilities from the Société de Notre-Dame in 1663. More than 300 years after its construction, the seminary still serves as the residence for the Sulpicians.

Across the square stands the English businessman's retort to Notre-Dame's assertion of indomitable French-Canadian values: the serene neo-Classical **Banque de Montréal**, built in 1847. During banking hours the main hall is open to visitors, as is a tiny but interesting museum.

Walking east past the shops and cafes on rue Notre-Dame, you encounter on the north side the old Napoleonic-style **Palais de Justice** with its silver dome, and on the south side the less graceful "new" Palais de Justice with its august pillars and heavy doors. Both buildings are government offices today.

Opening off the south side of rue Notre-Dame lies **Place Jacques Cartier Ⓚ**, a center of much less serious activity than Place d'Armes. Cobblestoned, floriated, peopled, and surrounded by restaurants and terrace cafes in buildings a century and a half old, it preserves the charm and human scale of another era. At the top of the square stands **Nelson's Column**, the city's oldest monument and the first in the world to be dedicated to Admiral Nelson. Lest the monument should be thought a rather diminutive replica of the column in Trafalgar Square, know that Montréal's pre-dates London's by 34 years.

Facing Nelson across rue Notre-Dame is the **Hôtel de Ville** (city hall), an elegant Second Empire-style building with slender columns and mansard roofs. Opposite, on the south side, stands the **Château de Ramezay** (1705), looking like a sturdy farmhouse, but nevertheless the focal point of more than a century of early Canadian history. Today, the château is a private museum (daily 9.30am-6pm; www.chateauramezay.qc.ca) with some impressively equipped 18th-century living quarters and many fascinating artifacts. Look out for North America's first paper money: playing cards authorized as legal tender when a cargo of coins was delayed on its way across the Atlantic.

Yet another site to see here is **Le Vieux-Port**, now an entertainment area that offers summer evenings of music, dancing, and beer under the stars with the city skyline as a backdrop. The port also provides the best view of the **Marché Bonsecours**, which served as the Lower Canada Parliament during its construction (1849–52), but for almost a century was Montréal's principal marketplace. Its long, classical facade and silver dome greeted thousands of immigrants and travelers in the 19th century. Now it houses *café-terrasses* and boutiques that showcase Québec artists, designers, and artisans.

Besides the Marché Bonsecours, and overlooking the river, stands the **Chapelle Notre-Dame-de-Bon-Secours**, also known as the Sailors' Church as sailors have traditionally come here to give thanks for being

Tip

Visit Maison Sir Georges-Etienne Cartier, 458 Notre-Dame Est, for a peek into the life of a 19th-century statesman of Québec (Wed-Sun 10am-5pm).

Taking a break on Rue de la Commune.

ORATOIRE ST-JOSEPH

One of the greatest of Montréal's monuments is the Oratoire St-Joseph on Mont-Royal. It was the dream-child of Alfred Bessette, Brother André, who was porter at the nearby Collège Notre-Dame when he developed a reputation as "the miracle worker," because of the many cures he performed. The secret of his cure was the application of "oil of St Joseph" to the bodies of the sick. Soon the sick were flocking to him by the thousands.

People were asked to donate money to its construction and the church began to take shape in 1924. When money ran out during the Depression, Brother André recommended that a statue of St Joseph be placed in the center of the roofless church. "If he wants a roof over his head, he'll get it," he said. Two months later money was found to continue with the building.

⊙ Tip

For water transport, Quai Jacques Cartier is the departure point for Parc des Iles ferries, jet-boats to Lachine Rapids, water taxis, and even a paddle steamer.

saved from a shipwreck. Built in 1658, it is Montréal's oldest stone chapel. Within it, the **Musée Marguerite Bourgeoys** (May to Thanksgiving Tue–Sun 10am–6pm, mid-Oct to mid-Jan and Mar–Apr 11am–4pm, closed mid-Jan until end of February; www.margueritebourgeoys.org/en) is dedicated to the history of the chapel and the life of Marguerite Bourgeoys, Montréal's first teacher.

FROM CHURCHES TO MODERN ARCHITECTURE

Until the 1960s, religion as much as language set French Canada apart from the rest of North America. In the middle of the anglo business district Monsignor Ignace Bourget built **Cathédrale Marie-Reine-du-Monde** ⓟ, a one-third scale replica of St Peter's in Rome. But nowhere is the role of religion more obvious than at **Oratoire St-Joseph** ⓠ, the church that rises 152 meters (500ft) above the street on the western summit of Mont-Royal. It rose up out of a wave of popular devotion to St Joseph, the patron saint of the worker, led by

Jogger at Parc Mont-Royal.

the humble Brother André who became famous for his curative powers during the first half of the 20th century. If the exterior is more remarkable for its size than its beauty (only the dome of St Peter's in the Vatican is larger), the austere simplicity of the modern interior is more lovely. Impressive in quite a different way is the crypt with its rows of crutches, donated by the miraculously healed, and banks of devotional candles. Brother André's tiny living quarters still stand in the shadow of the oratory.

The buildings of the 1960s in Montréal are monuments not to the church but to modernity. **Place-Ville-Marie** ⓡ, perhaps the most successful creation of the famous urban architect I.M. Pei (responsible for the pyramid outside the Louvre in Paris), with its cruciform tower and underground plaza, pioneered the concept of the shopping mall in 1962. For Expo 67 Moshe Safdie, a student at McGill University, designed **Habitat 67**, a sort of Cubist representation of the mountain made out of 158 concrete apartment units.

⊙ THE LACHINE CANAL

The Lachine Canal runs for 14.5km (9 miles) from the Vieux-Port to Lachine on Lac St-Louis. A National Historic Site operated by Parks Canada, it was constructed in the 1820s and later enlarged to allow cargo vessels heading for the Great Lakes to circumvent the Lachine Rapids. By the mid-19th century the canal had helped to launch Canada's Industrial Revolution, but after the construction of the St Lawrence Seaway in 1959, the Lachine Canal stood unused for several decades.

It finally reopened to leisure boat traffic in 2001. Today the old factories and warehouses have been transformed into loft apartments and trendy bars and restaurants.

The towpath and the surrounding area is a city park, and the canal can be explored by boat, by bike (allow at least half a day to cover its entire length) or on foot. Worth a visit are a couple of small museums, a sculpture garden, and the house where jazz great Oscar Peterson was born (3007 rue Delisle at the Union United Church). Parks Canada added various podcasting options, to bring the canal's rich history to life more vividly from a digital perspective. From the Vieux-Port head west to the Lachine Lock, or stop by the Visitor Center at 500 chemin des Iroquois.

PARC JEAN-DRAPEAU

The site of Expo 67, on two man-made islands in the St Lawrence, is now Parc Jean-Drapeau. The world exposition drew no fewer than 50 million visitors during the summer of Canada's centennial year, 1967. Several of the 83 supposedly temporary structures were so sturdy and impressive that it made no sense to demolish them. **Ile Ste-Hélène** and **Ile Notre-Dame** can be identified by Buckminster Fuller's geodesic dome, built to house the US pavilion. The **Biosphère musée de l'environnement** ⑤ (June–Nov daily 10am–5pm, Dec–May Wed–Sun 10am–5pm), on Ste-Hélène, is now home to an environmental observation center focusing on the St Lawrence-Great Lakes ecosystem. An amusement park, **La Ronde**, (mid-June to late Aug daily, mid-May to mid-June, Sept–Oct Sat–Sun only) is on the island's eastern tip. Nearby is the **Vieux Fort** (1822), with summer re-enactments of maneuvers by the Fraser Highlanders. The **Musée Stewart** (10am–5pm late June–early Sept Tue–Sun, early Sept–late June Wed–Sun; www.stewart-museum.org/en) covers the period from the native occupation until today, including early European exploration and the settlement of New France. By night on the Ile Notre-Dame, Montréalers and visitors try their luck at the **Casino de Montréal** ⑦ with its river and city views (daily 24 hrs).

HOCHELAGA-MAISONNEUVE

On the eastern end of the island, Hochelaga-Maisonneuve was Canada's fifth-largest city before it was annexed to Montréal in 1918. Known for its striking collection of Beaux-Arts architecture, one of the best examples is the **Marché Maisonneuve**, which opened in 1912 and is now popular for its organic and regionally grown products.

The neighborhood's most prominent and modern monument is the **Parc Olympique** ⑪, one of the world's most ambitious sports complexes, located on rue Sherbrooke Est. Designed by French architect Roger Taillibert, the futuristic, grandiose, impractical, and incredibly expensive stadium was built for the 1976 Summer Olympic Games and is famous for its suspended

Montréal Biosphere.

retractable roof and for its tower, the highest inclined tower in the world (late June–early Sept Mon 1–8pm, Tue–Sun 9am–8pm, early Sept–early Oct until 6pm, early Oct–late Dec until 5pm, closed Mon; www.parcolympique. qc.ca). It has one of the best views in the city, extending about 80km (50 miles), and includes an unobstructed westward view of Mont-Royal and the city skyline, with the St Lawrence River winding from the left. There is also a vertiginous view into the stadium. At its base, the impressive sports center includes six huge swimming pools.

Next to the stadium is the **Biodôme de Montréal** (mid-June to Labor Day daily 9am–6pm, closed for renovations until the summer of 2019; www. espacepourlavie.ca), a showcase for flora and fauna from four different ecosystems: rainforest, polar, marine, and forest. The **Rio Tinto Alcan Planetarium** (Sun–Wed 9am–5pm, Thu–Sat 9am–8pm, closed Mon in autumn–winter), next to the Biodôme, opened in a cutting-edge modern building in 2013, offering a unique experience of the universe in its two extraordinary immersive shows.

Opposite the Parc Olympique is the **Jardin botanique de Montréal**, considered among the world's best, with 75 hectares (185 acres) of flora. If Montréal, with its harsh winters, seems an unlikely setting for one of the world's largest botanical gardens, consider the pleasure of sitting in the warmth of the tropical greenhouse, among pineapple plants and orchids, during a December blizzard. Although nine greenhouses protect the tropical flora from the elements, spring and fall are the best seasons for a visit, since the vast majority of plants are divided among the various outdoor gardens. Different plant groups bloom each month between April and October.

More than 250,000 species are housed in the **Insectarium** (Labor Day to Oct daily 9am–9pm, Tue–Sun and shorter hours rest of the year). Part museum and part zoo, the project was designed to educate children and adults about creatures that usually receive only negative attention from humans. An extraordinary variety of perfectly preserved insects, from butterflies to golden scarab beetles, is mounted on the walls, while an assortment of living insects is housed behind glass. Brave visitors may want to time their visit to coincide with the annual insect tasting event.

DISCOVERIES BY BIKE

One of the increasingly popular ways to explore Montréal's neighborhoods is by bike – specifically a Bixi bike. Since their arrival in 2009, Bixi has become a hugely popular way to take a spin around town among both locals and tourists, May through November. Cyclists can borrow (and return) a bicycle for a nominal fee from 516 Bixi stations across the city. Since Montréal is one of North America's most cyclist-friendly cities, this is an excellent way to explore. Favorite rides include the Lachine Canal, Parc Jean-Drapeau and right downtown along boulevard de Maisonneuve.

Bixi bike station.

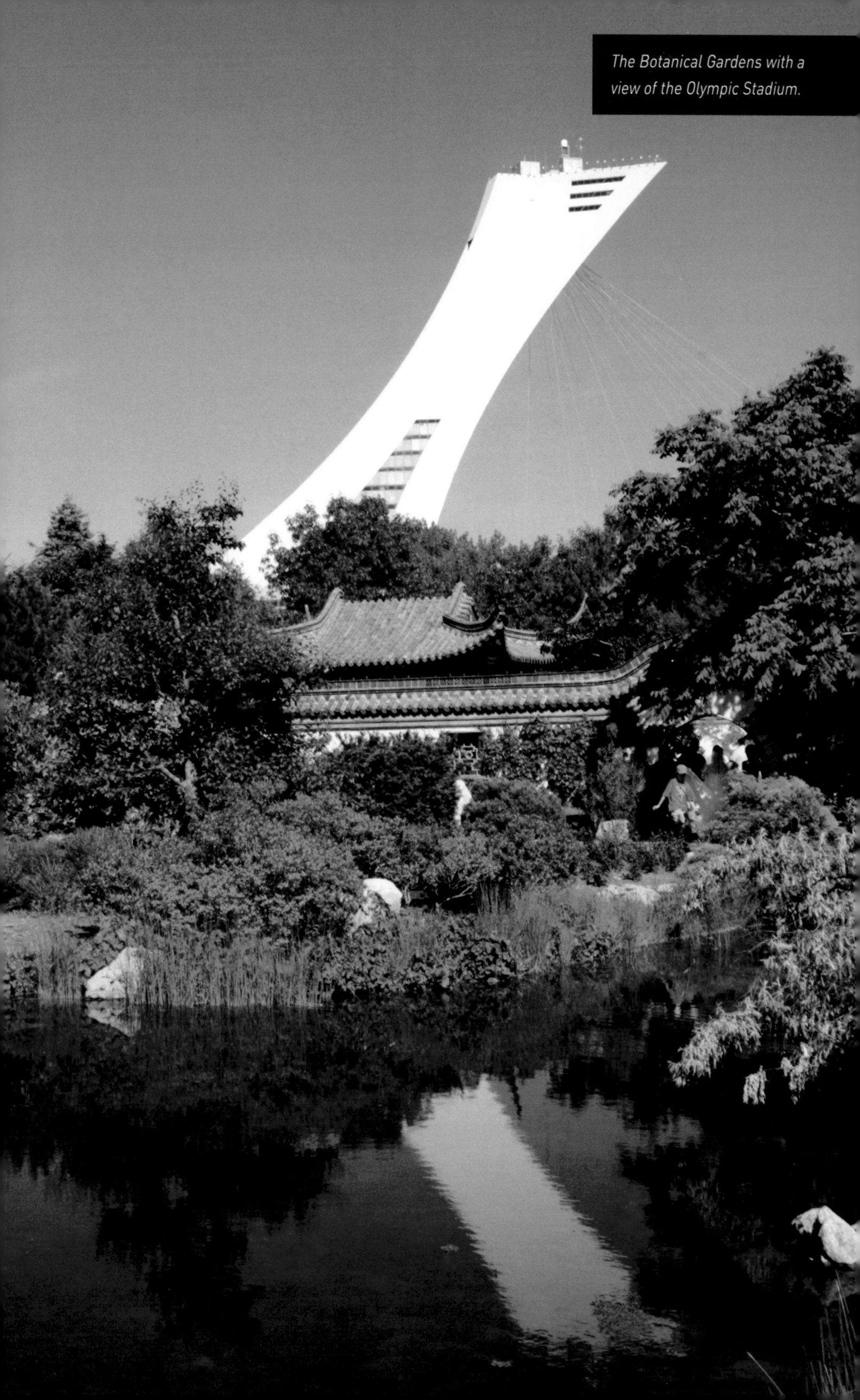

The Botanical Gardens with a view of the Olympic Stadium.

📷 THE GREAT OUTDOORS

The country's huge land and water masses and varied climate provide countless opportunities for outdoor pursuits and sports – not just ice hockey.

Canadians are avid tourists in their own country. Some families spend entire summer vacations in their favorite national and provincial parks in pursuit of outdoor activity. Others have vacation homes, known as "cottages," regardless of their size. Boaters head for the waters, tenters to the backroads. Birdwatchers, fishermen, and canoeists, too, find plenty of space for these gentle pursuits. If all that sounds too tame, there is plenty of scope for white_water rafting, heli-hiking, even heli-fishing. Parks have campgrounds, supervised beaches, hiking, and cycling trails.

Even city-dwellers can enjoy walking and cycling trails cut through municipal parks well endowed with wooded areas, rivers, and lakes.

PARTICIPANT SPORTS

In the realm of participant sports, golf and tennis are summer's favorites, but cricket and soccer also have their adherents. Lacrosse, which originated as a rough native tribal contest, has been tamed to a seven-a-side game.

In winter, ice and snow are welcomed by many. That's when city walking and cycling paths are transformed into cross-country ski and snowshoeing trails, fishermen cut holes in the ice, dog-team enthusiasts have race meets, amateurs enjoy sleigh rides, while alpine skiers head for the mountain slopes.

Hiking takes you to the true heart of the country and parks have well-marked trails, graded for most abilities.

Canada's magnificent scenery and wildlife are often best observed from the water.

Horse-riding is a very popular activity in the west and on the prairies, where novices can improve their technique on a ranch holiday. Best of all is trail-riding in the Rockies' national parks.

Hockey is popular in Canada and a favorite family pastime.

Sports Worth Watching Out For

Baseball, hockey, and Canadian football all have amateur and professional teams and hordes of enthusiastic supporters. In summer youngsters play "little league" baseball. A treat for the kids around Toronto is to visit the Rogers Center to watch the Toronto Blue Jays play American opponents.

In winter little-leaguers trade baseball mitts for hockey skates and take to community ice rinks. While the origins of ice hockey (known in Canada simply as "hockey") are murky, there is no doubt it is Canada's sporting gift to the world. This is a major spectator sport, with teams competing from all over North America. If the Edmonton Oilers, Montréal Canadiens, Ottawa Senators, Winnipeg Jets, Calgary Flames, Vancouver Canucks or Toronto Maple Leafs arrive at the annual Stanley Cup game in late spring, the entire country comes to a halt to watch.

Canadian football, which has its origins in 19th-century English rugby, is played by high-school and university teams as well as commercial league teams. Football's high point is the Grey Cup in late November or early December. Parades and post-game festivities bring Grey Cup fever to a high pitch; the game itself often has well-fortified fans cheering their teams on.

Canada's lakes, rivers, and coastlines provide a haven for fishing enthusiasts. Permits are required.

Wakeboarding on a lake in Ontario.

The South Nahanni river, which flows through Nahanni National Park in the Northwest Territories, offers some of the most thrilling white water in the country.

Tremblant ski resort at twilight.

QUÉBEC

Fiercely proud of its French-speaking traditions, the province of Québec, from the frozen north to the fertile land along the St Lawrence, has developed its own distinct culture.

At 1,504,687 sq km (594,860 sq miles), Québec is the largest eastern province, lying between Ontario and New Brunswick, the Hudson Bay and the Gulf of St Lawrence. Montréal, Québec City, and the other main population centers are along the St Lawrence River and on the east coast. The 8.2 million Québécois are deeply aware of being surrounded by almost 300 million Anglophones whose culture seems to impinge on their own. Don't be surprised if you sometimes encounter a protective and proud attitude toward language and culture, two great local preoccupations.

THE UPPER RICHELIEU RIVER

To the east of Montréal, the tourist region of Montérégie is split into two parts – the area north of the St Lawrence (St Laurent) River and the territory to the south of the city. The spine of Montérégie – and the most interesting part for a visitor – is the 130km (80-mile) **Richelieu River**, which flows out of Lac Champlain, then snakes north before emptying into Lac St-Pierre at Sorel.

A logical starting point is **Chambly ❶**. The first impression of the river, named for Cardinal Richelieu, the ruthless chief minister of Louis XlII, is that of a sleepy backwater. In Québec's early days it was part of a bustling

transportation network – a vital link in New France's fur trade and, during the 19th century, a strategic route for the British military.

The imposing Fort Chambly National Historic Site (mid-June to early Sept daily, 10am-5pm, early Sept to mid-Oct and mid-May to mid-June Wed–Sun) is perched on the edge of the Richelieu Rapids, and the names of the heroes of New France are carved in stone at its gates. A towering stone structure, it was part of a chain of military installations that in the 17th and 18th centuries

Main attractions
Mont Orford
Mont-Tremblant
Place Royale, Vieux Québec
Musée de la civilisation, Québec City
La Citadelle, Québec City
Plains of Abraham
Saguenay
Percé Rock
Jardins de Métis

Maps on pages 186, 192

Canoes at sunset.

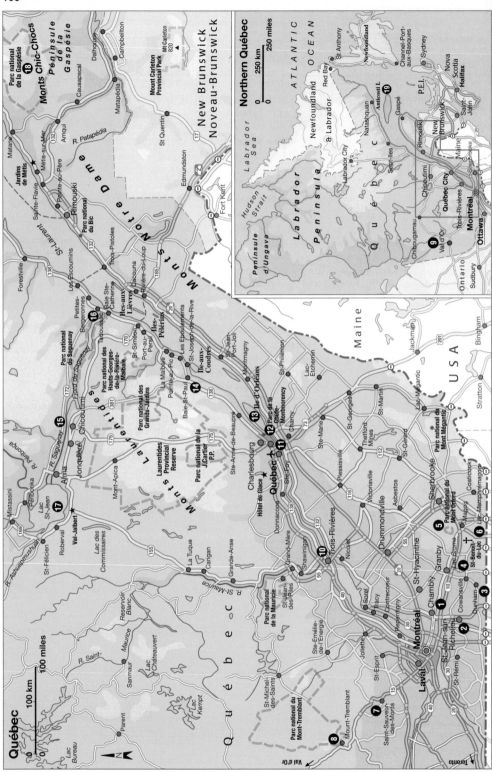

Québec

0 100 km
0 100 miles

Northern Québec

0 250 km
0 250 miles

Parc national de la Gaspésie
Monts Chic-Chocs
Péninsule de la Gaspésie
Mt Carleton 820
Mount Carleton Provincial Park
New Brunswick
Noveau-Brunswick

Campbellton
Dalhousie
Causapscal
Amqui
Matapédia
St Quentin
Edmundston
Fort Kent

Matane
Métis-sur-Mer
Jardins de Métis
Sainte-Flavie
Pointe-au-Père
Rimouski
Parc national du Bic
Trois-Pistoles
Les Escoumins
Forestville
Petites-Bergeronnes
Tadoussac
Baie-Ste-Catherine
Îles-aux-Lièvres
Rivière-du-Loup
Cacouna

Parc national du Saguenay
Fjord du Saguenay
St-Siméon
Port-au-Persil
Les Éboulements
La Malbaie
Pointe-au-Pic
Baie-St-Paul
Parc national des Hauts-Georges-de-la-Rivière-Malbaie
Parc national des Grands-Jardins
Laurentides Provincial Reserve
Parc national de la J. Cartier P.P.

Mistassini
St-Félicien
Roberval
Val-Jalbert
Péribonka
Alma
Lac St-Jean
Jonquière
Chicoutimi
Mont-Apica

R. Ashuapmushuan
Lac des Commissaires
Péribonka
R. Péribonka

Îles-aux-Coudres
St-Joseph-de-la-Rive
Île-d'Orléans
Parc de la Chute-Montmorency
Hôtel-de-Glace
Québec
Charlesbourg
Ste-Anne-de-Beaupré
Ste-Foy
Donnacona
Grondines
Grand-Mère
Shawinigan
Parc national de la Mauricie
La Tuque
Carignan
Grande-Anse

Reservoir Blanc
R. St-Maurice
Ste-Émélie-de-l'Énergie
St-Jean-des-Piles
Joliette
St-Esprit
St-Michel-des-Saints
Parc national du Mont-Tremblant
Mont-Tremblant
Saint-Sauveur-des-Monts

Sanmaur
Parent
Lac Chàteauvert
R. Saint-
Lac Kempt
Lac Bureau

St-Jean-Port-Joli
Montmagny
St-Philémon
Lac Etchemin
Lac-Frontière
St-Georges
St-Martin
Lac-Mégantic
Parc national du Mont Mégantic
Stratton
USA
Maine
Jackman
Bingham

Ste-Marie
Thetford Mines
Plessisville
Victoriaville
Asbestos
St-Gérard
Coaticook
Magog
Lac Memphrémagog
St-Benoît-du-Lac
Sherbrooke
Parc national du Mont Orford

Drummondville
Nicolet
Trois-Rivières
Sorel
Tracy
Contrecoeur
Repentigny
St-Hyacinthe
Granby
Cowansville
Dunham
Chambly
St-Jean-sur-Richelieu
Montréal
Laval
St-Rémi
St-Remi
Toronto
Val d'Or

Northern Québec (inset)

ATLANTIC OCEAN
Labrador Sea
Newfoundland & Labrador
St Anthony
Red Bay
Labrador City
Sept-Îles
Natashquan
Anticosti I.
Gaspé
Rimouski
New Brunswick
Maine
Sherbrooke
Québec City
Trois-Rivières
Montréal
Ottawa
Chicoutimi
Val-d'Or
Chibougamau
Hudson Strait
Labrador Peninsula
Péninsule d'Ungava
Québec
Ontario
Sudbury
Nova Scotia
Halifax
P.E.I.
Saint-John
Channel-Port-aux-Basques
Sydney
Newfoundland

Peninsule de la Gaspésie
Monts Notre Dame
Monts Laurentides
St-Laurent
R. Patapédia

guarded the corridor from New York to Québec City. It takes its name from Captain Jacques Chambly, of le Régiment de Carignan-Salière, who built the first (wooden) fort on the site in 1665 to defend against Iroquois attack.

The first European settlement on the Richelieu River grew up around the fort, becoming the town of Chambly. In 1709–11 the wooden building was replaced by the massive, imposing structure with five-sided corner bastions that stands today, and it was occupied by the French until 1760, by the English until 1775 and by the Americans under General Montgomery until 1776. It later held American prisoners during the War of 1812 and rebels during the Patriot Rebellion of 1837–8.

Nearby, the Chambly Canal opened in 1843. Now the **Canal Chambly National Historic Site**, it was used for over a century by heavily loaded barges carrying lumber from the forests of Québec's interior, bound for the United States. From the closest three locks to the fort you can watch boaters "locking through" or you can go canoeing in the Chambly basin, which is just below the Richelieu rapids. The former towpath is now a 19km (12-mile) recreational trail for hikers and cyclists.

South of Chambly, the old part of **St-Jean-sur-Richelieu ❷** is a historic military town in a graceful riverside setting. During the exciting nine-day August festival of **l'International de Montgolfières de Saint-Jean-sur-Richelieu**, colorful hot-air balloons float over the rooftops and steeples of the town.

THE EASTERN TOWNSHIPS

For hundreds of years, the Eastern Townships have been a place of refuge and of peace. Once predominantly English, the region is now 90 percent French (though the majority can speak both languages) and is now known as Les *Cantons-de-l'Est*. During the American War of Independence, many who preferred to stay loyal to the British Crown settled in these parts, and it has retained an English and American flavor throughout its history. It also drew benefit from the American Civil War, when southerners who felt

Snowboarding at Mont Tremblant.

⊘ E. TOWNSHIPS SKIING

Like the Laurentians, the Eastern Townships (Les Cantons-de-l'Est) is prime skiing country, with four major centers within a one-hour drive of the city of Montréal: **Bromont**, which is lit at night; **Mont-Orford**; **Mont-Sutton**; and **Owl's Head**. However, the choice of winter sports is not limited to skiing alone. Other popular activities include cross-country skiing, snowshoeing, dogsledding, ice-fishing and winter camping. The area is also well known as the capital of snowmobile country, with around 2,000km (1,200 miles) of designated trails. It's an exhilarating experience bobbing along on the snow at high speed. The fastest way to reach the Cantons from Montréal is along Autoroute 10 Est.

uncomfortable in the northern states would spend holidays in one of the Townships' many fine old hotels. But no friction between the Townships and New Englanders survives, and today they are the closest of neighbors.

Highway 10 from Montréal will get you into the Townships in about one hour. **Granby**, just north of the highway, 84km (52 miles) east from Montréal, is known for its zoo and collection of fountains.

WINE COUNTRY

Heading south from Granby, you'll pass through Cowansville with its handsome Loyalist buildings, where you'll start seeing blue and white signs indicating the *route des vins* (wine route) leading to **Dunham ❸**, Québec's wine-growing country. A picturesque hamlet with old stone houses, Dunham's farmland is rich and fertile, supporting fruit and vegetables as well as vines. It might seem surprising that grapevines can grow in an area better known for its ski hills, but this part of the Townships has a mild microclimate that allows the plants to survive the Québec winters.

There are 18 wineries in the region, offering tastings and tours. **Vignoble de l'Orpailleur** also has a small museum documenting the history of wine.

LAC BROME AND SUTTON

Another popular destination In the Eastern Townships, to the south of Granby, is **Lac Brome ❹**, a village and a lake, though the largely English-speaking village is commonly known by its former name, **Knowlton**. A millpond cuts through the heart of the Victorian village, and colorful shops in 19th-century houses give it a festive air. Brome Lake Books is one of the few places in this neck of the woods that stocks English-language books and magazines.

Knowlton is a pleasant spot for lunch, brunch or coffee, and is known for its white ducks, raised at a factory on the edge of town. Local restaurants serve this gourmet specialty, especially during the annual Duck Festival (end Sept to early Oct).

In stagecoach days, Knowlton was a stop on the Boston–Montréal run. The old coaching Inn – Auberge Knowlton,

Rooftops of Old Québec.

⊙ THE OTHER TOWNSHIPS

Unsurprisingly, the most frequented part of the Eastern Townships is closest to Montréal. Sherbrooke is the stepping stone into lesser-known le Haut-St-François, which describes itself as "the other Townships."

In its eastern reaches, Mégantic is the Townships' most mountainous region and spectacularly beautiful. Granite has been quarried here since the 1890s. At 1,102 meters (3,615ft), Mont-Mégantic is said to be the highest mountain in the province that can be climbed by car. At the summit, astronomical research is conducted in the Mont-Mégantic Observatory, which houses a 24-tonne telescope, the eastern seaboard's largest. The multimedia AstroLab (www. astrolab-parc-national-mont-megantic.org) looks at all things universe-related.

built in 1849 – still stands today, anchoring rue Lakeside and chemin Knowlton, the main crossroads.

Continuing south, **Sutton** bustles with hikers and skiers bound for the winding, wooded trails of **Mont-Sutton**, as well as shoppers bent on finding quilts and woven rugs, ceramics and pewter at **Farfelu**, the local artists' co-operative. The main street of this ski resort at the base of Mont-Sutton is flanked by graceful old houses, auberges, craft stores, art galleries, and tempting restaurants and outdoor cafes.

From Granby it's another 45km (37 miles) east toward **Mont Orford** ⑤ (well worth taking the ski resort's chairlift or panoramic gondolas to the summit during the fall Festival of Colours) and **Magog**, through the most beautiful country. The gentle hills and valleys are an extension of the ancient Appalachian mountain range, and with its intricate network of lakes and streams, its country villages, dairy cattle, sheep, and strawberry fields, this part of Québec has a bucolic charm that is unusual in the often rugged terrain of the province. Indeed, **North Hatley** (on Route 108 at the north end of Lake Massawippi) rests in a shielded valley, warmed by sunlight reflected from the lake, giving it a microclimate that prolongs summer and softens winter enough to make it the home of hummingbirds and flora normally found far to the south.

Long, slender **Lac Memphrémagog** ⑥ is the largest in the area; boat cruises and a variety of water sports are available at the town of Magog on its northern tip. On its west shore, the beautiful hillside Benedictine monastery of **St-Benoît-du-Lac** (daily May–Oct until 6pm, Nov–Apr until 5.00pm) produces cheese and chocolate.

THE LAURENTIANS

Spring, which in Québec lasts about a day and a half, is the only season in which Montréalers avoid the Laurentians (this is due to it being muddy from the melt water and the presence of blackfly). It is the playground just beyond the backyard of the metropolis; though its wooded lakes and hills are

The chic streets of Québec City.

still lovely, the difficulty is often where to get away from it all when everyone has come to do just that.

Winter is ski season. North America's first alpine ski rope-tows were erected in the Laurentians at Prévost in 1930 and at St-Sauveur-des-Monts in 1934. Montréalers soon flocked to the region to try the new-fangled sport and the glamor and fun of skiing began to catch on, enduring to this day. Today, acrobatic skiing, snowboarding, cross-country, skiing by torchlight, tubing (which involves scooting down a hill on a large inner tube), and tobogganing, or sledding as Québecers call it, are all hugely popular. Almost everyone in Montréal skis either cross-country or downhill. In summer, families pack up the car and head to the cottage for swimming, sailing, windsurfing, and waterskiing. In fall, the leaves turn those deep shades of red and orange that draw hikers irresistibly to the hills and valleys.

Heading north from Montréal, you pass a cluster of villages named after what sound like saints – St-Jérôme, St-Sauveur-des-Monts, Ste-Adèle, Ste-Agathe-des-Monts, and so on. In fact, the majority of these Laurentian "saints" were local politicians or entrepreneurs who, in pioneer days, helped to build up the community, opening businesses, constructing homes, and building churches.

The main road north is Autoroute 15 but, if time permits, take the more scenic and slow Rte 117, the old road that was in place before the Laurentians became a major resort area.

In the beginning, skiers used to head up north on **Le Petit Train du Nord**, the little train that opened up the Laurentian wilderness to the outside world and helped to launch the fledgling tourism industry. The construction of the highways rendered the train obsolete, but in 1996 its route was reborn as a 200km (124-mile) linear recreation trail. Running from St-Jérôme at the southern end of the Laurentians, it terminates in Mont-Laurier. In summer and autumn it's popular with cyclists, while cross-country skiers use it in winter.

St-Sauveur-des-Monts ❼ (or simply St-Sauveur) heralds the start of the Laurentian tourist region. It's the archetypal French-Canadian village, with a huge, silver-spired Catholic church and a main street lined with small, brightly painted wooden houses. It is also a great shopping destination, with boutiques, art galleries, craft shops, studios, and restaurants housed in those old-fashioned buildings.

Continuing north, **Ste-Adèle** is a lively ski resort and a thriving writers' and artisans' colony by the shores of Lac Rond and the slopes of Mont-Ste-Adèle. Chocoholics will relish a visit to **À la Chocolaterie Marie-Claude**, for an insight into the process of making confectionery the traditional way, in small batches.

Just beyond Val-Morin are 38-meter (125ft) high **Mont-Condor** and the awesome 22-meter (72ft) **Condor Needle**,

Street scene, Québec City.

one of the few rock pinnacles in eastern Canada. Rock climbers flock to both to test their skills. Continuing north, Val-David is well known for its abundance of traditional Québécois houses with steep roofs, its attractive inns and fine cuisine.

To get an idea of the Laurentians' old-guard wealth, take a quick cruise around Lac des Sables in Ste-Agathe-des-Monts on the *Bateau Alouette (May to Oct)*. You'll see the estate built by 20th Century Fox tycoon William B. Fox and the 42-room "summer cottage" that belonged to a millionaire who kept his own orchestra to play for him day and night, and a greenhouse in which he cultivated only roses.

About 140km (87 miles) from Montréal, you finally come to **Mont-Tremblant** ❽. The town of Mont-Tremblant is both the Laurentians' largest resort and one of eastern North America's foremost all-year travel destinations, with 94 ski and snowboarding runs and four top-ranking golf courses for summer visitors. The Laurentians are among the oldest mountain ranges in

the world, so for the most part erosion has softened peaks into gently rounded hills perhaps 300 meters (1,000ft) high. Mont-Tremblant is the region's highest mountain at 875 meters (2,870ft); chairlifts operate year-round to transport visitors up to the summit.

The "trembling mountain" was given its name by the First Nations, who lived here long before the Europeans. One version of the story (and there are quite a few) is that when you look into Lac Tremblant, a 14km (8-mile) long lake, you can see the shimmering reflection of the mountain behind it.

The resort at the base of the mountain, known simply as Tremblant, was the brainchild of the now-defunct Intrawest Corporation, once one of Canada's flagship companies. The prototype for the Tremblant Resort, which the company started developing in the early 1990s, was Whistler/Blackcomb in British Columbia, one of the best ski resorts in North America and the main site for the 2010 Winter Olympic Games. The pedestrian-only holiday village at Tremblant Resort,

Laviolette Bridge.

The Virgin and Child within Ste-Anne-de-Beaupré Church.

which curves around the base of the mountain, is actually a smaller version of its western Canadian cousin. Tremblant sits beside **Parc national du Mont-Tremblant**, a vast 1,500-sq km (579-sq mile) expanse in which the area's tranquility and natural beauty are easily appreciated. More than 400 lakes and hiking trails are scattered throughout the park. It is a canoer's dream. The Rouge, Matawin and du Diable rivers provide great swimming and fishing for trout or landlocked salmon, and there are riverside camping places. If you've never tried canoeing, that most Canadian of water sports, this is the place to learn, and there's kayaking along the 15km (9-mile) Rivière Assomption, with rapids ranging in difficulty from levels I to IV.

The park is thick with maple and pine forests, and it shelters all manner of Canadian wildlife – black bears, deer, lynx, wolves, beaver, and nearly 200 bird species. Birdwatchers can tramp along the trails armed with a checklist, spotting such common birds (at least in these parts) as great blue herons, blue jays, and pileated woodpeckers. Listen out for the haunting cry of the loon (the bird that features on the one-dollar coin, giving it the nickname "loony"), most commonly heard at dawn or dusk.

Val d'Or ❾ means Valley of Gold, and it lies at the eastern extreme of the Cadillac Break, a gold-rich fault that extends west to Kirkland Lake in Ontario. The glittering metal was first discovered in 1914, and high gold prices kept the miners working until 1985. Now the Lamaque mine has been converted into an interpretation center, La Cité d'Or (The City of Gold). A visit includes donning miner's gear and descending 90 meters (300ft) for a tour of the mine and exploring **Bourlamaque** – first built by the mining company for its employees – a well-preserved historic quarter of 75 pinewood houses and a small museum. More recently, the town found another source of prosperity: its strategic location on the road north from Montréal to

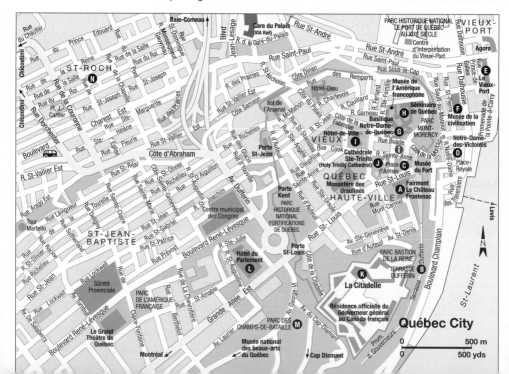

Québec City

the vast James Bay hydroelectric project.

PAPER TOWN

Ten percent of the world's newsprint, 2,500 tonnes a day, once came from **Trois-Rivières** ⑩, 142km (88 miles) northeast of Montréal. Though still important commercially, it struggles to overcome its image as a lackluster industrial town. It has prospered since 1610, but the fires that regularly swept through all Québec's communities have left little to show from the town's first two centuries. In rue des Ursulines, the **Manoir de Tonnancour** (Tue–Fri 10am–noon, 1.30–5pm, Sat–Sun 1–5pm; free), housing temporary art exhibitions, the **Maison Hertel-de-la-Fresnière** (also used for visiting exhibitions), and the **Musée-des-Ursulines** (late June to early Sept daily 10am–5pm, May–Nov Tue–Sun 10am–5pm, Mar–Apr Wed–Sun 1–5pm, www.musee-ursulines.qc.ca) survive, at least in part, from the early 18th century.

The town's attractions are modern: the **Grand Prix** races through the streets in August, the **International Poetry Festival** takes place in September and October, the **Laviolette Bridge** spans the St Lawrence. The revitalized area at the port is also well worth a visit.

Nowhere in the vicinity draws as many visitors as the shrine, 10km (6 miles) north of Trois-Rivières, called **Notre-Dame-du-Cap**, in the small town of Cap-de-la-Madeleine. The little church of Notre-Dame-du-Rosaire was built in 1714 and drew a moderate number of pilgrims until the day in 1883 that Father Frederic Jansoone and two others saw the statue of the Virgin open her eyes.

Trois-Rivières stands at the confluence of the St-Maurice and the St Lawrence rivers, begging the question: where is the third river? In fact, there isn't one. If you travel up the St Lawrence by boat, as Jacques Cartier and Samuel de Champlain did, the two delta islands at the mouth of St Maurice give the impression that *trois rivières* end here. The name survives from then.

QUÉBEC CITY

"The impression made upon the visitor by this Gibraltar of North America: its giddy heights; its citadel suspended, as it were, in the air, its picturesque streets and frowning gateways; and the splendid views which burst upon the eye at every turn: is at once unique and everlasting."

Remarkably, Charles Dickens's comment on **Québec City** ⑪ is still appropriate more than a century after his visit. It retains its 18th-century ambience with narrow, winding streets, horse-drawn carriages, and fine French cooking behind charming facades. The only dramatic change in the Old Town is the construction at the turn of the 19th century of a castle-like

Fairmont Le Château Frontenac.

A government building on Place d'Armes.

Changing of the Guard at the Citadel.

hotel that perches on its promontory overlooking the St Lawrence River: the **Fairmont Le Château Frontenac** .

The province's cryptic motto, *Je me souviens* (I remember), insists upon the defense of Québécois tradition, language, and culture. Here in the provincial capital, reminders are everywhere that this was once performed by soldiers with guns from turrets and bastions. Today, the politicians and civil servants of Québec City have taken over the job, using the milder instruments of democracy, but are hardly less ardent in their purpose. Québec City still stands sentinel over the St Lawrence, the only walled city on the continent north of Mexico. The views are as lovely as ever: from the **Terrasse Dufferin** in front of the Château Frontenac, one looks out at the blue Laurentian hills and Mont Ste-Anne, the rolling countryside and the boats passing on the shimmering St Lawrence 60 meters (200ft) below.

Parks Canada recently undertook an archeological dig beneath the Terrasse Dufferin, revealing the remains of the St-Louis Forts and Châteaux, the residence of colonial French and British governors. Although the dig has been completed, fascinating guided tours of the site are offered (May–Oct daily).

Diagonally opposite **Place d'Armes** , the former drill and parade ground, rue du Trésor runs down to rue Buade. This lane, named after the building where colonists used to pay their dues to the Royal Treasury, is today the artists' row; it is hung with quite decent watercolors, etchings, and silkscreens. Rue Buade winds downhill to **Parc Montmorency**, opposite the grand **Ancien Bureau de Poste** with its rather pompous monument to Bishop François-Xavier de Laval-Montmorency, first bishop of Québec and founder of its largest university.

Côte de la Montagne drops steeply to the left, winding down into the Lower Town, following the ravine that Québec's first settlers used to climb from the Lower Town to the Upper. Just beyond the **Porte Prescott**, a recent reconstruction of the original erected here in 1797, is **L'Escalier**

Casse-Cou, the "Breakneck Stairway." This staircase, not quite as daunting as it sounds, leads to the narrow Petit-Champlain, which is lined with crafts shops.

THE LOWER TOWN

From the foot of L'Escalier Casse-Cou, **Place Royale** is just around the corner. Thus one tumbles from the Château Frontenac into the cradle of French civilization in North America.

Place Royale was the business center of Québec City until about 1832. Its name derives from the bust of Louis XIV, the great Sun King of Versailles, which was erected here in 1686. Today it is the scene of constant play and concert performances, usually recreating the culture of the 17th and 18th centuries. **Eglise Notre-Dame-des-Victoires** , dominating the square, was built in 1688 and reconstructed after Wolfe's devastation of the Lower Town in 1759. The church is named for two early victories against the Anglo-Americans – or rather, one great victory and one lucky accident. A Bostonian, Sir William Phips (knighted for discovering 32 tonnes of shipwrecked bullion), sailed to Québec with 34 boats and 2,000 men in October 1690, and demanded its surrender.

Governor Frontenac promised to reply with his cannon, and during six days of fighting his guns hammered the fleet. By land, snipers, fighting Indian-style against Phips's troops drawn up in formal battle-order, killed 150 men with only one loss to their own party. Phips withdrew on the sixth day, unaware that the French had just run out of ammunition. The lucky accident – or to the French, Our Lady's victory – was the storm in the Gulf of St Lawrence that destroyed the enormous British fleet of Sir Hovendon Walker in 1711, saving Québec from almost certain defeat. Both these events are depicted in little scenes above the odd, turreted altar.

Crossing the road on the waterfront, rue Dalhousie, you leave the 18th century behind and enter the more modern world of the port. On the right is the entrance to the government-operated ferry services to **Levis** ("leh-vee") on the other side of the river, while straight

Québec City port.

ahead the MV *Louis-Jolliet*, a colorful and popular cruise boat, docks.

Walking north beside the river leads to the new commercial and community complex, called **Le Vieux-Port ⓔ** despite its thoroughly contemporary design: overhead walkways of red and silver tubing and plexiglass walls connect spacious, functional pavilions. The complex surrounds the **Agora**, a 6,000-seat amphitheater used for cultural events, particularly evening concerts throughout the summer. The award-winning modern **Musée de la civilisation ⓕ** (June 24 to Labor Day daily 10am–5pm, Labor Day to June 23 Tue–Sun 10am–5pm; www.mcq.org) in the center of Le Vieux-Port has exhibitions on such subjects as language, thought, the body, and society.

THE UPPER TOWN

The easiest way to get back to the Upper Town is by taking the little funicular at the head of rue Sous-le-Fort, which is worth the small charge to save wear and tear on the feet in this city-made-for-walking. It shinnies

Parc de la Chûte-Montmorency.

up the cliff from the house of Louis Jolliet (the explorer of the Mississippi river) to the Terrasse Dufferin (daily Oct–Mar 7.30am–11pm, Apr–mid-June and early Sept–Oct until 11.30pm, mid-June–early Sept until midnight).

At the intersection of rue Buade and Côte de la Fabrique is the Baroque cathedral of Québec City, **Basilique Notre-Dame-de-Québec ⓖ** (Mon-Fri 7am-4pm, Sat 7am-6pm, Sun 8am-5pm; Confession Mon-Fri 11.30am-12pm, Sat 4.30pm-5pm, Sun 9am-9.30am, 11am-11.30am and 1.45pm-3.45pm). The city's main church has been here since 1633 when Samuel de Champlain built Notre-Dame-de-la-Recouvrance in gratitude for the recovery of New France from the British. Next door stands the **Séminaire de Québec ⓗ** and the **Université Laval**. The Jesuits established a college here in 1635, a year before Harvard opened, but the seminary was officially founded only in 1663 by Bishop Laval (guided tours in summer).

The university still exists, though its modern campus is now in the suburb of **Ste-Foy**, and these buildings serve their original purpose as a seminary and high school. The seminary's museum, known as the **Musée de l'Amérique francophone** (June 24 to Labor Day daily 10am–5pm, Labor Day to June 23 Sat–Sun 10am–5pm; www.mcq.org) is the oldest museum of history in Canada. Now part of the Musée de la civilisation, its permanent exhibition looks at the economic and social role the seminary played, as well as the religious and educational aspect. Across the street from the cathedral is the monument to **Cardinal Taschereau**, looking formidable, as if ready to carry out his threat to excommunicate any worker who joined a union. Behind is the gray, ample **Hôtel-de-Ville ❶**.

Around the corner stands the only rival to the Château Frontenac on the city's skyline, the **Price Building**. With 19 stories, it just about qualifies as the Old Town's only skyscraper. One is enough, and fortunately the 1937 Art Deco style is not out of keeping with the neighborhood. Straight on, however,

stands the **Holy Trinity Cathedral ❶**, the first Anglican cathedral built outside the British Isles and thoroughly English, from its design (on the model of St Martin-in-the-Fields in London's Trafalgar Square) to its pews made of oak imported from the Royal Windsor Forest.

Lively **rue St-Louis**, with its snug little restaurants and *pensions*, slopes up from the end of rue Desjardins to the Porte St-Louis, rebuilt in a grand neo-Gothic style (complete with turret and crenellated gun-ports) to replace the 17th-century original. Just in front of the gate is the lane that leads to **La Citadelle ❶**, the star-shaped bastion on the summit of **Cap-Diamant** (daily May–Oct 9am–5pm, Nov–Apr 10am– 4pm), 100 meters (400ft) over the St Lawrence.

The Citadel, with its Changing of the Guard ceremony (June 24 to Labor Day daily 10am) and Beating of the Retreat (July–Aug Wed 4pm), appeals to childhood notions of soldierly glory and adventure. But however colorful, it continues to play a military role as

Art for sale on Rue du Trésor, Québec City.

the headquarters of Canada's French-only Royal 22e Régiment, known as the "Vandoos" (the nickname a corruption of *les vingt-deuxième*).

Built by the British in the early 1800s according to plans approved by the Duke of Wellington, with double granite walls and a magnificent position above a sheer cliff, it was considered one of the most impregnable strongholds in the Empire.

BEYOND THE CITY WALLS

Beyond the wall's confines, the city becomes suddenly roomy, opening out onto the **Grande Allée** and the lawns of the **Hôtel du Parlement ①**, the seat of the National Assembly, Québec's provincial government. Though not old by the city's standards (building began in 1881), the elaborate French Renaissance design by Eugène-E. Taché does seem to embody Québec's distant roots in the court of Louis XIII. Its symbols, however, are purely Québécois; the important figures of her history are all there, each trying to outdo the other's elegant pose in his alcove on the facade: Frontenac, Wolfe, Montcalm,

The Saguenay River.

Lévis, Talon... Below, Louis-Philippe Hébert's bronze works include dignified groups of Indians, the "noble savages" of the white man's imagination.

Outside, the terraces of the Georgian houses that border the Grande Allée west from the National Assembly are cluttered with tables where visitors and civil servants enjoy the cuisine, the wines, and the serenading violins of some of Québec's liveliest restaurants. A block south, there is gentle peace. **Parc des Champs-de-Bataille ⓜ**, or the **Plains of Abraham**, runs parallel to the Grande Allée with spectacular views across the St Lawrence to the Appalachian foothills. Its rolling lawns and broad shade trees have known far more romance than fighting, many more wine-and-cheese picnics than violent deaths, but however incongruously, it commemorates a vicious 15-minute battle in which Louis-Joseph, Marquis de Montcalm, lost half of North America to the British. It wasn't quite that simple, but the fact remains that the Indian fighting style of the Canadians had won them success after success against the British until the Marquis de Montcalm, a traditionalist and a defeatist, became head of the land troops. Always ready to retreat even after a victory, and rarely pressing an advantage, Montcalm steadily reduced the territory that he had to defend.

General Wolfe, who sailed down the St Lawrence with half as many troops as Montcalm held in the fortress of Québec City, never really hoped to succeed in taking it and so he destroyed 80 percent of the town with cannon fire.

Montcalm would not emerge to fight a pitched battle and, in a last-ditch, desperate attempt, Wolfe took 4,400 men up the cliff in silence by cover of night to the heights where there was no hope of turning back. Montcalm had been expecting Wolfe at Beauport, north of the city, and he rushed back to fight on the plains. Throwing away every advantage – time, the possession of the city stronghold, and the sniping skills of his men – Montcalm fought the kind of European-style set battle that his troops were improperly trained for. Wolfe was killed, Montcalm mortally wounded and, though the British held only the plains at the battle's conclusion, the French surrendered the city.

At the far end of Parc des Champs-de-Bataille, just beyond the now-vacant jail called the **Petit Bastille**, stands the **Musée national des beaux-arts du Québec** (late June to early Sept daily 10am–6pm, Wed until 9pm, early Sept to late June Tue–Sun 10am–5pm, Wed until 9pm; www.mnbaq.org), the imposing neo-Classical home of a large proportion of the best Québec art. Painters such as Alfred Pellan, Marc-Aurèle Fortin, and Jean-Paul Riopelle are not quite household names throughout the world, but the work of these modern artists ranges from expressionistic landscapes to frenetic abstracts.

A 15-minute walk west from Vieux-Québec, the neighborhood of **St-Roch** , offers sharp contrast to a city steeped in hundreds of years of history. Reclaimed by cutting-edge entities in art, technology, food, fashion, and music, it has become one of the hippest parts of the city.

CHÛTE-MONTMORENCY WATERFALL

Pack your bathing suit when you head east for 10km (6 miles) either by the upper Route 360 or the lower road, Route 138, to **Parc de la Chûte-Mont-morency** ⓬ (June 24 to late Aug daily 8.30am–7.30pm, rest of the year hours vary greatly, check at www.sepaq.com; park free). These falls at 83 meters (272ft) are considerably higher than Niagara Falls, though less dramatic because they are so much narrower. Here, however, instead of looking at the falls from the top down, you approach the base, which means that the closer you get, the wetter you get from the spray. The province has thoughtfully built a large granite platform at the

Maple leaves in the fall.

Chûte-Montmorency waterfall.

⊙ Tip

The best observation points for spotting whales in the St Lawrence are in the area of the Parc du Saguenay at Pointe-Noire Promontory and Cap-de-Bon-Désir.

base of the falls so that visitors can actually stand inside the chilly cloud of spray. In winter, the spray forms a solid block that grows up from the bottom into a "sugarloaf" of ice and snow, providing a splendid slope for tobogganing.

ILE D'ORLÉANS

Just a mile (1.6km) south of the falls, the bridge over the **Ile d'Orléans** ⑬ turns off the autoroute. In 1970, the provincial government declared the island a historic district to prevent the encroachment of the city and the tourist trade from destroying the milieu of one of Québec's most picturesque and historic regions. The exceptionally fertile soil brought prosperity early to the island. In the 1600s there were as many inhabitants here as in Montréal or Québec, and farming is still the vocation of most of the families here.

Few visitors can resist indulging themselves at the roadside stands that offer fat strawberries swimming in lakes of thick, fresh cream topped off with maple sugar. **Ste-Anne-de-Beaupré**, a nearby town on the St Lawrence's north shore, houses a cathedral that millions of Catholics have visited. The fountain of St Anne, in front of the church, is said to have healing powers.

CHARLEVOIX, SAGUENAY, AND LAC ST-JEAN

Stretching over 200km (124 miles) along the north shore as far as the Saguenay River, the Charlevoix region's immediate selling point is its sheer beauty. Here, the Laurentian Mountains plunge sharply down to the St Lawrence. Dense forests, fertile valleys, racing streams, and cascading waterfalls backdrop picture-perfect towns of silver-spired churches and steep, red-roofed houses. In the early 1900s, Canadian artists such as A.Y. Jackson, Clarence Gagnon, and Jean-Paul Lemieux came to capture its magic on canvas – and painters, photographers, and writers continue to come here for inspiration. Many of them stay in historic **Baie-St-Paul** ⑭, where the **Musée d'art contemporain de Baie-St-Paul** (mid-June–early Sept daily 10am–5pm, early Sept–mid-June

Cottages on Perce Rock.

Tue–Sun 11am–5pm; www.macbsp.com) hosts an international symposium of contemporary art in August.

Among all Québec's uncountable lakes and waterways, perhaps none can match the splendor of the **Saguenay ⑮**, its ragged cliffs looming hundreds of meters over the broad, blue river. Vikings and Basque fishermen came and went long before Jacques Cartier named it "the Kingdom of the Saguenay" when he came seeking a western passage to the Orient in 1535. Its spectacular beauty survives today, and the whales never fail to gather in the deep estuary each July, staying until December, when they swim away to unknown destinations. The cruise boats that leave from the wharf at **Baie-Ste-Catherine**, 71km (44 miles) north of Québec on Route 138, can virtually guarantee whale sightings.

A ferry takes passengers and cars across the river to **Tadoussac ⑯**, where North America's oldest wooden church, **Petite Chapelle de Tadoussac** (early June to mid-Oct daily 10am–6pm), has stood since 1647, and New France's first fort, built in 1600, has been reconstructed. If the **Tadoussac Hotel** looks familiar, it's because the movie *Hotel New Hampshire* was filmed here.

Farther inland, the terrain levels out onto the fertile plain of the **Lac St-Jean ⑰** region. Fur-trading companies held a monopoly on the area until the mid-19th century, and it was barely settled until railroads brought pulp and paper developments after 1883, followed by large hydroelectric and aluminum smelting plants.

For visitors, however, the industry is relatively insignificant except in the commercial centers of Chicoutimi, Jonquière, and Alma. The rich soil produces 4.5 million kg (10 million lbs) of blueberries a year and, coupled with award-winning local cheeses, these provide the materials for an endless supply of mouth-watering blueberry cheesecakes. Less decadent regional specialties include various *tourtières* (spiced meat pies) and a dried-bean soup called *soupe à la gourgane*. Local fish – trout, pike, doré, and plentiful freshwater salmon – complete the menu.

> **⏱ Fact**
>
> The mountains, meadows, limestone cliffs, and sandy beaches of Gaspésie's Parc national de Forillon are home to a wealth of flora and fauna (daily).

Sightings of whales are quite common.

Beyond the commercial centers, several beautiful small towns cluster around Lac St-Jean, such as **Péribonka**, the setting of Louis Hémon's novel *Maria Chapdelaine*, and **Mistassini**, the blueberry capital. **Val-Jalbert**, a ghost town since 1927, has been partially restored, preserving its original character and buildings. The old mill stands against the 72-meter (236ft) **Ouiatchouan Falls**.

PÉNINSULE DE LA GASPÉSIE

Route 132 loops around the **Péninsule de la Gaspésie**, beginning and ending at **Ste-Flavie**, in a 560km (348-mile) circle that strings together the sleepy fishing villages of the eastern coast. The Mi'kmaq called it *Gespeg*, "the end of the earth." Though the Gaspé has been settled since Shakespeare's time, it has suffered almost no industrial development. Even the roads and trains that came with the later part of the 19th century left its rural tranquility and Québécois culture largely the same as ever.

From Ste-Flavie, the road cuts southeast down the Matapédia Valley,

A floral window display.

following the "river of 222 rapids," which cascades through a deep gorge at the edge of the Chic-Choc Mountains. At the village of **Matapédia**, 150km (93 miles) south, the road turns northeast and follows the Baie des Chaleurs. Once known as the "Canadian Riviera," the bay is thankfully too wild and unspoiled to merit the name today. The road weaves among coves and villages, some with English names such as New Carlisle, New Richmond, and Douglastown, given to them by loyalists who settled here to escape the American War of Independence. Eventually the coast wends northward and meets the red, rocky cliffs where the Chic-Chocs veer down to the sea. The road rounds a curve, and suddenly the massive **Percé Rock** appears, a 400 million-tonne block of limestone jutting improbably, and almost out of nowhere, from the sea. Roughly oblong in shape, there were once as many as four arches driven by the tides through this treeless crag, which also goes by the name "pierced rock." Nearby, the bird sanctuary on **Ile Bonaventure** is home to 50,000 gannets.

The north coast of the Gaspé is more rugged: the road winds along the bluffs at the edge of the highest mountains in eastern Canada. **Mont Jacques-Cartier** rises 1,268 meters (4,160ft) a few miles inland at the edge of the **Parc national de la Gaspésie** ⑱. This stretch along the south St Lawrence shore provides perhaps the most dramatic scenery on the Gaspé: the road hugs the steep cliffs that the sea washes below. At **Mont-St-Pierre,** near Ste-Anne-des-Monts, a hang-gliding festival – Fête du Vol libre – is held each July, its competitors jumping like Icarus over the St Lawrence.

A number of families who live along the shore are descended from Irish immigrants whose boats were destroyed on the coast. Stories are told of the day in 1914 when the *Empress of Ireland* collided with another boat and sank in 15 minutes, with the loss of 1,014 lives. A gentler civilization reappears at **Jardins de Métis** (or Reford Gardens in English) near Métis-sur-Mer, where Lord George Stephen built **Reford House** in the last century with its beautiful English garden displaying more than 3,000 floral varieties (June–Sept daily).

The round trip from Québec City covers 1,600km (1,000 miles) – not exactly a Sunday afternoon drive, but worthwhile if you can afford a couple of Sundays, and the week between.

ANTICOSTI ISLAND

Like something coughed up out of the mouth of the St Lawrence, the 8,000-sq km (3,000-sq mile) **Ile d'Anticosti** ⑲ may seem a little remote. Surrounded by steep cliffs and treacherous reefs, Anticosti was known as "the graveyard of the gulf." About 400 shipwrecks scatter the coast, some of them quite recent. These days, populated by 300 people, Anticosti is an ecotourist's haven. It is home to the fourth-largest population of bald eagles in North America.

The island is now divided between three outfitters (SEPAQ Anticosti, Safari Anticosti, and Pourvoirie du Lac Geneviève), with the exception of the village of **Port-Menier**. Reservations with an outfitter are definitely recommended for hunting and fishing (mainly sea trout, salmon, and speckled trout), and permits are required for fishing and hunting anywhere in Québec. Access is convenient: flights leave from **Havre-Saint-Pierre**, and a ferry boat, the *Nordik Express*, takes passengers from Rimouski or **Sept-Iles** to Port-Menier.

There is one hotel in Port-Menier, **Hôtel de l'île,** and three others scattered around the Island – **Auberge de la Pointe Ouest**, at Pointe Ouest, approximately 20 minutes from Port-Menier, Auberge de Chicotte on the south shore, and Auberge McDonald on the north shore. There are also six campgrounds offering numerous campsites. Though a vast area is untouched by humans, centuries of occasional habitation have left their mark: ghost towns, overgrown cemeteries, an old railroad, and the 4,000-year-old remains of its earliest inhabitants.

Pointe Carleton lighthouse on Ile d'Anticosti.

Peggy's Cove lighthouse, Nova Scotia.

Horses in New Brunswick.

THE EAST

Canada's four Atlantic provinces are bound by seafaring traditions, yet each has its own rich cultural identity.

An iceberg in Trinity Bay.

The host to Canada's first European visitors, and with the freshness of air laden with sea spray, the East Coast is perhaps one of the most startlingly beautiful regions of Canada. Here are the achingly lonely beaches of Nova Scotia, the distinctive sense of humor and charming friendliness of the people of Newfoundland and Labrador, the old-world, unembarrassed potato obsession of the Prince Edward Island farmers, and the graceful elegance of New Brunswick's towns.

The four provinces that constitute Canada's eastern region are bound together by their proximity to the Atlantic Ocean – nowhere is more than 160km (100 miles) from the sea, and most of the land is much closer – yet each possesses its own singular charm. On one side, Atlantic waves crash against soaring cliffs; on the other, the more sheltered waters of the Gulf of St Lawrence are calmer and warmer.

New Brunswick's rugged coastline begins the section and reveals the province's unusual blend of eastern reserve and wanton wildness in its towns and landscape. Nova Scotia, "New Scotland," is explored by following its circuitous coastline and stopping to examine some of its unusual cities and delightful towns.

Newfoundland and Labrador is perhaps the most quirky of all the provinces, and its rugged beauty and remoteness serve as a background to a portrait of the area's friendly inhabitants.

The East section ends at Prince Edward Island, Canada's tiniest province. Surrounded by singing ocean and covered with potato fields, it offers some of the area's most beautiful beaches.

Colorful houses in Saint John.

Fresh lobster, caught off the coast of New Brunswick.

NEW BRUNSWICK

New Brunswick serves as a perfect beginning to experiencing the East Coast lifestyle. Settled by both the French and Anglo-Loyalists, it is a province rich in traditions.

Here in New Brunswick the pace is slow and the friendly people take the time to talk. Magnificent wild forests cover 85 percent of the land, supporting a substantial pulp and paper industry. Under these lie lead, copper, and zinc, providing a healthy mining industry. And then there is the mining of the sea: fishing.

THE ACADIANS AND LOYALISTS

The first people to settle in this region after the Mi'kmaq and Maliseet First Nations were the French in 1604. They arrived with Samuel de Champlain and called the land they worked Acadie; it covered the Atlantic provinces and Maine. The Acadians were constantly fighting battles with the British during the Anglo-French wars of the 17th century. French rule ended in 1713 and mainland Nova Scotia was controlled by the British. In 1755 the British governor, Charles Lawrence, delivered an ultimatum to the Acadians – take an oath of allegiance to the British Crown, or face deportation. The Acadians did not want to take the oath for fear of being forced to fight fellow Frenchmen on behalf of Britain. The infamous Deportation Order forced 14,600 Acadians into exile. Many settled in Louisiana, where the Cajuns survive to this day. When peace was

declared between England and France in 1763, most of the Acadians returned to Nova Scotia, only to find their land had been occupied by new English colonists. Once again they moved on and settled in what is now New Brunswick. Today almost 33 percent of the province's population is French-speaking, and New Brunswick is Canada's only officially bilingual province.

For the descendants from the British Isles, the deportation was a windfall that started a trend. Many New Englanders moved, and during

Main attractions

Kings Landing Historical Settlement
Historic Garrison District, Fredericton
Fundy Islands
Fundy National Park
Hopewell Rocks
Village Historique Acadien

Map on page 210

Living history at Kings Landing.

the American Revolution even more crossed the border. They were known as the Loyalists. With them they brought the maritime traditions of the seafaring colonies.

ST JOHN RIVER VALLEY

The St John River is New Brunswick's lifeblood. It was the route traveled by Maliseet and Mi'kmaq, Acadians and Loyalists, Scots and Danes. In the northwestern region of the province it creates a border with Maine and from there the waterway can be traced along its winding course to Saint John.

New Brunswick's westernmost outcrop, a thumb-like parcel of land bordered by Québec, Maine, and the St John River, is popularly known as the Republic of Madawaska. The region's inhabitants created this mythical realm in the 1800s because they were fed up with being pawns in border negotiations between Canada and the United States. With their own leader (the mayor of Edmundston) and their own flag, the Madawaskans (mostly francophones) are both proud

The water-powered sawmill at Kings Landing.

and exuberant. At no time is their spirit more in evidence than during the festival called *La Foire Brayonne* (the French in this region are known as Brayons, after a tool used in processing flax). The midsummer event features both folk dancing and lumberjack competitions. **Edmundston ❶**, an important pulp and paper center and the capital of Madawaska, is situated where the St John and Madawaska rivers converge. Of particular interest to visitors is the Church of Our Lady of Sorrows, containing woodcarvings (the Stations of the Cross) by New Brunswick artist Claude Roussel.

To the south, the beautiful and productive St John River Valley has always been a major thoroughfare. The northern segment of the valley, from Saint-Léonard to Woodstock, is known as the "potato belt." This tuber is a major regional crop, celebrated each year, around the end of June, at the Potato Festival in **Grand Falls ❷**, during which flower-strewn boats are sometimes launched over the town's

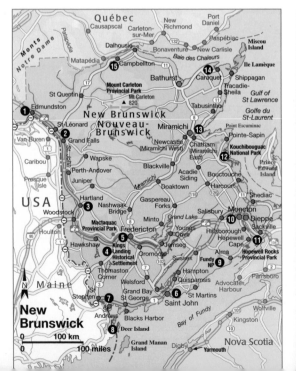

waterfalls. The gorge into which the water plunges is one of the largest cataracts east of Niagara Falls. Lying 80km (50 miles) downstream is the small agricultural town of **Hartland** ❸, known for its majestic covered bridge spanning the St John River. This is not just any covered bridge, but the world's longest, with seven spans, traversing 391 meters (1,282ft).

Just south is **Woodstock**, whose residents pride themselves on their tradition of hospitality. A landmark here is the restored Old Courthouse, which over the years has served not only as the seat of justice, but as a social hall, a coach stop, and a political meeting house. It's only fitting that such a busy little town should be the birthplace of Canada's first dial telephone system in 1900.

For a look at Loyalist life in the valley throughout the 1800s, visit **Kings Landing Historical Settlement** ❹ (early June to early Oct daily 10am–5pm), 37km (23 miles) west of Fredericton. This reconstructed village, built on the banks of the St John River,

depicts daily life among the Loyalists of that era. In 1783 Loyalists exploring the valley came upon the area and, realizing its natural advantages, settled here the same year. After enduring the hardship of a very severe first winter, they proceeded to build a town whose spirit exists to this day – **Fredericton** ❺, "Atlantic Canada's Riverfront Capital." It is an appellation that befits this provincial capital.

Fredericton is the cultural center of the province, thanks in large part to the generosity and high profile of the publisher and statesman Lord Beaverbrook, who never forgot his boyhood home. The **Beaverbrook Art Gallery**, Queen Street (Mon–Sat 10am–5pm, Thu until 9pm, Sun noon–5pm, closed Mon Oct–Apr) www.beaverbrookartgallery. org), houses a marvelous collection from the 15th century on, including the work of Dalí, Constable, Gainsborough, Botticelli, Henry Moore, and even Winston Churchill.

The Legislative Building (late June– late Aug daily 10am–5pm, Sep–late June Mon–Fri 9am–4pm; free) displays

⊙ Fact

New Brunswickers are extremely particular about never abbreviating Saint John, perhaps to avoid confusion with St John's across the sea in Newfoundland.

The covered bridge at Hartland.

⊙ COVERED BRIDGES

The covered bridge at Hartland is one of 58 still standing in New Brunswick. Built like old barns from hand-hewn timbers, they capture the essence of bygone times. They were first erected in the late 19th century, to assist those traveling from A to B with rivers to cross. New Brunswick had an ample supply of rivers, lumber, and skilled labor eager to connect the ever-expanding settlements. By protecting the bridge from the elements, the wood did not rot as quickly, which could extend the bridge's lifetime to 50–60 years, compared to the more typical 10 years of a conventional structure. Many of them had colorful names such as The Bridge to Nowhere (built to service a community that was ultimately not built) or the Plumweseep Bridge, a Maliseet word for 'salmon river'.

○ Eat

Saint John's City Market is the place to sample dulse, a dried, deep-purple seaweed from the Bay of Fundy; and fiddlehead greens, a type of fern, which tastes similar to asparagus.

portraits by Joshua Reynolds as well as a rare copy of the Domesday Book. The city's most elegant structure is Christ Church Cathedral. Completed in 1853, it is considered one of North America's best examples of decorated Gothic architecture.

The Historic Garrison District beside the river is the hub for museums, art galleries, outdoor concerts, and heritage walking tours. It incorporates the **Fredericton Region Museum** (July–Sept daily 10am–5pm, Apr–June, Sept–Nov Tue–Sat 1–4pm by appointment, Dec–Mar by appointment), which chronicles Fredericton's military and domestic past. If you show up and the door is locked, feel free to ring the bell. You may be let in. Re-enactments of the Changing of the Guard (July–Aug daily 11am and 4pm, Tue and Thu also 7pm; free) take place in Officers Square. Modern military life can be found by following the St John River southeast from Fredericton to Oromocto, home of Canada's largest military training base and a military museum.

FIRST CITY

Weathered **Saint John** ❻, Canada's oldest city, sits along the Bay of Fundy at the mouth of the St John River, famed for its reversing rapids which flow toward the bay at low tide and away from it at high tide. Samuel de Champlain landed here in 1604 and gave the location its name, but its true birth came in 1783 with the arrival of 3,000 Loyalists from New England.

"The Loyalist City," as it is known, celebrates its heritage each July during Loyalist Days. The festivities include a three-day jazz and blues festival, the annual Buskers on the Boardwalk Festival, and various summer theater presentations.

Determined, energetic, and ambitious, the Loyalist citizenry catapulted their new home into the forefront of wooden shipbuilding. The thriving port city declined following a disastrous fire in 1877 along with the eventual obsolescence of wooden ocean-going vessels. Recent waterfront development and urban renewal have provided Saint John with a much-needed transfusion.

View of historic Prince William Street, Saint John.

It is now a major cruise ship port of call, which has had a significant effect on the city's economy. It also claims the first police force in North America, and the first newspaper and bank in Canada.

To catch up with the city's past there are three walking tours: Prince William's Walk, a Victorian Stroll, and the Loyalist Trail. One attraction the tours are sure to include is **Barbour's General Store** (early June to early Oct Mon–Sat 10am–6pm, Sun noon–6pm), a restored and fully stocked 19th-century store in which thousands of artifacts, including 300 "cure-all or kill-alls," bring the past to life.

Saint John's Loyalist roots are nowhere more evident than at King Square (opposite the Loyalist Burial Ground), landscaped in the form of the Union flag; and at **Loyalist House** (mid-May–June Mon–Fri, July to mid-Sept daily, rest of year by appointment), a Georgian mansion completed in 1817 after taking seven years to build. Occupied for about a century and a half by Loyalist David Daniel Merritt and his descendants, it is the oldest structurally unaltered edifice in the city; indeed, one of the few buildings to survive the Great Fire of 1877. With most of its original furnishings still intact, Loyalist House is a tribute to the fine craftsmanship of 19th-century Saint John. In 2017, the building celebrated its 200th year.

Saint John's City Market is another survivor of the Great Fire. This institution has provided unflagging service since 1876, making it Canada's oldest market. Then, as now, the market clerk rings a bell to close commercial proceedings. The building, filled with New Brunswick produce, is a pleasure to the eye, with its ship's-hull roof, its big game trophies, and its ornate iron gate.

The gem of Saint John's revitalized downtown waterfront district was officially christened Market Square in 1983. Its success has brought business, tourism, employment, and pride back to the city. An early 19th-century brick facade serves as an invitation to a warm and lively center for shopping and dining. There is a boardwalk by the sea, a grand Food Hall and a regional library with a fine collection of early Canadian printed work.

In Market Square, the country's oldest museum, the **New Brunswick Museum** (Mon-Fri 9am-5pm, Thu until 9pm, Sat 10am-5pm, Sun 12pm-5pm; www.nbm-mnb.ca), has treasures from around the world, and particularly artifacts pertaining to the history of New Brunswick. Its Hall of Great Whales is one of the most arresting displays.

For a panoramic view of the city and its waterfront, visit Fort Howe and the Carleton Martello Tower.

THE FUNDY COAST

West of Saint John, the idiosyncratic Fundy Coast is characterized by picture-perfect fishing villages and the highest tides in the world (up to 50ft/15meters, twice daily). This is where United Empire Loyalists

Woodcarvings in the Loyalist Plaza, Saint John.

Fountains in Fredericton.

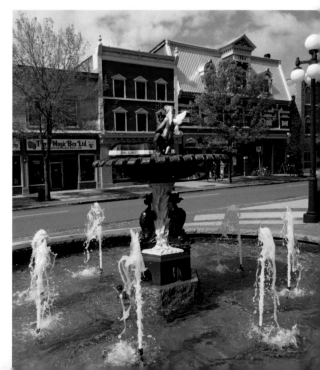

settled en masse after the American Revolution.

Carved out of the Bay of Fundy, between Maine and New Brunswick, is Passamaquoddy Bay. At its eastern edge sits **Blacks Harbour**, famed for possessing the Commonwealth's largest sardine factory.

Rounding the bay takes you through **St George**, where visitors can meander about one of the oldest Protestant graveyards in Canada, while nearby Oak Bay is the site of a beachfront park and campground.

Probably the best-known community on the bay is **St Andrews ❼**, a fishing village, resort, and marine biological research center, studded with 18th- and 19th-century mansions. Founded by Loyalists following the American Revolution, some families floated their homes here (one piece at a time) when the border with Maine was determined in 1842 – hence the New England atmosphere. St Andrews is home of the Algonquin Resort, one of Canada's oldest resort hotels; but its most distinctive landmark is **Greenock Church**.

This pristine structure, encircled by a white picket fence, is embellished with a carved oak tree design, a clock, and a weathervane.

The multi-award-winning **Kingsbrae Garden** (daily 9am-6pm, Jul-Aug until 7pm) was created from the grounds of several of St Andrew's grand old estates, offering a delightful mix of old and new gardening styles. The village also houses the Huntsman Marine Science Centre, and its newly opened **Fundy Discovery Aquarium** (mid-May–mid-Oct daily 10am–5pm) gives visitors a chance to see just what swims around the Bay of Fundy.

St Stephen, New Brunswick, stands face to face with **Calais**, Maine. These border towns have traditionally been the best of friends – even during the War of 1812 when St Stephen loaned Calais gunpowder for its Fourth of July celebration. Today, the towns hold joint festivities each summer. The world's first chocolate bar is thought to have been invented here at the Ganong candy factory in 1910.

ROOSEVELT'S PARADISE

A paradise for birdwatchers, whale-watchers, fishermen, and other outdoor types exists on the **Fundy Islands** where Passamaquoddy Bay widens into the Bay of Fundy. The beauty and natural riches of the islands have attracted nature lovers, from James J. Audubon to Franklin Delano Roosevelt.

Grand Manan Island is the largest and farthest from the coast. It is a particular favorite of ornithologists, with about 360 species of birds, including the puffin, which has become somewhat of a symbol here. For the artist there are lighthouses and seascapes to paint or photograph. **Campobello**, the "beloved island" of F.D. Roosevelt, is accessible by bridge (from Lubec, Maine). It brings you to the **Roosevelt-Campobello International Park** (Mid-May to mid-Oct sunrise–sunset; free), a natural preserve in the southern portion of the island.

Puffins can be seen on the Fundy Trail.

Visitors can see round Roosevelt's 34-room "cottage" (end May to mid-Oct daily 9am–5pm; free), built in the Dutch Colonial style and preserved almost entirely as it was in 1920, from where he viewed so many sunrises.

Located smack on the 45th parallel (and proud of it), **Deer Island ⑧** is a mere 12km (7.5 miles) long. It compensates for its size by having the world's largest lobster pond and, offshore, the largest tidal whirlpool in the western hemisphere, "Old Sow," named because of the auditory experience it provides.

THE SOUTHEAST

The southeast region of New Brunswick, from Saint John to Moncton, reveals the cultural texture of the province; towns and villages gradually reflect a transition from areas settled by Loyalists to those settled by Acadians.

Beyond the sea coast village of St Martins is **Fundy National Park ⑨**, 80km (50 miles) east of Saint John, a showcase for the spectacularly dramatic Fundy tides and coastal terrain.

It once reverberated with the clamor of a thriving lumber industry, which, along with intense trapping in the area, nearly destroyed its natural gifts. By 1930 the population of Alma, on the eastern edge of the park, once a roaring lumber town, was reduced to two struggling families. The park covers an area of rugged shoreline, forests, and gorges. Trails provide views of the Bay of Fundy and the chance to see rare birds. The towering cliffs at Cape Enrage offer the best view of the area.

Thanks to Parks Canada, the region is now being returned to a wilderness state, with its forests protected and wildlife and fish stocks, particularly salmon, being reintroduced.

Hopewell Rocks, 40km (25 miles) east of Alma, is perhaps better known than the national park, and it is also better known as home of the "Flowerpot Rocks," which is what these peculiar formations look like at low tide, when you can explore the tidal pools surrounding them. In 2016, the famed Elephant Rock formation collapsed into the sea.

⊙ Tip
Early July is the time of the Lobster Festival in Shediac, when lobster suppers, a lobster-eating contest, and a parade feature on the itinerary.

⊙ FUNDY TRAIL

Linking Fundy National Park and Hopewell Rocks, the 16km (10-mile) Fundy Trail offers access – by car, bike, or on foot – to one of the last remaining wilderness coastlines between Florida and Labrador. Carved out of the Fundy escarpment, the trail hugs the top of 250-meter (820ft) cliffs, high above the Bay of Fundy's famously high tides, and connects to paths and stairways leading to pristine beaches and tumbling waterfalls. As these waters are the breeding habitat for right whales, this is one of the best places for viewing marine and wildlife. A suspension footbridge above the Big Salmon River Interpretive Center crosses to the start of the rugged Fundy Footpath – a separate entity to the Fundy Trail – that winds some 41km (24 miles) through thick forests to the boundaries of Fundy National Park.

Saint John City Market.

Beyond the Fundy Coast is the city of **Moncton** , an old railroad town, called the "hub of the Maritimes." It was first settled by Middle Europeans, but following the era of deportation and the influx of Acadians into what is now New Brunswick, it became known as the unofficial capital of Acadia. The Université de Moncton is the only French university in New Brunswick. Moncton is also a good place to observe the phenomenon of the Fundy tides.

Sackville is a tiny town that resembles an English village. It is the home of Sackville Harness Limited, which has the distinction of being the only place on the continent where horse collars are still made by hand. Sackville is also a university town. The first degree given to a woman in the British Empire was handed out by the town's Mount Allison University in 1875.

Nearby Fort Beauséjour–Fort Cumberland National Historic Site is where the French and English last battled in this region. Today, there is little echo of its past, but a rather magnificent panoramic view of the surrounding area.

Hopewell Rocks.

THE ACADIAN COAST

The coastal region of New Brunswick, east of Moncton, is known as the "Acadian Coast." Washed by the warm tides of the Northumberland Strait, it is primarily to this region that the Acadians returned following the deportation. In Bayfield, at the foot of Confederation Bridge to Prince Edward Island, 8 miles/13km across the water, the **Cape Jourimain Nature Centre** (mid-May to mid-Oct daily 9am-5pm; donation) on Jourimain Island offers lovely coastal views, a historic lighthouse, an interpretation center, walking trails, and excellent birdwatching opportunities. Farther up the coast, they say that **Shediac** has the warmest salt water north of Virginia. It also bills itself as the lobster capital of the world.

Tiny Acadian fishing villages are strung along the coast. **Bouctouche** is particularly well known for its oysters, and for the Irving Eco-Centre: La dune de Bouctouche, which introduces visitors to the ecosystem of one of the last great sand dunes on North America's northeastern coast. The **Kouchibouguac National Park** , 100km (62 miles) north of Moncton, has preserved miles of deserted but fine sand beaches. It is a pleasant drive out to Point Escuminac, a place that has never forgotten its distinction as the site of the province's worst fishing disaster. A powerful monument to the men who lost their lives here in 1959, carved by New Brunswick artist Claude Roussel, stands with its back to the sea, as a constant reminder of this tragedy.

Farther north along the coast is the city of **Miramichi** , an amalgamation of Chatham and Newcastle, early lumber towns that have preserved some British culture.

This area is famous for its ballads and folklore, as well as for its illustrious native sons. Chatham's once-busy shipyards have now been replaced by port facilities for exporting local wood products. Newcastle was the boyhood home of Lord Beaverbrook, who was exceedingly generous in his bequests to this town.

Acadian flags, a French tricolor with a yellow star in the upper part of the blue stripe, become increasingly visible as you continue northward. Shippagan is a typical fishing village, home of the exceptionally fine **New Brunswick Aquarium and Marine Centre** (late May to end Sept daily, 10am-6pm), devoted to the world of fishing in the Gulf of St Lawrence. A ferry will transport you to the delightfully deserted beaches of Miscou Island.

Caraquet ⑭, 20km (12 miles) west of Shippagan, is the most prosperous town on the Acadian coast and a cultural center for the region. Le Festival Acadien each August draws celebrants from up and down the coast and includes the traditional blessing of the fleet. The town also has one of the largest commercial fishing fleets in New Brunswick and the only provincial fisheries school. There are boat builders and fish markets on the wharf. Caraquet's **Village Historique Acadien**

(mid-June to Sept daily, 9.30am-6pm) has recreated an Acadian settlement reflecting the century from 1780 to 1949, a time of re-establishment here following the deportation. It is nestled near the marshland *levées* constructed by early Acadian settlers.

Off the coast are the waters of Baie des Chaleurs, literally "Bay of Warmth." Named by Cartier in 1534, the bay is notorious for a phantom ship, which has been sighted along the coast from Bathurst to Campbellton. Some people believe it to be the ghost of a French ship lost in battle, while others suggest there must be a more scientific explanation.

Dalhousie and **Campbellton ⑮** at the western end of the Chaleur Bay were settled by Scots, Irish, and Acadians, and a fine-tuned ear is needed to place the accents. Campbellton rests at the foot of Sugarloaf Mountain; it is a center for salmon fishing and winter sports, and a gateway to Québec.

Beyond, to the south and east, lie Nova Scotia, Newfoundland and Labrador, and Prince Edward Island.

Fishing in the mists of New Brunswick.

Grande Anse lighthouse, near Baie des Chaleurs.

Buoys in Nova Scotia.

NOVA SCOTIA

This Maritime province, where French, Loyalist, and Scottish cultures predominate, has a rich seafaring past. Its rugged coast and sheltered inlets were home to pirates and shipbuilders alike.

The name of Nova Scotia brings to mind a vision of craggy highlands, echoing with the sound of bagpipes. But before Highlanders fled to "New Scotland," there were Mi'kmaq, French, British, and Loyalists from the American colonies. All have left a stamp on this province. Today, of the more than 920,000 residents, some 80 percent of Nova Scotians are of some British descent and 11 percent of French (Acadian) extraction. Nova Scotia also has a large black population, beginning with the arrival of the first recorded black person on these shores in the early 1600s.

Nova Scotians are as close to the sea as they are to the past – inextricably bound to it by their nature, by economics, and by geography. Part of the province, Cape Breton, is an island; and the mainland is attached to Canada by the Isthmus of Chignecto.

Appropriately, the shape of the province resembles a lobster, with no point more than 56km (35 miles) from the sea. People are drawn to Nova Scotia for its overwhelming friendliness, exemplified by the traditional Gaelic greeting *Céad míle fáilte* – 100,000 welcomes.

HISTORICAL CONTEXT

The original inhabitants of Nova Scotia, the Mi'kmaq, still inhabit this area, though their numbers are greatly reduced.

It is thought possible that Norsemen visited here around AD 1000, and some evidence of this has been substantiated. Centuries later, John Cabot, exploring under the English flag, touched upon northern Cape Breton Island. And French and Portuguese fishermen caught and cured fish here in the 16th century.

The French called this land Acadie. It encompassed what is now Nova Scotia, New Brunswick, Prince Edward Island, and Maine. They settled along the Bay of Fundy and on the marshy land

Main attractions

Historic Properties, Halifax
Maritime Museum of the Atlantic, Halifax
Pier 21, Halifax
Peggy's Cove
Lunenburg
Port Royal
Grand-Pré National Historic Site
Cabot Trail
Cape Breton Miners' Museum
Fortress of Louisbourg

Map on page 220

All smiles at the Royal Nova Scotia International Tattoo.

surrounding the Annapolis river, developing what is still the most fertile land in Nova Scotia.

A sense of Maritime pride and tradition still runs strong in Nova Scotia, but great prosperity largely abandoned the province with the advent of the 20th century. Over the years, central Canada has often looked upon the area as a liability because of the financial aid it receives from the federal government.

Long before the St Lawrence became the foremost river of commerce, with the creation of the St Lawrence Seaway in 1959, the area's importance as a transportation channel had been greatly diminished. Steam-powered, steel-hulled vessels rendered the wooden sailing ships obsolete, and killed off an all-important industry and economic base. Coal mining later supplanted shipbuilding economically, only to falter after World War II.

But the province also has other natural endowments to fall back on: forestry is a significant provider of jobs; there are abundant freshwater and saltwater fishing grounds; and the rich productive land of the Annapolis Valley, once so highly prized by the Acadians. And then there is tourism, which is a longstanding tradition here and a major contributor to the economy of the region.

TWIN CITIES

The first and second-largest Nova Scotian cities respectively, **Halifax**, the provincial capital, and **Dartmouth ❶** sit on opposite sides of one of the world's great harbors, connected by two suspension bridges. Magnificent **Halifax Harbour** is one of the world's largest natural harbors, as well as being free of ice year-round. The Mi'kmaq called it *chebucto,* meaning "big harbor." It has long been a bustling international port and naval base.

As the commercial and educational center of Atlantic Canada, Halifax is unquestionably the more dominant and favored of the twins, yet Dartmouth is not without its charms. Though known for its industry, they call it the "City of Lakes" for its 25 sparkling bodies of water.

This allows Dartmouthians to enjoy freshwater fishing and canoeing all

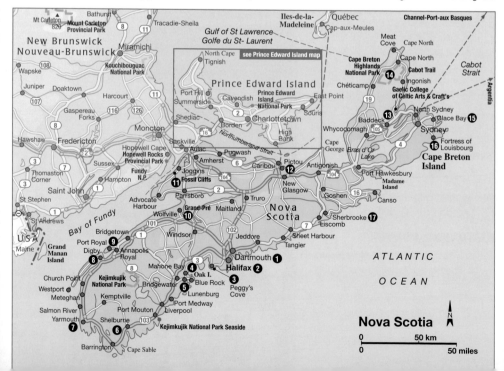

through the summer without leaving the city, and lake-top skating parties in the winter. Dartmouth was founded in 1750 (a year after Halifax), when British troops from across the harbor came on woodcutting expeditions. It was to develop largely in response to Halifax's needs, and as early as 1752 it began operating a ferry between the two settlements. The boats continue to ply the harbor, in what is the oldest saltwater ferry service in North America.

Quakers from Nantucket Island settled here between 1785 and 1792 following the American Revolution. They made Dartmouth the headquarters of a whaling company whose operations were centered at what is now the **Dartmouth Shipyards**. They also left behind a number of homes. These simple structures, with their front doors placed off-center, were built to endure; a stroll down Ochterloney Street shows several, including the historic **Quaker House**, probably the oldest house in Dartmouth (June–Aug Tue–Sun 10am–1pm, 2–5pm).

On Dartmouth's Main Street, the **Black Cultural Centre for Nova Scotia** (daily Mon–Fri 10am–4pm, June – Sep Sat 12pm-4pm) offers a powerful perspective on a little-known part of the region's history – the black immigrants, who first arrived in here in significant numbers almost a century before Canadian Confederation in 1867.

The twin waterfronts of Halifax and Dartmouth have undergone a significant transformation, as have waterfronts across Canada. Halifax's restoration and redevelopment have been the most dramatic.

In the mid-1960s the people of **Halifax ❷** took it upon themselves to transform their city's gray image. The waterfront area now known as **Historic Properties**, which began construction during the Napoleonic wars, was saved from demolition and is now Canada's oldest-surviving group of waterfront warehouses. Tourists can shop, dine, and explore in this cobblestoned area, which externally appears as it did in the 19th century when privateers used it to cache their goods. Nearby, off Lower Water Street, are the more recently restored **Historic Farmers' Market** and

Alfresco dining in Halifax.

Windsurfing at Lawrencetown Beach, Halifax.

A lonely beacon at Peggy's Cove.

the Maritime Museum of the Atlantic. Alexander Keith, the one-time mayor of Nova Scotia, built his brewery in 1820, and its courtyards and arched tunnels are filled once again with spirit. The **Maritime Museum of the Atlantic** (May–Oct daily, Nov–Apr Tue–Sun; http://maritimemuseum.novascotia.ca) not only boasts a magnificent view of the harbor, plus more than 24,000 artifacts and 20,000 photos, but a huge hydrographic ship, the CSS *Acadia*. Now moored behind the museum, the *Acadia* once plied the frigid waters of the Arctic and North Atlantic while charting northern coastlines.

The **Halifax Seaport Farmers' Market** (July–Oct daily, Nov–June Tue–Sun), where more than 250 vendors sell fresh fruit and produce, organic meats and cheeses, baked goods and artisan crafts, is in a recently converted building at Pier 20.

Heading south along the waterfront you come to **Pier 21** (May–Nov daily, Dec–Mar Wed–Sun, Apr Tue–Sun; www.pier21.ca), the portal for the 1 million immigrants who entered Canada between 1928 and 1971. Pier 21 documents their experiences through interactive displays.

Just to the west of the waterfront is Halifax's business district. Amid the office towers and hotels is the **World Trade and Convention Centre**. Easily spotted by its huge weathervane depicting the schooner *Bluenose*, it plays host to shows, conventions, and live concerts. North on Prince Street beside the Old Montreal Trust Building is where 14 newspapers used to be published. The eight pre-Confederation buildings, where the likes of Charles Dickens and Oscar Wilde are said to have stayed, have been incorporated into an attractive complex called **Founders Square**.

Halifax was founded in 1749 not only because of its great harbor, but as a fortress to counter the French installation at Louisbourg. On a hill overlooking downtown Halifax is the **Citadel** (early May to Oct daily, Nov to early May grounds only). The current star-shaped 19th-century structure is the fourth to occupy this pedestal. It no longer serves as a military installation, but as a National Historic Park,

housing the expansive collection of the **Army Museum** (early May to Oct daily; admission included with Citadel; www.armymuseumhalifax.ca), while affording a spectacular view of downtown and the waterfront. This is the best vantage point from which to see the **Town Clock**. With its four clock faces and belfry to ring the hours, Haligonians (residents of Halifax) need not wear wristwatches. Its construction was ordered by Prince Edward, Duke of Kent, a stickler for punctuality.

Two churches not to be missed are **St Mary's Cathedral Basilica**, topped by the world's tallest polished granite spire, and **St Paul's Anglican Church** (1750) on Grand Parade, the oldest Protestant church in Canada. The Grand Parade also serves as an open-air venue for Maritime artists. Nearby on Hollis Street is **Province House** (July–Aug daily, Sept–June Mon–Fri; free), Canada's oldest-standing legislative building. Charles Dickens referred to it as "a gem of Georgian architecture."

At the foot of the citadel are the **Public Gardens**. Established in 1867, these are the oldest Victorian formal gardens in North America. Near the gardens on Summer Street is the **Museum of Natural History** (daily Tue–Sun; http://naturalhistory.novascotia.ca), headquarters of a province-wide system incorporating 27 sites. Celebrating over 150 years, the collection here is devoted to the natural and social history of Nova Scotia, particularly Mi'kmaq artifacts, some dating back 11,000 years.

Going back to the waterfront, at the southern tip of the peninsula that Halifax occupies is **Point Pleasant Park**. The federal government rents this piece of greenery to the city for one shilling a year under the terms of a 999-year lease. The martello-style **Prince of Wales' Tower** (site is open year round; the inside of the tower is not open to visitors) was raised here in 1796 and still stands, the first in a series of these circular stone sentinels to be constructed along the coastal

regions of North America and the British Isles. The park, a favorite with joggers, hikers, swimmers, picnickers, and ship-watchers, is said to be the only place on the continent where Scottish heather grows wild (from seeds shaken from the mattresses of British soldiers). At the other end of Halifax stands **Fort Needham** Park, in memory of the **Halifax Explosion** in 1917.

THE SOUTH SHORE

The rugged and idiosyncratic Atlantic coastline, southwest from Halifax, is known as the **South Shore** and promoted by the tourist bureau as the "Lighthouse Route." It is an accurate appellation, yet despite these sentinels of the night, this beautiful, mysterious, and punishing coastline is no stranger to shipwrecks. Nor are its people strangers to the wrath and bounty of the sea.

The circuitous South Shore, with all its bays, coves, inlets, and islands, was a favorite of pirates and privateers. At **Indian Harbour** and **Peggy's Cove ❸**, 45km (28 miles) from Halifax, fishing villages nestling among and atop the

⊙ Eat

Seafood enthusiasts should visit the acclaimed Five Fishermen Restaurant, across from St Paul's Anglican Church. The restaurant is housed in the building that used to be the first school of art in Canada. Its patron, Anna Leonowens, was the English governess whose adventures inspired the book *Anna and the King of Siam*, which later became the musical *The King and I*.

Halifax Public Gardens.

granite outcroppings are treasures of a different sort. The latter has become a semi-official showcase for the province and is said to be the most photographed fishing village in the world. Yet it has not been robbed of its simplicity and authenticity. There is some quandary over the name Peggy's Cove. Some believe it to be a diminutive of St Margaret's Bay, while others believe it was named after the sole survivor of a shipwreck, who subsequently married one of the local men.

The late William E. de Garthe (1907–83), a marine artist who resided here, apparently sided with the latter theory. Taking a decade to complete, he carved the images of 32 local fishermen, their wives, and their children, in a 30-meter (100ft) face of granite rock located behind his house, which became known as the "Fisherman's Monument." De Garthe also included the image of the young woman of the shipwreck legend. The **Lighthouse**, combined with post office, is a landmark that draws many to Peggy's Cove. Sadly, the tragedy of a Swissair jetliner that plunged into the ocean off Peggy's

Cove in the summer of 1998, with 229 people on board, is a memory that the locals – who played a heroic role in the rescue and salvage operations – will be living with for a long time to come. There are a few memorials to those that died around Peggy's Cove.

St Margaret's Bay, named by Samuel de Champlain in 1631, is known for its fine sand beaches and summer cottages. It is followed by the notorious **Mahone Bay ❹**, with its 365 islands. This was once the realm of pirates, and its name was probably derived from the French *mahonne*, a low-lying craft used by these sea raiders. Other names echo that era, such as **Sacrifice Island** and **Murderer's Point**, but **Oak Island** is the most intriguing. Long the site of treasure hunts, it is said that Captain Kidd buried another part of his treasure here. The island was once densely covered by large oaks and, according to local legend, the mystery of the buried treasure will not be solved until all the oaks have died and seven lives have been lost. (Six persons have so far lost their lives and only a few trees remain standing.)

Lunenburg harbor.

HOME OF THE *BLUENOSE*

"A Snug Harbor since 1753." That's what they say about **Lunenburg ❺**, one of Canada's most important fishing ports. Nowhere in Canada are the traditions of the sea more palpable – carried on by sailors, fishermen, and shipbuilders. The renowned schooner *Bluenose,* the "Queen of the North Atlantic," winner of four international schooner races, was built here in 1921.

A symbol of pride for the people of Lunenburg, she was ultimately lost off the coast of Haiti in 1946. The shipyards of this city later made the ship used in the film *Mutiny on the Bounty*; it was sailed to Tahiti by a Nova Scotian crew. Unfortunately, the ship sank during Hurricane Sandy in 2012. This inspired the creation of *Bluenose II*, a replica of the original, built by the same shipwrights, which is open to visitors when in port. The ship has recently undergone a $17 million restoration.

On the waterfront, the **Fisheries Museum of the Atlantic** (daily 9.30am–5.30pm; https://fisheriesmuseum.novasc otia.ca) will give you a vivid sense of the history of sailing and fishing along Nova Scotia's coasts including their living fish exhibit. Old Town Lunenburg has dozens of beautifully maintained historic buildings dating back to 1760. Many have been converted into attractive inns, restaurants, shops, and galleries. Summer is lively, with the Lunenburg Craft Festival in July; and in August, the Lunenburg Folk Harbour Festival and the Nova Scotia Folk Art Festival.

Across the harbor, walk over the cliffs to The Ovens. These caves were the scene of a mini gold rush in 1861, when New Englanders poured into the area to pan nuggets from the shale on the beach. A museum contains some of their tools and a few bits of gold.

Lunenburg Academy, an outstanding landmark, is now a public school.

CARIBBEAN TRADING PORT

Quiet now, **Port Medway** was a major port in the late 19th century, engaged in a brisk Caribbean trade: fish and lumber in return for rum and molasses. Things are still bustling in **Liverpool**, 142km (88 miles) west of Halifax, which is built on the banks of the Mersey river like its English counterpart.

Sailboats at sunset, Halifax harbor.

⊘ THE HALIFAX EXPLOSION

During World War I, Halifax harbor was constantly crowded with wartime shipping. The city's population was swollen with troops, as well as those who came to benefit from copious work. On December 6, 1917, a catastrophic explosion shook Halifax, causing enormous loss of life. A French munitions ship, the *Mont Blanc*, loaded with a cargo of ammunition and explosives, including TNT, collided with a Norwegian relief ship, the *Imo*, in Halifax harbor. As the ships burst into flames, people came rushing down to the waterfront to watch. Suddenly the *Mont Blanc* exploded. Two thousand men, women, and children lost their lives in an instant, many thousands more were injured, and a large area of northern Halifax was destroyed. Windows were shattered as far away as Truro, 100km (60 miles) from the city. It is said to have been the largest man-made blast prior to the bombing of Hiroshima in 1945.

Halifax picked up the pieces and symbolically placed a sculpture containing remnants of metal from the *Mont Blanc* – some discovered several kilometers away – in front of the Halifax North Memorial Library as a monument to those who lost their lives.

The event features beside the *Titanic* in an exhibition of Nova Scotia's seafaring past at the Maritime Museum of the Atlantic, Water and Prince streets (May–Oct daily, Nov–Apr Tue–Sun).

Privateering figures prominently in the city's history, and this heritage is celebrated for three days each July during "Privateer Days" with music, battlefield re-enactments, and more. Of particular interest here is the **Perkins House & Store Museum** (June to mid-Oct daily), built in 1767. Perkins kept a diary that chronicled life in colonial Liverpool, and his home is a showcase for the same.

West along the coast is **Port Mouton**, a pleasant fishing village named by Sieur de Monts and his party in 1604 when one of their sheep was lost overboard here. Tiny **Port Joli** is a bird sanctuary, a favorite spot of Canada Geese supporting some 4-5,000 geese annually. This makes up some 40 percent of the wintering Canadian Geese in the Atlantic provinces.

Shelburne 6 lies 67km (41 miles) west of Liverpool. A treasure trove of 18th-century history, it's referred to as "The Loyalist Town," for it was settled by 16,000 United Empire Loyalists from America between 1783 and 1785. It became an instant boom town – bigger than not only Halifax, but also Montréal. The population dropped abruptly after 1787 with the termination of government support and by the 1820s fewer than 300 people called this home. Shelburne's **Ross-Thomson House** (June to 15 Oct daily), built in 1784, is a Loyalist home and store – thought to be the only surviving 18th-century store in Nova Scotia. It now functions as a provincial museum, fully stocked and decorated to reflect the 1780s.

Edging north toward the **Bay of Fundy** brings you to **Yarmouth 7**. Following a five and a half hour ferry ride from Maine, USA you can disembark here to start your adventure. During the golden age of sail this was one of the world's great ports.

THE FRENCH SHORE

The **French Shore**, home of Nova Scotia's largest Acadian population, is synonymous with the municipality of **Clare**, midway between Yarmouth and Digby, which locals are fond of saying rivals Toronto's Yonge Street as the longest main street in the world, for it

Shelburne Waterfront Heritage District.

consists of 27 villages, more than half of which sit along the main thoroughfare. Many Acadians returned to this area following the deportation to start anew, some on foot through the wilderness. In **Meteghan**, 40km (25 miles) north of Yarmouth, a short path takes hikers in **Smuggler Cove Provincial Park** down to a secluded beach with a natural cave, purported to have been a cache for contraband rum during the days of Prohibition in the United States.

Most Acadian villages are dominated by their church, and in **Church Point** (*Pointe d'Eglise*) this is particularly true. **St Mary's Church**, built early in the 20th century, is the tallest and largest wooden church in North America. Its 56-meter (184ft) spire, swayed by bay breezes, is stabilized by 36 tonnes of ballast. This landmark sits on the campus of the **Université Sainte-Anne**, the only French university in the province. As a center for Acadian culture, the institution hosts the **Festival Acadien de Clare** for the first two weeks of August.

East of St Mary's Bay, at the southern tip of the Annapolis basin and overlooking Digby Gut, is **Digby ❽**. The town has a long maritime history and was named for the commander of a ship that carried Loyalists here from New England in 1783 (among them, the great-grandfather of inventor Thomas Edison). This is home of the renowned **Digby Scallop Fleet** (the world's largest), which is celebrated each August during the Digby Scallop Days Festival.

THE ANNAPOLIS VALLEY

Champlain wrote of the Annapolis basin: "We entered one of the most beautiful ports which I had seen on these coasts." His compatriot Marc Lescarbot considered it "a thing so marvelous to see I wonder how so fair a place did remain desert." Although orchards and other farmlands have replaced the primeval forest along the Annapolis basin and river, this completely transformed region is still beautiful to behold.

Built in the 1780s, **Old St Edward's Loyalist Church** in **Clementsport** is situated high on a hill within an ancient cemetery. It was one of the province's

Tip

For unsurpassed views of St Mary's Bay on the northwest coast, hike along the trail that heads out along the clifftops between Cape St Mary and Bear Cove.

Fort Anne, Annapolis Royal.

earliest museums, showing off not only its own architectural integrity, but a fine collection of Loyalist artifacts. Its elevated setting also provides one of the best vantage points from which to appreciate the Annapolis basin.

On the other side of the basin is **Port Royal National Historic Site** ❾, 10km (6 miles) from Annapolis Royal, with its reconstructed **Habitation** (late June to early Sept daily, late May to late June and Sept to early Oct Tue–Sat), the settlement built by Sieur de Monts and Samuel de Champlain in 1605. It is a place that witnessed many firsts: the first permanent North American settlement north of Florida; the first Roman Catholic Mass celebrated in Canada; the first Canadian social club (Champlain introduced the Order of Good Cheer as an antidote to the prospect of another dismal winter); and the first Canadian dramatic production (*Le Théâtre de Neptune* orchestrated by lawyer and writer Marc Lescarbot in 1606). Burned by the English in 1613, its reconstruction in 1939, after years of research, was one of the first great successes of Canada's

historic preservation movement. In 2019, the palisades and gun platform will be closed to visitors.

The Annapolis Valley, sheltered by the North and South Mountains and extensively diked by Acadian settlers, is an agriculturally and scenically gifted area, known particularly for its apples. In spring the scent of apple blossoms lingers in the air, and the **Apple Blossom Festival** is celebrated.

Though settled primarily by Planters and Loyalists following the deportation, the valley pays homage to Acadians – nowhere more poignantly than in **Grand-Pré** ❿, the village immortalized by Longfellow in *Evangeline*. Grand-Pré was the most important Acadian settlement in Nova Scotia before the deportation. Longfellow's *Evangeline – A Tale of Acadie* (1847) describes the separation of a young couple during the deportation and the subsequent search by the woman for her lover.

At **Grand-Pré National Historic Site** (mid-May to mid-Oct daily), a simple stone church contains many artifacts relating to Acadian culture. Outside the church stands a statue of Longfellow's tragic heroine.

Southeast of Grand-Pré, where the Avon and St Croix rivers converge, is the town of **Windsor**. Anyone fond of expressions such as "raining cats and dogs," "quick as a wink," and "an ounce of prevention is worth a pound of cure," should visit Windsor's **Haliburton House** (*c.*1839). Now a museum, it was once the home of judge, humorist, and author Thomas Chandler Haliburton, who created *Sam Slick*, the fictional Yankee peddler who spouted his witticisms on his travels through Nova Scotia (June–Oct Mon–Sat 10am–5pm, Sun 1–5pm; https://haliburtonhouse.novascotia.ca).

CHIGNECTO ISTHMUS

The northern aspect of mainland Nova Scotia is washed by the Bay of Fundy, with the highest tides in the

Grand Pré, The Annapolis Valley.

world; and, on the other side of the Chignecto Isthmus, by the Northumberland Strait. Whereas some bizarre natural phenomena occur only once in a lifetime, the Fundy tides put on their show twice daily, with a repertoire that varies according to the location. **Burntcoat Head**, on the **Minas Basin**, is the point at which Canada's highest tides have been recorded – a difference of 16.3 meters (53.5 feet) between low and high.

Perhaps this atmosphere of extremity inspired William D. Lawrence to construct Canada's largest wooden-hulled ship in nearby **Maitland**, 20km (12 miles) west of Truro. His namesake, a fully rigged sailing vessel, was launched in 1874 and was a technical and financial success. Lawrence's stately home, now the Lawrence House Museum, contains artifacts and memorabilia relating to ships and shipbuilding, including a model of the record-breaking *William D. Lawrence*.

Truro was originally settled by Acadians (they called it Cobequid), and later by people from Northern Ireland and New Hampshire. It is a good place to observe the tidal bore, or "wall of water," in which the incoming Fundy tide rushes into the Salmon river at the rate of 0.3 meters (1ft) a minute. East across the isthmus is a region washed by the Northumberland Strait, strung with beaches and often echoing with the sound of bagpipes. It is said that more clans are represented in Nova Scotia than in Scotland, and a good number of them can be found right here. To the west of Truro, the 300 million-year-old fossils at **Joggins Fossil Cliffs** ⑪ have been designated a World Heritage Site by UNESCO (visitor center and guided tours late Apr–Oct daily).

Pictou ⑫, 76km (47 miles) east of Truro, is the "Birthplace of New Scotland," where the first Scottish Highlanders landed, aboard the *Hector* in 1773. This fine harbor saw many subsequent waves of Scottish immigration. Today it is a center for shipbuilding and fishing. Each July brings the three day **Pictou Lobster Carnival**.

⊘ JOGGINS FOSSIL CLIFFS

During the "Coal Age" 300 million years ago, Joggins was covered by lush forests that ultimately created the coal deposits that gave this period of history its name.

Today, embedded within some 15km (9 miles) of cliff face along the Bay of Fundy, is the world's most complete fossil record of life at that time, including the earliest reptiles entombed within once-hollow trees. The first true reptile, *Hylonomus lyelli* – the ancestor of all dinosaurs that would rule the earth 100 million years later – was discovered here by Canadian-born scientist Sir William Dawson. With the Bay of Fundy's extreme tides rising and falling 15 meters (47ft) twice daily, new fossils are constantly exposed, and a new crop of fossils is revealed every three of four years.

Joggins Fossil cliffs, Bay of Fundy.

Like Pictou, **Antigonish**, 74km (46 miles) southeast, took its name from the Mi'kmaq and later became characterized by the culture of Highland Scots. The annual week-long **Highland Games** draw competitors from far and wide every July, in what is the oldest such spectacle in North America. With Scottish music, dance, and sports, they also feature the ancient caber toss.

CAPE BRETON ISLAND

Alexander Graham Bell once wrote: "I have traveled around the globe. I have seen the Canadian and American Rockies, the Andes and the Alps, and the highlands of Scotland; but for simple beauty, Cape Breton outrivals them all." Bell's words have not gone unheeded; **Cape Breton Island** is the most popular tourist destination in Nova Scotia. Ironically, the island is also the most economically depressed region in a province less affluent than much of the rest of Canada, due in some part to the decline in coal mining.

Cape Breton has always been a place apart – occupied by the French longer than the rest of Nova Scotia (they called it *Ile Royale*) and a separate province until 1820. The **Canso Causeway**, an umbilical cord to the "Mainland," was not constructed until 1955.

The Cabot Trail, which is named after the explorer John Cabot, is a 298km (185-mile) loop which rollercoasts around the northern part of Cape Breton. This road is popularly thought of as one of the most spectacular drives to be found in North America, winding through lush river valleys, past (and often clinging to bluffs high above) a rugged and dramatically beautiful coastline, through dense forest lands, and over mountains.

It was once a series of death-defying footpaths and, later, equally treacherous trails. By 1891, a narrow wagon trail forged its way circuitously over Cape Smoky, which has a sheer rock cliff on one side and a 366-meter (1,200ft) plunge to the sea off the other. Automobiles began taking their chances here in 1908; one of these early motorists' tricks was to tie a spruce tree behind the car to prevent it running away downhill. The trail still has its hair-raising stretches and most people drive it in a clockwise direction, clinging to the inside of the road.

Alexander Graham Bell, himself born in Scotland, built a summer house in **Baddeck** ⑬, the official beginning and terminus of the Cabot Trail, and spent his last 35 years here. As a teacher of the deaf, he directed Helen Keller's education and undertook research that led to the invention of the telephone. **The Alexander Graham Bell National Historic Site** (mid-May–Oct daily 9am-5pm), through photographs and exhibits, is a monument to Bell – the teacher, inventor, and humanitarian. The Cabot Trail, traveling clockwise beyond Baddeck, traces the **Margaree River**, renowned for its beauty and an abundance of trout and salmon.

Cape Breton at sunset.

The stretch of Gulf of St Lawrence coastline from the Margaree to the Cape Breton Highlands National Park is dotted with Acadian fishing villages, inhabited by descendants of the mainland French who came here at the time of the deportation.

Just as the Acadian language has retained its 17th-century flavor, the culture of the people here has remained relatively undiluted. Acadian flags fly in the sea breeze, and a church steeple signifies the next community. Such is the case with **Chéticamp**, the biggest town in these parts. **Cape Breton Highlands National Park ⓮** begins a few miles north of Chéticamp, extending from the Gulf to the Atlantic and bordered on three sides by the Cabot Trail. This magnificent wilderness preserve is a paradise for hikers, swimmers, campers, golfers, and other lovers of the great outdoors.

The trail reaches its northernmost point at **Cape North**, and from here another road heads farther north to the fishing village of **Bay St Lawrence**. En route, at the base of **Wilkie Sugarloaf mountain**, is the site where Cabot is believed to have landed in 1497. At the eastern exit from the park are the **Ingonish**, a group of communities that have long been a great attraction for visitors. Just beyond Ingonish Harbor is Cape Smoky, its head in the clouds, rising 366 meters (1,200ft) above the sea. Tourists can ski its slopes in winter while looking out upon the Atlantic. In summer, a ride on the chairlift to the top of Cape Smoky provides a breathtaking view (weather permitting) of this rugged, misty isle.

The stretch from Cape Smoky to Baddeck is known as the **Gaelic Coast**. Skirting the coast of St Ann's Bay will take travelers to the **Gaelic College of Celtic Arts and Crafts**. As the only institution of its type in North America, it serves as a vibrant memorial to the Highland Scottish who settled here, and has been nurtured by their descendants. In early August the clans are well represented as they gather for the annual **Gaelic Mod**, a seven-day festival of Celtic culture. While on campus, visit the **Great Hall of the Clans** (mid-May–Oct Mon–Fri). It tells the story of the Great Migration from the highlands, while interactive displays focus on the music, dance, song, stories, and crafts of Nova Scotia Gaels.

COAL AND STEEL COUNTRY

Jumping off the Cabot Trail into what is called **Industrial Cape Breton** becomes an introduction to a world of smokestacks and steel mills. Coal was once king in this area. Today the Nova Scotia government still uses coal for the majority of its electrically generated stations.

Cape Breton Miners' Museum in **Glace Bay ⓯** has developed into one of Nova Scotia's finest museums (late May–mid-Oct daily, mid-Oct–May tours by appointment only; www.minersmuseum.com). Artifacts and photographs chronicle the history of coal mining in this town and commemorate the men

A moose foraging in the leaves.

The Jack Pine and Coastal Trails in Cape Breton Highlands National Park.

who risked their lives working in the depths; but the highlight of any visit here is the mine tour. Salty veteran miners bring visitors down into the **Ocean Deeps Colliery** (carved from under the ocean floor), and tell stories of pain, death, pride, hard work, low wages, and camaraderie. Let yourself be transported back to what it was like to work these mines in the 1930s.

Coal has been mined in the vicinity of Glace Bay since the 18th century, when soldiers from nearby Louisbourg were assigned this duty.

THE LAST FRENCH STRONGHOLD

Passing by the sentries into **Fortress of Louisbourg ⓰** (mid-May to Oct daily, Nov to mid-May by appointment) is like stepping back in time to the summer of 1744. Fortress Louisbourg was the last great military, commercial, and governmental stronghold of the French in the region that was once Acadia, but by 1758 it was in ruins. The site remained untouched until two centuries later when reconstruction began, in what

The annual Scarecrow Festival in the town of Mahone Bay celebrates the arrival of fall.

has been termed the most ambitious project of its kind ever undertaken in Canada.

From the costumed staff (performing roles of fishermen, merchants, and soldiers) trained in 18th-century deportment, to the authenticity of the structures and their furnishings, Louisbourg never fails to impress. You will need a full day to do it justice.

A center for scuba diving is **Louisbourg Harbour**, and the waters off the southern coast of Cape Breton are known as fertile ground for "wreck-hunting" – the legacy of centuries of maritime activity.

Off the south shore, just before reaching mainland Nova Scotia, is **Isle Madame**, reached by a small bridge across the Lennox Passage. A scenic loop meanders through Acadian fishing villages. Of particular note is **LeNoir Forge Museum** (June Mon-Fri 10am-5pm, July-Aug Tue-Sat 10am-5pm, Sun 1pm-5pm; all other times by appointment; requested donation) in Arichat, a restored stone blacksmith shop with working forge, in what is the

oldest building on the island (1793). At Little Anse, a trail leads to **Cap Rouge** at land's end. From here you can look out upon **Green Island** with its lighthouse, one of the last remaining manned beacons in the province.

THE EASTERN SHORE

The eastern shore of Nova Scotia, between Cape Breton and the Twin Cities, is characterized by its unspoiled beauty, an abundance and variety of fishing opportunities, and its traditional personality. Locals maintain that things have changed little over the years.

Closer than all other mainland communities to the great Atlantic fishing banks, **Canso** has developed into a center for fishing and fish processing. Its harbor has witnessed the history of this region, from the early European fishermen and traders to the British fleet that made its rendezvous here before the final assault on Louisbourg.

Along the banks of St Mary's river is the village of **Sherbrooke** ⑰, 80km (50 miles) west of Canso. It was a French fur-trading post in the 17th century, but the first permanent settlers came here in 1800 attracted by the tall timber and the river, then as now, filled with salmon. Sixty-one years later something happened to change the face of this town for all time – they discovered gold. The boom, referred to as "Sherbrooke's Golden Age," lasted only 20 years.

Sherbrooke became quiet again, left alone except for seasonal visits by salmon fishermen, until the 1970s, when a restoration project was established. The heart of town is now almost entirely restored to the period from 1860 to pre-World War I, and certain streets have been closed to traffic to create **Sherbrooke Village**.

It's inhabited by people in costume going about their daily business, so visitors can walk through 21st century

Sherbrooke and happen upon a town steeped in another era.

In use since the 1870s, **The Blacksmith Shop** produces items used in the restoration and sold in the Emporium, as does **Sherbrooke Village Pottery**. Most fascinating of all is the jail, built in 1862 and used for 100 years. Not a jail really, but an ordinary 19th-century home inhabited by a jailor, his family, and the offenders.

Continuing for 85km (52 miles) west along the coastal road brings visitors to **Tangier**, home of an enterprise known to gourmets and gourmands the world over – J. Willy Krauch and Sons. Krauch, now joined by his sons, has spent the better part of his life smoking Atlantic salmon, mackerel, and eel, using the Danish system of wood-smoking.

A farther 30km (18 miles) west at **Jeddore Oyster Pond** is the **Fisherman's Life Museum** (June–Sept Mon–Fri). The museum is the modest homestead of Ervin and Ethelda Myers and their 13 daughters, restored to reflect the period after the turn of the 20th century.

Sea kayaking in Nova Scotia.

📷 WHALE-WATCHING IN COASTAL WATERS

For the Inuit, whaling meant survival; for the Europeans it was big business. Today whales live under the watchful eyes of scientists and tourists.

While Christopher Columbus and Jacques Cartier were still recounting their New World discoveries, Basque whalers were quietly making fortunes on the Canadian coast. Their Red Bay, Labrador, whaling station employed 1,000 men, and refined up to 2 million liters (440,000 gallons) of valuable oil each season. At the same time, unknown to the Basques, Inuit were catching whales in the Arctic Ocean far to the west, and the Nootka people were hunting off Canada's West Coast. Other European and later American whalers joined the Basques, expanding their hunts to the edges of the known world on each of Canada's three coasts. They would pursue the whale in a small boat, thrust their harpoon into the mammal, and let out a line. The frenzied whale would take the boat on what became known as a "Nantucket sleigh ride" until, exhausted, it would fall victim to its hunters. Then its carcass would be towed ashore for stripping.

When the 19th century brought steamships, and harpoon guns to shoot a missile that exploded inside the animal, whale stocks went into decline.

WHALING GIVES WAY TO WHALE-WATCHING

By the onset of World War I, profitable whaling had ceased in the Canadian Arctic, but it continued along the British Columbian and Newfoundland coasts with the introduction of factory ships for processing. The International Whaling Commission began controlling catches in the late 1940s, but stocks off Canada's coasts diminished at a dramatic rate. Commercial whaling was ended by the government in 1972. Today only the Inuit are allowed to take whales, for their own consumption.

Canada's coastal waters provide a habitat for various species of whales: bowhead and white whales are found around Baffin Bay, while orcas and gray whales can be seen off British Columbia.

Inuit were the most skilled at finding a use for almost every part of the whale. They ate the skin, blubber, and flesh, used the bones for weapons and the oil for light and heat.

Tourists watching killer whales from a boat off the coast of British Columbia.

Where to Spot a Whale

Newfoundland's east-coast ports, including those in Trinity and Bonavista bays, date back to the heyday of whaling. Today operators combine whale-watching with sighting bald eagles and other rare bird species. A bonus here is a close-up look at spectacular icebergs as they drift south.

The **Bay of Fundy** has krill-rich waters stirred by enormous tides. These attract families of huge right whales, so called by whalers, who found them valuable and easy to catch. The most popular spot for viewing is New Brunswick's Grand Manan Island, where expeditions are run by marine biologists. Whale-watching boats also leave from St Andrews, NB and Nova Scotia.

At the confluence of **Québec's** Saguenay and the Gulf of St Lawrence, whales are readily seen from the shore and on guided expeditions. Several species here include a permanent – although dwindling – colony of small white beluga whales, the only such group found outside the Arctic.

Churchill, on **Manitoba's** Arctic coast, also includes belugas among its whale species. In addition to the traditional excursions, visitors here can go snorkeling among the whales.

On **British Columbia's** coast, excursions leave from Vancouver and Victoria and many smaller ports. Gray whales, which migrate each spring down the west coast of Vancouver Island, are best seen between mid-March and early April. There is also a resident population of orcas (killer whales), whose numbers appear to be, unfortunately, shrinking in recent years.

A reconstructed whalebone roof frame near Resolute, Nunavut.

beluga whale (Delphinapterus leucas) lifts its head from *e water.*

rcas (or killer whales) can be spotted off the west coast *f Canada.*

PRINCE EDWARD ISLAND

The birthplace of the Canadian Confederation and the setting for L.M. Montgomery's novel *Anne of Green Gables*, Prince Edward Island is the tiniest province in a land of vast horizons.

Prince Edward Island (P.E.I.) rests in the Gulf of St Lawrence, cut off from the mainland by the Northumberland Strait. Less rugged than its fellow Atlantic Provinces, P.E.I.'s quaintness seems untouched by the modern world and it has a gentle, rural atmosphere. Agriculturally, the land (which is bright red in color) is well groomed and cultivated. Some go so far as to describe the island as two beaches divided by potato fields. The importance of potatoes cannot be overestimated; they are the pre-eminent crop. Tourism is second in economic importance. There are more than 145,000 inhabitants on the island, most of them the descendants of early French, Scottish, English, and Irish settlers.

P.E.I. is an island begging to be explored. Since 1997 it has been joined to the mainland by the Confederation Bridge, an imposing 12.9km (8-mile) structure between Borden and Cape Jourimain, New Brunswick. There is also a ferry service between Wood Islands and Caribou, Nova Scotia.

THE WEST: NORTH CAPE COASTAL DRIVE

P.E.I. is geographically separated into three parts: traveling from west to east – **Prince**, **Queens**, and **Kings**. The westernmost region is less developed

than the other two in terms of tourism, but it is no less attractive.

North Cape Coastal Drive meanders around a deeply indented coastline; past sandstone cliffs and sun-bleached dunes; and through tiny villages, many of them ringing with the sounds of Acadian French (almost 5 percent of P.E.I.'s population is French-speaking).

The route begins and ends in **Summerside ❶**, the second-largest of only two cities in P.E.I. (its capital, Charlottetown, is the largest). Located on **Bedeque Bay**, the town was

◉ Main attractions
North Cape Coastal Drive
Green Park Provincial Park
Charlottetown Festival
Central Coastal Drive
P.E.I. National Park
Green Gables House
Points East Coastal Drive
Orwell Corner Historic Village
Basin Head Fisheries Museum

◉

Map on page 238

Catch of the day.

presumably named for being on the warmer or "sunny-side" of P.E.I. Once a center for shipbuilding, the waterfront is now crowded with vessels loading up with potatoes. One highlight of Summerside's calendar comes in mid-July with three days of gustatory merriment known as the Lobster Carnival. On a musical note, the one-of-a-kind College of Piping and Celtic Performing Arts of Canada offers high-energy performances of Celtic music and dance during July and August. Check their website (www.collegeofpiping.com) for seasonal performances.

The spires of **St John the Baptist Church**, one of the island's loveliest churches, announce one's arrival in **Miscouche**, 10km (6 miles) west. It was in this town that the National Acadian Convention decided to adopt the red, white, and blue Acadian flag in 1884. Today, this banner can be seen throughout French-speaking regions of Atlantic Canada. Miscouche is also home of **Le Musée Acadien** (late June–mid-Oct daily 9am–5pm, shorter hours rest of the year), whose collection of antique tools, household items, religious artifacts, photographs, and documents aims to preserve the culture of these early settlers.

OYSTER CENTER

Five kilometers (3 miles) north of Miscouche is **Malpeque Bay**, where the world-renowned Malpeque oysters were first discovered. The Tyne Valley Oyster Festival celebrates these bivalves annually in August. Malpeque Bay is also known for its fine sand beaches and for having been a great center for shipbuilding in the 19th century, a part of the island heritage commemorated at **Green Park Provincial Park** in **Port Hill** ❷ to the west of the bay. Green Park is the former estate of shipbuilding magnate James Yeo, Jr, which today includes his restored home, Yeo House (c.1865), a shipbuilding museum and a recreated 19th-century shipyard (June Mon–Fri 9am–4.30pm, July–Aug daily 9am–4.30pm, closed rest of year).

Beyond Port Hill is a causeway leading to **Lennox Island**, and the largest

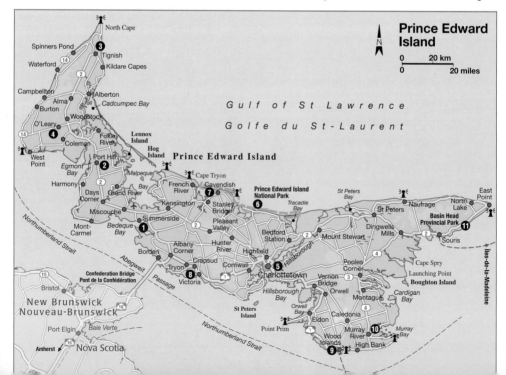

community of Mi'kmaq in P.E.I. Lennox Island's Indian Art & Crafts of North America specializes in the sale of beaded and silver jewelry, clay pottery, woodcarvings, woven baskets, and ceremonial headdresses made by First Nations peoples from many different ations.

The **Cape Kildare** area, 45km (28 miles) north of Port Hill, is where Jacques Cartier dropped anchor in 1534, thereby "discovering" the island. Inland 12km (7 miles) to the north is **Tignish** ❸, a community founded in 1799 by a group of Acadians who were later joined by two Irishmen. Both cultures are still well represented and, typically, the church is the focal point of the community. The **Church of St Simon and St Jude** has a fine pipe organ, which is played at recitals during July and August (times advertised locally).

The northernmost tip of P.E.I., **North Cape**, is a continually eroding point, so much so that the lighthouse and the road that encircles it have been moved inland several times. Its strategic location prompted development of the **Atlantic Wind Test Site**, a national facility for the testing and evaluation of wind generators, where visitors are welcome.

South from North Cape, along the Northumberland shore, tourists are likely to see Irish moss drying by the road or perhaps, following a storm, being gathered and hauled by horse-drawn carriages and pick-up trucks along the beach. The area around Miminegash is particularly known for the harvesting of this commercially viable seaweed. Sightings of a ghost ship, full-rigged and aflame, are frequently reported between **Campbellton** and **Burton** on this shore. Legends abound here, from Mi'kmaq lore to tales of Captain Kidd's buried treasure at **West Point**.

Inland from West Point is **O'Leary** ❹, in the center of one of P.E.I.'s richest and largest potato-producing areas, home of the Canadian **Potato Museum** (part of the **O'Leary Museum**). If you're hungry you can try some potatoes at their kitchen and restaurant. The museum is also host to the annual Potato Blossom Festival (July).

Lobster traps are stacked on the quayside at Malpeque harbor at the start of the lobster fishing season.

Fresh oysters.

⊘ ABEGWEIT

According to Mi'kmaq legend, the Great Spirit molded brick-red clay into "the most beautiful place on earth" and gently placed it in the Gulf of St Lawrence. He presented it to his people and they came here in summer to camp and to fish nearly 2,000 years ago. They called it *Abegweit*, "land cradled on the waves." Today the Mi'kmaq account for less than 1 percent of the population of the island.

The first European to covet the island was Jacques Cartier, who claimed it for France in 1534. It became the breadbasket for the French stronghold at Louisbourg, and the island still serves a similar function for the region as the "Garden of the Gulf."

Tracing **Egmont Bay**, approaching the Summerside area, is the Région Acadienne – punctuated by the villages **Abram-Village**, **Cap-Egmont**, and **Mont-Carmel**. There are some excellent opportunities to experience Acadian culture and *joie de vivre* during the summer season, including *l'exposition agricole et le festival acadien* in early September. The latter both include agricultural competitions, step dancing, fiddling, lobster suppers, the Blessing of the Fleet, and more. Abram-Village is also a center for crafts (particularly quilts and rugs), which are demonstrated and sold at the local Handcraft Co-operative.

The seaside community of Cap-Egmont has a rather unusual attraction – **The Bottle Houses**, a recycling project (undertaken in retirement) of the first magnitude. Edouard T. Arsenault built his glass houses and chapel from bottles (the first called for 12,000 of them). After a "long winter cleaning bottles," the former fisherman and carpenter began work in 1980, lovingly laboring over the project until

his death four years later. Arsenault's typically Acadian spirit, a mixture of creative energy and humor, shines through the walls.

THE ISLAND'S CAPITAL CITY

Not the least of **Charlottetown's** ❺ considerable charms is that it is still predominantly wooden (structurally, but decidedly not in demeanor). It is the center of all things for P.E.I. – government, commerce, and culture – though it seems more like an elegant small town, complete with a town crier and gaslights. Historically, Charlottetown is best known for being the "Cradle of the Confederation." The 1864 meeting, which led to the formation of the Dominion of Canada three years later, was held in **Province House** (reopening in 2019 after restoration), the province's first public building. Ironically, P.E.I. was at first hesitant to join Canada, and it did not enter the Confederation until 1873. This neo-Classical stone structure is now a National Historic Site and the chamber where the Fathers of Confederation met has

Colorful houses in Charlottetown.

been restored, though it still houses the legislature.

Next door is the **Confederation Centre of the Arts**. Established to commemorate the centennial of the main event, the center showcases the talents of Canadian artists, year round. Each province contributed 15 cents for each of its citizens to help to finance construction. It includes gallery and theater spaces and is host each summer to the **Charlottetown Festival**. Running from mid-June until mid-September, it is Canada's best-known music and theater festival. One of the loveliest parts of town is **Rochford Square**, its beautiful shade trees the legacy of Arbor Day 1884. Adjacent to the square is **St Peter's Anglican Church** (1869) with a notable attachment, **All Souls' Chapel**, created in 1888 as a memorial to one of the cathedral's first clergymen. It was a labor of love for William Harris, who designed it, and for his brother Robert, who created luminous wall paintings. Harris specified that island materials be used, from the rich, red sandstone exterior to the wood and stone used for interior carvings – a testament to the spirit of both brothers, and to the skill of island craftspeople.

THE CENTER: CENTRAL COASTAL DRIVE

The central region of P.E.I. is traced by the route known as the **Central Coastal Drive**, which comes full circle at Charlottetown. It is distinguished by fine beaches – white sand along the Gulf shore and red sand along the Northumberland shore – colorful fishing villages, *Anne of Green Gables*-related attractions (an Island sub-industry), and community lobster suppers. Every summer night throughout P.E.I.'s small towns and districts, amazing feasts are organized and prepared by local women. Held either in churches or big halls, as many as 400 to 500 people are fed. For a reasonable price travelers can experience some of the best homemade food and lobster dishes they will ever taste.

Most of **Queens County's gulf coast** belongs to **P.E.I. National Park ⑥**,

A Prince Edward Island lighthouse.

Harvesting Irish moss on Cavendish Beach.

24km (15 miles) northwest of Charlottetown, with some of the best beaches in eastern Canada (year-round). The Victorian mansion of Dalvay-by-the-Sea, now a hotel, near the eastern entrance to the park, was built in 1896 by the oil magnate Alexander Macdonald.

Rustico Island, part of the national park, is the summer home to a colony of great blue herons, the possessors of 2-meter (6ft) wing spans, while North Rustico is a traditional fishing village. You can purchase seafood practically off the boats here, pass the time talking with locals, or go out on a tuna charter. In late July, the Rendez-vous Rustico Festival offers three days of traditional and contemporary Acadian music.

GREEN GABLES HOUSE

Still within P.E.I. National Park, 10km (6 miles) west of the Rusticos, is Cavendish ❼, the center of *Anne of Green Gables* country. Visitors come from far and wide to see the settings described by Lucy Maud Montgomery

A resident mariner of Prince Edward Island.

in her book about an orphan girl, published in 1908, and other works of fiction, as well as to explore landmarks in the author's life. The lovely Green Gables House itself, on Highway 6, has undergone restoration following a fire in 1997. The L.M. Montgomery Birthplace (mid-May to mid-Oct 9am–5pm, daily) can be found in New London, 15km (9 miles) southwest. A brochure sets the stage by stating: "As you walk through the rooms of the Birthplace, you will thrill to the realization, that it was in this house that Lucy Maud first saw the light of day."

Victoria ❽ (its residents like to call it Victoria-by-the-Sea), 30km (18 miles) southwest of Charlottetown facing the Northumberland Strait, is an English-flavored town, which is both an active fishing port and a center for antiques. From end June to mid-September, theater performances take place at the restored Victoria Playhouse. The Provincial Park, which is edged by red sand, is a good place to have a picnic.

THE EAST: POINTS EAST COASTAL DRIVE

The easternmost piece of P.E.I., most of it corresponding to Kings County, is encircled by the Points East Coastal Drive. This is the longest of the three routes. In the Orwell Corner Historic Village (June, Sept, Oct Mon–Fri 8.30am–4.30pm, July–Aug daily 8.30am–4.30pm), 30km (19 miles) east of Charlottetown, the atmosphere of a late 19th-century rural crossroads community has been recreated. Most of the early settlers here were Scottish, and in summer the sounds of the Highlands can be enjoyed at a weekly *ceilidh* (pronounced kay-lee) in July and August. Beside the village, the Sir Andrew Macphail Homestead (June–Sept Tue–Fri; Sundays for brunch) reflects the life and times of a prominent Islander at the turn of the 20th century.

In 1803 a Scotsman by the name of Lord Selkirk financed the immigration of three shiploads of Highlanders to P.E.I., and the "Selkirk Pioneers" settled in **Eldon**, 13km (8 miles) south of Orwell. Over time, the settlement became the **Lord Selkirk Provincial Park**. In early August, it is the site of the annual P.E.I. Highland Games & Festival, hosted by the Caledonian Club of Prince Edward Island.

SCULPTORS AND SEALS

At **Wood Islands** ❾, a boarding point for the Nova Scotia ferry, the museum at the **Wood Islands Lighthouse** (early June to late Sept daily) offers a spectacular 360-degree view and is an interpretive museum with themed displays covering the way of life for lighthouse keepers, rum-running during Prohibition, and phantom ships.

Eighteen kilometers (11 miles) beyond Wood Islands is **Murray River** ❿. This lovely town was once a center for shipbuilding, but today wood is worked on a much smaller scale. **Murray Bay** is the home of a large natural seal colony. These sleek creatures can be best observed from the **Seal Cove Campground** in **Murray Harbour North**, cavorting in the sun on their offshore sandbar.

Approaching the easternmost tip of P.E.I., you reach **Bay Fortune**, washed by a string of legends. There is talk of the early 19th-century murder by a tenant of landlord Edward Abell at **Abell's Cape**, of buried treasures along the sandstone cliffs, and of actor Charles Flockton, who in the late 19th century bought the cape and spent each summer here with his comedy company. American playwright Elmer Harris was inspired to feature nearby **Souris** as the setting for his book *Johnny Belinda* (based on the local legend of a deaf and mute girl). Today Souris is an embarkation point for passengers heading for the nearby Iles de la Madeleine.

Basin Head ⓫, 12km (7 miles) east of Souris, is home of the **Fisheries Museum** (July–Aug daily 9.30am-5pm, June and Sept Mon–Fri, 9.30am-5pm). The museum is located beside a particularly beautiful stretch of dunes, where the sand "sings" as you walk. Rounding **East Point** (called *Kespemenagek*, "the end of the Island," by the Mi'kmaq) brings one to **North Lake**, the "Tuna Fishing Capital of the World." Tourists flock here in pursuit of the giant bluefin tuna – regarded as the ultimate in sport fishing.

Heading back to Charlottetown one realizes that in 2,000 years little has changed. The Mi'kmaq were right in calling P.E.I. *Abegweit* – it is indeed a "land cradled on the waves." The Gulf Coast provides endless water activities for travelers, from fishing and boating to swimming and digging a clam dinner out of the brick-red sand beaches. Inland, the flat, quaint terrain is perfect for adventurous trekkers and cyclists.

Animal rights activists on the ice floes near the Gulf of St Lawrence.

NEWFOUNDLAND

While settlements are sparse and many areas are only accessible by boat or light plane, the province's craggy coastline, mountains, lakes, and rich history appeal to visitors worldwide.

Newfoundland's mountains are not as high as the Rockies and are much less accessible. There are no theme parks or world-class art galleries. Tourist facilities, while adequate, are rarely luxurious. Yet Newfoundland's remoteness has cultivated the most individualistic part of North America. Imagine a land mass three times the area of New Brunswick, Nova Scotia, and Prince Edward Island combined, then remember that the rugged terrain is home to less than four people per square mile. A third of the total population live around St John's on the east coast, while the rest live in smaller inland communities, or in coastal towns and villages, known as "outports." English is the most common language spoken, and 96 percent of the people were born here. Jokes about Newfies can be heard across the country, but Newfoundlanders have their own brand of humor, calling Newfoundland simply "The Rock."

THE FIRST EXPLORERS

To understand Newfoundland, one must understand some of its history. The **Grand Banks** are the fishing grounds southeast of Newfoundland that have been worked by European fishermen since the 15th century. Giovanni Caboto from Italy (also known as John Cabot) sighted this coast in 1497

and claimed the land for the English king, Henry VII, who had financed his voyage. Henry, who had hoped the expedition would find gold, gave him £10 and had to be content with fish. Cabot reported that the cod were so numerous that, "they would fill a basket lowered over the side." The Spanish, Portuguese, and French who also fished in the area, salted their catch to preserve it for the trip home. But the English, who lacked a source of cheap salt, had to dry their cod, and to do this the fleets needed to go ashore.

Main attractions

Gros Morne National Park
Terra Nova National Park
Bonavista Peninsula
L'Anse-aux-Meadows
    National Historic Site
Cape Spear National
    Historic Park
Signal Hill National
    Historic Site, St John's
The Rooms, St John's
Battle Harbour

Map on page 246

The unique architecture of St. John's, Newfoundland.

Britain originally did not want a colony and actively discouraged settlement. In fact it was illegal for anyone to winter in Newfoundland. The "Masterless Men" were the first European settlers after the Vikings to come to Canada. They were sailors who jumped ship, preferring life in one of Newfoundland's many natural harbors to life aboard. Their independence and spirit of survival are still very much a part of Newfoundlanders' character today.

The Viking settlements ("Vinland") of the early 11th century did not survive, perhaps because of climate change or a vitamin deficiency causing a weakening of the bones. Stories of Vinland have indicated that the first child born in the Americas of European origin was Snorri Torfinnsson. When Christopher Columbus visited Iceland in the 1480s, before his "discovery" of the New World in 1492, he probably would have heard the stories of the Newfoundland voyages that the Vikings made. The site of Vinland is at L'Anse-aux-Meadows – at the northern tip of the Great Northern Peninsula.

ORAL TRADITION

Since St John's is closer to Ireland than to Toronto, its language is not surprising. It is a unique blend of dialects from England's West Country and southwest Ireland, brought over by the original settlers and left largely unchanged by the passing centuries. It is the closest dialect in the modern world to Shakespearean English and the only place where many words and expressions that were common in the 17th century still survive.

A tradition preserved in Newfoundland is storytelling. The oral form of handing down stories from generation to generation is still alive. Times are changing, but not all Newfoundlanders will change with them. Guglielmo Marconi was dubbed an "irrepressible dandy" when he came to Newfoundland to receive the first transatlantic wireless message in 1901. The "old days" are described as the times when, "most people could neither read nor write, but my, how they could talk!" Modern times differ only in that people can now read and write as well.

In fact, Newfoundland is Canada's most recent province. Confederation

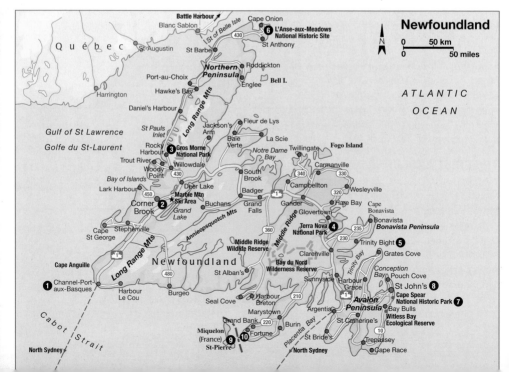

(union) with Canada was, and sometimes still is, one of the liveliest topics for discussion in Newfoundland. It did not take place until 1949 and was a hard-won victory for the federalists.

MODERN LIFE

Until well into the 20th century the majority of Newfoundlanders lived along the coasts making a difficult living from the sea. Cod, which was the foundation of Newfoundland's economy, has virtually disappeared from the waters off Canada's East Coast. As a result, a 10 year moratorium was implemented in 1992, and cod fishing is now highly restricted – as Fisheries Department scientists insist it is the only way the cod stocks will return to healthy levels. Nevertheless, it is still available at supermarkets and fish-and-chip restaurants. In recent years, reports indicate that the cod (and haddock) populations are returning to their former (and healthy) levels.

Sealing, however, remains an annual ritual, and almost all Newfoundland fishermen continue to be proud of their humane killing methods and adherence to quotas. However, adhering to the quota has become less of an issue. In 2015, the federal government set seal quotas at 400,000, although only 35,000 seals were killed — less than 10 percent of the quota. Due to the success of animal rights groups, there has been a significant drop in international demand for seal pelts, which is just as well as the changing sea temperatures and lack of sea ice have started to impact on the seal population's ecosystem.

In the last 50 years, the importance of forestry in Newfoundland has declined. However, a huge nickel deposit discovered in Labrador in the 1990s is now being mined, and three offshore oil developments – Hibernia, Terra Nova, and White Rose – discovered off the coast rival those in the North Sea. A massive reserve of shale oil was also discovered and in recent years efforts have been undertaken to extract it.

Hydroelectricity produced at Labrador's Churchill Falls is also now a major contributor to the province's economic health. Tourism is a relatively recent phenomenon in Newfoundland. However, there are plenty of B&Bs and hotels throughout the province – and also two lighthouses – where tourists can sleep and enjoy Newfoundland home-cooking.

Screech, found in many households and taverns, is the dark rum drink for which Newfoundland is famous, and has been popular since salt fish was first shipped to the West Indies and exchanged for rum. It is rather like the Newfoundland character – more interesting than it is refined. While screech is still popular, so are iceberg vodka and various berry-based wines, which are also made here. For the seafood lover, Newfoundland homes are the ideal venue. Fish is served as often and in as much variety as one could wish: halibut, crab, Atlantic salmon, cod, lobster, and much more.

EXPLORING THE PROVINCE

The independent traveler will need a car. There are bus services to virtually

> ## ⊙ Fact
>
> First-time visitors are invited to taste screech, the local distillation, at a "screeching-in" ceremony held in town halls. A scroll is issued as proof of passage.

Historic buildings in Trinity, Newfoundland.

Over 7,000 moose have made their home in Gros Morne National Park.

all locations, but the farther off the beaten path, the more infrequent the service. There are still many locations that are best reached or only accessible by boat. The main road in Newfoundland is **Highway 1 (Trans-Canada Highway)**, which runs through Newfoundland on an indirect path between **Channel-Port aux Basques** 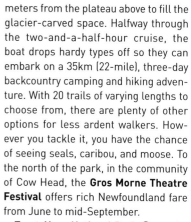 in the west (terminus for the ferry from North Sydney, Nova Scotia), to St John's in the east. It's 905km (562 miles) long and is the life-line of the province. Right off the Trans-Canada Highway, 200km (137 miles) northeast of Channel-Port aux Basques, **Corner Brook** ❷ is the scenic business center for Newfoundland's west coast.

The national parks are a source of pride for Newfoundlanders and a source of delight for the visitor. On the west coast is mountainous **Gros Morne National Park** ❸, a Unesco World Heritage Site, which puts it in a class with the Grand Canyon and Australia's Great Barrier Reef. It's best known for its fjords, which are best seen by boat. Around **Western Brook Pond**, one of the area's lakes, waterfalls tumble hundreds of

meters from the plateau above to fill the glacier-carved space. Halfway through the two-and-a-half-hour cruise, the boat drops hardy types off so they can embark on a 35km (22-mile), three-day backcountry camping and hiking adventure. With 20 trails of varying lengths to choose from, there are plenty of other options for less ardent walkers. However you tackle it, you have the chance of seeing seals, caribou, and moose. To the north of the park, in the community of Cow Head, the **Gros Morne Theatre Festival** offers rich Newfoundland fare from June to mid-September.

Terra Nova National Park ❹, on the east coast, is a piece of typical Newfoundland fishing coast. Here there is boating, fishing, and moonlight cruises on beautiful **Clode Sound**. Inland in the park there is good camping and hiking, and the water in the lakes is warm enough to swim.

East of the park lies the **Bonavista Peninsula**. This region attracted worldwide attention in 1997 when, in a re-enactment of Cabot's voyage 500 years earlier, a replica of his boat, the *Matthew*,

sailed from Bristol, England, and landed amid great ceremony at Cape Bonavista.

Visitors can get a feel for life on this isolated cape at the **Cape Bonavista Lighthouse**, restored to the 1870s period (mid-May to early Oct daily), which includes admittance to the **Mockbeggar Plantation Provincial Historic Site** (mid-May to early Oct, 9.30am-5pm), whose intriguing story traces the evolution of the Newfoundland fishery. Centrally located on the peninsula, the 12 communities of **Trinity Bight ➎** offer historic sites, delightful B&Bs, and good paths for walking off the excellent Newfoundland fare – in particular the 5.3km (3.3-mile) Skerwink Trail, rated among the top 35 trails in North America by *Travel & Leisure Magazine* for its unforgettable views.

At the most northerly tip of Newfoundland, **L'Anse-aux-Meadows National Historic Site ➏** (June to early Oct daily) is also worth a visit. Dwellings from an 11th-century Viking settlement have been reconstructed and Norse artifacts found on site are displayed at the Visitor Center.

Cape Spear Lighthouse National Historic Site ➐ is the most easterly point of both Newfoundland and the continent. Take a boat tour to see and listen to a school of whales. Even the shortest boat ride off the coast will remind you of the power of the sea.

Sport fishing opportunities are as many and as varied as the Newfoundland coast and all the rivers and lakes inland. Fishing lakes are known as "ponds." Salmon, arctic char, and northern pike are the favored catches.

ST JOHN'S

The capital of Newfoundland and Labrador, **St John's ➑**, sited on the northeast of the Avalon Peninsula, is one of the oldest cities in North America. Its streets were originally cow paths wandering up from the harbor. **Government House** has what is commonly (and mistakenly) referred to as a moat – in fact, the 'moat'

is a cost-effective 19th century (when the mansion was built) method of allowing more light through the basement windows.

Signal Hill National Historic Site (June – early Sep daily 10am-6pm) must be seen: more events of historical importance have taken place on this site than in most other provinces. In 1762, Signal Hill was the site of the last battle of the Seven Years War. Visitors can still see fortifications ranging from the Napoleonic Wars to World War II. It was also here, high up the hill in one of three hospitals, the Diphtheria and Fever Hospital, that Guglielmo Marconi received the first transatlantic wireless signal from Cornwall on December 12, 1901. Today, in the **Cabot Tower** (mid-May to early Sep; free), built in honor of Queen Victoria's Diamond Jubilee, an exhibition on Marconi's ultimately successful endeavors is well worth visiting. Despite its historic significance, Signal Hill got its name originally from the practice of putting up flags to let people know of ships in the harbor. Views from here of downtown, the harbor, and down the

> **⊙ Tip**
>
> Whales can often be seen in the waters off Cape Spear in spring and summer – ask a park ranger where to look. This is also a good place to see icebergs.

Getting to grips with Viking boat building at L'Anse-aux-Meadows National Historic Site.

Cabot Tower on Signal Hill, St John's.

Evening on Water Street, St John's.

coast to Cape Spear are extraordinarily good. If you have good walking shoes and the weather is clement, the steep North Head trail down to The Battery, an old neighborhood at the entrance to the harbor, is an exhilarating walk.

The best way to get a sense of St John's is to walk down Water Street, the oldest street on the continent. When Newfoundland joined Canada in 1949 most of the province lived in poverty, but Newfoundland had more millionaires (they were known as "Water Street Men") per capita than anywhere in North America.

The Rooms on Bonaventure Avenue (May-Sep Mon-Sat 10am-5pm, Wed until 9pm, Fri until 10pm, Sun 12pm-5pm; Oct-Apr Tue-Sat 10am-5pm, Wed until 9pm, Sat until 10pm, Sun 12pm-5pm, closed Mondays) house the provincial museum, the provincial art gallery, and the provincial archives. Perched high above downtown St John's, the striking building is based on the buildings and shoreline structures found in outport Newfoundland and Labrador.

The museum recounts the human history of the island, and how nature interwove with the lives of the peoples who lived here from 9,000 years ago to 1730. Five fires devastated St John's in the 19th century. One of the few buildings to escape was the clapboard **Commissariat House**, King's Bridge Road, now restored to reflect the 1830s. **Quidi Vidi Village**, 3km (2 miles) north of Signal Hill, has the typical "pocket" harbor of an outport.

Make time to visit the **Presentation Sisters' Motherhouse** (Mon–Fri 10.30am–noon, 2–4pm; donation) to see the beautiful *Veiled Virgin*, carved from one piece of marble by Giovanni Strazza, which was brought from Rome in 1856.

OUTPOST OF FRANCE

Not only is Newfoundland closer to Ireland than Toronto but it is also closer to France than to Nova Scotia. Just off Newfoundland's southern coast are the islands of **St Pierre** and **Miquelon** ❾, the remnants of France's once-great empire in North America. The islands can be reached by a passenger-only ferry from

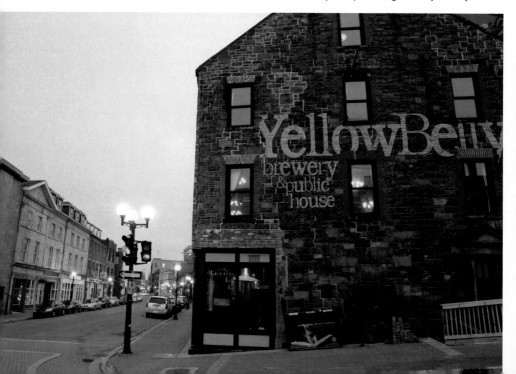

Fortune ❿ or by air, and a passport is usually required.

JOURNEY TO LABRADOR

For the truly adventurous, Labrador beckons, just 17km (10 miles) across the Strait of Belle Isle from northern Newfoundland. Subject to the weather, ferries make the short crossing from **St Barbe** to **Blanc Sablon** on the Labrador–Québec border. From here, Route 510 (also known as the Labrador Coastal Drive) connects a string of coastal settlements, including the fishing village of **L'Anse-au-Clair**, founded by the French in the early 18th century; **L'Anse-Amour**, where aboriginals are known to have lived 9,000 years ago; **Red Bay**, site of a Basque whaling station (c.1550); and **Cartwright**, 400km (248 miles) from the Québec–Labrador border. Only the first 84km (52 miles) of Route 510 are paved. On an island about an hour's ferry ride from Mary's Harbour, **Battle Harbour** is possibly the province's best-preserved traditional outport, and was declared a national historic district in the mid-1990s.

CHANGING TIMES

Newfoundland's first day as a Canadian province was April 1, 1949. In the last 40 years, the changes here have been profound. Between 1954 and 1972 more than 27,000 people from more than 220 isolated outport communities were resettled in larger centers, although some 700 outports are still home to many tenacious Newfoundlanders. The impact of multimillion-dollar oil projects off the east coast of St John's has also been huge. Countless new restaurants offer cuisine from around the world, and trendy boutiques have replaced the traditional Water Street merchants. Nightlife ranges from dinner theaters and pubs to launch parties and live music, particularly of the traditional Irish sort.

In many ways, Newfoundland and Labrador is Canada's most unusual province, and in others it is the most typical. It is a land of beauty and of hardships, and a place where even the short-term visitor may gain memories to last a lifetime.

> **⊘ Fact**
>
> Quidi Vidi Lake is the site of the annual Royal St John's Regatta. Held since, at least, 1816, it is the oldest continuing sporting event in North America.

Signal Hill, St John's.

Mother polar bear and cub, Manitoba.

Merritt, the country music capital of Canada.

THE WEST

From Manitoba to the Pacific coast, western Canada offers a rich diversity of landscapes and cultures.

After more than a century of off-handed treatment from Ontario and Québec, over the past 40 years the West has emerged as a powerful presence in Canada. Rich in minerals, oil, and natural gas, the Prairie provinces, in particular Alberta, are now economic forces to be reckoned with.

Canada Place, Vancouver.

Sometimes referred to as Canada's "Garden of Eden," British Columbia, Canada's most westerly province, enjoys the most temperate climate. It contains part of the splendid and irascible Rocky Mountains range, as well as a twisted coastline with fjords as spectacular as those in Norway.

The West's most well-known destination is of course Vancouver, Canada's third-largest city and its window on the Pacific. It's also regularly voted one of the best places to live in the world and it's the heart of the province of British Columbia (BC). The province's capital city, Victoria lies offshore on Vancouver Island. BC is rich with parks and hiking trails that will appeal to all levels of skill and its massive wilderness is breathtaking.

The region then sprawls away from the Pacific coast, inwards to the Prairie provinces: Alberta, Saskatchewan, and Manitoba. These three provinces provide wonderful contrasts between mountains, wide open prairie, and the more than 200,000 lakes in this part of the country. Alberta begins the search for the "prairie existence" and demonstrates its diversity by journeying up into Canada's vast playground: the Rocky Mountains. Banff's splendid beauty contrasts with the modern and bustling city-life of Edmonton and Calgary. Saskatchewan is explored through its rich history and its proud and prolific cultural features. Manitoba, concluding the section, provides an experience of the prairie itself: wide open spaces, no longer shaded by forests, rolling on to a distant horizon.

Taking a break in Riding Mountain National Park, Manitoba.

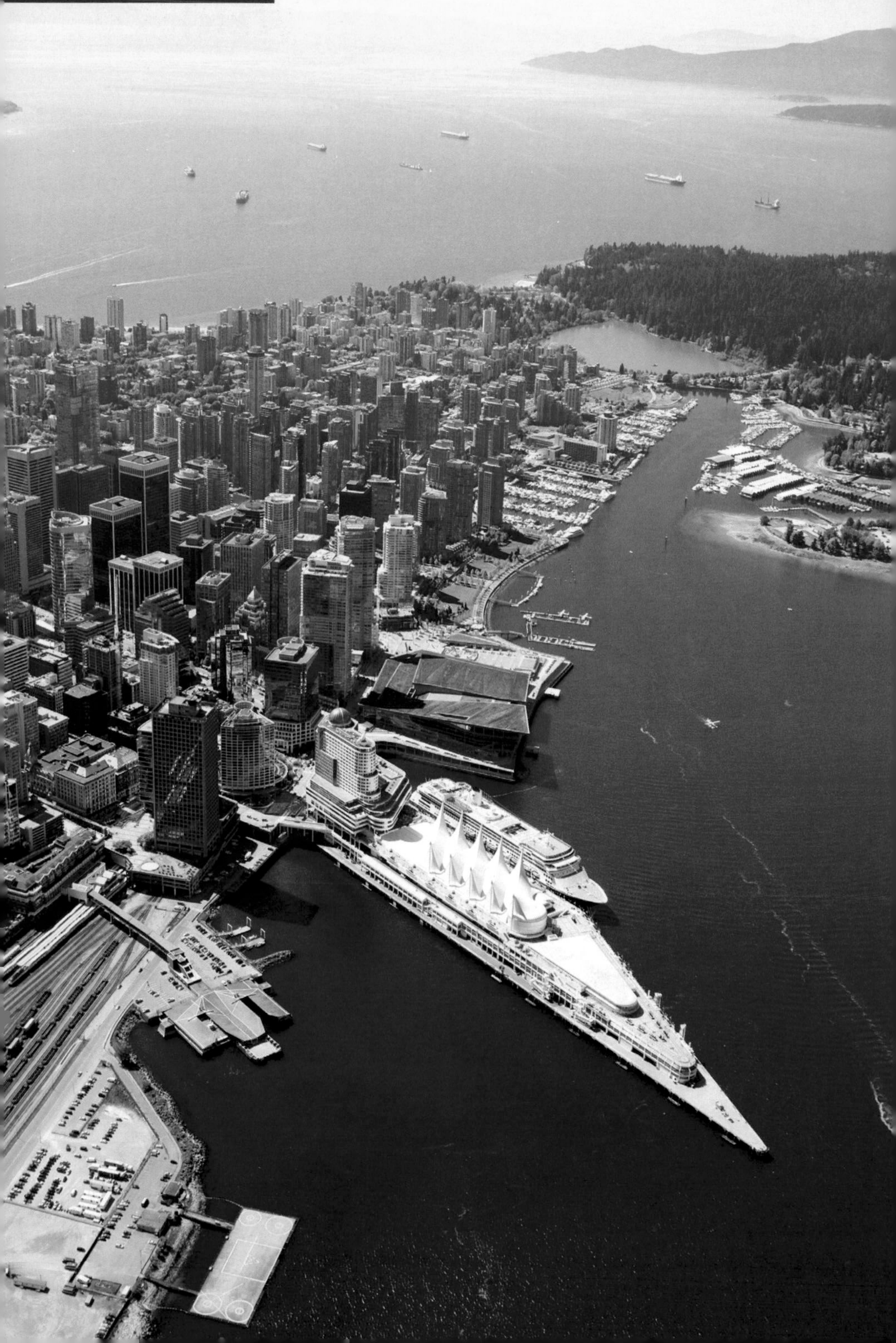

Aerial view of downtown Vancouver.

VANCOUVER

Set perfectly between the Pacific Ocean and the Rocky Mountains, this green and vibrant city combines a thriving arts and cultural scene with the wholesome goodness of the great outdoors.

The mainland city of **Vancouver** is more than the West Coast's shining star. It is invariably selected as one of the top cities in the world for quality of life.

Evidence of prosperity can be seen in the elegance of its luxury hotels downtown, including two built to coincide with the Expo 86 World's Fair, the Fairmont Waterfront Hotel and the Pan-Pacific Hotel Vancouver, the latter adjoining **Canada Place Ⓐ**. Canada Place, built as the Canada pavilion for the fair, is meant to approximate a cruise ship leaving port – similarities to the Sydney Opera House (it has five large sails for a roof) are apparent. The building forms the central focus of the Trade and Convention Center, with an expansion to the west that opened in 2009, just in time to host the international broadcasters for the 2010 Winter Olympics. The expansion was built according to the highest environmental standards, boasting seawater heating and cooling, an on-site water treatment plant, and a 2.4-hectare (6-acre) "living roof" that houses thousands of indigenous plants while also recovering rainwater for irrigation. The sails also house the main cruise ship terminal for the trip to Alaska, so it is frequently an image that rests in the mind of visitors.

STANLEY PARK

If Canada Place is the first sight, **Stanley Park Ⓑ** is the first stop for the rest

of the senses. This 405-hectare (1,000-acre) thumb of forest jutting into the Burrard Inlet is home to Douglas fir, cedar, hemlock, and is a National Historic Site. This evergreen oasis was dedicated in 1889 in the name of a governor general, Lord Stanley, the same Stanley whose name stands for supremacy in professional hockey: the Stanley Cup.

Stanley Park has a 10km (6-mile) perimeter sea wall that offers a panoramic view of the water and the city skyline, and entertains visitors and locals alike with every type of vessel,

Main attractions
Canada Place
Stanley Park
Museum of Anthropology
Telus World of Science
Vancouver Art Gallery
Chinatown
Granville Island Public Market
Grouse Mountain
Whistler Village

Map on page 258

Queen Elizabeth Park.

⊙ Tip

For some of the best views of the harbor, city, and mountains, take a 15-minute ride on a seabus plying the waters between downtown and north Vancouver.

from kayak to sailboat to yacht to cargo ship. Cruise ships plying the Pacific West Coast north to Alaska dock regularly in the harbor from May through September. Vancouver is Canada's foremost West Coast port, shipping bulk tonnage such as coal, grain, sulfur, potash, liquid chemicals, and fuel oil. Additionally, it is the general container cargo port for inbound goods to the west. A steady parade of cargo vessels and cruise ships, plus recreational boaters, makes for fascinating viewing.

Among the many attractions in the park is the collection of nine totem poles near Brockton Oval. Three First Nations, Kwakwaka'wakw, Haida, and Squamish, are represented here. The recent addition of three carved gateways created by Coast Salish artist Susan Point creates a welcoming entry to the area. In summer, those with a bit more time may also head to Klahowya Village, a First Nations cultural experience centered around artists and performers of many different nations. Visitors can experience storytelling, performance, carving demonstrations, and plenty of activities for children, including a miniature train (mid-June to mid-Sept).

One of the other highlights in the park is the **Vancouver Aquarium** (end-June to early Sept daily 9.30am–6pm; early Sept to end-June daily 10am–5pm; www.vanaqua.org). The aquarium holds more than 70,000 creatures, including docile beluga whales and gregarious dolphins, but it is the tanks holding nurse sharks that devour huge pieces of meat in the blink of an eye that draw the biggest crowds. Recent additions, Lakina and Balzak, are two young walruses that are starting to steal the show. The focus of this aquarium is definitely on research and education, so it's a great spot to learn and be entertained at the same time.

MUSEUMS AND GALLERIES

Vancouver's list of museums of history and fine art is extensive. Leading these on the campus of the University of British Columbia is the **Museum of Anthropology ©** (daily 10am–5pm, Tue until 9pm, mid-Oct to mid-May closed Mon; www.moa.ubc.ca), which contains an

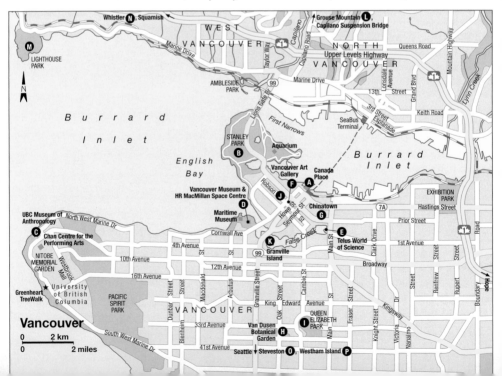

Vancouver

outstanding collection of totem poles, including a full-size replica of a West Coast native village complete with longhouses. There are also significant artifacts from the South Pacific, as well as many other parts of the world. Contemporary works by living First Nations artists demonstrate how the art and culture is being kept alive. The small museum shop has an excellent selection of pieces – and their authenticity is certain. Located between the university and downtown is the **Vancouver Museum ⓓ** (Tue–Sun 10am–5pm, Thu until 9pm; www.museumofvancouver.ca), Canada's largest civic collection, which traces the history of the city, from the first settlement by native peoples through to the arrival of European settlers and the modern history of the city.

Also here on the grounds of the city museum is the **H.R. MacMillan Space Centre** (Mon-Fri 10am-3pm, Sat 10am-5pm, Sun 12pm-5pm, observatory Sat 7pm–11pm, Sat evening astronomy shows 7.30pm and 9pm; www.space-centre.ca), a planetarium, observatory, motion simulator, and theater.

Close by is the **Vancouver Maritime Museum** (Daily 10am-5pm, Thu until 8pm; www.vancouvermaritimemuseum.com), preserving the RCMP Arctic-exploring schooner, the *St Roch*. This hardy little ship made two passages of the ice-laden Northwest Passage and established Canada's supremacy over the region. The Franklin Exploration pop-up display is worth a look. Nearby, at Heritage Harbor, historic ships are moored during summer months. It's a great open space for kids to run around and adults to get a maritime history fix. Serious kite flying nearby can also mesmerize the whole family on a breezy day.

Hugely popular with kids is **Telus World of Science ⓔ** (daily 9am-5pm, Fri-Sat until 6pm, hours are seasonal; www.scienceworld.ca) at the waterfront Expo 86 site. The ultimate hands-on experience, the dome has more than 350 interactive displays, focusing on entertaining kids of all ages while educating. There is also an **OMNIMAX Theatre**, the largest screen of its kind in the world.

Fall leaves in Stanley Park.

On the corner of Robson and Howe streets is the **Vancouver Art Gallery** ❻ (daily 10am–5pm, Tue until 9pm; www.vanartgallery.bc.ca), which has an impressive collection of the works of both Canadian and international artists. It is home to a superb collection of paintings by Emily Carr, a world-renowned British Columbia-born artist who painted the skies, forests, and native cultures of the area in the first three decades of the 20th century.

ENTERTAINMENT

The theater season runs from September through June and offers every kind of performance. The **Orpheum** on Smithe Street, a completely refurbished movie theater built in 1927, is home to the Vancouver Symphony Orchestra, while opera can be found at the **Queen Elizabeth Theatre** on Cambie Street which opened in 1959. The **Chan Centre for the Performing Arts**, renowned for its acoustics, is surrounded by gardens on the idyllic UBC campus.

Entertaining and comedic plays are performed at the **Arts Club** on Granville Island, and outdoor Shakespearean theater is presented all summer long at **Bard on the Beach**, near the Vancouver Museum. In September, theatrical tradition pushes the envelope with a world-class Fringe Festival that takes over numerous theaters and performance spaces on and around Granville Island. It's a great opportunity to see a lot of shows in a short time, with all box office revenue going directly to the actors.

GARDENS, GARDENS, GARDENS

It's true that Vancouver gets a lot of rain – the annual rainfall is 111cm (42ins) – but, aside from the dark days of November, the rain here is often little more than a drizzle. Locals have umbrellas but rarely use them, opting more often for hoods. While the lack of sun can be depressing in winter, people here are very aware that the rain and mild climate create the best in parks and gardens in Canada.

The **Dr Sun Yat-Sen Classical Chinese Garden** (daily 1 May–15 June and Sept 10am–6pm, 15 June–31 Aug

Museum of Anthropology.

9.30am–7pm, 1 Oct– 30 Apr 10am–4.30pm, closed Mon between 1 Nov –30 Apr; www.vancouverchinesegarden.com, $12) in **Chinatown**  is the first such garden to be built outside China, and includes special river rocks, pavilions, and covered walkways, most of which were imported from China. A more conventional garden, **Van Dusen Botanical Garden**  (daily June–Aug 9am–8pm, shorter hours rest of the year; http://vandusengarden.org) stretches across 22 hectares (55 acres) and is home to more than 250,000 plants. It's a garden that has something to offer no matter what the season, but some of the most popular areas are the rhododendron walk, the maze, the Japanese maples, and, in early spring, the crabapples and flowering cherries. Check their website for information on their full bloom schedule. The interpretive center is a "living building," its construction inspired by the form of a native orchid, with a green roof that seems to float over the center. At **Queen Elizabeth Park**  (daily), a 130 acre park houses a rose garden, quarry-pit garden, conservatory, tennis courts, and miniature golf circuit make this a popular place for locals and visitors. Along with its numerous sandy beaches, the quarry-pit garden is one of Vancouver's most popular places for wedding photos.

Back out at the UBC campus, **Nitobe Memorial Garden** (mid-Mar–Oct daily 11am–4.30pm, Nov–mid-Mar Mon–Fri 10am–2pm) is considered one of the top five traditional Japanese gardens outside Japan. In spring, the cherry blossoms are magical, while summer seduces with irises, and fall delivers a magical experience with the brilliant hues of maple trees. Nearby, the **Greenheart TreeWalk** (daily Apr–Oct 10am-4pm) is a 308-meter (1,010ft) aerial trail system where visitors traverse bridges suspended in trees that are more than 100 years old. The trails are 15–20 meters (50–65ft) above the ground, with several viewing platforms joining the walkways.

NEIGHBORHOOD LIFE

Like all great cities, Vancouver offers a variety of fascinating neighborhoods. These are the places where people and buildings are not just anonymous cogs in some swirling commercial mass, but where they take on a character of their own, and live out a culture unique to their block or avenue. Vancouver has several distinctive neighborhoods that give it this kind of life.

The stores along **Robson Street**  are a far cry from the schnitzel houses and small European delicatessens that reflected the European immigrants who came to Vancouver after the war. By the late 1970s, the street that was frequently called Robsonstrasse was heading for a transformation. The high-rises of the downtown business core and the apartment blocks of the West End met along Robson Street and entrepreneurs responded with more shopping and better restaurants. The street now offers exceptional dining and great window shopping, with all the international brands crammed along the blocks closest to Burrard Street.

There are many exotic species of birds at the Bloedel Conservatory in Queen Elizabeth Park.

⊘ THE BEACHES OF VANCOUVER

Life in Vancouver seems to be bound up with the ocean. In winter, even in the wind and rain, people are out walking along the beaches. When summer comes, the rest of the city moves in to make the most of the golden stretches of sand. Despite being located right in the center of a large city, the beaches and waters are relatively clean, clean enough for people to swim as soon as it is warm enough.

One of the closest to downtown and therefore one of the most popular is **Kitsilano Beach**, invariably referred to as "Kits." Games of beach volleyball are often in progress, and the safe swimming makes it popular with families.

Farther west, **Jericho**, **Locarno**, and **Sunset** beaches have a huge hinterland and are popular for families and groups of friends who need the space for barbecues of epic proportions. The shallow shore extends out well into **English Bay**, so low tide offers an expanse of sand with a margin that challenges the best skimboarders.

Beyond all the other beaches, below the cliffs of the University of British Columbia, lies the internationally-acclaimed **Wreck Beach**, for decades the one beach where you can bare all. It's not remotely voyeuristic, and the fine sweep of sand is cared for by its own society.

Robson is the city's busiest shopping street, which means it is also one of the best people-watching places. In early August the streets are closed so that more than 500,000 people can watch and participate in the Pride Parade.

The **Granville Island Public Market**  (daily 9am-7pm except around Christmas and New Year) is more than just a food market located in the middle of the city. The island began as an experiment in the late 1970s to turn a collection of abandoned buildings and heavy industry into a place where people would come to buy fresh fruits and vegetables. Some of the industry stayed – there is still a working cement plant, complete with brightly painted cement trucks rumbling on and off the island all day long. Several of the old sheds were combined to create a farmers' market that has evolved into one of the most successful public markets in North America. Here you will find scores of small producers of everything from artisanal chocolates to wild mushrooms and seaweeds, with an emphasis on locally grown and created products. There are restaurants and bars, as well

Granville Island Public Market.

as two brewing companies and even a sake maker. Buskers entertain in five or six different locations, providing free entertainment, from magic shows to a Chapman stick musician to teenagers playing classical violin. Local artisans, ranging from jewelers and woodworkers to violin and furniture makers to glassblowers and printmakers also adorn the food market and occupy small workshops all over the island. If one only had a day to get a feel for Vancouver and pick up a few unique gifts to take home, this is the place.

Another urban food mecca is **Chinatown**, close to the downtown core, but a world apart. It's one of the largest Chinatowns in North America, vying for size with San Francisco and New York. While it offers a diversity of shopping from cooking supplies to furniture, the main attraction is food. Dim sum restaurants provide the neophyte a great opportunity to point and choose. Small dishes of delicacies come hot out of the kitchen and waiters wander through the restaurant offering them to patrons. The waiters keep a running tally of the dishes selected, and the final bill is generally far less than expected. The Asian community is well established here: the first wave of Chinese immigrants helped to keep the gold rush going when white frontiersmen had lost interest and left for home, and a second wave was in large part responsible for the construction of the Canadian Pacific Railway.

Successive waves of immigrants from most European countries after World War II, followed by more recent arrivals from India, Pakistan, Hong Kong, Taiwan, China, Korea, Vietnam, and other Asian countries has created a truly cosmopolitan city. While English is still the dominant language, more than 90 languages are actively spoken in Vancouver, including Mandarin, Cantonese, Punjabi, Tagalog, and German. It is estimated that today more than 40 percent of all school children in Vancouver are raised speaking a language other than English at home.

VANCOUVER SUBURBS

The city of Vancouver is just a small part of the urban sprawl that stretches west to east from the ocean up the Fraser river Valley and north to south from the mountains to the US border. While many of the suburbs are relatively new residential communities, they are also the gateway to the great outdoors that surrounds the city. Across Burrard Inlet, in North Vancouver, the **Grouse Mountain Skyride** Ⓛ (daily 9am–10pm; www.grousemountain.com) offers a panoramic city view, and this is one of the four local mountains that offer skiing, snowshoeing, and other winter sports. Grouse Mountain is famous for its "Grouse Grind" – a 2.9km (1.8-mile) path up the mountain that is promoted as "Nature's Stairmaster." It's steep: with an elevation gain of more than 850 meters (2,800ft), the average time for a fit person to complete the trail is about an hour, with novice hikers taking two hours or more. A better choice for novices would be one of the walks through the forests at the top. More adventurous visitors can opt for ziplining or paragliding. On the way, the **Capilano Suspension Bridge** (daily) is more than a 137 metre (450 feet) suspension bridge; it also offers a First

Grouse Mountain's cable cars.

⊘ Fact

Capilano Suspension Bridge in North Vancouver is a sight not to be missed. This 137-meter (450ft) undulating steel cable bridge crosses a dramatic canyon, 70 meters (239ft) above the Capilano river.

Nations' Cultural Center, complete with demonstrations of traditional weaving, beadwork, and carving.

Heading west into West Vancouver along Marine Drive, Ambleside is another example of a neighborhood, with small shops along a main street that has a small-town feeling. A few blocks away, the public walkway runs along a beach that mirrors the main street: everything is slower over here, away from the hustle and bustle of Vancouver. Even farther west, the community of Horseshoe Bay, best known for its ferry terminal, is a great place to explore nature away from the crowds. **Lighthouse Park** offers both easy and more challenging trails through old growth Western red cedar and Douglas fir trees.

NORTH OF VANCOUVER

About 100km (62 miles) north of Vancouver is **Whistler Village** , co-host of the 2010 Winter Olympics (with Vancouver). Whistler is an international destination, attracting more than 2 million visitors a year, almost equally split between winter and summer. The two mountains of Whistler and Blackcomb compete for honors as skiers' preferred slopes, with snowboarding, cross-country skiing and other winter sports making it a destination for all ages and levels of fitness. The two mountains are linked by the 2nd longest (1.88 miles / 3.03km) free span between ropeway towers and, is still, the highest (1,430ft/436meters) cable car span in the world, the Peak 2 Peak Gondola. In summer, golf, mountain biking, and hiking trails attract visitors for the day or for much longer.

Another 32km (20 miles) north of Whistler, a pleasant half-hour walk along the Green river leads to **Nairn Falls**. Although not particularly high, its powerful tumble is loud and very impressive.

SOUTH OF VANCOUVER

Now a neighborhood with a small-town feel, the fishing village of **Steveston** has a rich history. In 1887 a single Japanese fisherman came to this tiny town for the salmon season. Just 40 years later there were 3,000 Japanese here, mostly fishermen. Salmon was the main

The ascent to Blackcomb Glacier.

⊘ WHISTLER

Whistler has evolved from a gondola and a few t-bars serving local diehard skiers to the top ski resort in North America. While this is partly due to the careful creation of a European-style village, the real reason is the spectacular mountains that have been developed to yield their best. Two separate mountains, Whistler and Blackcomb, share accommodations and entertainment.

There are activities all year long to keep both avid adventurers and those less accustomed to outdoor activity more than satisfied.

Exceptional food and drink reward a day of hiking, skiing, or braving the zipline, a series of 10 individual steel cables strung across 2,400 meters (8,100ft) of forest, interspersed with suspension bridges and viewing platforms.

catch, and canneries soon sprouted up all along the foreshore. Today, the Gulf of Georgia Cannery offers tours (daily 10am-5pm; www.gulfofgeorgiacannery.org), including one that brings the machines back to life. Nearby, the small Japanese village fills out the picture of life in a fishing village at the turn of the century, where fishermen got by despite government bureaucrats placing quotas on the number of fishing permits allowed to Japanese immigrants.

All Japanese communities along the coast were dealt a more severe blow when the government began forcibly evacuating Japanese families from coastal areas during World War II. Virtually the entire village of Steveston was evacuated, and all its boats and fishing equipment was confiscated. Many people were interned in camps in northern Ontario and central Alberta. Freed after the war, many returned to Steveston.

Today Steveston is a great place to browse in the shops and wander down to the wharves where the day's catch of salmon, tuna, snapper, prawns, crab, and herring is sold right off the boat.

The **George C. Reifel Migratory Bird Sanctuary** (daily 9am-4pm) on **Westham Island** Ⓟ at the mouth of the Fraser River supports the winter home of the snow goose, and the largest wintering population of waterfowl in Canada. The 300-hectare (850-acre) habitat and estuarine marsh serves as a sanctuary to more than 195 regularly occurring species of bird.

In November, vast flocks of migrating lesser snow geese arrive from their Arctic breeding grounds. The flocks then split up, with up to 65,000 birds remaining here for the winter, while the balance head south to the Sacramento river Valley in California. While the snow geese are dramatic by virtue of their numbers, there are a host of other exciting species to see for avid birders and neophytes alike. In spring, millions of western sandpipers pass through, along with hawks, eagles, cormorants, and ospreys, these latter birds following the salmon as they make their way down the Fraser to the ocean. Midsummer, close to 50 species can be spotted, including elegant sandhill cranes, often accompanied by gawky offspring.

⊙ Tip

Westham Island, site of the Reifel bird sanctuary, is also a great spot for picking up fresh fruits, vegetables, honey, and even award-winning fruit wines.

Whistler Village.

WINES OF BRITISH COLUMBIA

It may come as a surprise to some that British Columbia produces wine at all, let alone world-class wine.

Compared to other areas like California, Washington, even Ontario in eastern Canada, production is small, and the majority of the province's wine is enthusiastically consumed at home. But B.C. wines – especially those of the Okanagan Valley – have received accolades in the most distinguished circles. A breakthrough came in 1994 when a Chardonnay from the Okanagan Valley's Mission Hill Estate Winery captured the Avery's Trophy for Best Chardonnay at the UK's prestigious International Wine and Spirit Competition.

The real turning point for B.C. wines took place earlier still. It was prompted by the 1988 Free Trade Agreement, which stripped away the protected status enjoyed by Canada's largely moribund wine

Blasted Church vineyard.

industry. By 1990, barely 560 hectares (1,400 acres) of vines were left in B.C. after the government paid to have two-thirds of them pulled out. Since then, the B.C. wine industry has reinvented itself by taking simple steps: planting the right clones of the right premium varietals on the right plots of land; attracting talented winemakers and giving them the resources to build state-of-the-art facilities; and establishing a structure to allow small estate wineries to flourish. It's a small but impressive wine industry. The Vintners Quality Alliance (VQA) appellation system was established in 1990 to ensure origin and quality of B.C.-produced wines. This "branding" of B.C. wine made it easy for consumers to choose wines with varietal character; it gave consumers the confidence to take a chance on B.C. wines.

More than ninety percent of B.C.'s wine is produced in the Okanagan Valley, a region of distinct microclimates and diverse soil types, stretching over 160km (100 miles) from north of Lake Okanagan to the US border. Nestled between mountain and lakes, the region now has more than 3,200 hectares (8,000 acres) dedicated to grape growing, and is expanding rapidly. There are now in the range of 120 wineries in the Okanagan Valley compared to 14 before Free Trade, and scores more in other pockets of the province. They range from exclusive boutique wineries to large-scale operations, with varietals from Merlot and Chardonnay to Syrah, Sangiovese, and even Malbec. The winemakers are learning which grapes suit which terrain. Where the land and climate are not hospitable to grapes, tree fruits and berries alike are coaxed into quite acceptable fruit wines.

How can a region so far north produce such great wines? Start with near-desert conditions, more so in the south. Add hot, dry summers with long hours of sunlight, and lengthy hang time in the autumn. Of course, the moderating influence of the lakes and the protection of the mountains help. Pick a suitable location, a cliff or a hillside, irrigate sufficiently, and healthy grapes are certain. When the weather drops below freezing, some of the vines are at risk, but the prudent viticulturist knows which varietals can tolerate the colder plots of land – it's all factored into their choice of plantings.

Touring a few wineries from the hot, arid south to the wetter, cooler north of the Okanagan:

Osoyoos: Nk'Mip Cellars, North America's first aboriginal winery, produces superlative Merlot, Chardonnay, and Icewine.

Black Sage and the Golden Mile: In this area, reds and whites are produced with bright, intense fruit flavors. Much-awarded Tinhorn Creek Vineyards offer great value across the board, with a Cabernet Franc that wows in some vintages. The on-site restaurant Miradoro provides the perfect place to dine and taste while overlooking the Golden Mile. Black Hills is known for its iconic "Nota Bene," but its Carmanere and white blend ("Alibi") are worth trying as well.

Okanagan Falls: Blasted Church may have fanciful labels, but those in the know choose the wines for their consistent quality. Wild Goose can't compete on labels, but their wines, particularly the Pinot Blanc and Gewurztraminer, are exceptional and frequent gold winners at international competitions.

Naramata Bench: Wineries dot winding roads and picturesque rural countryside, each with an impressive offering, from Lake Breeze, named the 2016 'Best Small Winery' in British Columbia, and its stunning Pinot Gris and Pinot Blanc to Nichol Vineyard with its shockingly good Syrah. Other must-taste wines come from Poplar Grove and Kettle Valley.

Summerland: Sumac Ridge, one of the original 14 wineries, offers superb wines as well as great food on a picture-perfect patio. A bit further south, Thornhaven produces fine Pinot Noir.

Westside: Two must-see wineries are on the slopes of Mount Boucherie. Unveiled in 2003, Mission Hill's grand mission-style winery with a 12-story bell tower sits dramatically above Lake Okanagan. Quails' Gate, a highly regarded medium-sized winery surrounded by sweeping vineyards, features the elegant Old Vines Patio & Restaurant.

Kelowna and Lake Country: The first vines in B.C. were planted in Kelowna by Father Pandosy, who established a mission in 1859. B.C.'s oldest continuously operating winery, Calona Vineyards, produces premium wines under the "Sandhill Vineyard" label. One of Okanagan's most acclaimed wineries, Cedar Creek offers brilliantly crafted wines. A champion of organic grape growing, Summerhill Pyramid Winery practices what it preaches both in the winery and at the Summerhill Sunset Bistro with innovative organic cuisine.

A bit further afield, but on the way if you take the scenic route between Vancouver and the Okanagan:

Similkameen Valley: West of the Okanagan Valley, this narrow stretch of lowland, lined with tall mountains, is home to newer wineries, including Corcelettes Winery with its fine Pinot Noir, Merlot and Cabernet Sauvignon/Syrah wines.

The wineries in the rest of the province are worth exploring, but you may find you are tasting wines that are partly made from grapes from the Okanagan, as winemakers try to produce something to sell in the tasting room while their vines mature. Still, at these smaller operations, chances are you may get to meet the owners and see the passion in their faces as they tell you about their babies.

Wine festivals take place in BC throughout the year, one of the most famous being the Okanagan Fall Wine Festival, which takes place all through the valley in early autumn.

Useful websites:
www.winebc.com
www.winesofcanada.com
www.johnschreiner.blogspot.com
www.thewinefestivals.com

Ripe for the Icewine harvest, Okanagan Valley, British Columbia.

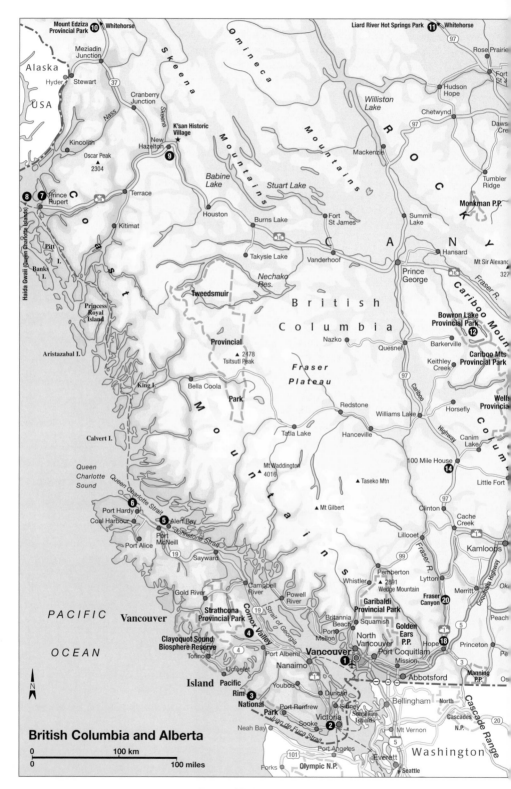

Mount Edziza Provincial Park **10** Whitehorse

Liard River Hot Springs Park **11** Whitehorse

Rose Prairie

97

Meziadin Junction

O m i n e c a

Fort St J

Alaska

Hyder • Stewart

37

Cranberry Junction

S k e e n a

Williston Lake

Hudson Hope

USA

Chetwynd

97

Daws Cre

New Hazelton

K'san Historic Village ★

9

M o u n t a i n s

Mackenzie

Kincolith

Oscar Peak ▲ 2304

R

O

C

Tumbler Ridge

Babine Lake

Stuart Lake

Monkman P.P.

8 7 Prince Rupert

Terrace

16

Houston

Burns Lake

Fort St James

Summit Lake

Hansard

K

Haida Gwaii (Queen Charlotte Islands)

Kitimat

16

Takysie Lake

Vanderhoof

Mt Sir Alexand 327

Banks I.

Pitt I.

S

Nechako Res.

Tweedsmuir

British

Prince George

16

Cariboo Moun

Fraser R.

Princess Royal Island

t

Columbia

Bowron Lake Provincial Park

12

Aristazabal I.

Provincial

▲ 2478 Tsitsutl Peak

Nazko

Quesnel

Barkerville

Cariboo Mts Provincial Park

King I.

Bella Coola

Fraser Plateau

97

Keithley Creek

Calvert I.

M

Park

Redstone

Williams Lake

Horsefly

Wells Provincia

Cariboo

Highway

Canim Lake

Tatla Lake

Hanceville

Colum

Queen Charlotte Sound

o

Mt Waddington ▲ 4016

▲ Taseko Mtn

100 Mile House

14

Little Fort

Queen Charlotte Strait

6

Port Hardy

Coal Harbour

5 Alert Bay

▲ Mt Gilbert

Clinton

97

Cache Creek

Port McNeill

u

Lillooet

1

Port Alice

19

Johnstone Strait

Sayward

n

99

Fraser R

Kamloops

Gold River

Campbell River

Powell River

Whistler

Pemberton

▲ 2891 Wedge Mountain

Lytton

20

Fraser Canyon

Merritt

Oka

Coquihalla Highway

PACIFIC

Vancouver

Strathcona Provincial Park

t

19

Comox Valley

a

Strait of Georgia

Britannia Beach

Squamish

Garibaldi Provincial Park

Golden Ears P.P.

5

Peach

Clayoquot Sound Biosphere Reserve

4

Port Mellon

North Vancouver

Hope

18

Princeton

Pa

OCEAN

Tofino

4

Port Alberni

n

Vancouver 1

Port Coquitlam

Mission

3

Nanaimo

1

Abbotsford

Manning P.P.

Os

N

Island Pacific

Youbou

Duncan

Bellingham

North

Rim

3

Sidney

Saltspring Islands

Cascades N.P.

20

National

Park

Port Renfrew

Victoria

2

Mt Vernon

Cascade Range

Neah Bay

Sooke

Juan de Fuca Strait

5

British Columbia and Alberta

101

Port Angeles

Washington

0 _____ 100 km

Forks

Olympic N.P.

Everett

0 _____ 100 miles

Seattle

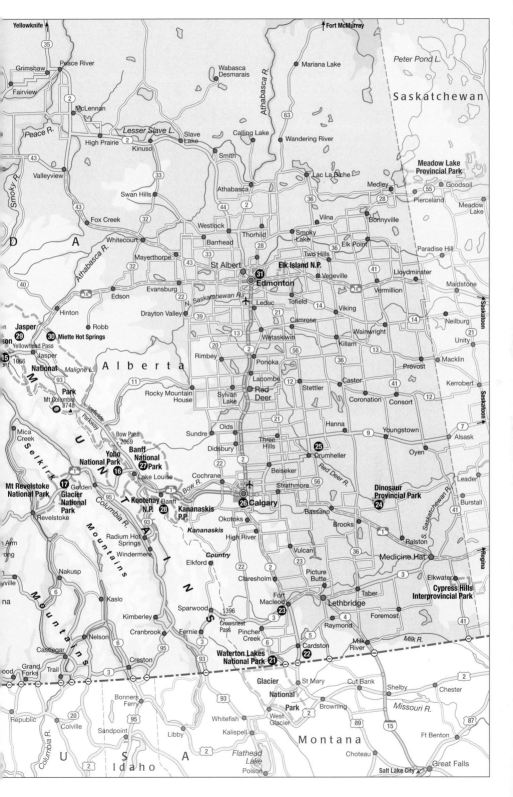

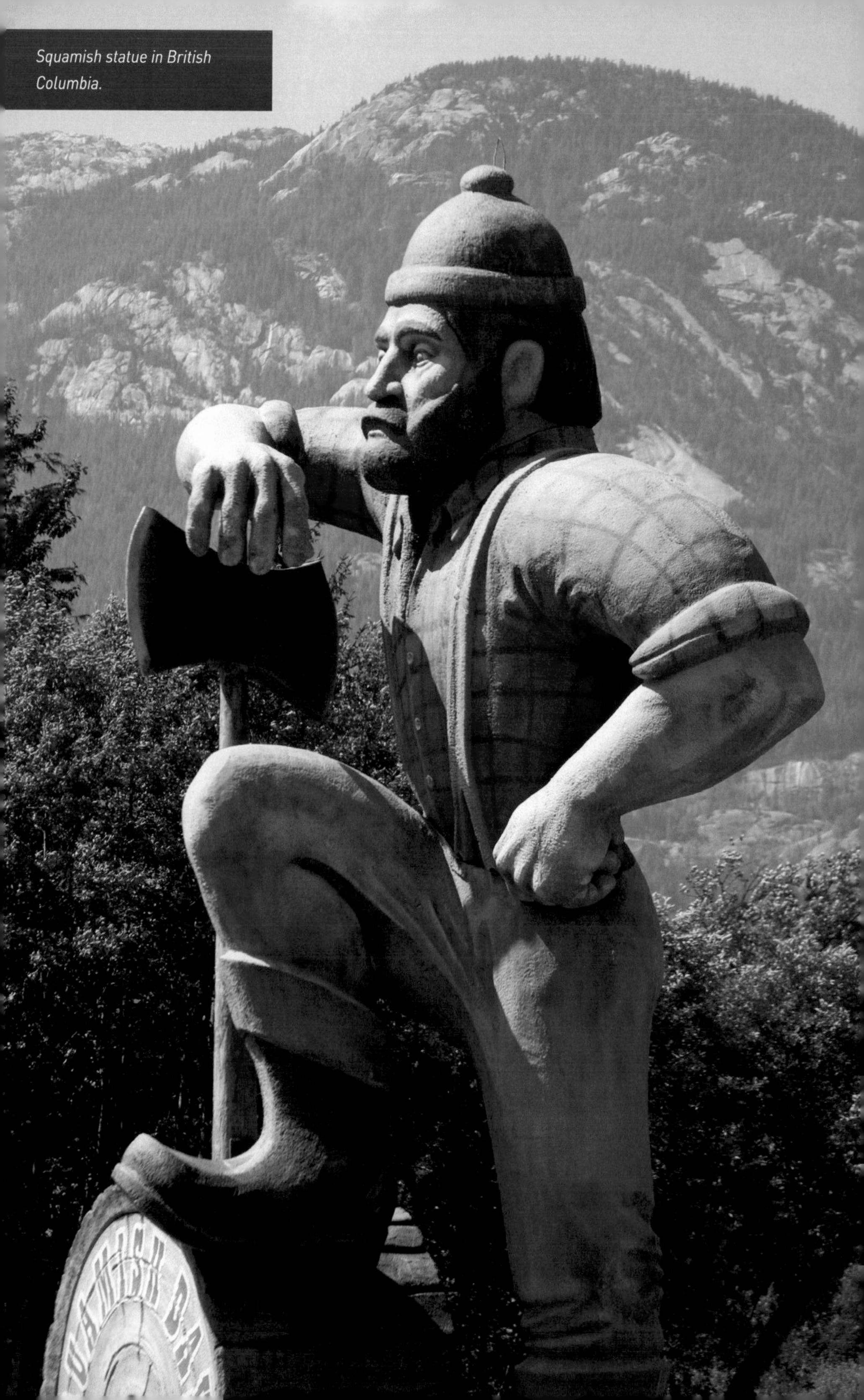

Squamish statue in British Columbia.

BRITISH COLUMBIA

People are drawn to the overwhelming natural beauty of British Columbia – its rocky coastline and thick forests, teeming mountains, mild temperatures – and to its relaxed lifestyle.

Almost half the people who live in British Columbia (B.C.) were born somewhere else. With its diverse interests and great beauty, the area has attracted health enthusiasts, diehard hippies, monarchists, trade unionists, and profit-oriented businesspeople. Nearly 5 million residents can't be wrong about B.C.'s appeal. Nor can the millions of visitors who come to explore **Vancouver ❶** and the surrounding province each year.

The natural beauty and the hospitable climate prompted many First Nations peoples to settle all along the Pacific coast. Each community developed its own unique and complex lifestyle based on the assured harvest of the annual salmon runs, and the abundance of forest products. They developed intricate trading relationships with both coastal neighbors and inland nations.

Today, pride of culture and history is increasing among First Nations communities across the province, as they work to overcome some of the legacies of the prohibition of their culture and the wholesale shipment of their children to residential schools.

For West Coast First Nations, first contact with Europeans came in 1778, when Captain Cook claimed the land for Britain. Over the next century, explorers mapped the interior of the

area, exploring its rugged canyons and raging rivers. Simon Fraser, of Scottish descent, but born in New York during the American Revolution (1776–1862), made the exploration of the northwest his life's work, whilst working for the North West Company. He established the Fraser River as an important fur-trading route.

Fur trading in the 19th century was big business, and the competition for control of this new market marks the early history of British Columbia. The North West Company was chartered

⊙ Main attractions
Victoria
Pacific Rim National Park
Comox Valley
Haida Gwaii
Bowron Lake Provincial Park
Wells Gray Provincial Park
Okanagan Valley

⊙ Maps on pages 268, 272

Enjoying the view.

by the British government specifically to develop the resources of the northwest. The company had to fight for trade routes and profits with the Hudson's Bay Company, an older "eastern" company that already had a monopoly on Canadian trade with Europe.

The Nor'west, as the company became called, established an inland trading post, Fort George, which is now the city of Prince George. The Hudson's Bay Company, being the larger of the two enterprises and appreciating the value of the fur trade as well as the future of lumber and mining, bought out Nor'west in 1821 and maintained virtual monopoly control over the area until 1858.

THE 49TH PARALLEL

In the 19th century, the fur trade along the Columbia River was carried out by a combination of French Canadians and Americans, although the American population grew much faster. The desire of the southerners to control the river trade became increasingly clear. The American battle cry "Fifty-Four-Forty or Fight!" (referring to the latitude that marked the northern boundary of the territory) prompted the British to build Fort Victoria in 1843.

The territory was finally divided in two at the 49th Parallel. This handed most of the Columbia River, and the best fur-trading territory, over to the United States.

The British Loyalists needed to find an "all-British route" inland to the fur trapping territory. In 1856 James Douglas, a bear-like man with political skill, called for Vancouver Island's 774 European immigrants (half of whom were under the age of 20) to elect their first legislature. Two years later Queen Victoria named the region British Columbia and made Douglas the first governor.

GOLD AND ITS AFTERMATH

In April 1856, gold was discovered in the North Thompson river, just above Kamloops. A survey team subsequently reported that there was gold in B.C.

Stacked logs at Merritt lumberyard.

and the rush, in often perilous conditions, was on.

As the mainland developed, the city of Victoria suffered from an economic hangover. Its glory days were over, and the bust that followed the gold rush left Vancouver Island economically dependent on the rest of the colony. New industry was needed to diversify the island's economy and to provide jobs for the thousands of men who didn't make their fortunes in the gold fields of the Cariboo along the upper Fraser River.

Gold was not the first wealth offered by the rich land, it had simply replaced furs. Looking around, the European settlers on Vancouver Island looked at the vast forests and saw the future in lumber. The Alberni Sawmill, the first sawmill west of the Rockies in Canada, was built on Vancouver Island in 1860, on land casually appropriated from the native people. The tension this created was exacerbated by the hierarchy of labor created by the sawmill: "whites" were paid 25 cents an hour to log and work the mill, while "Asians and Indians" were paid a mere 15 cents.

This was not the glorious future imagined by the gold-rushers of 1858. The river beds had been panned out, and working in a sawmill or a gold mine was similar to the factory work they had abandoned to come here: low-wage labor and difficult to get.

The independent spirit of the colony came into harsh conflict with the economic reality of its need for the outside world. With the promise to build a Canadian Pacific Railway, which would link the young city of Vancouver with the rest of Canada, British Columbia became a Canadian province in 1871. It took another 14 years to complete the railway and deliver on the promise. Today, with natural resources subject to currency shifts and other factors influencing commodities, British Columbians have had to diversify away from the lumber and mining industries. While forestry is still important, many mills have closed permanently, leaving rural areas to shift efforts to tourism and other service industries.

> **⊙ Fact**
>
> Not only gold, but lumber attracted the Europeans. George Vancouver described the land in the 1860s, "well covered with trees of large growth principally... pine."

Freight train in Canadian Rockies, Banff National Park.

While tourism is generally more environmentally sound, the development of infrastructure has been slow in some areas. It's a province of contrasts, with a cosmopolitan population that sees its future in attracting visitors to enjoy both its modern urban beauty and its remote wilderness.

VICTORIA

Just as the history of British Columbia begins in **Victoria ❷**, the capital is often the "first" city in the province for many tourists. Victoria, a city with the mildest climate in Canada, is located on the southern tip of Vancouver Island approximately 56km (35 miles) from the city of Vancouver, reached by navigating past the lush Gulf Islands. The most common access is via BC Ferries, large car ferries that travel to the outskirts of Victoria from the major terminal south of Vancouver called Tsawwassen. It is also accessible from Seattle by passenger ferry. Although this proximity to its southern US neighbor should imply shared characteristics, Victoria is not only thoroughly Canadian, it is more British than most other places in Canada. Some would say it is more British than Britain.

The **Parliament Buildings ❹** (mid-May to early Sept daily 9am–5pm, early Sept to mid-May Mon–Fri 9am–5pm; www.leg.bc.ca; free) make an excellent place to begin a tour of this province. Built in 1897, they were erected by someone with a playful sense of what might best evoke merry old England. There is a bit of London's St Paul's Cathedral in the huge central dome topped by a gilded statue of Captain George Vancouver. The neo-Romanesque arched entrance recalls London's Natural History Museum, and the smaller domed turrets suggest an Englishman's castle. The fairytale effect is enhanced at night when thousands of light bulbs outline the building.

But if the political rhetoric there proves tiresome, instant relief can be found by joining people who still celebrate the British monarchy in style at the **Fairmont Empress ❺**. Named after Queen Victoria, Empress of India,

Victoria's Legislative Building.

the hotel was designed by English-born Francis Rattenbury and completed in 1908 at a cost of $750,000. It was designated as a National Historic Site of Canada in 1981. It has been renovated numerous times, the latest in 2016–17, when it underwent an extensive $30 million restoration during which a new lobby lounge, spa, and restaurant were added. Afternoon tea is a major tourist attraction, drawing over 100,000 people a year. The 464 rooms are refurbished on an ongoing basis, always in keeping with the stature of the building.

Between these two Victorian edifices sits the **Royal British Columbia Museum** (daily 10am–5pm, open until 10pm Fri–Sat in summer; www.royalbcmuseum.bc.ca) with its exceptional First Peoples gallery depicting life both before and after the arrival of Europeans. Its Modern History exhibit spans 200 years of fur-trading, the gold rush, farming, and the influx of immigrants from all over the world. There are also displays covering the natural history of the province and the impact of environmental changes.

History buffs will appreciate **Emily Carr House** (May–Sept ,Tue-Sat 11am–4pm), the artist's childhood abode; **Craigdarroch Castle** (daily 10am–4.30pm, 9am–7pm in summer), the mansion built by a ruthless coal baron in the late 19th century; while, for the nautically inclined, the **Maritime Museum** is worth a visit. A bit further afield, **Fort Rodd Hill** and **Fisgard Lighthouse** (mid-May–mid-Oct daily, mid-Oct–Feb Sat–Sun, Mar–mid-May Wed–Sun) are contained in a park with a long military history and sweeping views across the Strait of Juan de Fuca separating Canada from the US.

Near the Swartz Bay ferry terminal in Sidney, the **Shaw Centre for the Salish Sea** (daily from 10am–4.30pm; www.salishseacentre.org) is an aquarium focused entirely on the astonishingly diverse marine life of the surrounding waters. It's much more of an interactive experience than just looking at sea life in huge tanks, although the tank of Pacific sea nettles is definitely mesmerizing.

The city has several fine art collections – notably the **Art Gallery of**

Eat

Experience the world of gracious living by taking afternoon tea in the Tea Lobby of the Fairmont Empress (served from noon on; reservations required; dress code smart casual).

Victoria harbor at sunset.

Tip

The Swartz Bay ferry terminal is close to Sidney, a perfectly charming seaside spot for coffee and a visit to the Shaw Centre for the Salish Sea.

Greater Victoria ⓓ on Moss Street (mid-May to mid-Sept Mon–Sat 10am–5pm, Thu until 9pm, Sun noon–5pm, mid-Sept to mid-May closed on Mon; www.aggv.ca). The equivalent of Vancouver's Stanley Park, **Beacon Hill Park** ⓔ, east of Douglas Street and south of downtown, offers tranquil visits to see the swans after a busy day of shopping along **Government Street**. For children, a highlight in the park is the petting zoo (daily; requested donation), where the most popular pen is the goat petting area. On weekends, there are often free concerts going on.

North of the city, en route to the ferry terminal, the century-old **Butchart Gardens** (daily) are a world-renowned quarry garden in a 22-hectare (55-acre) display of seasonal splendors. Allow at least a couple of hours to see the garden properly; there are numerous other gardens open to the public that are impressive, but not as large.

Without a doubt, the greatest of the island's offerings are outdoors. In fact, the whole province is a vast fisherman's paradise – saltwater and freshwater fishing, game fishing, and, for those more interested in the results than the process, just plain good eating. On the coast, salmon reigns supreme, followed closely by halibut, which can come in at over 40kg (100lbs). The freshwater angler will find rainbow trout in scores of lakes. Fishing regulations are enforced, so it is essential to obtain proper licenses and understand the rules, which not only limit the time and place one can fish, but also the species and quantities that can be kept.

VANCOUVER ISLAND

A trip to **Barkley Sound** on the west coast of Vancouver Island offers top-notch fishing, and the scenery of the **Pacific Rim National Park** ❸ (year-round, fully operational mid-Mar to mid-Oct). Here is an excellent view of the Pacific Coast in all its glory: rocky islands, sea lions playing in the crashing surf, harbor seals hiding in the coves, and sea birds hovering above. The area also holds a wealth of backpacking opportunities. The **Broken Group Islands**, off the southwest coast

Off Botanical Beach, Vancouver Island.

of Vancouver Island, are accessible by boat, and **Long Beach,** on the mainland, has hiking trails and sunsets into the endless Pacific. The small town of Tofino is famous for its surfing; icy waters mean that wetsuits are essential, but countless surf schools make sure their students are safe and successful in their quest to ride the waves. In winter, the massive storms have created another tourist attraction: storm-watching. Tofino gets close to 5 meters (16ft) of rain annually, and most of it comes down between November and March. Choose a hotel that has ocean views from the rooms in case it is just too inhospitable to go outside.

While the 75km (46-mile) **West Coast Trail** (May–Sept; reservations to hike are mandatory) is the serious hiker's dream, it is suitable for experts only – it is defined by steep hills, narrow, muddy paths, nearly impenetrable forests, and stretches along the beach that can only be traversed at low tide. The trail offers spectacular views of gray whales, sea lions, seals, rock formations, and two lighthouses.

More civilized backpacking and hiking is available in any of British Columbia's numerous provincial parks. They offer excellent views, trails, and invigorating exercise, as well as a closeness to nature that can make every tree seem like a unique experience in color.

Between Vancouver Island and Vancouver, the stunning **Gulf Islands** offer unique communities, known for their laid-back lifestyles and sometimes eccentric inhabitants. The islands share the same gentle climate as Victoria, offering up rugged, forested coastlines that appeal to sailors and kayakers alike. The larger islands have regularly scheduled ferry services. It's a good idea to make reservations for all ferries around weekends during summer.

The east coast of Vancouver Island is the more populated part of the island outside Victoria, with pockets of retirement communities dotted along the coast. As one of the most hospitable places in Canada's often brutal winters, this is where people from the prairies and even farther afield choose

Totem poles in B.C.

Long Beach, Vancouver Island.

⊘ LONG BEACH

Some of the most spectacular scenery in British Columbia lies along the west coast of Vancouver Island. The towns of Tofino and Ucluelet effectively bookend Long Beach, where brave souls in wetsuits surf and children build sandcastles. In winter, storm-watching tourists keep hotels and restaurants busy along this tourist-driven area.

To the north, the Clayoquot Sound was recognized by the United Nations in 2000 as a World Biosphere Reserve, a refuge for thousands of gray whales and hundreds of thousands of shore birds that migrate along the Pacific coast. The people of the Nuu-Chah-Nulth First Nations, protectors of the lands that have been inhabited for at least 5,000 years, are also amazing artists, creating spectacular carved masks and bentwood boxes.

⊘ Tip

The best time to sail north from Port Hardy to Prince Rupert along the Inside Passage is in summer, when the ferry makes the 15-hour trip in daylight.

to retire, with dreams of year-round golf and no snow to shovel.

The first scars the forestry industry etched into the landscape while opening up the dense forests in the 20th century are fading. First growth forest is rare, and much of the second growth has been harvested, with replanting creating homogeneous carpets of trees, a contrast with the unlogged jumble of cedar, hemlock, spruce, along with numerous deciduous species. Logging, although much reduced, still continues here; the big upsides are employment in a generally depressed area, as well as a network of logging roads that offer an excellent entree into the back woods. Locals are very careful about which roads they use and when, as an encounter with a logging truck on a one-lane active road is potentially fatal. Active logging roads are generally identified, but caution is still essential.

The east coast of Vancouver Island offers at least a day or two of adventure for nature lovers. Instead of the main highway, the oceanside route weaves its way much closer to the

St John the Divine church and museum at Yale, north of Hope.

ocean, offering up the sandy beaches at Parksville and Qualicum for an impromptu picnic.

The **Comox Valley** ❹ is home to an extensive ski resort, Mount Washington. In summer, the walking trails and hiking seem custom-designed for every level of fitness and ambition. There are wooden walkways through the meadows that branch off to steeper more remote areas, each one promising a spectacular vista. At the end of the day, the three communities of Comox, Courtenay, and Cumberland that lie below the mountain each offer their own appeal and attractions.

Mostly, the Comox Valley is about the scenery and outdoor activity. While most active communities boast of their triathlon or marathon, the Snow to Surf race held in late April has a bit of everything to challenge an athlete. Teams of nine people compete: A downhill skier runs in ski boots up a slope at Mount Washington, races down the run to hand off a baton to a cross-country skier, who speeds through an 8km (5-mile) course to hand off to a runner,

⊘ TIDAL WATERS

The waters between Vancouver Island and the mainland generate tides that can exceed 5 meters (16ft). Beachcombers at low tide will find much more than beach glass and driftwood. At Kye Bay, just outside Comox, the herons, kingfishers, eagles, ravens, sea ducks, gulls, and assorted shore birds ensure that even a casual birder can tally 15 species on an afternoon stroll at low tide. The marine biologist in the family will be enchanted by thousands of sand dollars, gigantic moon snails, starfish in shades of purple and orange, snails, chitin, barnacles, oysters, clams, and cockles. Crab shells accumulated at the base of a one of the glacial erratics (massive rocks left when the last ice age retreated) may signify an octopus's lair.

who starts running down the mountain, handing off after 7 or 8km (5 miles) to a second runner who heads off on a logging road for about the same distance, leading to the start of the mountain bike leg of the race. Tired yet? The mountain biker heads up into forest trails, for a 12km (7.5-mile) ride, including some single track – a bit difficult when there are more than 180 teams on the track. A kayaker awaits at one end of Comox Lake, paddling about 5km (3 mile) to the starting point of the road cyclists, who have a short 30km (19-mile) ride down to the water, where two canoeists patiently wait their turn. As the last leg, the 5km (3-mile) paddle in Comox Bay ends at the Comox marina, where team members have congregated to cheer the canoes at the finish line.

This may seem silly, but the fact that every year more teams want to compete than can be accommodated does underscore the general level of fitness of the community, as well as the ample opportunity to experience the outdoors.

Heading toward the top of the island, stop at **Port McNeill**, 350km (217 miles) north of Victoria, and take the short ferry to **Alert Bay** ❺ for a chance to see important art forms of the northwest in the right context: totem poles and masks. Alert Bay is a Kwakwaka'wakw village that dates back more than 8,000 years, and one of the best accessible places to see totem poles, including the world's tallest (56 meters/173ft). The masks and other pieces on display at the **U'mista Cultural Centre** (July–Labor Day daily 9am–5pm, early Sept–June closed Sun-Mon; www.umista.ca) tell the heartbreaking story of the prohibition of potlatch, the traditional gathering outlawed by government in 1884, labeling it "immoral" and "heathen." Potlatch went underground, but in 1921, the activity was captured and masks and regalia confiscated. Some masks and other pieces were sold, while some were sent off to museums. After the law restricting potlatch was finally abolished in 1951, efforts began to recover the pieces, which by then were dispersed as far away as England. Most of the collection has been returned and it now represents a focal point of a people

Zip wiring in the British Columbia wilderness.

⊘ Tip

Popular with climbers and hikers, Glacier National Park on the Trans-Canada Highway has more than 130 glaciers, best seen by taking a mapped trail. Be warned, though – the terrain here is steep and most of the hikes in the park are ranked as challenging.

Fishing on the Fraser river.

proud of their heritage and committed to preserving it. In summer only, the T'sasala Dance Group performs magnificent traditional Kwakwaka'wakw dances that are well worth the visit (July–Aug Thu–Sat at 1pm).

UP THE PACIFIC COAST

The best way to see the coast in all its lush-green mountainous glory is to take the trip on the **Prince Rupert Ferry**. Once the only way to get from Victoria to Prince Rupert or Alaska, the B.C. Inside Passage route ferry still makes the 15-hour journey, leaving from **Port Hardy** ❻ at the northern tip of Vancouver Island (reservations required). In summer (mid-May to Sept), the trip is scheduled to take advantage of the long days. In winter, the same trip is scheduled for night, stopping in a few more ports and stretching to 22 hours.

From **Prince Rupert** ❼ another seven-hour ferry will take travelers to spectacular **Haida Gwaii** ❽ (formerly known as the **Queen Charlotte Islands**), a collection of more than 150 islands located

about 200km (125 miles) offshore. At **Skidegate**, the **Haida Heritage Centre** (July–Aug daily 9am-6pm, Thu until 8pm, Sept 9am-5pm, Oct-Apr Tue–Sat 9.30am–5pm, May Mon–Sat 9am–5pm, June Mon–Sat 9am–6pm; www.haidaheritagecentre.com) showcases the woodcarving, craftsmanship, and culture of the Haida peoples, who have lived here for more than 12,000 years. The beaches at **Sandspit** are where legend says the raven *Ne-kil-stlas* landed and discovered a cockle shell that contained the first people – the origin of the human race.

Back on the mainland, it is possible to visit a number of other sites where native carving is practiced, including 'Ksan (year-round; charge for guided tour) near **New Hazelton** ❾, where the Gitxsan people work in a full-size recreation of a traditional native village.

NORTHERN LAKE COUNTRY

Heading inland from Prince Rupert the amount of open land becomes overwhelming. The choice of direction is limited by the distinct lack of roads. Aside from the main East/West

⊘ THE GOLD RUSH TRAIL

The forested plateau of the Cariboo, lying north of Lillooet, between the Coast Mountains and the Cariboo Mountains, may not be the most scenically spectacular region of British Columbia, but its rich history more than compensates the visitor.

Gold was discovered in the area in the late 1850s, but it was in 1862 that Billy Barker, a Cornish sailor, struck the vast quantities at Williams Creek that sparked the Cariboo Gold Rush. Boom towns such as Barkerville appeared within months, and a 640km (400-mile) supply road was constructed in a remarkable feat of engineering along the inhospitable Fraser river canyon from Yale in the south. At its peak, some 10,000 people lived in Barkerville, not only fortune-seeking gold prospectors, but also every kind of support service, from saloon to general store, from church to post office. But within 10 years the gold deposits were exhausted.

Today Highway 97 and Highway 26 follow the route of the original Cariboo Highway to Barkerville, restored as a living museum with all the atmosphere of a gold-rush town (mid-May to late Sept daily 8am–8pm; www.barkerville.ca). Among the original buildings there are stores, saloons, and hotels; from May to September, there are in-depth tours of the town and activities for all ages. In winter, visitors are free to wander amongst the buildings at no charge.

Highway (the Yellowhead Highway 16), most are unpaved and only one-and-a-half lanes wide, designed for logging rather than for tourism.

One of the longest and most beautiful roads north is Highway 37 from **Terrace**, which takes more than 12 hours of driving before intersecting the Alaska Highway near **Watson Lake**, Yukon. It offers numerous side trips, including **Mount Edziza Provincial Park** (no vehicle access; entrance on foot, horseback, or float plane) and the town of **Stewart**. From Stewart one can cross over to **Hyder**, Alaska, where viewing platforms allow observers to see both grizzlies and black bears fishing for salmon at the river's edge. The road to Stewart passes through the Cambria snowfield and offers spectacular views of **Bear Glacier**.

Aside from bears, everything from moose and caribou to the bald eagle can be seen here. The lakes to the south have rainbow, lake , and brook trout, and the delicious Dolly Varden – a member of the char family, not as heavy as salmon, but meatier than trout. Farther north in the **Peace River Area** the fishing action turns to the arctic grayling and the northern pike.

One wonderful stop in the northeast corner of the province is the remote **Liard River Hot Springs Park** ⓫ (year-round) at Mile 493 of the Alaska Highway. The springs are naturally heated, slightly sulfurous pools of water, surrounded by orchids and tropical vines as thick as the northern forests just a few yards away. The water is over 43°C (110°F) and has created a microclimate. It is so relaxing, and almost impossible to get up the steps out of the water. The Alpha pool remains open while the Beta pool was closed in 2013 following a bear attack.

CARIBOO GOLD RUSH ROUTE

South of **Prince George**, through **Quesnel** and south all the way to **Cache Creek**, travelers can trace the history of the gold rush. The **Cariboo Highway** now follows roughly the same route as the old Cariboo Wagon Road. Ironically, the completion of the road, as well as the exhaustion of easily panned gold,

Backpacking through Monkman Provincial Park.

helped to end the frontier phase of the gold rush and made way for more organized shaft-mining operations. While gold continued to be mined in quantity until the 1870s, the romance was gone.

The fact that the rush is over should not discourage tourists from trying their hand at panning for wealth at historic **Barkerville**, a reconstructed gold-rush ghost town with dance hall girls and plenty of western fun. The town is open all year round to visit the outside of the buildings, but is really "open" in summer only (mid-May to Sept). Two days' panning might generate enough "dust" to buy a newspaper back in Vancouver. Visitors may prefer to hike along the streams that have beds of raw jade stone, although the green stone might not be as impressive as the gold. Nearby **Bowron Lake Provincial Park** ⓬ (year-round, camping mid-May to Sept) offers a famous collection of interlocking lakes for canoe enthusiasts. The circuit takes 6–10 days, depending on skill level. The park is a wildlife sanctuary, and it's

not unusual to see deer, moose, bears, and caribou. The forest cover is mainly white spruce and alpine fir.

Campgrounds abound in the many provincial parks in this area. One of the largest is the **Wells Gray Provincial Park** ⓭ (year-round, camping May–Oct). It has all the beauty that the rest of B.C. has shown, along with old homesteads abandoned by families that did not survive the 19th-century frontier days. There are five major lakes here as well as a multitude of waterfalls and rapids.

This is also cowboy country, where much of the province's cattle industry is located. Here travelers are able to see modern-day cowboys, in addition to helping the area to celebrate the old glories with rodeos and horseback riding. The hub of much of this summer activity is **100 Mile House** ⓮, which started as a stagecoach rest stop during the gold rush. One of the original Barnard Express stagecoaches is on display at the north end of town. Winter activities include snowmobiling, dog sledding, ice-fishing, and cross-country skiing.

Continuing south and west, all roads begin to lead to Vancouver, but there is still plenty to see in the areas that border the US. For example, while Banff and Jasper in Alberta are more famous, there is no denying the beauty of the **British Columbia Rockies**, and the parks that preserve it are well worth visiting: **Mount Robson Provincial Park** ⓯ contains the highest point in the Canadian Rockies, while **Yoho** ⓰ and **Glacier** ⓱ **National Parks** have camping, skiing, and views of snowfields. Heading back toward Vancouver via **Hope** ⓲ along the four-lane divided Coquihalla Highway is both fast and scenic.

LAND OF FRUIT AND WINES

About four or five hours east of Vancouver by car, the geography begins to change. The rainfall is less frequent,

Cowboy country.

there are arid hills and even sagebrush. This is Canada's best-known fruit belt – the Okanagan Valley. Water from **Okanagan Lake ⓳** is used for irrigation and, combined with long hot sunny days, creates a lush garden. Apples, peaches, plums, grapes, cherries, apricots, and pears all grow here in abundance. The area is also known for its sandy beaches and lakes. Kelowna is the marketing center for the Okanagan fruit belt and is famous for its **regattas** held throughout the summer. Unfortunately, it feels more like an endless collection of big box stores along a strip of road punctuated by stop lights. The smaller towns along the road between Kelowna and Osoyoos, nestled up against the US border, are much more interesting. Here, the pace is less frenetic and the people friendlier. Penticton has two beaches, one fronting on Okanagan Lake and Skaha Lake. On the east side of town, a lovely winding road leads along the Naramata Bench, where vineyards compete for the best view over the lake.

The valley is a destination for wine lovers, who compare the wines and the valley to Napa Valley of the 1980s, full of potential and excitement. Scores of wineries propose tastings and wine sales. (See page 266 for more detail on the wines of British Columbia.)

The particular appeal to this area is the abundance of lakes warm enough to play in all summer long, a short distance from the mountains that offer great skiing in winter.

Down in the southeast corner of the province, **Nelson** grew up as supply town to the gold miners. Nelson has more than 300 heritage buildings, which is probably one reason why the town has served as a backdrop to several feature films. It's a small town that seems to live in a time warp, but a good one – with great food and a focus on lifestyle, culture, and the outdoors, the people who live here seem to have everything – and they know what a good life they have.

The whole province seems to offer up beautiful routes just to drive along. Highway 3, the "Crowsnest Highway," offers spectacular views for those not in a hurry – most of the road is two lanes, so a slow-moving camper can hold up the traffic. Closer to Vancouver, the Duffey Lake Road is essentially an extension of Highway 99 from Vancouver to Whistler (also known as the Sea to Sky Highway). It's a part of what is known as the Coast Mountain Circle Tour, a 600–700km (370–435-mile) trip that is well worth the time it takes. The road is winding and feels isolated, a real chance to enjoy the province's natural beauty. This road is well loved by motorcyclists, who enjoy taking the loop in both directions – the view and the feel of the road is quite different each way. Taking the whole loop will also give you a wonderful treat, driving through the **Fraser Canyon ⓴**, where it's easy to imagine the early Scottish explorers making their way through the wilds, not exactly sure where they were headed.

The mountains of British Columbia.

📷 FLORA AND FAUNA

Stretching from the 49th Parallel to the North Pole, western Canada provides diverse habitats for a rich array of plants and wildlife.

Western Canada is blessed with a multitude of different environments. The north has tundra and some of the continent's loftiest mountains, while the south includes prairie grasslands, thousands of lakes, and mountain ranges. It even has the northern tip of the central American desert, and yet a few hundred kilometers away you can find lush temperate rainforest. Given this huge assembly of habitats, western Canada's flora ranges from lichens clinging to permanently frozen rocks through varieties of cacti and lush ferns to such exotica as rhododendrons, azaleas, and wild orchids. Perhaps most striking are the fir trees and aspens which make up forests stretching to the horizon.

TRADITIONAL EMBLEMS

In spring, Canada bursts into color with a host of wild flowers, in the north with the Yukon's brilliant pink fireweed and the Northwest Territories' pretty mountain avens. The western dogwood is British Columbia's floral representative, Alberta has the wild rose, Saskatchewan the prairie lily, and Manitoba the prairie crocus. Among its fauna, beavers are traditionally recognized as Canada's emblem because their valuable pelts were a major stimulus to early exploration. Their dams and intricate lodges are readily apparent, as are the stumps of trees they harvest with sharp incisors.

Above the timber line in the Rockies, and across Arctic Canada, a wide variety of plants, especially alpine fireweed, survive freezing winters to burst into bloom in the summer months.

Hunting and disease have seriously depleted bison populations and those that remain in Canada can be found in protected areas and parks.

The bald eagle, symbol of the United States, is common along Canada's Pacific coastline. Although no longer endangered, the eagle is a protected species.

A bear in remote Ontario.

Running Wild in Canada's Parks

The national and provincial parks of Canada provide natural habitats for many species. For spectacular beauty, rich in wildlife, few areas in the world can match the Yukon's Kluane National Park, with its herds of Dall sheep, mountain goats, caribou, and bears.

While black bears are found all over Canada, grizzlies are confined to the forests and scrub lands of the West. Many are regular campground visitors, so it's wise to heed the rangers' warnings – even baby bears should be considered dangerous, since they are bound to have a very big mom lurking nearby.

White-tailed deer, with Bambi-like spotted fawns, are commonplace in the parks. So are the huge, prehistoric-looking moose, readily spotted in the swamplands. In the Rocky Mountains' parks there are elk, wild goats, and mountain sheep, coyotes, and wolf. Cats, including lynx and cougars, are there, but rarely seen.

The largest population of bison is in Wood Buffalo National Park on the Northwest Territories/Alberta border. Some 5,600 free-roaming wood bison live here, as do white pelicans, rare whooping cranes, eagles, and wolves, but, since this park is the size of Switzerland, you will need a guide to help you locate them.

Inuits lead safaris across the Arctic in search of polar bears between Oct–Nov.

Colorful maple leaves in Ontario.

Caribou are known as tuktu, or tuktuk, by the Inuit who depended on them for food, clothing, tools, and weapons.

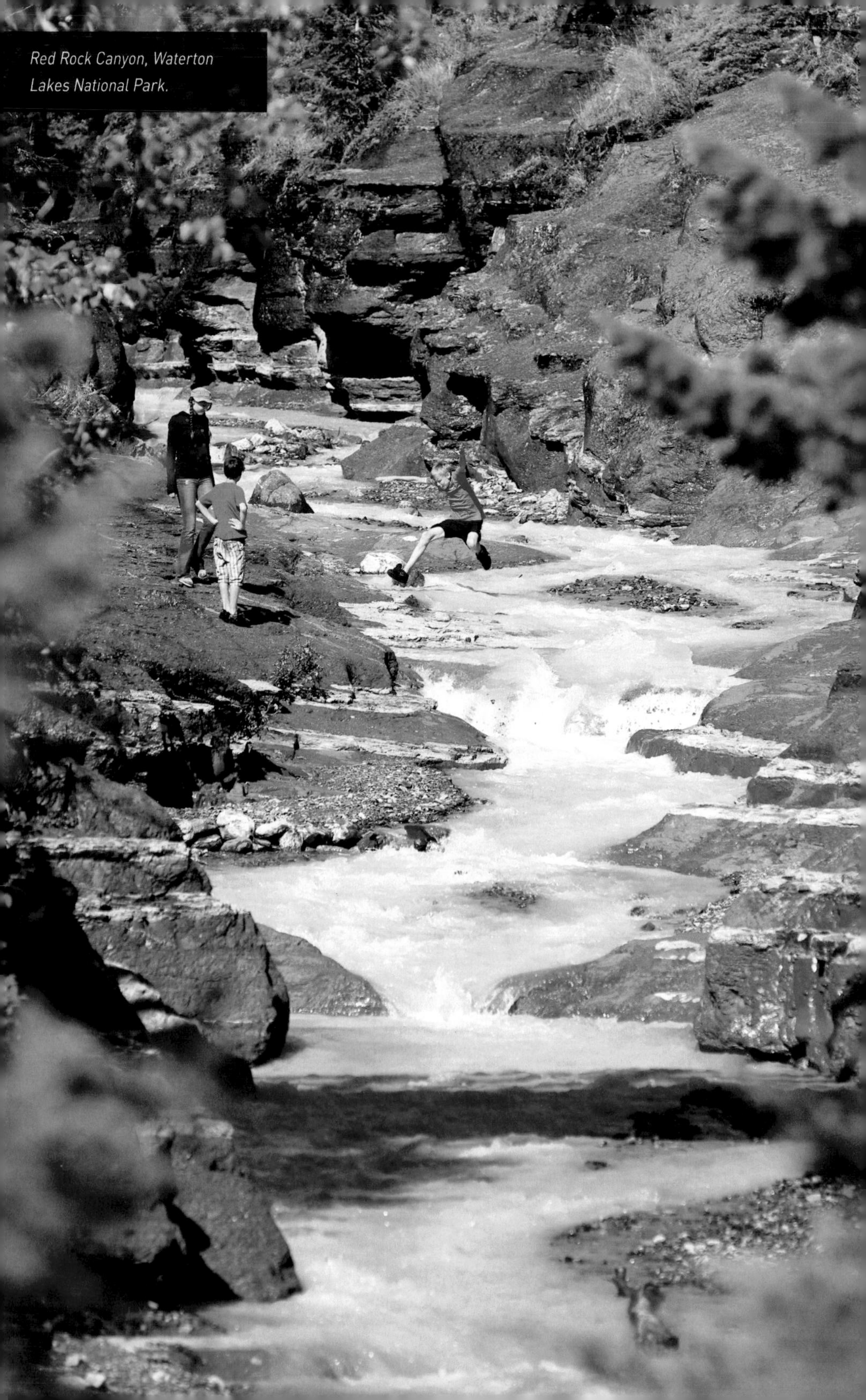

Red Rock Canyon, Waterton Lakes National Park.

ALBERTA

From the soaring peaks of the Rockies to wide open prairies, Alberta is a province of dramatic contrasts. Discover the variety of snow-capped national parks, arid dinosaur trails, modern cities and provincial towns.

If a province could walk, Alberta would swagger just a bit, chest out, chin up, eyes fixed firmly on the future. And why not? It has the best of the west: fertile farmland; oil, gas, and coal in abundance; modern cities like Calgary and Edmonton; and the incomparable blue Canadian Rockies for a playground. Albertans exuberantly inform the rest of the country about the virtues of their province, and their pride sounds to some like flat-out American bragging. The petroleum industry, which fueled Alberta's tremendous economic growth in the 1970s, was founded mostly by American companies that parachuted some of their brightest and sometimes brashest from Texas oil country. Their can-do spirit, essential in a business that rewards risk-takers, seems to have rubbed off on everyone else.

OIL-RICH ALBERTA

Rancher John Lineham didn't risk much when he sank a well in 1902 among the oil-seepage pools along the Akamina Parkway in the southwest corner of the province. The Kutenai, First Nations people in the area, had been using the oil for centuries as a balm to heal wounds. Lineham's well, the first in western Canada, produced 300 barrels a day until the flow ebbed after four years. The site of **Discovery Well** is prominently marked in

Waterton Lakes National Park ㉑, 250km (155 miles) south of Calgary.

The park's landscape changes abruptly from rolling grasslands to snowcapped peaks chiseled by Ice Age glaciers. Boat tours on the lakes pass outstanding glacier-carved formations, including hanging valleys high up mountain walls. A hiking trail winds through **Red Rock Canyon**, streaked with the red, purple, green, and yellow of mineral deposits; another path leads to **Cameron Lake**, a blue gem set in a bowl-shaped valley.

Main attractions
The Rocky Mountains
Alberta Badlands
Calgary
Banff National Park
Jasper National Park
Edmonton

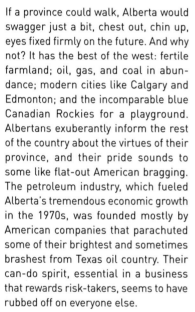

Map on page 268

The famous Calgary Stampede.

Calgary City Hall.

Buffalo skulls at Head Smashed-In Buffalo Jump Centre, Fort Macleod.

Canada's first Mormon temple, a pristine white marble edifice finished in 1913, gleams in the prairie sun at **Cardston ㉒**, 45km (28 miles) east of the park. It was founded by Charles Ora Card, a son-in-law of Brigham Young. Visitors can tour the grounds and Card's 1887 cabin. The Mormons emigrated from Utah in 1887. They developed Canada's first major irrigation project soon after their arrival, digging 96km (60 miles) of canals out from the St Mary River, and growing bumper crops of vegetables.

Less community-minded American immigrants were the traders who came up from Montana in the 1870s to swap furs and buffalo hides with the local native population for a shot of rotgut whiskey. **Fort Macleod ㉓**, 60km (37 miles) north of Cardston, was built in 1874 and manned with North West Mounted Police (precursors to the Royal Canadian Mounted Police) who halted the trade. The Fort Museum tells about daily life around the post; interpretive guides dressed in 1870s police uniforms parade on horseback

(May–June daily 9am–5pm July–Labor Day until 6pm, Sept–Thanksgiving (early October) Wed–Sun 10am–4pm; www.nwmpmuseum.com).

Lethbridge, some 75km (46 miles) northeast of Cardston, is home to the first and most notorious of the whiskey forts the Mounties put out of business, **Fort Whoop-up** (Mon–Sat 10am–5pm, Thu until 9pm, Sun 1–5pm). Nearby, the last major battle between First Nations (the Cree and Blackfoot Nations) in Canada is commemorated at **Indian Battle Park**. Locals claim Lethbridge gets 2,400 hours of sunshine a year, making it one of Canada's sunniest cities. The town's role in a dark chapter of the country's history is brightened by the **Nikka Yuko Japanese Garden** (mid-May–mid-Oct daily 10am–6pm; www.nikkayuko.com), a serene oasis of water, rocks, and willows. The garden was built by the city in 1967 for Canada's centenary, inspired by the contributions of the Japanese Canadians who were interned here during World War II and stayed on to make it their home.

⊙ HEAD-SMASHED-IN

Alberta is home to five of the 19 Unesco World Heritage Sites in Canada, each showcasing fascinating geology and geography. One of these sites falls into the category of "cultural" heritage – Head-Smashed-In Buffalo Jump, near Fort Macleod.

It's a unique opportunity to understand how the Blackfoot and other First Nations lived for close to 6,000 years, herding buffalo past hundreds of stone cairns that guided them into a narrow valley and over a steep cliff to their death, then stripping the carcasses, using every part of the animals. Skeletal remains at the base of the cliff several meters thick, plus a good interpretative center, tell the story of a way of life. An estimated 60–80 million buffalo roamed the North American plains at the time of the arrival of European explorers.

PREHISTORIC FINDS

The **Alberta Badlands**, once part of a subtropical swamp that sheltered a vast array of prehistoric life, contain one of the world's finest repositories of dinosaur fossils. The most spectacular badlands are preserved along the Red Deer river in **Dinosaur Provincial Park 24**, 175km (108 miles) east of Calgary, a Unesco World Heritage Site since 1979. From a lookout near the park entrance, visitors can survey 7,000 hectares (18,000 acres) of this gnarled sandstone landscape with its weirdly eroded formations. A circular 5km (3-mile) drive with side trips on foot leads to dinosaur fossils preserved where they were found. Other areas of the park are accessible on organized bus tours and hikes. Amateur paleontologists can even participate in a real dig for fossils (May–Oct; reservations tel: +1 403-378-4342).

The town of **Drumheller 25**, 138km (86 miles) northeast of Calgary, lies deep within the badlands, which drop abruptly here below the lip of the prairie. The sheer unexpectedness of the scene shocks the eye and delights the imagination. A 48km (30-mile) circular drive called the **Dinosaur Trail** takes motorists from the impressive **Royal Tyrrell Museum of Paleontology** (mid-May–Aug daily 9am–9pm, Sept daily 10am–5pm, Oct–mid-May Tue–Sun 10am–5pm; www. tyrrellmuseum.com), 6km (4 miles) northwest of Drumheller, containing one of the best collections of dinosaur fossils in the world, up to the rim of the mile-wide valley. Highlights of the trip are the lookout at **Horsethief Canyon** and the **Bleriot Ferry** (summer only), one of the last cable ferries in the province.

CALGARY

The city of **Calgary 26** feels different from any other Canadian city. First and foremost, it is a boom and bust town, its rollercoaster ride over the past 50 years closely linked to the price of oil. Suburbs sprawl in all directions, and in boom times, the city lavishly

creates public structures such as the Jack Singer Concert Hall, home of the Calgary Philharmonic Orchestra; and the 17,000-seat Scotiabank **Saddledome**, Calgary's premier sports arena. The arena was built for the hockey and skating competitions of the 1988 Winter Olympics, but it is now better known as the home base for the Calgary Flames hockey team.

When oil prices plummet, Calgarians tighten their belts and demonstrate that pioneer spirit that saw their forefathers through the Depression. There is an eternal optimism that seems to come with the southern Alberta territory – a firm belief that things will turn around. So far they have, and, with each economic recovery, the city seems to jump higher and faster than other Canadian cities, attracting ambitious people with a love of action and excitement.

Part of the price for this rapid growth is downtown congestion. The light rail "C trains" help, and pedestrians have the advantage of elevated promenades. Most of the downtown core is connected by "Plus 15s" – skyways 5

View of the Badlands in Dinosaur Provincial Park.

Tip

Don't miss the Prehistoric Park at Calgary Zoo, with more than 100 species of plants and a collection of life-sized dinosaurs – the triceratops is particularly realistic.

meters (15ft) over the traffic that link office towers, shopping complexes, and hotels. Repairs are performed regularly so always check. At an elevated indoor park called **Devonian Gardens**, office workers on their lunch break brown-bag it on benches scattered amid waterfalls, ponds, and greenery. There is also a five-block pedestrian mall along Stephen Avenue, a civilized thoroughfare of two-story buildings and street-level shops, with benches to sit on and wandering musicians to provide entertainment. It also has convenient entrances to some of the higher-end shopping in the city.

RODEO DAYS

The slicker the city gets, the more it seems to revel in the down home fun of the Calgary Stampede, one of the world's largest rodeo, with $2 million in prize money. For 10 days in early July residents and visitors alike don Stetson hats and cowboy boots and let loose at flapjack breakfasts, square dancing, and parades. Beer flows freely and a party atmosphere pervades the whole city. Long-time residents generally leave town, but it's a great place to get caught up in the romance of the rodeo. The most thrilling and popular event on the **Exhibition Grounds** is chuck-wagon racing.

Pioneer days are also relived at **Heritage Park Historical Village** (mid-May–early Sept daily 10am–5pm, early Sept–early Oct Sat–Sun 10am–5pm; www.heritagepark.ca), on Heritage Drive, an extensive first-rate collection of reconstructed buildings and authentic structures gathered from all over the province. A vintage steam train tours the site, and a replica paddlewheeler plies the **Glenmore Reservoir**.

Delve further into the past at the **Glenbow Museum** (Tue–Sat 9am–5pm, Sun noon–5pm; www.glenbow.org), which displays the best collections of prairie-dwelling First Nations peoples' artifacts in the world. Other sections of the museum show what the early lives of settlers were like and how oil exploration and cattle ranching fostered the strong survival instinct that pervades the Alberta approach to life.

Moraine Lake, Banff National Park.

If Calgary's hectic pace becomes overwhelming, a visit to the **Calgary Zoo** (daily 9am–5pm) will put things back in perspective. The zoo spans **St George's Island** in the Bow river and a huge swath of land on the north side of the river. There is a comfortable transition from the present to the past, with life-size reproductions of dinosaurs occupying their own piece of the park, adjacent to the Canadian Wilds exhibit, which boasts endangered species like the whooping crane, along with the ever-popular bears, bison, wolves, and bighorn sheep.

Travelers heading for the mountains can get a taste of the alpine adventure to come by ascending the 190-meter (626ft) high **Calgary Tower** (daily 9am–9pm, July-Aug until 10pm; www.calgary-tower.com). Below lies the sprawling city, and to the west the serrated ridge of the **Rockies**, much of which is protected by national and provincial parks. One such area is **Kananaskis Provincial Park**, a 45-minute drive southwest of Calgary, containing foothills, mountains, ice-caps, and sparkling lakes. Dirt-bike trails thread its forests, fishermen try their luck in dozens of prime trout streams, and downhill skiers challenge the slopes at **Nakiska**. One of the best ways to enjoy the Kananaskis is to stay at a guest ranch, where greenhorns work up mountain-size appetites on trail rides or hiking trips and then satisfy themselves with hearty, home-cooked fare, including large portions of Alberta beef.

JEWEL OF THE ROCKIES

Crown jewel of the Rockies, **Banff National Park** ㉗ has some of the continent's finest mountain scenery within its confines along the eastern flank of the Continental Divide. The park was founded more than 125 years ago as Canada's first national preserve to protect hot springs just outside the present-day town of **Banff** ㉘ to the southeast.

Visitors can take a dip in the sulfurous waters at **Upper Hot Springs**,

Mountain Avenue, where the mineral water thrust up more than 2,000 meters (6,560ft) in a fault between Mount Rundle and Sulphur Mountain is kept steady at a 37–40°C (98.6–104°F). The bathhouse has been restored to its early 1930s glory (daily).

A gondola ride up **Sulphur Mountain**, 3km (2 miles) from Banff (daily), ends at a summit cafeteria and a full-serve restaurant where mountain sheep are often seen snuffling for snacks. Here, a boardwalk trail leads to the restored 1903 weather observatory. In winter, **Mount Norquay**, 8km (5 miles) out of town, also affords panoramas of encircling peaks from the top of its ski lifts. Other world-class ski resorts include Lake Louise and Sunshine, a little farther from Calgary, but offering great variety of terrain and deep, dry snow, ideal for powder skiing.

Jutting above the trees are the granite spires of **The Fairmont Banff Springs Hotel**, a massive 770-room Victorian edifice built in 1888, styled after a Scottish baronial castle. Sunday brunch is a popular outing.

The Calgary Stampeders football team in action.

⊘ Tip

Take a rubber-tired SnoCoach along the Athabasca Glacier, 105km (65 miles) south of Jasper (Apr–Sept 9am–5pm, Oct 10am–4.30pm; buses depart every 15–30 minutes).

Banff has all the flavor of an alpine town. In summer, its sidewalks are crowded. Strollers browse in the dozens of gift shops or munch on delights in the Cascade Plaza. In winter, après-ski life abounds. Stores stay open late and there is a wide variety of restaurants.

To escape the crowds, wander the grounds of **Banff Centre**, a world-class conservatory of fine arts, music, and drama. In this Salzburg of the Rockies, the summer-long Banff Arts Festival showcases opera, dance, cabaret, musical theater, and jazz.

GLACIER COUNTRY

Lake Louise, 90km (56 miles) north of Banff, a jade gem set against the backdrop of Victoria Glacier, is one of the Rockies' most photographed spots. A Scottish piper wanders among the flowers and pines in the grounds of the **Fairmont Château Lake Louise**; the echo of his skirling resounds from surrounding peaks. Romantics rent canoes and sigh as they paddle around the edge of the lake. The more ambitious hike the moderately difficult trail (7km/4.5 miles

round trip) to **Lake Agnes** to a teahouse perched near the top of a waterfall.

The junction of Highways 93 and 11, 76km (47 miles) north of Lake Louise, is the starting point of the **Icefields Parkway**, one of the world's great mountain drives. The supreme beauty of Lake Louise is challenged within 40km (25 miles) by **Peyto Lake**, set in the **Mistaya river Valley**. A platform at the end of a half-mile trail off the parking lot affords unobstructed views of the deep, turquoise-colored lake, 240 meters (800ft) below.

The parkway continues north in the valley of the Mistaya (Cree for "grizzly"), then follows the braided channels of the North Saskatchewan river to the Rockies' apex: the **Columbia Icefield**, at 325 sq km (125 sq miles) the biggest ice cap in the range. This "mother of rivers" feeds three systems: the Columbia, the Athabasca, and the Saskatchewan. **Athabasca Glacier**, one of dozens that flow from Columbia's bowl of ice, extends almost to the Parkway.

Here, the Parkway enters **Jasper National Park ㉙**, the largest and most northerly in the Rockies. Take the scenic alternate route, 93A, along the west bank of the Athabasca River to Athabasca Falls, which thunder over a 30-meter (100ft) high ledge and hurtle through a narrow canyon. A self-guided trail along the gorge provides close-ups of the violent beauty of the powerful cataract.

Another highlight along the way is **Mount Edith Cavell**, a snow-covered dome of rock rising sheer from **Angel Glacier**. Fur traders in the early 1800s called this the "mountain of the great crossing"; in World War I it was renamed after a heroic British nurse who was executed for helping Allied troops. A hiking trail climbs into alpine meadows spangled with colorful wild flowers; another path wanders across the boulder-strewn outwash of the glacier.

The town of **Jasper**, smaller and quieter than Banff, is the starting point

The Muttart Conservatory, Edmonton.

for dozens of scenic hiking trails, bicycle routes, and driving tours. The **Jasper Tramway** (end Apr to early Oct, 10am–5pm, weather permitting), 4km (2.5 miles) south of the town, whisks sightseers close to the stony summit of **The Whistlers**, a 2,464-meter (8,084ft) mountain. From its summit, looking 77km (48 miles) northwest into British Columbia, on a clear day you can glimpse the highest peak in the Rockies, the imposing Mount Robson (3,954 meters/12,972ft).

Jasper's answer to the Banff Springs Hotel is the less imposing but no less luxurious **Fairmont Jasper Park Lodge**, a hotel with an additional cluster of 56 cedar chalets along **Lac Beauvert**. Room service comes on a bicycle, bears have been known to commandeer the lawns, and a moose once took over a pond on the golf course.

The **Maligne Valley Drive** offers spectacular views of **Maligne Canyon**, 11km (7 miles) east of Jasper, where the river plunges into a steep-walled limestone gorge; **Medicine Lake**, 16km (10 miles) southeast, drained by a vast underground river system; and **Maligne Lake**, a further 10km (6 miles) on, which can be explored by boat in summer and is a cross-country ski center in winter.

En route to Edmonton, take a side-trip to the **Miette Hot Springs** ㉚, 60km (37 miles) north of Jasper, the hottest in the Rockies. The waters are cooled from 54°C (129°F) to 40°C (104°F) before being fed into a huge swimming pool (mid-June–early Sept daily 9am–11pm, early Sept–early Oct daily 10.30am–9pm; swimsuits, towels, lockers available for rent).

Travelers reluctantly leave the Rockies behind as they head east through the parklands and forests of northern Alberta. Locally sourced products make up the menu at the Stony Plain Pie Shoppe at the **Stony Plain Multicultural Heritage Centre** (daily; charge for food; museum by donation), 20km

(12 miles) west of Edmonton, may take the edge off the disappointment. On Saturdays during the summer, don't miss the farmers' market for a sample of other regional food.

EDMONTON

Provincial capital and Canada's most northerly metropolis, **Edmonton** ㉛ is noted for its scenic river valley and numerous arts festivals. The **West Edmonton Mall** is the largest in North America, with an astounding 800 stores, 100 restaurants and fast-food outlets, and a massive indoor amusement park. Other local attractions include the **Citadel Theatre**, housing live theater with five separate venues all under a single roof; and the **Telus World of Science** (Sun–Thu 9am–5pm, Fri–Sat 9am–6pm), a great place to engage kids in science through interactive exhibits.

Oil deals are made at the head offices in Calgary; the actual work of turning black gold into commodities such as gasoline and diesel occurs in Edmonton. The city flexes its industrial

⊙ **Fact**

Yellowhead Highway 16, heading northeast from Jasper, follows the route of the fur traders. Viewpoints offer dramatic glimpses of the terrain they endured.

Mistaya Canyon, Banff National Park.

muscle along the unofficially named **Refinery Row**, a glittering galaxy of tubes, giant storage tanks, and gas flares that light up the night sky like a scene from a science-fiction movie.

But Edmonton is no blue-collar town. In fact, it seems more sophisticated in some ways than its southern rival, where the backyard mountains attract lots of outdoors types more interested in backpacking than Bach. Seat of provincial government and home of the **University of Alberta**, Edmonton has opera and classical ballet companies, a symphony orchestra, and several professional theater groups. Crystal chandeliers even adorn a couple of its rapid transit stations!

SUMMER CELEBRATIONS

All this refinement is inclined to be overshadowed in late July during K-Days, a 10-day revival of the Klondike Gold Rush. The city's vast **Northlands Park** is lit up by midway lights and nightly fireworks, rocked by the sounds of the country's best bands, and clouded with the dusty haze of the chuck-wagon

and thoroughbred races. It is followed by Heritage Days in August, an ethnic festival celebrating more than 80 cultures with music, dance, and, above all, food. Visitors buy tickets to sample delicacies from all parts of the world, from Afghani *shami kabobs* to *Gweru* (chicken stew) from Zimbabwe.

An outdoor museum beside the river, **Fort Edmonton Park** is perhaps a clearer window on the past (end May to end Sept). Thirty-five buildings along three small-town streets recapture the flavor of three separate eras: 1846, 1885, and 1920. Old Strathcona, the city's original commercial district, preserves along its narrow streets early structures such as the **Old Firehall**, **Strathcona Hotel**, and **Princess Theatre**. This is also the site of the **International Fringe Theatre Festival**, North America's oldest and largest fringe festival, attracting performers from all over the world every August for 10 days. The streets echo with mime, music, puppet shows, and plays.

An impressive urban greenbelt preserves riverbank along the North Saskatchewan River, where you can hike, cycle, picnic, and ride horseback on more than 100km (62 miles) of trails. Guides at a nature center near Fort Edmonton conduct walks in all seasons. Four glass pyramids nestled in the valley house the **Muttart Conservatory** (daily 10am–5pm, Wed–Thu until 9pm), a showcase of plants from the tropics to the deserts of the world.

The valley is also the site of a manmade wonder that expresses Alberta's exuberant spirit. As his contribution to the province's 75th anniversary celebrations back in 1980, artist Peter Lewis installed a series of water pipes along the top of the **High Level Bridge**. Until 2009, on civic holidays in summer, a tap was turned and the bridge became a spectacular waterfall higher than Niagara Falls. While, there are no plans to start the falls again, the pipes are still in place, so the possibility remains viable.

Irish dancers performing at the Edmonton Heritage Days Festival.

RODEOS: AN ALBERTA PASSION

Almost any summer or autumn weekend you'll find a rodeo somewhere in Alberta's cattle country.

Rodeos, big or small, will give you a day of excitement and fun along with a generous slice of western Canadian culture. In fairgrounds across the province, locals urge neighbors on as they compete at bronco-busting, steer-wrestling and calf-roping, while big city stadiums attract professional rodeo riders from all over North America competing for valuable purses.

Originating in 16th-century Mexico, rodeos are designed to demonstrate cowboy skills. For example, the broncobuster riding the wild horse must adapt to its bucking gait, while keeping his spurs above the animal's shoulders, all without touching it with his hands.

The niceties of bull-riding may be lost on the average tenderfoot tourist, but still it is one of the most exciting rodeo events. With only one hand on the single halter, a contestant has to ride the back of a huge Brahma bull for eight seconds. Then, after the inevitable fall, he escapes the enraged animal's flailing horns and hooves in his race for safety. The rider's sole protection is a team of fleet-footed rodeo clowns who run interference across the bull's path. To the crowd's delight they must sometimes take refuge in barrels strategically placed around the arena.

Tension gives way to hilarity in the wild cow-milking contest, in which participants are required to get at least some milk into their pails. Calf-roping calls for yet a different set of skills, including excellent horsemanship. Speed is everything here as the rider lassoes his sturdy calf, then dismounts and ties its legs. All the while the horse keeps the lasso rope taut, positioning the calf for branding.

These are just some traditional features of Alberta's rodeos. For pure drama, the larger events add chuckwagon races. They hark back to an era when cowboys slept in bedrolls under a prairie sky and depended on these primitive mobile kitchens for meals.

On Saturday afternoons they would race their wagons home, and the last driver to reach home bought the first round in the town saloon. Now, with prizes as high as $100,000, modern races are held in heats of four competing wagons, each drawn by four horses with its own team of outriders. Each outfit must race around a figure-of-eight course, then dash to the finish line, where the iron stove is unloaded and a wood fire coaxed into flame. Unsurprisingly, given the number of horses involved on a tricky course, accidents are commonplace.

The rodeo circuit spans all four western provinces, with events every weekend from mid-April through mid-October. They culminate with the Canadian Finals Rodeo held every late Oct or early November in Edmonton, pitting the country's top cowboys against the top-ranking bucking bulls and horses, the finale of a summer-long quest to be recognized as the best.

For "The Greatest Show on Earth," plan to attend the annual Calgary Exhibition and Stampede, 100 years old and going strong. Street parades, fireworks, pancake breakfasts cooked and served on city sidewalks, agricultural exhibitions, and funfairs are all part of the big show. During stampede week most locals and visitors go about their business dressed in western clothes. If that seems a bit ambitious, you should at least buy a ten-gallon hat. It's part of the rodeo tradition.

See Travel Tips for more on the Calgary Exhibition and Stampede.

A rodeo rider at the Calgary Stampede.

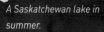
A Saskatchewan lake in summer.

SASKATCHEWAN

Canada's Old Northwest lies at the very heart of Saskatchewan, a province of highlands, plains, deserts, and lakes, once home to gangsters, gunrunners, and fur traders.

A hush falls over the crowd as the solemn jurors return to the courtroom with their verdict. They pass the dock where the defendant, Louis Riel, kneels in prayer. Riel has been charged with high treason for leading the Métis people in rebellion against the Crown. Riel rises to meet his fate. The clerk of the court asks the foreman if the jury members are agreed upon their verdict. "How say you: is the prisoner guilty or not guilty?"

"Guilty."

The foreman asks the judge for leniency, but the judge passes his sentence: Riel will hang. This scene from *The Trial of Louis Riel*, a play by John Coulter, is re-enacted every July at the Royal Saskatchewan Museum, Regina. Each time the jury finds Riel guilty beyond a shadow of doubt.

Traitor to some, hero to others, Louis Riel twice tried to defend the rights of his people, the mixed-blood offspring of aboriginal women and French fur traders. In 1869 he established a provisional Métis government in Manitoba, an ill-fated experiment in self-determination that ended when the Canadian militia put down the insurrection. Riel fled to Montana, where he lived quietly as a schoolteacher.

Louis Riel, leader of the Métis.

MÉTIS UPRISING

In 1884 federal agents began surveying Métis lands in the Saskatchewan river Valley in preparation for the coming of white settlers. Métis leaders again called on Riel, who returned to Canada to lead a ragtag army against the Canadian militia. The Métis' brief uprising ended in defeat at Batoche on May 15, 1885. Riel was tried in Regina, and was hanged later that year.

Saskatchewan has a hard time with heroes, especially with Riel, a fiery, French-speaking Catholic who once

⊙ Main attractions

Regina
Qu'Appelle river Valley
Moose Mountain
    Provincial Park
Cypress Hills
    Interprovincial Park
T. Rex Discovery Centre
Saskatoon
Battleford National
    Historic Park

⊙ Map on page 298

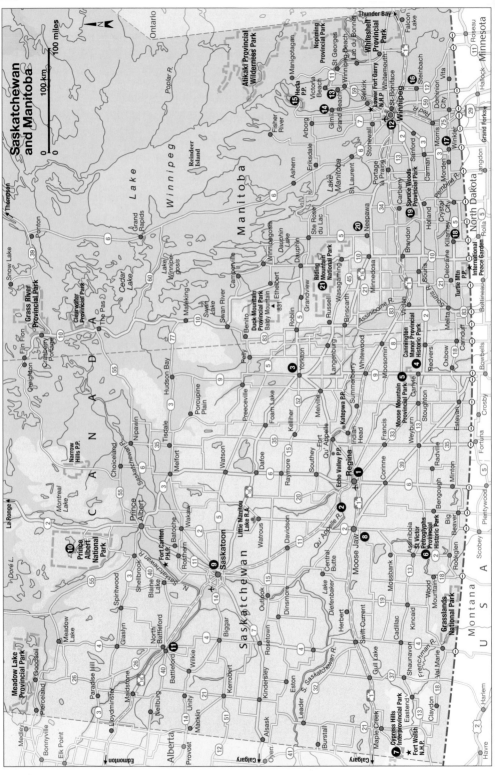

Saskatchewan and Manitoba

called himself "Prophet, Infallible Pontiff, and Priest King." That sort of talk delayed his acceptance as an authentic folk hero for about 80 years; this province demands humility, even from its hockey stars.

Saskatchewan's indifference to Riel has been due in part to another tragedy that looms larger in prairie hearts and minds: 10 lost years called the Great Depression, when hail, grasshoppers, and drought destroyed millions of acres of wheat, leaving the prairie provinces destitute. The inaction of government nurtured a cautious people sceptical about the pronouncements of politicians.

The 1930s will colour provincial perceptions as long as anyone who lived through the era is alive. But the experience also produced sturdy self-reliance. Take Regina, for example – provincial capital and Queen City of the Plains. Its less than regal setting prompted Sir John A. Macdonald, Canada's first prime minister, to remark in 1886: "If you had a little more wood, and a little more water, I think the prospect would be improved."

THE MAKING OF REGINA

When **Regina** ❶ was named capital of the newly formed province of Saskatchewan in 1905, city leaders took Macdonald's suggestion of "more wood" to heart. They dammed muddy Wascana Creek to create a small lake, erected the Legislative Building, planted trees, laid out formal gardens, and splashed it all with fountains, including one from London's Trafalgar Square.

The result was **Wascana Centre** (daily; free), still an oasis of woods and water. Cyclists and joggers circle the lake, and birdwatchers are seduced by the prospect of eight types of woodpeckers, six heron species, and more than 25 types of ducks at the waterfowl sanctuary.

You can also admire the Egyptian sculpture in the **University of Regina's**

art gallery, or visit the **Saskatchewan Science Centre** (Closed Mondays), featuring the human body, astronomy, and geology. The **Royal Saskatchewan Museum** (daily 9.30am–5pm; www.royalsaskmuseum.ca/rsm; donation requested) offers an excellent introduction to the province's flora and fauna, both present-day and tracking back to the days when dinosaurs ruled the plains. Its First Nations Gallery traces 10,000 years of aboriginal history and culture.

WIDE AND OPEN PRAIRIES

To the northeast of Regina the **Qu'Appelle River Valley** ❷ is a welcome change from the Queen City in topography and tempo. Carved by glacial meltwaters, this verdant furrow in the brown prairie divides the flat and open plains to the south and rolling parkland to the north. The valley is best appreciated from Highway 56 where it flanks the **Fishing Lakes** – four broadenings in the Qu'Appelle river. **Echo Valley** and **Katepwa** provincial parks offer camping, fishing,

Playing on the beach in Saskatchewan.

⊙ **Fact**

Grasslands National Park is Canada's only national prairie park and a perfect spot to view the wide open landscapes of the prairies.

swimming, and nature trails that wind through wooded ravines.

Eastern spires crown many churches northeast of the Qu'Appelle, testifying to the predominance of Ukrainian settlers. In **Yorkton** ❸, a stroll through the **Western Development Museum** (Mon–Fri 9am-5pm, Sat–Sun noon–5pm) reveals household scenes of early settlers. A colourful Ukrainian pioneer kitchen, brightened with ceramic tiles and embroideries, contrasts with an austere English parlor. In early August, the museum sponsors the Threshermen's Show, with wagon rides, threshing competitions, and square dancing.

BRITISH ECCENTRICITY

Eccentricity is a traditional English export, and few were more flamboyant than the aristocrats who tried to recreate a corner of their sceptered isle on the bald prairie at **Cannington Manor** ❹ (Mon–Fri 8am-5pm, closed weekends), now a historic park 200km (125 miles) southeast of Regina. Here, in 1882, Captain Edward Pierce established a manorial village, where blue bloods bred racehorses, played rugby and cricket, and hired immigrants to do the farming. When the railroad bypassed Cannington, the settlement became a ghost town. Still standing are five furnished buildings, including a carpenter's shop, and **All Saints Anglican Church**. Beside the log church is the grave of Captain Pierce, far from his beloved England. **Moose Mountain Provincial Park** ❺, 27km (17 miles) northwest, is a favorite with birdwatchers, who scan the skies for turkey vultures, teal, ducks, and dozens of other species. It is also offers lots of family activities including golf (including the miniature variety), various water sports, snowmobiling and more around Kenosee Lake,

THE BADLANDS

At the turn of the century the **Big Muddy Badlands** south of Regina sheltered a community every bit as strange as Cannington Manor. Law enforcement was finally established in the American territory of Montana to the south, so outlaws such as Bloody

The Royal Canadian Mounted Police on parade.

⊙ THE MOUNTIES

Once headquarters for the North West Mounted Police (1882–1920), Regina is home to Canada's training academy for the Royal Canadian Mounted Police (RCMP). The history of the Mounties is central to Saskatchewan. In 1874 a detachment of North West Mounted Police was sent from Manitoba to establish law and order in the northwest, where the illegal trade in whiskey, guns, and fur was growing apace. Today the interprovincial highway has been named the Red Coat Trail after their epic 1,300km (800-mile) trek west on horseback. They set up posts across the province, many of which have been restored and are open to visitors, including Fort Walsh National Historic Site in the Cypress Hills and Fort Battleford National Historic Site to the north.

The **RCMP Heritage Centre** (daily 11am–5pm) in Regina houses displays that trace the history of the force, from the early days of establishing law and order on the frontier to its modern role in solving crime through technology. Prized artifacts include the handcuffs worn by the rebel Louis Riel, and the crucifix he carried to his execution on a site just outside the museum (daily). In summer, the Sunset-Retreat ceremony includes a troop drill display in the famous scarlet tunic, military music, the lowering of the Canadian flag, and the March Past (July–mid-Aug, weather permitting, Tue 6.45pm; free).

Knife and the Pigeon Toed Kid moved their base of operations north to the empty badlands, hiding out in caves between cattle-rustling raids on Montana ranches. The rock formations depict 65 million years of history, glaciers advancing and retreating, carving rocky plateaus and riverbeds.

St Victor Petroglyphs Provincial Historic Park ❻, 150km (93 miles) southwest of Regina, tells a bit of the human history at a weirdly eroded sandstone outcrop, where prehistoric peoples carved dozens of designs in the soft rock. The outcrop also affords a panorama of chessboard crops, alkali lakes, escarpments, and brightly painted grain elevators, those "cathedrals of the plains" which give prairie towns their distinctive (and often only) skylines. South-central Saskatchewan is the province's predominantly French-speaking region, but English is spoken just as readily.

Wood Mountain, 50km (30 miles) southwest of St Victor, briefly became a refuge to Sitting Bull and his band of Sioux after the Battle of Little Big Horn in 1876. The barracks and mess hall

of a Mountie post established to watch over the Sioux have been recreated in the **Wood Mountain Post Historic Park** (June–Aug daily 10am–5pm; donation requested). If the museum happens to be closed, the area also doubles as a great place to picnic.

Cypress Hills Interprovincial Park ❼, on the southwest border with Alberta, is situated in one of the few parts of western Canada left uncovered by Ice Age glaciers. The hills rise like a long, green wedge near **Eastend** and extend west into Alberta. This oasis of coniferous forests, cool valleys, and rounded buttes has long been a refuge for travelers from the hot and dusty plains. Campgrounds, cabins, tennis, golf, and skiing are all available at **Loch Leven**.

There is history here, too, at **Fort Walsh National Historic Site** (July–Aug daily 9.30am–5pm, May, June, Sept Tue–Sat 9.30am–5pm), built by the North West Mounted Police in 1875 to bring order to the region, controlling the whiskey traders and horse thieves. They tried to manage the influx of Lakota refugees from the Great Sioux War of 1877–8.

The Mountie barracks at Fort Walsh.

From 1878 to 1882 the fort served as the headquarters of the North West Mounted Police. The officers' quarters, commissioner's residence, and various other buildings have all been recreated.

It's worth making a quick detour into Eastend to visit the **T. Rex Discovery Centre** (Victoria Day weekend to Labor Day daily 10am–6pm; donation requested), a state-of-the-art facility housing the area's astounding fossil finds – including a complete Tyrannosaurus Rex skeleton. There are tours throughout the day and a visit to an active quarry may be possible.

Lying 50km (30 miles) north of Cypress Hills, the "Old Cow Town" of **Maple Creek** drowses beneath its canopy of cottonwoods. Capital of bone-dry ranchland, Maple Creek is about as Old West as Saskatchewan gets.

Heading back toward Regina, sheltered in a broad valley 312km (194 miles) east on Highway 1, **Moose Jaw ❽** is a quiet city with a lively past. In the 1920s bootleggers and brothels flourished along **River Street**, and Chicago gangsters cooled their heels here. In the

city's historic center, **Temple Gardens Mineral Spa** (Daily 8am-10pm) has a natural geothermal mineral water pool. It's attached to a hotel, but the public can visit after 10am. Beneath the city, visitors can experience the **Tunnels of Moose Jaw** (July–Aug Mon–Fri 10am–7pm, Sat-Sun 10am-8pm; 10.30am-4.30pm rest of the year), in which bootlegging tales are brought to life on interactive tours. Moose Jaw's **Western Development Museum** (Apr–Dec daily 9am–5pm, Jan–Mar Tue–Sun 9am–5pm) emphasizes early transportation.

SASKATOON'S TEMPERANCE DAYS

Bootleggers never darkened the streets of **Saskatoon ❾**, founded in 1884 as a temperance colony, a legacy that endures only in the sign for **Temperance Avenue**. One of the city's most defining features is the **North Saskatchewan River**, which flows between high, wooded banks protected from development by parks. The summer cruise boats pass riverside landmarks such as the turreted Delta Hotels **Bessborough** and the graystone buildings of the **University of Saskatchewan**. The university gives Saskatoon a cultural and cosmopolitan cachet. Five theater groups and a symphony orchestra perform here, and restaurants can be found that border on the bohemian.

Six weeks each summer, from early July to mid-August, sold-out audiences fill riverside tents during **Shakespeare on the Saskatchewan**. For almost 30 years, the festival's innovative productions have made Shakespeare's plays as pertinent to today's audiences as they ever were. The Persephone Theatre at the Remai Arts Center offers accessible national and international repertoire year round.

HISTORIC SITES NORTH OF SASKATOON

On the northern edge of Saskatoon, the **Wanuskewin Heritage Park**

Dog sledding, one of the best ways to get around in winter.

(pronounced Wah-nus-kay-win, Cree for "peace of mind"; daily 9am–4.30pm; www.wanuskewin.com) portrays 6,000 years of Northern Plains Indian culture. Here, with the help of native elders, visitors can see what life was like in a Plains Indian encampment, with cultural demonstrations and a restaurant serving authentic native cuisine.

Continuing north toward Prince Albert, a high bluff commands a mighty bend of the South Saskatchewan River where the Métis made their last stand during the Northwest Rebellion of 1885. The only remains of the Métis "capital" at **Batoche National Historic Site** are a simple white church, which served as Louis Riel's headquarters, and a bullet-scarred rectory. A few miles west stands palisaded **Fort Carlton** (late May – Labor day Mon-Fri 9.30am-5.30pm, late Jun-Sep also weekends 9.30am-5.30pm), once the most important fur-trade depot between the Red River and the Rockies.

Eighty kilometers (50 miles) northeast of this battle-scarred valley is **Prince Albert**, gateway to the province's northlands, famous among fishermen for both its pristine lakes and its record-size trout.

Straddling a transition zone between parkland and boreal forest is **Prince Albert National Park** ⑩. Pines scent the air of **Waskesiu Lake**, park headquarters and an attractive year-round resort town. Sailboats and fishing boats are available at the townsite.

About 160km (100 miles) southwest of the park, **Battleford** ⑪, the former capital of the Northwest Territories, occupies a wooded setting far superior to that of its successor, Regina. The **Fort Battleford National Historic Site** (late May–June Mon–Fri 10am-4pm, July–early Sep daily 10am-4pm), a Mountie post where Canada's last public execution took place in 1885, contains officers' quarters and residences, and other restored buildings. The fort's most poignant artifact recalls Louis Riel: the Gatling gun used in the battle of Batoche. The weapon's brass is as shiny as a century ago, when the dreams of the Métis died on a bluff above the North Saskatchewan River.

⊙ Tip

In Prince Albert National Park, little-visited lakes, including Ajawaan, former home of the enterprising British naturalist Archie Belaney, aka Grey Owl, can be seen at their best by canoe. Canoes can be rented at Wakesiu Lake Marina.

Horseback riding by the South Saskatchewan River.

Polar bear in Manitoba.

MANITOBA

A traveler coming from the east through the forests of Ontario will find Manitoba bursting upon the senses with space, light, and color, with towns and cities as varied as the settlers themselves.

Ah, thinks the traveler, approaching Manitoba along northern Ontario's corridor of ragged trees, the prairie at last! Suddenly the land rolls on and on to a distant horizon. The sky, once confined to a gray strip above the highway, expands into a dome of deep blue.

Well, yes and no. The boreal forest is close by, blanketing the northern two-thirds of Manitoba with a lake-dotted wilderness that remains virtually unpopulated, and the sunny south refutes the old equation of prairie equals flat. West of Whiteshell Provincial Park, the land rises in stone and gravel ridges, flattens around Winnipeg, turns marshy south of Lake Manitoba, dips into the valleys of the Pembina and Assiniboine rivers, then rises again in the western uplands.

THRIVING COMMUNITIES

The towns and cities are as varied as the land, and herein lies Manitoba's special appeal. Settlers from Europe and eastern Canada established towns with character, not just as supply centers for farmers, and proudly added their ethnic flavor: French Canadians at Ste Anne, Icelanders at Gimli and Russians at Tolstoi.

The vigor of these communities is remarkable considering the overwhelming presence of **Winnipeg** ⑫, provincial capital and home to 670,000

The Winnipeg Mint.

people, more than 60 percent of Manitoba's population.

PROVINCIAL CAPITAL

Winnipeg sometimes startles visitors with its canopy of trees contrasting visibly with the surrounding treeless prairie. There's no mistaking the junction of Portage and Main, however, reputedly the widest, windiest street corner in Canada. But downtown avenues curve with the Assiniboine and Red rivers, giving some buildings delightfully quirky angles and avoiding the West's

Main attractions
Winnipeg
Grand Beach
Gimli
Hecla Island
Steinbach
Killarney
Spirit Sandhills
Neepawa
Riding Mountain National Park

Map on page 298

usual rigid street grid. **The Forks**, dubbed Winnipeg's meeting place, is the site of several summer festivals. Inaugurated in 2014, the Canadian Museum for Human Rights at The Forks (Tue-Sun 10am–5pm, Wed until 9pm; www.humanrights.ca), is a huge and stunning building, the only museum in the world solely devoted to human rights awareness.

Outstanding green swathes are a feature in Assiniboine Park. Behind the pavilion is the Lyric Outdoor Stage for performances, including the Royal Winnipeg Ballet's annual Ballet in the Park. In the park you will also find Canada's Diversity Gardens and the **Zoo** (daily summer 9am–5pm, winter until 4pm) with over 2,000 animals representing more than 200 distinct species. Visit the new International Polar Bear Conservation Centre to learn about climate change and its impact on polar bears.

Winnipeg is also an old city in a young land. The first Europeans to build on this site were French fur traders, who constructed Fort Rouge in 1738 near the flood-prone confluence of the Red and Assiniboine rivers, silt-laden waterways which eventually gave the city its Cree name of *Win-nipi* (muddy water). After the French came those fierce fur-trade rivals, the London-based Hudson's Bay Company and the North West Company of Montréal. During the late 18th and early 19th centuries, the two companies built a series of palisaded forts within shooting distance near the Assiniboine and Red rivers.

In 1812 Scottish crofters, who had been turned out of their homes by the Highland Clearances, arrived on the scene with a few farming implements and a bull and a cow named Adam and Eve. The trip, tools, and livestock were courtesy of the Scottish humanitarian Lord Selkirk, who established farming colonies throughout North America for homeless Highlanders. But, like cattle ranchers and sheep farmers, fur traders and settlers did not mix. Conflict erupted on June 19, 1816, when Métis employees of the North West Company slaughtered 20 settlers in what

Inuit inukshuk on the Legislative Building grounds, Winnipeg.

became known as the Seven Oaks Incident.

Lord Selkirk heard the bad news in Montréal, and promptly marched west with a private army. He arrested the fur traders and their Métis employees, then re-established his settlement, which eventually prospered. There are several reminders of the fur-trade era in Winnipeg. **Grant's Old Mill** (June–Aug; Tue–Sun 10am-6pm; donation) is a working replica of the settlement's first gristmill, built in 1829 by Cuthbert Grant, leader of the Métis at the massacre.

The **Ross House Museum** (June–Aug Wed–Sun, 10am-4pm, free), home of the Ross family and the first post office in western Canada (1854), is worth visiting, as is the **Manitoba Museum** (mid-May to early Sept daily 10am–5pm, early Sept–mid-May Tue–Fri 10am–4pm, Sat–Sun 11am–5pm; www.manitobamuseum.ca). Its most impressive fur-trade display is a full-size replica of the *Nonsuch*, a Hudson's Bay Company vessel that in 1668 carried the very first cargo of furs from Canada to England.

The most evocative relic of this exciting era is the lone remaining gate of the last of the five forts built in the area, **Upper Fort Garry**, built by the Hudson's Bay Company in 1836, and now preserved in a quiet park in the shadow of the turreted **Fort Garry Hotel**. This hotel came from the later railway era, opened in 1913 as an elegant Grand Trunk Pacific Railway hotel for passengers breaking the long journey across the country.

MULTICULTURAL INFLUENCES

The city's economic good times arrived with the completion of the Canadian-Pacific Railway in 1885 and the hundreds of thousands of immigrants who followed the ribbon of steel: Europeans fleeing persecution, British city-dwellers hungry for land, Americans who saw their own West filling up. Almost all came through Winnipeg, and enough stayed on to swell the city's population.

Each year for two weeks in early August, Winnipeg remembers its rich ethnic mosaic with **Folklorama**, a festival held in some 40 informal pavilions scattered throughout the city. In the evening, church basements and school auditoriums are filled with the aromas of Polish sausage and Ukrainian cabbage rolls, and the strains of German polkas and Greek *sirtakis*, as each group celebrates its heritage with food, song, and dance. Today, Filipinos are Winnipeg's largest immigrant group making up more than 5 percent of the total population of the city.

Ukrainian Canadians are particularly prominent in Winnipeg. The pear-shaped domes of half a dozen major churches grace the skyline, and the **Oseredok Ukrainian Cultural and Educational Centre** contains a museum (Mon–Sat 10am–4pm, Sun 1pm-4pm) displaying such treasures as 17th-century church vestments, as

Nonsuch Ketch at the Manitoba Museum.

well as a series of rooms decorated with the hand-carved furniture and hand-painted ceramics typically found in village homes.

East across the Red River is **St Boniface**, bastion of French culture in western Canada, where streets are *rues*, and Orthodox domes yield to the belfries of **St Boniface Basilica**, built in 1908 and partially destroyed by fire in 1968. Close by, on the site of **Fort Gibraltar** (mid-May–mid-June Mon–Fri 9am–4pm, late June–late Aug Wed–Thu 10am–6pm, Fri–Sun 10am–4pm), a 1978 replica of the fort built by the North West Company in 1809 recaptures the height of the fur trade with a depiction of life at the fort in 1814. In February, the fort is the focal point for the 40-year old **Festival du Voyageur**, a 10-day celebration of the history of the province (complete with competitions ranging from snow sculpture to beard-growing to fiddling).

Visitors to Winnipeg between September and May can enjoy the Manitoba Opera Company, the Winnipeg Symphony Orchestra, mainstream plays at the Manitoba Theatre Centre, and experimental works at the intimate MTC Warehouse Theater. For more than 20 years, the New Music Festival at the end of January has been attracting fans from around the world to more than 200 world-premieres to challenge the boundaries of symphonic music. And if you're really lucky, the celebrated Royal Winnipeg Ballet will be in town during your visit.

Since 2011, winter visitors and locals alike have been able to once again watch the Winnipeg Jets of the National Hockey League. Winnipeg had been without a team since the mid-90s but following the relocation of the team from Atlanta, the city again claims the Jets as their own, bringing another historically Canadian team back to where hockey is considered king.

Once considered something of a dowager by the younger, upstart prairie communities such as Calgary and Edmonton, Winnipeg is turning its age into an asset with a flurry of sandblasting, wood stripping, and brass polishing. This fling with the past is centered

St Boniface Basilica.

on the historic **Exchange District**, a 15-block area which is bounded by Main and Princess streets, and William and Notre Dame avenues. Here, the largest concentration of commercial, early 20th-century architecture in the West has been given a new lease of life. It's an area alive with shopping, restaurants, and nightlife.

Visitors who want more tranquil pursuits can board the *Paddlewheel Queen* (its sister ship, the *Paddlewheel Princess,* was set on fire in 2017 by four teens), and cruise north on the Red river to **Lower Fort Garry National Historic Site** (mid-May to late August daily 9.30am–5pm), North America's last intact stone fur-trade fort, restored to the 1850s era. The landscaped grounds and the riverside setting are complemented by costumed attendants demonstrating how old-timers pressed beaver pelts into 41kg (90lb) bales for shipment back to Europe.

LAKESIDE RETREATS

Larger than Lake Ontario, vast **Lake Winnipeg** stretches north into the wilderness. Cottage communities ring its southern end: **Grand Beach** , 87km (54 miles) north of the provincial capital, **Winnipeg Beach** and **Victoria Beach**, all slightly commercialized and crowded but blessed with long stretches of white sand.

Seventy-six kilometers (47 miles) north on the western shore, the Icelandic community of **Gimli** remembers its past with a statue of a Viking and the **New Icelandic Heritage Museum** (summer, Mon-Fri 10am–4pm, Sat-Sun 1pm-4pm; www.nihm.ca), which tells the story of the Icelandic experience in North America and explains the fishing economy established on Lake Winnipeg by the town's forebears. **Hecla Island**, 50km (30 miles) north, once a self-governing Icelandic republic, is now part of a provincial park. Sunrise birdwatching safaris, hiking and cross-country ski trails, and a fine golf course are among the attractions.

Sculptures in Manitoba.

SOUTHERN MANITOBA

South of Winnipeg stretches flat farmland with rich, black gumbo soil of silt

Shoreline of Lake Winnipeg near Hillside Beach.

Polar bear and her cubs.

and clay. This land was described by the 18th-century fur trader Alexander Henry as "a kind of mortar that adheres to the foot like tar." In the middle stands **Steinbach** ⑯, whose tidy streets and freshly painted houses reflect the enduring values of the town's industrious Mennonite founders. The **Mennonite Heritage Village** (May, June and Sept Mon–Sat 9am–5pm, Sun 11.30am–5pm, July–Aug Mon–Sat 9am–6pm, Sun 11.30am–6pm, Oct–Apr Mon–Fri 9am–5pm; www.mennoniteheritagevillage.com) recalls the old ways with reconstructed thatched-roof cabins, a blacksmith's shop, and a wind-driven gristmill. Excellent borscht and spicy sausages are served at the museum restaurant.

West of the Red River and south to the American border lies the **Pembina Triangle**. Sheltered by the gentle Pembina Hills, the region has Manitoba's longest growing season and the only apple orchards between the Niagara Peninsula and the Okanagan Valley.

Seemingly every town in the region advertises the local agricultural specialty with theme fairs. Fields of sunflowers nodding in hot prairie breezes around **Altona**, 98km (61 miles) south of Winnipeg, inspired the Manitoba Sunflower Festival, held in July. Nearby **Winkler** ⑰, 24km (15 miles) west, settled by Anabaptist Hutterites, holds the Winkler Harvest Festival each August with barbecues, pancake breakfasts, and old-time sidewalk sales.

The **Pembina Valley** is steep enough at **La Rivière**, 61km (38 miles) west of Winkler, for a downhill ski run. The valley was carved by the willow-fringed Pembina River, which broadens into a chain of sparkling canoeing and fishing lakes – **Pelican**, **Lorne**, **Louise**, and **Rock**.

About 64km (40 miles) west, the attractive town of **Killarney** ⑱ has a small lake at its feet and a hill wooded with maple and oak at its back. This setting, said to be reminiscent of Kerry, Ireland, has produced Killarney's Celtic touches: a green fire engine, and Erin Park with its replica of the Blarney Stone.

The **International Peace Garden**, 32km (20 miles) southwest of Killarney, straddles the North Dakota–Manitoba border, near the geographical center of the continent. Dr Henry Moore, an ardent gardener from Toronto, tabled a modest proposal for a joint peace park in 1929 at a meeting of the Gardeners Association of North America. Three years later, his dream became a reality.

If all this cultivation creates a craving for wilderness, visit the **Spirit Sandhills** in **Spruce Woods Provincial Park** ⓳, 145km (90 miles) west of Winnipeg: grassy plains and barren sand dunes along the sinuous Assiniboine River. The sandhills were formed about 12,000 years ago when a mile-wide glacial river deposited a vast delta of sand, silt, and gravel. Ernest Thompson Seton, a naturalist-author who homesteaded near Carberry in the 1880s, made them the setting for his book *The Trail of the Sandhill Stag*. He spent every spare moment in what came to be known as "Seton's Kingdom" observing grouse, deer, and wolves. The self-guiding **Spirit Hills Trail** winds through barren dunes inhabited by rarities like hognose snakes, spadefoot toads, and northern prairie skinks. Fifty kilometers (30 miles) west lies **Brandon**, noted for handsome public buildings and gracious private homes dating from the early 1900s.

Highway 10 leads north past fields of wheat and rye interspersed with pothole lakes that attract millions of ducks and geese during spring and fall migrations. A short detour takes you to **Neepawa** ⓴, 75km (47 miles) northeast of Brandon, where you can visit the childhood home of the acclaimed Canadian author Margaret Laurence (daily 10am–5pm), before continuing north into the forests of **Riding Mountain National Park** ㉑.

Approaching the park from this direction, the usual reaction is: *Where's the mountain?* Patience will be rewarded on reaching the edge of the park, where the "mountain" rises abruptly, 450 meters (1,500ft) above a patchwork of crops: yellow rapeseed, brown squares of oats and barley, and rolling green and gold wheat fields.

◎ Tip

Explore Brandon on foot and discover its most notable historic buildings with the help of a walking tour brochure distributed by the Chamber of Commerce.

Northern Lights over Churchill.

Carcross, Yukon territory in fall.

THE NORTH

The long sunny days of summer lend themselves to exploring what is perhaps Canada's last uncharted frontier.

Delphiniums in the Yukon.

The hardest thing to understand about the Canadian North is its magnitude. Although the three territories combined are home to a barely more than 100,000 people, the land north of 60 degrees latitude comprises one-third of the country. It is massive, larger than India and about 10 times the size of Germany. Here it genuinely is bitterly cold in winter and some people do live in snow huts, with dogsled racing across the frozen tundra a popular form of entertainment.

Despite its formidable geography and vast distances separating remote outposts, the North is the natural habitat of the "first Canadians," the Inuit, who have survived here for thousands of years and who, in 1999, finally acquired their own territory of Nunavut.

Canada's northern hinterland is not the vaca-tion spot for everyone, as it is difficult to get to and offers limited accommodations and often challenging weather. But for those intrigued by unusual habitats, landscapes, and wildlife, the North presents an exciting adventure. The Yukon, the Northwest Territories, and Nunavut are regions of delicately balanced ecosystems and unparalleled natural beauty.

Musk oxen, Devon Island.

The Yukon is the first of Canada's three north-ern territories to be explored. Here, the reader can discover the significance of the gold rush for Canada's neglected North along with a descrip-tion of the Yukon's varied geography and spectacular vistas.

The Northwest Territories are treated in similar fashion, although with greater emphasis on geological formations and wildlife. As Nunavut is the most recently created territory, its political evolution is touched upon, along with the diverse range of activities awaiting its visitors.

The three chapters together present a compelling picture of the radi-cally different world looming over Canada's southern provinces. And, as the region being most drastically affected by climate change, it is the one which is evolving the fastest.

Hiking in Kluane National Park.

THE YUKON

Today, tourists trace the footsteps of the gold prospectors who once made their fortunes in this northerly outpost. Glaciers, wide plateaus, and magnificent mountains characterize the Yukon.

Before 1896, the northwest corner of Canada was a mountainous wilderness where few outsiders, besides the occasional whaler and fur trader, ventured. The Dene had lived here for perhaps 60,000 years, but it was terra incognita for the rest of the world. But in 1896 this forgotten land was suddenly overrun by man and beast. Gold, and lots of it, had been discovered in the Klondike.

The young Dominion of Canada had to deal with the headaches that accompany sudden wealth. If the government could not bring order (or at least a civilizing influence) to the North, it might lose millions in gold tax revenues. Therefore, the queen's ministers, in recognition of the sudden prominence of a land most only knew about from sketchy maps, decided to redraw those maps. In 1898, they roped off the northwest corner of the Northwest Territories and created the Yukon Territory. What the federal officials lassoed in their haste to reassert Canadian sovereignty is a territory larger than the New England states, double the land mass of the British Isles, and two and a half times the size of Texas.

This is a land of wild beauty and varied landscapes known as part of the Western Highlands. Along the eastern border of the territory the **Mackenzie Mountains** straddle the border with the Northwest Territories (NT) and gently roll up to the mouth of the **Mackenzie**

A totem pole in the Yukon territory.

River. Within this range there are rivers carved into the rock by ancient glaciers. One such river, the **Nahanni**, contains Virginia Falls. However, unlike Ontario's great Niagara, no one has ever attempted to go over these falls in a barrel or walk over them on a tightrope – they are twice the height, although much narrower and virtually unknown to anyone who hasn't been to the Yukon.

MOUNTAIN COUNTRY

Mountains are an omnipresent sight in the Yukon. The **Selwyn Mountains** lie

○ Main attractions
Whitehorse
Kluane National Park
Dawson City
Danoja Zho Cultural
  Centre

Map on page 318

to the west of the Mackenzie mountain range and to the north are the very ancient **Ogilvie Mountains**.

The best-known peaks are **St Elias** and **Mount Logan** on the province's southwest border with Alaska. Standing at 5,959 meters (19,550ft), Mount Logan, in Kluane National Park, is the highest peak in Canada and is second only to Mount McKinley in Alaska as the highest mountain in North America.

Many peaks in the St Elias Range poke through glaciers that are in part sustained by the "chill factor" associated with great heights. The St Elias Range, besides offering some of the most spectacular sights in the world, also acts to block much of the moisture coming off the Pacific Ocean. It is because of this that most of the interior of the Yukon receives little precipitation. The average in **Whitehorse ❶**, capital of the Yukon, is 26cm (10ins) a year. In the High Arctic there is less precipitation than farther south. Yet the Yukon does receive more precipitation than the Northwest Territories and, because of the relatively cold temperatures and high altitudes,

whatever snow falls in winter will not melt until spring. This snow helps provide excellent cross-country trails.

PLATEAU LAND

Between the mountain ranges are plateaus, the **Pelly**, the **Porcupine**, and the **Yukon**. Each plateau is named after the river that flows through it. The Yukon Plateau is the largest of the three. Although glaciers remain in Yukon Territory, much of the Yukon Plateau was untouched by the last glacial era, making it unique among geological areas in North America. Thus the Yukon river, unlike the other northern rivers that felt the effects of glaciation, flows gently through the plateau and is devoid of rapids, falls, and other such hazards that can make canoe trips a thrilling and dangerous excursion. Ice-free millennia have allowed the Yukon River to find its own path.

Within the plateau one finds mountains that have dome-like summits rising to heights of 1,800 meters (6,000ft). These domes were formed by a million years of sediment accumulating on top of the mountains. Unlike the neighboring

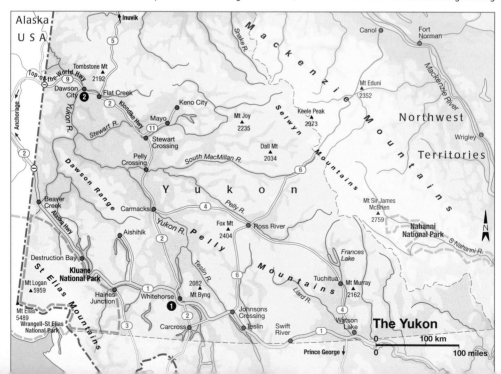

ranges, such as the Mackenzie or St Elias that have been scoured by glaciers and left with whittled-down, pencil-shaped peaks, the mountains of the Yukon Plateau have few rocky outcroppings.

This plateau is a relic of another age, one that stands apart from the geological violence of the last Ice Age. For that reason, ancient mastodon and mammoth species survived far longer here. Likewise, the plateau offered shelter for the people who entered North America across the Bering Strait thousands of years ago.

Owing to the plenitude of vegetation there is an excellent food supply to support the many species of animals, including moose, caribou, Dall sheep, mountain goats, cougars, grizzly, and black bears. Within the rivers of the Yukon there are usually large runs of salmon – they hatch in the creeks and rivers that empty into the Pacific, eventually returning to spawn and die.

GOLD RUSH DAYS

There was a time when not only thousands of salmon swam up the Yukon river, but thousands of men waded into her. Unlike the salmon that are driven by biological imperative, these men were driven by the promise of the placer gold that lay buried deep in the sediment of river beds.

In contrast to the manner in which it is extracted, placer gold is created by the eternally slow process of erosion. Gradually the river flows over a rock face, wearing down the quartz-bearing gold until it breaks off into pieces varying in size from that of a tennis ball to a microscopic speck.

This iridescent mineral lay complacently in Yukon river beds for thousands of years. Legend has it that an American, George Washington Carmack, and two Tagish First Nations scouts, Skookum Jim and Dawson Charlie, struck gold at **Rabbit Creek** (renamed **Bonanza**) on August 17, 1896, a day that is now a territorial holiday. Within two years, the population of Dawson City had exploded to more than 40,000. Eventually, close to

80,000 men would scurry northward to seek their fortune, with the gold stories that were published in William Randolph Hearst's hyperbolic newspapers rattling in their heads. The routes that some miners chose to take were rather bizarre. A group of Edmonton businessmen, for instance, advertised a trail through the rugged interior of Alberta and British Columbia. Little did those who took this passage know that Dawson City, the center of the gold rush, lay a few thousand miles away and that this "trail" was a hoax. Of the thousands who attempted this route, many lost their lives and only a handful managed to straggle on into the Yukon.

SOAPY SMITH AND SAM STEELE

A more conventional route was to travel by steamer to Skagway, Alaska, and then onward through either the White Pass or the Chilkoot Pass into Yukon. Although these trails were better than the Edmonton Trail, they posed many dangers: not the least of which was the other people encountered along the way. In Skagway a ne'er-do-well named

Gold panning on Discovery Creek.

"Soapy" Smith managed to gather around him a rather unscrupulous flock who fleeced many a would-be prospector of his stake long before he got to Dawson. The Wild West made quite a revival in northern Skagway. Soapy's downfall came when a group of armed townsfolk drew him and his boys out. The gang quickly scattered; Soapy held his ground and was shot dead, but not until he had managed mortally to wound the vigilante who shot him.

The Canadian authorities looked upon both the outlaw activity and the vigilantism with disdain. The Canadian cabinet ordered that 300 North West Mounted Police be sent to the Yukon.

They were headed by a man whose name almost stereotypically symbolized not only his own character but that of his police force – Sam Steele. Steele was charged with several tasks, the first of which was to enforce and impress upon the prospectors Canadian sovereignty. More than 90 percent of those entering the Yukon were Americans. Another of Steele's responsibilities was to ensure that every man and woman

The steamer SS Keno used to transport silver, lead, and zinc ore from the Mayo District to Stewart.

entering the Yukon had enough supplies to last an entire year. Steele stationed Mounties at all mountain passes and ordered that all would-be Yukoners with less than 1,000lbs (453kg) of equipment and food be turned back. This was a sensible order: you could hope for, but not depend on, charity in the Yukon.

Carrying the requisite equipment through mountain passes 1,160 meters (3,800ft) or more in height was a Herculean task. In April of 1898, with spring well on its way, 63 people were smothered to death in an avalanche at Chilkoot Pass. Within a day the pass was reopened and people continued their grim ascent.

BOOM TO BUST

During the early years of the gold rush in **Dawson City ②**, inflation was rampant: oranges sold for 50 cents apiece and a pint of champagne cost $40. Gold poured out of the Yukon. In 1896, $300,000-worth of gold was produced; the following year $2.5 million-worth was mined; in 1898, $10 million in gold was extracted; and by 1900, the peak year, more than $22 million-worth of gold was

⊙ THE YUKON'S CITIES

Whitehorse began as a Yukon River shantytown in the late 1890s, its population ebbing and flowing with the gold rush. Visit the steamboat SS *Klondike II* (mid-May to early Sept daily 9.30am–5pm; free), one of several hundred steamwheelers that once plied the river to Dawson City. Also worth a visit is the Miles Canyon, 9km (6 miles) south.

While the population has dwindled to less than 1,500 , Dawson City attracts more than 60,000 tourists a year who visit the original gold rush theaters, bars, and brothels. Start at the Front Street Visitor Reception Center, then head to the Dawson City Museum (mid-May to Labor Day daily 10am–6pm, Labor Day to Sept Tue–Sat 10am–2pm, Oct to mid-May, tel +1 867-993-5291 for appointment; www.dawsonmuseum.ca).

taken from the Yukon. Yet every boom has a bust, and the Yukon's halcyon days began to fade in 1902. There was simply less gold to be had. In addition, large companies began filing claims on many "used" claims and then reworking them. In this way corporations consolidated the gold industry and displaced the traditional small-time operators. They packed up and left, many of them seeking the next new frontier.

With the exodus of the original "sourdoughs" there followed the closing of the dancehalls, gambling parlors, and drinking establishments. The freewheeling and free-spirited days were over. At the height of the gold rush in 1898, Dawson City had a population of 40,000 and was the largest city in western Canada. By 1910 there were only 1,000 inhabitants. Today, just less than 2,000 people live there, and few are prospectors.

There has been speculation that both the Yukon and Canada missed a great opportunity to develop what would have become an indigenous industry. If the small-time operator had been encouraged to stay, perhaps a tertiary industry could have sustained the remarkable culture. Interestingly, there remain roughly 200 one- or two-man placer-gold outfits who are still working the rivers of the Yukon, long after the large gold companies have left.

Mining was the backbone of the Yukon's economy. When gold production began to slow, large zinc, lead, and silver deposits were discovered, allowing mining to continue.

THE YUKON TODAY

In recent years, tourism has played an increasingly important role in the Yukon. Since many of the outdoor activities require a high level of fitness and an adventurous streak, mainstream tourism focuses on Klondike nostalgia. So even if the gold boom broke more than 100 years ago, its legacy still pays a modest dividend. In Dawson City, the former capital of the Yukon and hub of the gold rush,

Canada's first legalized casino, Diamond Tooth Gertie's – with a gold-rush era theme, and a Klondike-style dance revue are strong reminders that the Yukon was founded by hustlers, gold diggers, and dreamers, not fishermen or farmers.

There are tours that will take travelers down the same rivers that paddlewheelers once traveled. Along the riverbanks and hiking trails are the remains of the prospectors' old camps and abandoned towns; tourists can relive the "golden days" of the Yukon's Klondike. Ironically, many in the tourist industry now wish to restrict or eliminate the activities of the modern placer-gold prospectors. Placer-gold extraction has done and can do tremendous environmental damage to riverbeds.

With all the emphasis on Yukon's faded "glory days," there is another perspective. To understand the region from a First Nations viewpoint, visit **Danoja Zho (Long Time Ago) Cultural Centre** (June–Sept Mon–Sat 10am–5pm, Oct–Apr by appointment), a community and heritage center for Tr'ondëk Hwëch'in culture.

The gold rush boomtown of Dawson City.

📷 LIVING IN A WHITE WORLD OF SNOW

In a country where people exist amidst a snowy white blanket for many months of the year, the necessity to respect and adapt to this harsh weather is essential for survival.

Snow angels practically define a Canadian childhood. You plonk yourself down on your back, flap your legs and arms up and down over the snow's soft surface, then leap up to inspect the enchanting result. This instinctive communing with nature frequently launches a lifelong affair with snow. Every winter, lakes, rivers, even back yards, are converted into ice rinks, where youngsters play hockey and their parents simply skate. Countless Canadians are addicted to outdoor winter activities from skiing to snowshoeing, snowmobiling, dog sledding, ice fishing, and horse-drawn sleigh rides.

INDOOR PURSUITS

Not all Canadians welcome snow with such enthusiasm. Fortunately winter also heralds a plethora of cultural activities, from experimental theater to symphony concerts and operatic galas, literary fests, and eye-popping art exhibits. Sports fans' weekends revolve around *Hockey Night in Canada*, a long-standing Saturday-night TV fixture. January and February's gloom is often brightened by extravagant culinary and wine-tastings, and by March stores are awash with sparkling springtime fashions and Easter bunnies.

In urban centers, snow is more easily avoided. From Calgary to Montréal, Canadians take refuge in networks of underground passageways where shops, restaurants, theaters, even ice rinks, offer diversions galore from the harsh reality of winter.

Igloo-building began in the fall, when snow was compacted into blocks. The inhabitants depended on further snow for insulation.

A man pulling a huge pike from under the ice.

A back-country skier jumping a cliff in British Columbia.

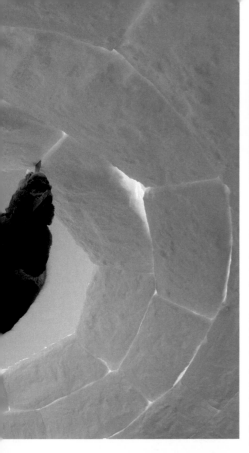

In the Yukon, much of the land lies under a snowy blanket from October to April, providing opportunities for exhilarating dog sledding.

Survival in the Far North

Hunting and trapping have been the lifeline of Arctic communities for thousands of years. Huskies (or *qimmiit*) were the workhorses of the Arctic, pulling wooden sleds *(qamutiit)* carrying Inuit hunters and their provisions for hundreds of miles during the fall, when extensive caribou hunts were necessary to provide sufficient food for the family. *Inukshuks*, which are slabs of rock piled high, were built to guide startled caribou into a blind where hunters waited with bows and arrows. Once the meat was removed, the skins were turned into clothing and blankets.

Winter was spent largely within their igloos, which were heated by *qulliqs* – soapstone oil lamps fueled by seal blubber. To break the monotony, storytelling, wrestling contests, throat singing, and drum dances took place in a *qaggiq*, which was a large snowhouse.

In the longer days of March, the huskies helped to locate seal breathing-holes in the ice, and the hunters then waited patiently with their harpoons for seals to emerge. Spring and summer saw the return of arctic char, birds, and an abundance of arctic berries. Inuit survival depended on the riches of both land and sea.

Snow buntings (Plectrophenax nivalis) in winter.

Traditional indoor games in Nunavut.

Creating popular maple-syrup snow candy during the annual Winterlude Festival in Ottawa.

The Nahanni River, Nahanni National Park Preserve.

THE NORTHWEST TERRITORIES

Far away from the pressures of urban life, the Northwest Territories conceal a sparkling landscape of mountains, rivers, and canyons. Here visitors can climb, canoe, fish, and watch wildlife.

Many would picture the Northwest Territories as a flat and perennially icy slab stretching from the 60th Parallel toward the North Pole, with the occasional polar bear or Inuit igloo to give some relief to the unvarying landscape. However, the landscape is anything but monotonous, and it is not one land but a multitude of lands – lands that are foreign to most people, and yet so mystical that each person who visits there is not so much a tourist as an explorer.

The Northwest Territories cover an immense area of almost 1.2 million sq km (over 450,000 sq miles). To gain some insight into how large this is, combine Spain, France, Switzerland, the Netherlands, and Belgium. The southern border touches Saskatchewan, Alberta, and part of British Columbia, along the 60th Parallel and stretches 3,400km (2,110 miles) up to the North Pole. This means that the total land mass of the N.W.T. (officially abbreviated to NT, but commonly referred to as N.W.T.) is larger than Texas, Oklahoma, Arkansas, and Louisiana combined, yet the area has a population of a mere 44,000.

More than half of these residents are aboriginal, some of whom have ancestors that lived on this land since the last Ice Age.

SCARS OF THE ICE AGE

Venturing north above the tree line into the tundra, where it is too cold for lush vegetation and forests to survive, the scars of thousands of centuries of geological history stand before the eyes. It was only 10,000 years ago that the last Ice Age, the Pleistocene, finally retreated from much of the area, leaving behind moraines, dry gravel beds, and drumlins.

There are also thousands of rivers and lakes that cover more than half of the territory's land mass. Many of

Main attractions

Yellowknife
Wood Buffalo National Park
Nahanni National Park
Prince of Wales Northern Heritage Center

Map on page 326

Aurora Borealis over Great Slave Lake.

Tip

To view the tundra and mountains north of the Arctic Circle, take the 730km (450-mile) Dempster Highway from Dawson City, Yukon, to Inuvik, NT.

these lakes and rivers, particularly those in the Mackenzie delta, were formed by glaciers creating indentations in the earth and leaving behind melted glacial ice.

Rivers and lakes notwithstanding, much of the territory is classified by geographers as desert. The stereotypical picture of the Canadian North being smothered in snow is surprisingly inaccurate. In fact, the mean annual precipitation for both the eastern and western Arctic is only 30cm (12ins), which is the equivalent of just a single Montréal snowstorm.

During the long Arctic winters, however, the sun may only appear for a few brief hours, if at all, so whatever snow does fall will not melt until spring. Temperatures in the region are legendary. At Inuvik, the territory's capital, two degrees north of the Arctic Circle, the average winter temperature drops to a perishing –31°C (–24°F) at night, with a record low of –56°C (–70°F), while in July, its warmest month, it averages close to 20°C (68°F) and is

more frequently than not closer to 30°C (89°F).

For a traveler trying to plan what clothing to pack for an adventure – which is what any trip to the Northwest Territories will be – the standard rule of lots of layers applies. The temperature may vary, but one thing does not. When summer arrives here the sun only just dips into the horizon before beginning its slow upward journey, and conditions are ideal for hiking or camping. In fact, summer in this region is remarkably similar to that in the rest of Canada, except of course that there is more sunshine and a much lower probability of rain.

BREEDING GROUNDS

While the Northwest Territories receive relatively few human visitors, it is estimated that 12 percent of North America's bird population breeds here during the spring and summer months. Close to 300 species are tracked here, with biologists looking to learn more about migratory habits. They believe that one of the main attractions to this part of

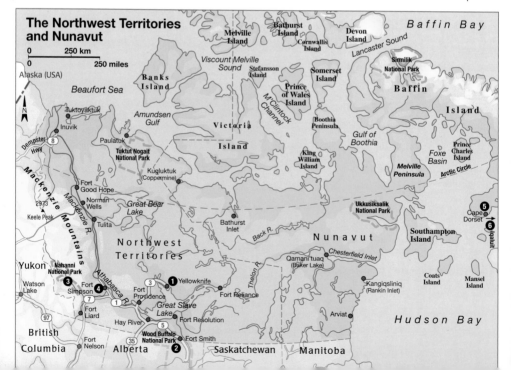

North America is the relative lack of predators and, in summer, an abundant source of food.

This is a birder's paradise, as it provides the potential of seven different species of owl, and a huge variety of eagles, hawks, and other raptors. Ocean birds, shore birds, and even songbirds can be spotted here, provided the right planning is undertaken. The land is so vast that it makes sense to rely on the tour operators who cater to keen birders and photographers for help with itineraries and timing.

Below the tree line, where the weather is less harsh and the trees offer protection from the elements, there are moose, beaver, marten, muskrat, red fox, timber wolf, and black bear. Massive herds of caribou migrate from their traditional calving ground near the Beaufort Sea southward. In select areas, the largest mammal in North America, the wood bison, also roams the grassy plains. Above the tree line there are arctic wolves with white coats, as well as arctic fox

and lemmings. Along the coastline and on the islands polar bears, seals, walrus, and even lemmings can be seen. **Banks**, **Victoria**, and **Melville Islands** in the far north are inhabited by the exotic, hirsute musk ox.

THE TUNDRA AND CLIMATE CHANGE

Perhaps one of the most remarkable facts about survival on the tundra is the dependency of all life on soil frozen to a depth of between 30 and 300 meters (100 to 1,000ft). This ground is appropriately called permafrost. During the summer, the sun's rays are able to melt topsoil here to a depth of 24 meters (80ft). It is within this layer of soil that small organisms, including lichen, grow. Lichen and low-lying vegetation are a main source of food for the mammals of the tundra.

In the summer season that is too short in length for plant life to grow, all species suffer losses. Decimated species eventually recover and restore the natural order, but this order becomes a precarious one and any external force

⊙ Tip

Just to the east of the Yukon, Nahanni National Park has gorges deeper than the Grand Canyon. Visit Fort Simpson to arrange tours, flights, and canoe rentals.

The Northwest Territories are a birdwatcher's paradise.

⊘ A RIVER RUNNER'S DREAM

The idyllic rivers of Canada's Northwest Territories are untamed, unpolluted, and flow through hundreds of miles of unmatched wilderness, offering some of the most wonderful and stimulating paddling experiences in the world. In boreal forest rivers including the Nahanni, the Natla-Keele, the Mountain, or the Slave, deep canyons, rapids, and spectacular plunging waterfalls prove great challenges to the paddler, whitewater canoeist, and photographer alike.

Farther north, Arctic rivers also have incredible appeal, meandering their way through the expansive open tundra, where the majority of plants grow no taller than a foot (30cm/12ins) high, and where great wildlife spectacles may include the midsummer migrations of the caribou or grizzly bears and tundra wolves.

can disrupt the fragile ecosystem. It is for this reason that the intrusion of southern development is seen as a dangerous threat.

The Canadian North is being closely examined by scientists concerned about climate change. As they observe the impact of the recent increases in temperature experienced here, they are trying to put the changes in the context of the delicate ecosystem and the countless plants and animals that have adapted themselves to survive here. Measuring the changes in permafrost temperatures and depth of seasonal freezing/thawing are key indicators of changes of climate in the Arctic.

Catch sight of the aurora borealis, or Northern Lights, here from late August through March, when the night sky comes alive with a dazzling display of colors.

EARLY EXPLORATIONS

Boats wait for the spring thaw on the Mackenzie River.

Since the first European explorers, the North has held a sense of mystery for all outsiders. Many believed there were untold fortunes to be made there, so they approached it with this in mind.

The first recorded European exploration of the Arctic was undertaken by the Elizabethan, Martin Frobisher, who searched for gold and the elusive Northwest Passage in 1576. Frobisher found neither gold nor the Passage on his first or many subsequent journeys. However, he did manage to bring back to England 700 tonnes of fool's gold from Baffin Island (now part of Nunavut).

Henry Hudson was another intrepid English explorer who set out to find the Passage. Hudson traveled extensively in the North for several years. Not only did he fail to find the Northwest Passage but his long-suffering crew mutinied, causing havoc. Hudson, his son, and seven other explorers were set adrift in a barque in the bay that now carries Hudson's name. The nine men were never seen again. Owing to the discouraging results of expeditions undertaken by Frobisher, Hudson, and others of the era, the British Crown and other financial backers

became disenchanted and abandoned the search for a northerly route to the Orient and India.

Within Canada, fur traders were searching for routes to markets in Europe. One such entrepreneur was Alexander Mackenzie, who in 1789 followed the Mackenzie river for its entire length (4,240km/2,630 miles) in the hope that it would eventually lead to the Pacific Ocean. It led instead to the Arctic Ocean. Little did Mackenzie realize in the 18th century that he had reached an opening to a sea that covered vast and lucrative oil deposits.

Even though this area had proven to have little commercial value in the 17th and 18th centuries, there were those in England during the 19th century who looked toward the Arctic region with a mixture of wide-eyed romanticism and genuine scientific curiosity. This era in Arctic exploration was similar to the period of space exploration of the 1960s and 1970s. The British Parliament offered prizes to any person who could find the Northwest Passage and/or discover the North Pole.

Daring explorers include William Parry, who managed to collect a purse of £5,000 for his excursion to the far Western Arctic islands (1819–21), and John Franklin, who, in characteristic, bloody-minded British bulldog manner, regularly risked his life while mapping the Arctic coastline.

On his final journey in 1845, Franklin departed from England with a crew of 129 men aboard two ships; their lofty objective was to find the Northwest Passage. Unfortunately the ships were locked in the ice for two years at Victoria Strait. In 1848, search parties were sent out, and eventually over the next eight years articles of clothing, logbooks, and mementos were found strewn across the chilly coastline. Of the 129 men on the Franklin expedition not one survivor was found.

TRAVELING TODAY

Today, however, travel to the Arctic is thankfully a great deal less hazardous. After the Franklin debacle, "outsiders" began to pay attention to the ways of the Inuit, the Dene and other

A lynx on the prowl in an aspen forest.

⊙ Fact

Yellowknife owes its existence to the discovery of gold here in 1934. Named after the copper knives of the local Indians, the city became capital of N.W.T. in 1967.

First Nations peoples who had not only survived in the North for millennia, but had also developed rich cultures with strong oral traditions, passing on practical information about how to thrive in such extreme and difficult conditions.

With the arrival of the airplane in the early 1920s, the Northwest Territories became far more accessible to the outside world. Air travel is now both routine and safe in the Territories. To reach many communities, air routes have become the "real" highways for the North. The area is served by several airlines from major cities in Canada to all large communities. Once there, approximately 30 scheduled and chartered services fly between cities and remote camps.

The N.W.T. has conventional highways too, which connect the majority of the large communities, including **Yellowknife ❶**, **Hay River**, **Fort Smith**, **Inuvik**, and **Fort Simpson**, with the outside world. These highways are all hardpacked gravel, rather than paved, so some adjustment to your driving style may be necessary. Yellowknife is also connected to Edmonton by a regular "black top" (asphalt) road.

Owing to a distinct lack of vehicular traffic, travel in the Territories can indeed be a relaxing experience and a great relief to those more accustomed to aggressive city driving. Drivers will see few vehicles on the roads, and are likely to see more wildlife than vehicles along the way. The **Dempster Highway** places restrictions on travel during fall and spring while herds of caribou, numbering in the tens of thousands, make their annual migration.

THE WESTERN ARCTIC

In all the territory west of **Great Slave** and **Great Bear Lake** up toward Inuvik – the Western Arctic – there are numerous equipment stores in the major communities. Below the tree line, canoe trips take place from late May to mid-September. In the tundra area most trips take place from mid-June to mid-August. In recent years, cross-country skiing trips have been set up during the spring so that tourists can witness the spectacular migration of caribou herds in style. Participants are flown into a base camp, and from there they glide onto frozen lakes and rivers to observe the caribou migration.

DOMAIN OF THE BISON

In the southern region of N.W.T. there are two spectacular national parks. **Wood Buffalo National Park ❷** is located on either side of the Alberta–N.W.T. border and was established in 1922 to preserve the bison. This objective has been a success, and one can now attend a "Bison Creep" to view these creatures. Occupying an area roughly the size of Switzerland, the national park covers a remarkable landscape of forests, meadows, sinkholes, and an unusual salt plain.

The second national park, further to the west, is located in the remote

A wild Woodland Bison near Yellowknife.

southwest corner of the territory on the Yukon border. **Nahanni National Park ❸**, which is a Unesco World Heritage Site, is in the Deh Cho Region, also known as the Nahanni-Ram. The region was once home to a mysterious people called Nahaa or Nahannis. Legends of wild mountain men, a white queen, evil spirits, lost maps, lost gold, and headless men are myths that prevail to this day.

Bird enthusiasts are one group that hasn't been deterred from venturing into the Deh Cho. In addition to seeing such exciting birds as white pelicans, peregrine falcons, and trumpeter swans, there are impressive river gorges, underground caves, and bubbling hot springs. The adventurous can take an exciting river-rafting trip down the South Nahanni river, one of the wildest rivers in Canada. Access to the park is by air only, from **Fort Simpson ❹**.

CULTURE IN YELLOWKNIFE

Yellowknife now promotes itself as "the diamond capital of North America," not only because of its proximity to the only commercial diamond mines on the continent, but because of the dazzling scenery that surrounds it. Overlooking Frame Lake in the center of town is the **Prince of Wales Northern Heritage Centre** (museum daily 10.30am–5pm, Thu until 9pm; www.pwnhc.ca; free), which houses excellent histories and artifacts of the Inuit, Dene, and Métis.

A UNIQUE EXPERIENCE

Much of the Northwest Territories is completely untouched by civilization. Here, the traveler sees first and foremost the land and how the plants and animals here have adapted to their environment. The impact of humans on this land has been minimal, allowing its delicate balance to survive. The impressive mountains, the barren grounds, the stunted forests, the overarching skies, the thousands of freshwater lakes and rivers of this vast land combine to create a unique and humbling experience.

⊙ Tip

Yellowknife has one of the N.W.T.'s few golf courses. However, the only course with grass greens (rather than sand) is at the Hay River Golf Club, on the southern shore of the Great Slave Lake.

Canoeing down the Nahanni River.

NUNAVUT

Nunavut – Canada's most recently established territory and home to more than half of the country's Inuit population – is a vast terrain of barren ground, plateaus, and mountains, and a hauntingly beautiful retreat.

Main attractions

Cape Dorset
Iqaluit
Auyuittuq National Park
  Reserve
Inuit Heritage Centre,
  Baker Lake

Map on page 326

The Eastern Arctic, including much of the Archipelago and the terrain east of Great Slave Lake, remained a hidden world until the age of the airplane. It became the new territory of Nunavut – which means "our land" in Inuktitut – on April 1, 1999, when the Northwest Territories were split into two. Approximately 85 percent of Nunavut's population is Inuit and it had been vying for independence since 1973, driven by the desire for a self-governed territory with firm control over its own future. The Nunavut Land Claim Settlement, proclaimed in July 1993, is now regarded as a global benchmark in aboriginal matters and includes title to nearly 356,000 sq km (138,000 sq miles), mineral rights, a share of federal royalties on oil, gas, and mineral development on Crown lands, and the right of first refusal on sport and commercial development of Nunavut's renewable resources.

THE GREAT OUTDOORS

Canada's newest territory is also its largest, occupying about 20 percent of the country's land mass, almost entirely above the timber line and spread across three time zones. Nunavut extends from the eastern shores of Baffin and Ellesmere islands, west to the plateaus and cliffs of the Arctic coast on the Coronation Gulf, and north to the High Arctic Islands and the North Pole. It is home to various outpost settlements and 28 communities, the largest of which is the capital, Iqaluit, with a population of around 6,700 citizens.

Although isolated and expensive to get to, the delights of Nunavut's great outdoors reward those who can afford the time and money to visit. As there are virtually no roads in Nunavut, other than a 21km (13-mile) stretch between Arctic Bay and Nanisivik, travel by air, snowmobile or dogsled are the only options. The challenging weather conditions may also mean frequent delays

Skiers admiring the view at Baffin Island.

and changed itineraries, but visitors agree it is worth it.

Most tourists come during the two- to three-month summer, when temperatures average 12°C (54°F). Nonetheless, some seasoned adventurers brave the frigid Arctic winter, when the mercury plummets to –46°C (–51°F), to accompany a traditional Inuit seal hunt or view the spectacular Northern Lights under winter's perpetually dark skies.

Irrefutably, Nunavut's main draw is the outdoors. Outfitters arrange packages from building igloos to polar-bear watching, dogsledding, and encounters with narwhals (one-tusked whales at one time believed to be cousins to the mythical unicorn).

BAFFIN ISLAND

Baffin Island is home to roughly a quarter of Canada's Inuit population and some of the oldest northern communities in the world. **Cape Dorset 5**, on the southwest coast, is the home of modern Inuit art, the understated simplicity of which expresses the harmonic Inuit vision of Arctic life. Examples are on display and for sale at the **West Baffin Eskimo Co-op** (tel: 867-897-8997). For action lovers, Cape Dorset also offers hiking, dogsledding, and cross-country skiing tours. **Iqaluit 6** (formerly known as Frobisher Bay), meaning 'place of fish', on the southeast coast, is the capital of Nunavut and another Baffin Island community rich in Inuit heritage. The glaciers on Baffin Island are another source of inspiration. The **Penny Ice Cap** is 6,000 sq km (2,300 sq miles) of ice and snow, 300 meters (985ft) deep in some areas. To view this glacier high up in the mountains of **Auyuittuq National Park Reserve** is to revisit the Ice Age. Sections of Baffin Island's east coast, where there are fjords and spectacular cliffs that rise to a height of 2,100 meters (7,000ft), higher than the walls of the Grand Canyon, also offer a taste of the Ice Age. Tours by snowmobile or dogsled to the floe-edge offer a fabulous way to experience Baffin Island's wildlife.

Summer is spectacular on the Arctic coast. The lure of abundant wildlife and a historic Inuit settlement make Bathurst Inlet a magnet for naturalists, birdwatchers, photographers, botanists, and archeologists alike.

BAKER LAKE

Situated on the shores of **Baker Lake** (its Inuit name – *Qamani'tuaq* – means "where the river widens") is the small community of Baker Lake, which is the geographical center of Canada. This is another popular base for delving into Arctic history and Inuit culture. Baker Lake is known for its soapstone carvings and exquisite prints. Northeast of here is the Thelon River, first explored by Europeans in 1893, when two brothers, James and Joseph Tyrell, descended the Thelon on behalf of the Geological Survey of Canada. Inuit art and heritage is well documented in the **Inuit Heritage Centre** (tel: 867-793-2598) in Baker Lake.

⊙ **Fact**

Nunavut seems to have been purposely designed for the nature photographer, with its estimated 750,000 caribou, 60,000 musk ox, and hundreds of millions of birds – more than 100 different species.

Aerial view of the glaciers, mountains and fjords of Auyuittuq National Park.

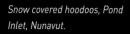
Snow covered hoodoos, Pond Inlet, Nunavut.

Gastown, Vancouver.

CANADA

TRAVEL TIPS

TRANSPORTATION

By Air

Many people choose to fly into Canada, then continue their trip by bus, train, plane, or rented car. Most major cities have direct air connections with US cities. Many international airlines connect Toronto, Montréal, and Vancouver with all parts of North and South America, Europe, and Asia. There are more limited services between Europe and Edmonton, Calgary, Halifax, and St John's, Newfoundland. Air Canada and several regional carriers, including Porter Airlines and WestJet, connect with extensive feeder routes operated by associated airlines.

Private plane pilots are required to file a trans-border flight plan prior to departure, and to land at a Canadian Customs port of entry. Full aircraft and personal documentation is required.

Airport Charges

A number of airports across Canada levy an Airport Improvement Fee (AIF) to all visitors departing from the airport. These fees are generally added to the ticket price, so there is no additional fee payable on departure. These fees can be as much as $30.

By Sea

There are car-ferry services between Maine and New Brunswick (Deer Island), and Washington State and British Columbia. Many cruise lines sailing from the US call at ports on the Atlantic and Pacific coasts, and there are also a few cruises in Arctic waters. Many yachtsmen sail to favorite Canadian cruising grounds on the coasts and within the Great Lakes, but in summer dock space can be tight. US and other foreign yachts are required to clear Canadian Customs at a designated port of entry.

By Road

From the US, passing through customs and immigration at the border can be a lengthy process, with line-ups of an hour or two not uncommon on weekends. If possible, avoid the border, traveling in either direction, on Friday or Sunday late afternoons and evenings.

The major bus company with routes into Canada is Greyhound (US) and its associated companies. Some routes end at a city just over the border, where you can subsequently transfer to a Canadian carrier, but there are also special packages from certain US cities (including Boston, New York, Chicago, and San Francisco) to Vancouver, Toronto, Montréal, and other destinations in Canada. Greyhound offers a variety of deals and discounts including student fares, web only fares and advance purchase fares. For further details, contact Greyhound Canada on 1-800-661-8747, www.greyhound.ca. In 2018, Greyhound discounted the majority of their routes in Alberta, Saskatchewan and Manitoba. In British Columbia, all routes were discontinued except for Vancouver to Seattle.

By Rail

Amtrak offers two direct passenger train routes into Canada: Seattle to Vancouver; and Washington and New York to Montréal. VIA Rail has similar services from New York to Toronto via Niagara Falls; and from Chicago to Sarnia, London, and Toronto. VIA Rail also offers group, family, and senior-citizen discounts, as well as flat-rate "CanRail" passes, which allow for travelling between Quebec and Ontario for 21 consecutive days (Corridor pass), or across Canada for 60 consecutive days (System Pass). Both first-class and coach accommodations are available, each with dining cars.

For further information, telephone the nearest train station or contact:

VIA Rail, PO Box 8116, SUCC CENTRE-VILLE, Montréal, QC H3C 3N33
Tel: 514-871-9830/1-888-842-7245 (from anywhere in Canada)
www.viarail.ca
To call **Amtrak** in the US dial 1-800-USA-RAIL; and in Canada dial 1-800-872-7245; or visit their website: www.amtrak.com

◎ Airlines

Air Canada
Tel: UK 00800 669 92222
Canada and US toll-free 1-888-247-2262
www.aircanada.com
Air Canada Jazz
Tel: toll-free 1-888-247-2262
www.flyjazz.ca
Air Transat (part of Air Canada)
Tel: toll-free 1-877-872-6728
www.airtransat.ca
First Air, Airline of the North
Tel: toll-free 1-800-267-1247
www.firstair.ca
Porter Airlines
Tel: 416-619-8622/1-888-619-8622
www.flyporter.com
WestJet Airlines
Tel: toll-free 1-888-937-8538 within Canada and from the US
Tel: UK 0800 279 7072
www.westjet.com

GETTING AROUND

For travelers who know where they want to go to in Canada, there are a number of different transportation options available.

By Air

Domestic air services are preferable, both for traveling long distances and for accessing any particularly remote areas, since driving can be very time-consuming. (A straightforward drive between Toronto and Montréal will take five hours.) While Air Canada is the main carrier, a number of smaller no-frills and discount airlines emerged after the collapse of Canadian Airlines in 2001. Some have not survived the fierce cut and thrust of Canada's passenger airline industry, but the survivors both compete with Air Canada on the most traveled routes, and offer services to smaller, less accessible communities.

Air Canada
Tel: 1-888-247-2262
www.aircanada.ca
Air Transat
Tel: 1-877-872-6728
www.airtransat.com
First Air (for the Northwest Territories)
Tel: 1-800-267-1247
www.firstair.ca
Porter Airlines (Toronto and east)
Tel: 1-888-619-8622
www.flyporter.com
WestJet Airlines
Tel: toll-free 1-888-937-8538 within Canada and from the US
www.westjet.com

By Rail

Railways are good for both short and long distances, although trains take five days to travel the 6,360km (3,950 miles) from Halifax in the east to Vancouver in the west. VIA Rail, Canada's major passenger train service, offers a range of cost-saving package discounts and travel passes. Ontario also operates some passenger rail services. Bear in mind that many routes sell out, so make sure you check availability early in the planning stages of your trip. For further information on routes, prices, and timetables contact:
Rocky Mountaineer
1100-980 Howe Street, Vancouver, BC V6Z 0C8

⊙ Steam trains

Canada is a beautiful country and it is possible to make your journey part of, or the main focus of, your vacation. With the railway playing such a vital role in Canada's development, it is not, perhaps, surprising that there are some terrific steam train rides to be enjoyed across the country.

In Ontario, the **Agawa Canyon Tour Train** offers a spectacular excursion, some 180km (114 miles) north from Sault Ste Marie, over towering trestle bridges, alongside pristine northern lakes and rivers, and through the granite rock formations and mixed forests of the Canadian Shield to the Agawa Canyon. It is especially popular during the fall, when advance reservations are an absolute necessity. For more information tel: 1-800-242-9287, www.agawacanyontourtrain.com.

Tel: 604-606-7245 (international) or toll-free in Canada and US 1-877-460-3200, toll-free UK 0-800-088-5541
www.rockymountaineer.com
Their two-day journey is billed as "the most spectacular train trip in the world."
VIA Rail Canada
For further information, call the following toll-free number: 1-888-842-7245 (from anywhere in Canada or the US); or, in Montréal, 514-989-2626.
www.viarail.ca

By Road

Buses

Buses are inexpensive and especially good for shorter distances or for getting to small towns not serviced by rail or air. Canada's major bus line, Greyhound Canada, offers a number of travel passes and packages, as well as discounts for early booking. For bus service through the Alberta and British Columbia Rockies, Brewster Transportation is another good alternative.
Brewster Transportation
Box 1140, 100 Gopher St, Banff, AB TIL IJ3
Tel: 403-762-6700/1-866-606-6700
Greyhound Canada

In Manitoba, **Prairie Dog Central Railway** (tel: 204-832-5259; www.pdcrailway.com), running on weekends during the summer and before Christmas (the Santa Express), takes passengers from the big city – Winnipeg – to rural Manitoba, visiting country markets in Grosse Isle and Warren, where the track terminates. The fully restored vintage rail coaches were built between 1901 and 1913 and the engine dates from 1882.

The 11km (7-mile) round trip on **The Spirit of Kamloops**, offered by the Kamloops Heritage Railway (tel: 250-374-2141; www.kamrail.com), travels through spectacular scenery, operating Mondays, Tuesdays, Fridays, and Saturdays, July and August. Passengers have the option of riding in a custom-designed open-air "Hayrack" car or reliving the past in a 1930s heritage coach.

877 Greyhound Way SW, Calgary, AB T3C 3V8
Tel: 1-800-661-8747
www.greyhound.ca

Driving

If general touring is on the agenda, it is usually straightforward to hire a car. Foreign drivers' licenses are valid in Canada, and accident liability insurance is required. Driving is on the right and conventions are similar to those in the US. Seat belts are mandatory, as are child seats. Highway speed limits are usually 100kph (60mph), but speed limits, seat-belt regulations, and other laws differ slightly from province to province. Provincial regulations are usually summarized in tourist literature and on many official road maps.

The Canadian Automobile Association, a federation of nine automotive clubs across Canada, is a good source for information, maps, and driving regulations. Members of European automobile associations can contact any of the nine clubs through the CAA's main website: www.caa.ca.

If you are traveling from the US check with your insurer before you depart to make sure it covers you during your stay in Canada. Be aware that most of Canada requires

⊘ Rules of the road

Besides remembering to drive on the right, there are few other safety considerations to keep in mind. As some traffic rules vary from province to province, ask your car rental company if you have any queries of this nature.

While Canada has an extensive and modern system of highways, most of which are well numbered and clearly marked, at times it is very helpful to know your north from south and your east from west. Speed limits are posted in kilometers per hour (kph) and they vary from 30 to 50kph (19–31mph) in built-up areas to between 80 and 100kph (50–62mph) on highways.

To improve highway safety, some Canadian provinces and territories require vehicles to be driven with headlights on for extended periods after dawn and before sunset. The headlights of most newer vehicles turn on automatically once the engine is started.

In all Canadian provinces except Québec, you may turn right at a red traffic light after coming to a full stop and making sure that the way is clear before you do so. In Québec you may turn right at a red light anywhere in the province except where prohibited by a sign or on Montréal Island.

School buses display flashing lights for around 150 meters (500ft) before stopping and 30 meters (100ft) after leaving a stop; drivers may only pass the bus at this time with caution. If the bus has stopped and is flashing its red lights, other drivers must stop behind that bus. Remember that pedestrians have right of way at all intersections without stop lights and crosswalks.

that you carry at least $200,000 in liability insurance.

Gasoline prices range from around $1.30 per liter (there are 3.8 liters in a US gallon and 4.5 liters in a Canadian imperial gallon).

Car Rentals

Several international car rental companies have offices throughout Canada and rentals can be easily arranged before arriving in the country. Call the following firms, toll-free, for information:

Avis
Tel: 1-800-879-2847 in Canada; 1-800-331-2323 in the US
www.avis.com
Budget
Tel: 1-800-268-8900 in Canada; 1-800-218-7992 in the US; 0844-544 3455 in the UK
www.budget.com
Hertz
Tel: 1-800-654-3131 in Canada and the US
www.hertz.com
National
Tel: 1-844-393-9989 in the US and 1-844-307-8014 in Canada; 0845-120-2071 in the UK
www.nationalcar.ca
Thrifty
Tel: 1-800-847-4389 in Canada and the US
www.thrifty.com

Motor Homes

If you plan to rent a camper/recreational vehicle (RV) in July and August you should book 3–4 months in advance. Or, if you have time to be flexible, check out the relocation and last-minute deals, where you can save half or more on the rental cost. Both companies listed below offer pick-up and drop-off at numerous locations across the country.
Canadream
292154 Crosspointe Dr, Calgary, AB T4A 0V2
Tel: 1-888-480-9726 in Canada and the US
www.canadream.com
Cruise Canada
11 Westhampton Ave, Meza, AZ 85210
Tel: 1-800-671-8042
(Also in Vancouver, Toronto, and Montréal)
www.cruisecanada.com

Car Ferries

There are numerous car ferries all over Canada which cross lakes and rivers large and small. Some are considered part of the highway system and are free, while others charge substantial fares. Of the large ferries, the most notable are those operated by BC Ferries along the British Columbia coast, and Marine Atlantic's between Nova Scotia and Newfoundland.

Province by Province

Alberta

By Air Calgary and Edmonton international airports are served by a number of airlines from elsewhere in Canada and from the US, Europe, and Asia, principally Air Canada, WestJet, Delta, Northwest, American, and United.
By Rail VIA Rail (tel: 1-888-842-7245; www.viarail.ca) has thrice-weekly services to Edmonton and Jasper (a five-and-a-half-hour ride apart) on its transcontinental route from Vancouver to Toronto.

Rocky Mountaineer (tel: 604-606-7245/1-877-460-3200 Canada/USA, 0-800-088-5541 UK, 0-800-451-247 New Zealand, 1-800-821-531 Australia; www.rockymountaineer.com) operates numerous sightseeing train excursions, including a seasonal two-day service from Calgary to Vancouver, with an overnight stop at Kamloops B.C., so patrons can enjoy the spectacular sightseeing that spans the 1,000km (625 mile) journey.
By Bus Red Arrow Motorcoach (tel: 1-800-232-1958; www.redarrow.ca) provide access to almost every Alberta community, while Brewster Transportation & Tours (tel: 1-877-606-6700; www.brewster.ca) provides major bus services to the parks and other tourist destinations.
By Car Trans-Canada Highway No. 1 runs west to southeast across Alberta, through Calgary. Highway 2 passes through Calgary on its way from the US border to Edmonton and points north. The major car rental companies are all represented, as well as a number of camper/RV rental agencies. Taxis are readily available in Calgary, Edmonton, Banff, and Jasper.

Calgary (403 & 587)
Calgary Transit (tel: 403-262-1000; www.calgarytransit.com) operates an express bus #300 from the airport to downtown or bus and light rail transit (LRT or the C-Train) to other parts of the city. City bus tours can be arranged through the tourist information center at the Calgary Tower on Center Street, or through most hotels.
Taxi: Checker Yellow Cab (tel: 403-299-9999).

⊘ Area codes

Telephone area codes are given in brackets after the place name. In general, the area code must be dialed before the number. For long distance calls (which will include some calls to other parts of the province you are in) you also have to dial the country code (1) before the area code.

Edmonton (780 & 587)
Edmonton Transit (tel: 780-442-5311; www.edmonton.ca/transportation.aspx) operates city buses and an efficient LRT line, including a dedicated bus, #747, to the airport.
Airport Transfer: Skyshuttle (tel: 780-465-8515).
Taxi: Yellow Cab (tel: 780-462-3456).

British Columbia
By Air Vancouver International Airport, located just south of the city in Richmond, is western Canada's major air hub. It is served by North American, European, and Asian airlines. Many smaller airlines and charters also serve northern B.C. and the Yukon. With flights between Vancouver and Victoria, Nanaimo and Comox, as well as up to the Sunshine Coast, Harbour Air's float planes offer a great way to see the coast and avoid the time involved in ferry crossings (1-800-665-0212; www.harbour-air.com).
Airport Transfer Quick Shuttle (tel: 1-604-940-4428; www.quickcoach.com) provides convenient transportation from Seattle. The best connection to the airport is the "Canada Line" rapid transit built for the 2010 Winter

Olympics; it is both faster and less expensive than a taxi. See Translink comments below under Vancouver.
By Sea There are numerous ships and services between Victoria, Vancouver, and other points along the coast. Of note is the "Inside Passage" as far as Prince Rupert (from Port Hardy at the north end of Vancouver Island): a scenic, 15-hour day cruise through deep fjords and narrow channels. Booking is mandatory, and can be done online at www.bcferries.com. Call 1-888-223-3779 (toll-free in Canada and US) for more details.
By Rail VIA Rail (tel: 1-888-842-7245; www.viarail.ca) operates passenger services connecting Prince Rupert with Alberta and the rest of Canada. Amtrak (tel: 1-800-872-7245; www.amtrakcascades.com) offers services from Seattle and points further south. In addition to its trips from Calgary, Rocky Mountaineer offers regularly scheduled services to Whistler.
By Bus Pacific Coach Lines (tel: 1-800-661-1725; www.pacificcoach.com) run from Vancouver to Victoria every two hours. Destination BC (www.hellobc.com) provides details of several other regional bus services.
By Car Interstate 5 in Washington becomes Highway 99 at the US border 48km (30 miles) south of Vancouver. Vancouver is a 3-hour drive from Seattle, potentially longer depending on the wait at the border. Highway 1, the Trans-Canada Highway, enters Vancouver from the east as does Highway 3, the Crowsnest Highway, which crosses southern B.C. From Alaska and the Yukon, the Alaska and Klondike

highways provide rugged routes into the province.

Vancouver (604 & 778)
Translink (tel: 604-953-3333; www.translink.ca) provides a mass-transit system for the whole region, with a rapid transit LRT service, buses and trolleys, and Seabus harbor passenger ferries to north Vancouver. The 15-minute Seabus ride is an inexpensive way to get a great tour of the Vancouver harbor, with a public market and plenty of restaurants in the area around the North Vancouver terminal.

Among others, Gray Line (tel: 1-877-451-1777; www.grayline.com) offers bus tours of Vancouver and environs, including Capilano Canyon and Grouse Mountain, and as far as Whistler. There are also numerous companies offering harbor cruises, some with deluxe buffet dinners.
By Taxi Blacktop (tel: 604-731-1111), Maclure's (tel: 604-831-1111), and Yellow Cabs (tel: 604-681-1111).

Victoria (250)
BC Transit (tel: 250-382-6161; www.bctransit.com/victoria/riderinfo) provides bus services throughout Greater Victoria. A number of tour companies, including Big Bus (Tel: 1-250-389-2229; www.bigbusvictoria.com), offer bus tours, some on trolleys and others on large, open-air buses. For slower, more romantic sightseeing, hire a horse-drawn carriage on Belleville Street, near the Royal British Columbia Museum.
By Taxi Blue Bird Cabs (tel: 250-382-2222) and Esquimalt Saanich Taxi (tel: 250-386-7766).
By Boat and Ferry BC Ferries (tel: 1-888-223-3779; www.bcferries.com) provides the main access to Victoria and Vancouver Island. From the US, Black Ball Transport (tel: 250-386-2202; www.cohoferry.com) operates car ferries daily between Victoria and Port Angeles, Washington. Victoria Clipper (tel: 1-800-888-2535; www.clippervacations.com) operates a daily passenger-only service between Victoria and Seattle. Washington State Ferries (tel: 206-464-6400; www.wsdot.wa.gov/ferries) travels daily between Sidney, north of Victoria, and Anacortes, Washington.

Manitoba (204)
By Air Winnipeg International Airport is served principally by Air Canada, and WestJet. There are also

Cruise ships are an excellent way to view Canada's scenic coastline.

a number of regional and charter carriers.

By Rail Winnipeg's Main Street Station is on VIA Rail's transcontinental passenger service and is the terminus of the line to Churchill for polar-bear viewing in winter (tel: 1-888-842-7245; www.viarail.ca).

By Bus Following the closure of many routes by Greyhound Bus Lines travel to and around Manitoba via long distance bus is in a state of flux. Many Canadian operators are vying to pick up the service.

By Car A reliable network of good paved roads extends across the southern part of the province and north to Thompson and Flin Flon. Several large car rental companies have offices in Winnipeg, both at the airport and downtown.

Winnipeg (204)

Winnipeg Transit System (tel: 1-877-311-4974; www.winnipegtransit. com) has an efficient bus system.

New Brunswick (506)

By Air Air Canada (tel: 1-888-247-2262) offers daily flights into the major airports at Moncton, Saint John, and Fredericton, with connections via associated airlines to smaller communities.

By Sea For ferry services connecting Blacks Harbor to Grand Manan Island call Coastal Transport (tel: 506-662-3724). For ferries between Deer Island and Campobello, call East Coast Ferries on 506-747-2159/1-877-747-2159; www.eastcoastferriesltd.com.

By Rail VIA Rail passenger services between Halifax and Montréal follow two routes within New Brunswick: three times a week via McAdam, Saint John, Sussex, and Moncton; and three times a week via Campbellton, Bathurst, Newcastle, Moncton, and Sackville. For details call 1-888-842-7245 or check www. viarail.ca.

By Bus Greyhound and Voyageur offer routes into New Brunswick and transfers to the province-wide service provided by Maritime Bus (tel: 1-800-575-1807; www.maritimebus.com).

By Car New Brunswick has excellent highways. Since the 1980s the province has undertaken an ambitious freeway construction program, the focal point of which is the Fredericton–Moncton Highway. The 12.9km (8-mile) Confederation Bridge, a toll facility, joins Prince Edward Island and Cape Jourimain, New Brunswick. A shuttle bus operates on demand.

Newfoundland and Labrador (709)

By Air Air Canada, Porter, and WestJet operate regular air services to Newfoundland and Labrador. Air Labrador also offers services through St Anthony to many points in Labrador. Provincial Airlines offers services throughout the province.

By Sea The large ferries of Marine Atlantic cross up to four times a day in summer from North Sydney, Nova Scotia, to Channel-Port-aux-Basques (6-hour journey) and Argentia, Newfoundland (18-hour journey). Marine Atlantic also operates freight/passenger services from St Anthony and Lewisport to the Labrador coast (www.marineatlantic.ca).

In addition, a ferry service operates between St Barbe and Blanc-Sablon, on the border with Labrador. There are a number of coastal ferries that carry a few passengers. For more information on these services contact Newfoundland and Labrador Tourism (tel: 709-729-2830/1-800-563-6353).

By Rail A 7-hour trip from Sept Iles, Québec to Emeril, Labrador (approximately 45 minutes' drive from Labrador City) is provided through Tshiuetin Rail Transportation Inc. (Sept Iles, QC, tel: 1-866-962-0988; www.tshiuetin.net).

By Bus DRL Coachlines connects the Port-aux-Basques ferry docks with St John's, a distance of some 905km (562 miles). Tel: 709-263-2171 in St John's or 1-888-263-1854; www.drl -lr.com.

By Car The major car rental agencies are represented at St John's and Deer Lake. Major highways are paved, though a few secondary roads are gravel-surfaced. The 80km (50-mile) stretch between the Blanc-Sablon ferry dock and Red Bay, Labrador, is paved, but Labrador highways are otherwise largely gravel-surfaced. Some car rental agencies have rules and regulations regarding travel along unpaved roads and may require you to rent a larger vehicle.

St John's

The city's Metrobus system (tel: 709-722-9400; www.metrobus.com) is efficient and inexpensive.

By Taxi It is often difficult to hail taxis on the street, so the best bet is to find one at a downtown hotel or to call Bugden's Taxi (tel: 709-722-4400).

Northwest Territories (867)

By Air Getting around this huge region is possible only by using a network of regional airlines. Centers of operation include Yellowknife, Inuvik, Hay River, and Fort Smith. Air Canada, WestJet, and the main regional carrier, First Air (tel: 1-800-267-1247; www.firstair.ca), all fly into Yellowknife from Edmonton. From Yellowknife you can travel elsewhere in the Northwest Territories and to the Yukon by First Air and Canadian North (tel: 1-800-661-1505 in Canada, internationally 1-902-406-1217; www.canadiannorth.com). Buffalo Airways (tel: 867-873-6112; www.buffaloairways.com) flies six days a week between Yellowknife and Hay River.

Numerous charter companies located in Yellowknife airport serve most northern destinations west of Hudson Bay.

By Bus Following the closure of many routes by Greyhound Bus Lines, long-distance travel to Yellowknife from Edmonton, with Greyhound, has stopped. Many local operators are vying to pick up the service.

By Car The territory has three highways, all hard-packed gravel. The Dempster Hwy stretches from Dawson City, Yukon to Inuvik on the Arctic Ocean. The Mackenzie Hwy runs between Edmonton and Yellowknife. The Liard Hwy runs from the Alaska Hwy near Fort Nelson, B.C. to Fort Liard, close to Nahanni National Park, and connects with the Mackenzie Hwy to Yellowknife.

For special precautions about driving in the north, see the Yukon Getting Around section. Note that highways here become impassable during the spring thaw and autumn freeze-up (usually May and November). Call 1-800-661-0750 for ferry schedules and the latest road information. Should visitors need to rent a vehicle, several agencies are available, but it is wise to reserve as far in advance as possible.

Nova Scotia (902)

By Air Air Canada (tel: 1-888-247-2262) connects Halifax and Sydney with the rest of Canada as well

Take your pick of canoe or kayak.

as the eastern US. Other carriers providing services to Nova Scotia include American Airlines, Delta Airlines, Icelandair, Porter, US Airways, and WestJet.

By Sea A number of car-ferry services are available, ranging from 1- to 6-hour voyages to a more luxurious overnight special with cabins and entertainment.

For travel from Wood Island, P.E.I. to Caribou, and from Saint John, N.B. to Digby, contact Bay Ferries (tel: 902-742-6800; www.ferries.ca). For travel from Port-aux-Basques, NFL to North Sydney, contact Marine Atlantic (tel: 1-800-341-7981; www.marineatlantic.ca).

By Rail VIA Rail provides services from Montréal to Halifax via Amherst and Truro. For schedules and fares call 1-888-842-7245.

By Bus Maritime Bus operates daily throughout Nova Scotia (tel: 1-800-575-1807; www.maritimebus.com), as does DRL Coachlines (tel: 1-888-263-1854; www.drl-lr.com).

By Car Nova Scotia highways are generally in very good condition. Four travelways converge in Halifax: the Marine Drive, Evangeline Trail, Glooscap Trail, and Lighthouse Route. Cars can be rented in downtown Halifax, Yarmouth, or Sydney, and at the two airports. Recreational vehicles can be hired out using the province's accommodations reservation system (tel: 1-800-565-0000).

Halifax

Metro Transit (tel: 902-480-8000; www.halifax.ca) operates a bus system in the Halifax/Dartmouth area. The system's pedestrian ferry service between Halifax and Dartmouth

is a truly delightful way to see the Halifax waterfront. Drivers will find that parking in downtown Halifax on business days can be difficult or expensive.

A number of tour companies, including Brewster Transportation (tel: 403-762-6700/1-866-606-6700), offer bus tours from the major hotels. However, the city is compact enough to explore on foot, either with a conducted group or on a self-guided tour, both of which are available from the Visitor Information Centre at Halifax Waterfront, Sackville Landing, 1655 Lower Water St. Tel: 902-424-4248. Taxis in Halifax are fairly inexpensive and easy to catch, as there are many cab stands.

For **Halifax Airport Shuttle** service to and from Halifax and Dartmouth contact Maritime Bus (tel: 1-800-575-1807; www.maritimebus.com).

Nunavut (867)

By Air Air Inuit (tel: 1-800-361-2965; www.airinuit.com), Calm Air (tel: 1-800-839-2256; www.calmair.com), Canadian North (tel: 1-800-661-1505; www.canadiannorth.com), First Air (tel: 1-800-267-1247; www.firstair.ca) have scheduled flights. There are also numerous charter air services available across Nunavut, using twin- or single-engine propeller aircraft. Helicopter charter services are also available, as they are sometimes more appropriate for the distances and terrain.

By Road As there is no road connecting Nunavut to the south, and only one 21km (13-mile) stretch of road within the territory, which connects

the communities of Arctic Bay and the mining town of Nanisivik, travel by bus or car is not an option.

Ontario

By Air Lester Pearson International Airport, just 30 minutes northwest of Toronto, is served by nearly all the major Canadian airlines as well as international carriers. Useful numbers are as follows:
Air Canada (tel: 1-888-247-2262).
American Airlines (tel: 1-800-433-7300).
British Airways (tel: 1-800-247-9297).
Delta Airlines (tel: 1-800-221-1212).
United Airlines (tel: 1-800-864-8331).
Union Pearson Express (tel: 1-844-438-6687; www.upexpress.com) provides a bus service every 15 minutes from Terminal 1 to downtown Toronto (journey time of 25 minutes). The service operates between 5.30am and 1am.

Ottawa's MacDonald Cartier International Airport (tel: 613-248-2125) is located 15 minutes south of the city. OC Transpo (tel: 613-741-4390; www.octranspo.com) bus no 97 connects the airport from Terminal 1 to the city.

Many of the province's northern hunting/fishing resort camps can be reached only by air. Usually, the price of a chartered air fare is included in a package deal. View the Explore the Possibilities in Northern Ontario magazine at www.ontariotravel.net.

By Rail Toronto's famous Union Station on Front Street is the city's main rail terminus, with direct access to the subway as well. VIA Rail (tel: 1-888-842-7245) can whisk you across Canada, including to and from US connections in Windsor and Niagara Falls. VIA Rail serves Ottawa from Toronto and Montréal. The Ottawa station is located at 200 Tremblay Rd, near the Queensway.

By Bus Toronto's bus terminal is located at 610 Bay Street, close to City Hall and the Eaton Centre. The two major carriers are Greyhound Canada (tel: 1-800-661-8747), which provides services throughout the province, and Coach Canada (tel: 1-866-488-4452), which provides services along the Highway 401 corridor, between Windsor, Toronto, and Montréal.

By Car The speed limit on Ontario highways is 100kph (60mph), unless otherwise posted. Remember that adults and children weighing over

40lbs (18kg) must wear seat belts; children smaller than this must be in child seats. In Ontario, drivers are allowed to turn right on a red traffic light, as long as traffic conditions make it safe to do so.

Ontario's road network is among the best maintained in North America, so your car should leave the province in as good shape as it came. Unless, of course, you travel the dirt and gravel sideroads of northern Ontario, in which case a post-vacation underbody flush will be appropriate. See the Getting Around introduction for toll-free car rental numbers.

Toronto (416 and 647)

Toronto has an excellent mass-transit system, including clean, efficient, and safe subways, with connections to punctual buses and trolley buses. For information call the Toronto Transit Commission (TTC; tel: 416-393-4636; www.ttc.ca). Route maps are often available at hotels.

Taxis are easily hailed on the street. Otherwise call Diamond (tel: 416-366-6868) or Beck Taxi (tel: 416-751-5555).

As in any large city, driving in Toronto can enervate the most patient of drivers, especially at rush hours. Parking, naturally, is expensive, although less so in municipal lots marked with a large, green "P". When a streetcar comes to a halt, stop behind it so that its passengers can exit through the right lane to the sidewalk. Whenever possible, it's more pleasant to walk or take the subway.

Ferries (tel: 416-392-8193) leave for Centre Island daily every 30 minutes from the foot of Bay Street.

Gray Line (tel: 1-800-594-3310; www.grayline.com) runs hop-on hop-off daytime Toronto excursions. Moreover, Gray Line offers pleasant, meandering bus tours to Niagara Falls.

To enjoy a harbor cruise call Toronto Harbour Tours (tel: 416-203-7786; www.harbourtourstoronto.ca) or wander through the Harbourfront area, where smaller outfits and privately owned yachts run tour cruises.

Ottawa (613)

Ottawa is served by OC Transpo (tel: 613-741-4390; www.octranspo.com). For tours of Ottawa contact Gray Line (tel: 1-800-472-9546). For taxis call Blue Line (tel: 613-238-1111).

Prince Edward Island (902)

By Air Air Canada (tel: 1-888-247-2262) and some of the smaller airlines fly into Charlottetown daily from numerous Canadian cities. Delta Air Lines offer direct seasonal services from Boston, New York, and Detroit.

By Sea From May to mid-December, Northumberland Ferries (tel: 1-877-762-7245; www.ferries.ca) leave hourly from Caribou, N.S., to Wood Islands, P.E.I., a 75-minute trip. The ferries are almost always crowded. Early morning and evening sailings have the shortest wait.

By Bus Maritime Bus provides services to the island. For information tel: 1-800-575-1807; www.maritimebus.com. There are few local bus services, but there are several taxi companies such as City Cab (tel: 902-892-6567) and Co-op Taxi (tel: 902-628-8200).

Prince Edward Tours (tel: 902-566-5466/1-877-286-6532; www.princeedwardtours.com) is one company that runs tours of Charlottetown, the North Shore beaches, and other island attractions.

By Car Confederation Bridge is a toll bridge that permits driving to the island from Cape Tormentine. NB: The island speed limit is 90kph (55mph). See Getting Around introduction for toll-free rental car numbers.

By Bicycle Cyclists adore P.E.I.'s rural lanes. Rent a bike by the day or week from one of a number of agencies. MacQueen's Bike Shop and Travel, 430 Queen St in Charlottetown (tel: 902-368-2453; www.macqueens.com) will design a customized itinerary, arrange accommodations, and provide all equipment – even an emergency road service.

Québec

By Air Montréal-Pierre Elliott Trudeau International Airport (tel: 1-800-465-1213) is located on the outskirts of the city. It serves domestic, US, and international flights. All major Canadian airlines and numerous international carriers fly into Montréal, including Air Canada (tel: 1-888-247-2262).

Visitors piloting private aircraft should check first with Transport Canada in Ottawa.

By Rail Contact VIA Rail (tel: 1-888-842-7245, or visit www.viarail.ca).

By Bus Greyhound provides services throughout Québec (tel: 514-844-4040/1-800-661-8747).

By Ferry Many ferries offer year-round or seasonal services on the

A seaplane departs from in front of the Fairmont Empress Hotel in Victoria, B.C.

St Lawrence and other major rivers. The CTMA Ferry service (tel: 1-888-986-3278; www.traversierctma.ca/en) travels between the Iles de la Madeleine and Prince Edward Island, while a passenger/cargo ship, the *Relais Nordik* (tel: 1-800-463-0680; www.relaisnordik.com), connects Lower North Shore between Havre-St-Pierre, Ile d'Anticosti, and Blanc-Sablon. Places on this ship should be reserved in advance in peak season.

By Car Perhaps the best way to travel to Québec is by automobile, which gives you the flexibility to explore, and the freedom to stop and sample the local cuisine and to meander through the exceptional provincial parks. While good maps are available from most service stations, bear in mind that north of the major population areas the roads are often unpaved and sometimes even impassable in winter. The speed limit on autoroutes is 100kph (60mph), and drivers and all passengers must wear seat belts. Turning right on a red light is permitted throughout the province except in Montréal, where it is strictly prohibited unless there is an additional green arrow.

Montréal (514)

The City Transit System, STM (tel: 514-786-4636; www.stm.info), services the city with buses and its excellent Métro. You can use a bus transfer for admission to the subway and vice versa.

If you drive, try to make overnight parking arrangements in advance with a hotel. Be prepared to pay $20 a day to park around the city. Taxis abound in Montréal. The base rate is around $4. For car rentals try:

Avis (tel: 800-879-2847)
Hertz (tel: 800-654-3131)
Budget (tel: 800-268-8900)

Québec City (418)

In the Old City, walking is by far the easiest and most convenient way to get around. Woe to those who drive: parking is scarce and expensive (check with your hotel). You can avoid traffic snarls by renting a bicycle from Cyclo Services (tel: 418-692-4052/1-877-692-4050; www.cycloservices.net).

Saskatchewan (306 & 639)

By Air Saskatchewan's two principal airports, situated in Regina and Saskatoon, are served by the following airlines: Air Canada (tel: 1-888-247-2262; www.aircanada.com), WestJet (tel: 1-888-937-8538 within Canada and US, 0800 279 7072 from the UK; www.westjet.com), There are also a number of regional and charter carriers offering flights across the area.

By Rail Saskatoon is on VIA Rail's transcontinental service, with bus links to Regina. For information call VIA Rail (tel: 1-888-842-7245; www.viarail.ca).

By Bus Following the closure of both the Saskatchewan Transportation Co. and Greyhound Bus Lines there is a lack of long-distance bus travel in Saskatchewan. Local providers are looking to step in, however profitability remains a concern.

By Car The speed limit in Saskatchewan is 100kph (60mph). Free maps can be obtained from Tourism Saskatchewan or from any other travel bureau in the province. Avis, Budget, Enterprise, National, and Thifty car rental agencies all have depots at both airports as well as Downtown.

Regina and Saskatoon (306 & 639)

Regina Transit (tel: 306-777-7000; www.regina.ca) runs several bus routes through the city and to the airport. In Regina, taxis are readily available downtown. Saskatoon Transit System (tel: 306-975-3100; www.transit.saskatoon.ca) provides a regular bus service. Taxis are available in Saskatoon, or call United (tel: 306-652-2222).

The Yukon (867)

By Air Air Canada (tel: 1-888-247-2262; www.aircanada.com) runs direct flights to Whitehorse from Vancouver and Calgary. Air North (tel: 1-800-661-0407; www.flyairnorth.com) offers services to Fairbanks, Alaska, and First Air (tel: 1-800-267-1247; www.firstair.ca) offers flights to Yellowknife, then connecting flights across most northern airports.

By Sea Most visitors arrive in the Yukon aboard cruise ships as part of a package tour. Independent travelers will find that Skagway, the Alaskan port close to three hours' drive from Whitehorse, is served by the Alaska Marine Highway System (AMHS; tel: 1-800-642-0066; www.dot.state.ak.us).

By Rail There's a seasonal sightseeing rail service between Skagway and Lake Bennett, about halfway to Whitehorse, with connecting buses to complete the journey. For details contact White Pass and Yukon Railway (tel: 1-800-343-7373; www.wpyr.com).

By Bus Following the closure of routes by Greyhound Bus Lines there is a lack of long-distance bus travel from Edmonton to Whitehorse, and Alaska Highways through Yukon. Regional bus lines do service the interior and connect with Alaska.

By Car Among the national car rental agencies Budget and National are represented in Whitehorse, and there are also a number of local car and RV rental companies.

The speed limit is 90kph (55mph). Yukon roads are well maintained and most major highways are paved. The Alaska Highway runs from Dawson Creek, B.C., through Whitehorse and on into Alaska. The Klondike Highway commences in Skagway and cuts north from Whitehorse to Dawson. There it splits into the Dempster Highway, which runs due north to Inuvik, the Northwest Territories, and the Top of the World Highway, which drops west into Alaska.

Although these are open year-round, travel is recommended only between mid-May and mid-September. Any trek should be planned and undertaken with great care, following these recommendations:

Headlights must remain on at all times.

When journeying between October and April, make sure that the vehicle is properly winterized.

Before starting, ensure that the vehicle is in good working order. Bring at least two spare tires and plenty of water.

Refuel frequently.

By Taxi For bookings in Whitehorse, call Yellow Cab at 867-668-4811.

⊙ Hitchhiking

Hitchhiking is permitted in most of Canada, except on high-volume highways where stopping for passengers constitutes a danger. It is prohibited in certain municipalities, so prospective hitchhikers should check with tourist boards about local regulations.

A - Z

Accommodations

Canadian accommodations are similar to those in the US in the range of choices available, but some lodgings in Canada are more personalized and service-orientated. Reservations are essential in the busy summer months. Hotels generally will hold a room until 6pm, but if you plan to arrive later, notify the establishment in advance. If you have not reserved, begin looking for accommodation early in the afternoon, particularly in peak seasons when most establishments (especially those along highways) fill up quickly. Almost all hotels, motels, and resorts accept major credit cards, but it's a good idea to check in advance, especially if you travel in remote areas. Many hotels are now completely smoke-free, so if you require a smoking room, make sure to ask. Bed and breakfasts and hostels are becoming increasingly popular. Generally cheaper and more friendly, they can be found throughout the country. Another place to stay is in one of Canada's 2,000 campgrounds, most of which accommodate recreational vehicles as well as tents.

Although the price ranges quoted are for the lowest current rack rate at the time of going to press, ask about special packages and promotions when making a reservation. Off-season rates can be much lower. The prices indicated are based on double occupancy.

Prairie Farms

Farm vacations are a great way to get a true sense of the prairies. Lasting from one day to a week or more, they offer a wide enough variety of different activities to suit almost any taste.

Manitoba Farm Vacations

For further information write to Manitoba Country Vacations Association, Sherry Lynn, Box 3, Waldersee, MB R0J 2G0 (Tel: 204-352-4096; www.countryvacations.mb.ca).

If you prefer a more urban setting, try Bed and Breakfast of Manitoba at www.bedandbreakfast.mb.ca.

Alberta's Guest Ranches

Alberta's "country vacation" program provides the chance to experience life on an Albertan farm or ranch. Like other packages of this sort, it's fun, inexpensive, and, if you choose, hard work. You can select from a list of accommodations ranging from large cattle ranches to small family farms (www.thecowboytrail.com).

Québec Farm Vacations

La Fédération des Agricotours du Québec and the Québec Ministry of Agriculture co-sponsor an inexpensive B&B farm vacation program which offers several possibilities. It's an interesting alternative for campers. L'Association de l'Agrotourisme et du Tourisme Gourmand du Québec, 4545 ave Pierre de-Coubertin, Montréal, PQ H1V 0B2, tel: 514-252-3138; www.terroiretsaveurs.com/en/ promotes the flavors of Québec; their website links to more than 1,000 vendors and producers, covering restaurants, accommodations, and stores that promote regional food.

Saskatchewan Farm Vacations

Time and again, travelers return home with glowing accounts of their stay on a Saskatchewan farm: the hearty home cooking, the fresh air, even sharing the chores, are often raved about. Camping on a farm can be arranged. Vacation farms are listed in Tourism Saskatchewan's annual *Accommodation, Resort & Campground Guide*, or you can look online at www.sasktourism.com. For information

on B&Bs in the province, write to Saskatchewan Bed and Breakfast Association, which also includes many farms among its members, at 172 Cambridge Avenue, Regina, SK S4N 0L2, tel: 306-789-3259; www.bbsask.ca.

Admission Charges

There is an unlimited supply of museums and art galleries that cover a variety of themes. Although many charge admission, discounts are generally available for children, students, and senior citizens.

National Trust for Canada (www.heritagecanada.org) has identified historically important buildings and gardens, maintaining a register and encouraging people to visit. Many historic buildings that are normally closed are now occasionally open to the public, often at no charge.

Budgeting for Your Trip

The daily costs for an average traveler in Canada vary considerably across the country. In the large cities – Vancouver, Toronto, and Montréal – the comfortable daily cost per person (assuming two people sharing a room) should be about $250 ($150 for hotel, $20 for breakfast, $25 for lunch, $50 for dinner, and $10 for public transport). Accommodations

⊘ Hosteling

Budget travelers interested in hostelling can contact **Backpackers Hostels Canada** (Tel: 807-344-1348; www.backpackers.ca) or **Hostelling International** (Tel: 1-800-663-5777; www.hihostels.ca).

and food costs decrease considerably away from the main centers, except in the far North. A thrifty traveler in the city – and an average traveler in more rural areas – might get away with about $100–130 per day ($50–75 for accommodations, $30 for restaurant food, or as little as $20 self-catering and $10 for fares), again assuming two people share a hotel room. For extravagant luxury in the city – and in hotspots such as Banff, Whistler, and Mont-Tremblant – you could pay $800–1,000 per day ($300–500 for accommodations, $40 for breakfast, $100 for lunch, as much as $300 for dinner, and $100 for taxi fares).

Children

North America generally, including Canada, is strongly oriented toward accommodating family travel. Many hotels have excellent packages that often allow children under a certain age to stay free of charge, and most restaurants will produce children's menus and a supply of paper and wax crayons to keep them happy. Shopping malls and parks frequently have children's play areas. Restaurants and movie theaters will also provide booster seats for smaller children. Across the country there are hundreds of attractions geared toward children, from toddlers to teens.

Climate

It is difficult to generalize about the Canadian climate. Most visitors come during the summer, when temperatures average around 24°C (75°F). During July and August, however, the mercury can climb into the 30s (90–100°F) on the prairies and in southern Ontario. In northern Canada, summer temperatures may stay at 15°C (65°F) during the day, but can drop close to freezing at night. Don't forget to pack some protection against mosquitoes and other biting insects, especially if you are traveling in the early summer.

Canadian winters have been slightly exaggerated in popular lore. Winter temperatures average between –5°C and 10°C (10°F and 25°F) from the Maritimes through southern Ontario. It gets colder and windier from northern Québec

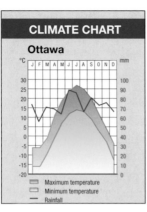

CLIMATE CHART

Ottawa

through the Rockies, with temperatures ranging from –18°C to –5°C (0°F to 10°F). In the Yukon, Northwest Territories, and Nunavut the mercury can drop to as low as –40°C (–40°F). On the balmy southern coast of British Columbia (B.C.), however, warm Pacific currents generally keep the temperature above freezing during the winter at sea level, while snow accumulates at higher levels.

Snowfall varies throughout Canada. Skiers can sometimes take to the slopes and trails by late November, and the snow lasts generally until April or even May in the mountains.

Crime and Safety

Generally speaking, Canada is one of the safest countries to visit. Its large cities, like any others, have areas that are best not visited, and it is not unusual to see homeless men and women on the streets, but they generally pose no threat to safety. Being aware of one's surroundings is always important.

Anyone in an emergency situation should phone **911**, and the call will be forwarded to police, fire department, or ambulance, depending upon the reason for the call.

In case your documentation is stolen, it's a good idea to have two photocopies of your passport identification page, airline tickets, driver's license, and the credit cards that you plan to bring with you. Leave one photocopy of this with family or friends at home; pack the other in a place separate from where you carry your valuables.

Pickpockets are not unheard of, especially in crowded places like a busy subway station, but it is not a huge problem in Canada, and simply requires being mindful of how you carry your wallet or any other valuables.

Customs Regulations

Canada's customs requirements for vacation visitors are fairly simple. Personal effects for use during the stay may be brought into the country. There is no problem with bringing rental cars from the US, but drivers should always carry a copy of the contract with them in the car (this is also important if stopped by police for any reason).

Hunting rifles and shotguns can be brought into Canada, but with restrictions. Consult the Canadian Firearms Program website: www.rcmp-grc.gc.ca/cfp-pcaf. Limits on duty-free tobacco, alcohol, and personal gifts are similar to other countries, but perhaps a bit stricter. For more details on Customs regulations and what you can bring to Canada, contact: Canada Border Services Agency, tel: 204-983-3500 or 506-636 5064 from outside Canada and 1-800-461-9999 from inside Canada; www.cbsa-asfc.gc.ca.

Pets require a veterinary's certificate of good health and vaccinations, etc. Many foods and plants are prohibited, so check the rules before arriving. The rules for a food type may be different depending whether you are coming from the United States or from another country. The Canada Border Services Agency website has full details: www.cbsa-asfc.gc.ca.

Citizens of the UK may bring home, duty-free: 200 cigarettes or 50 cigars; 2 liters of wine OR 1 liter of liquor; and additional goods totaling no more than £390 (Cdn$660).

Each American citizen who spends more than 48 hours in Canada may return with $800 worth of goods, duty-free. Some airports and border points feature duty-free shops, offering liquor and other goodies, but make sure you know your prices before jumping at the "bargains." Americans should direct their questions to any US Customs Office or visit its website at www.cbp.gov, while travelers from other countries should contact the Customs Office in their own country for information on what they can bring back.

Disabled Travelers

The Canadian Transportation Agency offers an online guide for disabled visitors traveling by air in Canada, which can be accessed at www.otc-cta.

gc.ca. Another useful online source for people with disabilities is the Government of Canada's www.travel. gc.ca/travelling/health-safety/disabilities.

Airlines, buses, and trains all offer wheelchair assistance, although you should allow extra time before commencing your journey. Taking a wheelchair on the train requires advanced notice, so it is recommended to call VIA Rail 48 hours beforehand (toll free tel: 1-888-842-7245, www.viarail.ca).

Disabled access, especially for those in wheelchairs, can be found in almost every public building across Canada, and most museums, tourist information centers, and visitor attractions have taken steps to make access easier. Hotels, especially those affiliated with chains, generally provide disabled accommodation and toilet facilities. Many national and provincial parks offer alternative trails that are accessible to disabled travelers. Designated spaces for disabled drivers are generally available at parking lots in cities, at shopping malls, and in the parking lots of large stores.

Eating Out

Download your free app for restaurant listings, see page 3.

Electricity

Canada operates on 110 volts in common with the US. Sockets accommodate plugs with two flat or two flat and one round pins, so an adapter is required for the use of European appliances.

Embassies and Consulates

While foreign visitors are traveling in and across Canada, they may need to contact their own country in case of an emergency. Consulates can be most helpful, for example, if a passport is stolen or if a message needs to be relayed quickly back home. The following list gives details of all the consulates located in the major Canadian cities.

British Columbia
Australia 2050-1075 West Georgia St, Vancouver, tel: 604-694-6160

France 1130 West Pender St, Ste 1100, Vancouver, tel: 604-637-5300
UK 1111 Melville St, Ste 800, Vancouver, tel: 604-683-4421
US 1095 West Pender St, 21st Floor, Vancouver, tel: 604-685-4311

Ontario
Australia 175 Bloor St E, Ste 1100, Toronto, tel: 416-323-4280
France 2 Bloor St E, Ste 2200, Toronto, tel: 416-847-1900
UK College Park, 777 Bay St, Ste 2800, Toronto, tel: 416-593-1290
US 360 University Ave, Toronto, tel: 416-595-1700

Québec
France 1501 McGill College, Bureau 1000, Montréal, tel: 514-878-4385
UK 2000 McGill College Avenue, Ste 1940, Montréal, tel: 514-866-5863
US 1155 rue Saint-Alexandre, Montréal, tel: 514-398-9695

Emergencies

Visitors are urged to obtain **travel medical insurance** before leaving their own country. Anyone using prescription medicine should bring an adequate supply with them, as well as a copy of the prescription in case it needs to be renewed. Travelers requiring medical attention needn't worry – Canadian hospitals are known for their high medical standards.

In an emergency requiring the **police**, an **ambulance** or **firemen**, immediate help can be summoned by dialing **911**. Emergency telephone numbers are listed in the front of all local telephone directories. If caught in a legal bind, foreign visitors should contact their consulates, a partial listing of which is shown in the Embassies and Consulates section.

Etiquette

Good manners are valued: hold doors open for people following you; don't jump the line; let people get off public transportation before you get on; offer your seat to older passengers or pregnant women; on escalators, stand on the right, walk past on the left. If you are a smoker, you'll have to look carefully to find a place to light up, as smoking is banned in most public places.

Festivals

Canada Day, the national holiday is typically celebrated on July 1st is celebrated with parades and parties. Smaller cities tend to have more interesting parades, which often boast floats from community groups and civic services like the fire and rescue groups. It's not as focused on patriotism as the American July 4th activities, but there are fireworks and a festive feeling prevails.

Alberta

May–August *(Banff)*
Banff Summer Arts Festival
Professional dance, opera, and music presented by artists from around the world, as well as showcases of the visual arts. www.banffcentre.ca

Second week of July *(Calgary)*
Calgary Stampede and Exhibition
The most famous annual Canadian event – 10 days of raucous western showmanship and celebration, with rodeo events, chuck-wagon racing, and more. Make hotel reservations well in advance (by some estimates, Calgary's population doubles at this time), and book tickets for main events early. Tel: 403-269-9822/1-800-661-1767; www.calgarystampede.com

All dressed up for the Gay Pride Parade in Toronto.

July *(Drumheller)*
The Canadian Badlands Passion Play
Set in a natural amphitheater, the similarity of the site to the Holy Land enhances the drama. A popular affair that draws people from across North America every year. www.canadianpassionplay.com

Late July *(Edmonton)*
K-Days
Formerly known as Klondike Days and Edmonton's Capital EX, the renamed festival focuses on celebrating Edmonton today, including Global Connections and Northwest Originals. http://k-days.com

Mid-August *(Edmonton)*
Edmonton's International Fringe Theatre Festival
Fabulous Fringe event, second only to Edinburgh in size. www.fringetheatre.ca

British Columbia

April *(Whistler)*
World Ski and Snowboard Festival
North America's largest annual snow sports and music celebration – serious skiing and snowboarding competitions for 10 days straight, film, music, and partying every night. www.wssf.com

May–June *(Vancouver)*
Vancouver International Children's Festival
A week of entertainment for kids of all ages – it's been around for more than 35 years, so it is a bit of an institution. www.childrensfestival.ca.

Late June- first week in July *(Williams Lake)*
Williams Lake Stampede
Five thousand spectators come to watch top contenders in one of Canada's best rodeo events. www.williamslakestampede.com

Mid-July
Vancouver Folk Music Festival
Folk musicians from all over the world come to Jericho Beach for this three-day music festival. www.thefestival.bc.ca

Mid-July *(Kimberley)*
Julyfest
A celebration of all that "Canada's highest city" has to offer, including the Canadian bocce championships and extreme skateboard racing. www.kimberleyjulyfest.com

Late July *(Vancouver)*
The Honda Celebration of Light
Held annually, this international pyrotechnics competition attracts hundreds of thousands to any space close to English Bay. hondacelebrationoflight.com

Early August *(Comox)*
Filberg Festival/Comox Nautical Days
Artisans from all over western Canada vie for exhibition space at a prestigious festival that attracts visitors from all over, looking for that special carving, painting, piece of pottery or glass, all while enjoying music and food in a 3.6-hectare (9-acre) garden. Down at the harbor, a fishing derby, canoe jousting, craft booths, and activities for the kids provide a friendly alternative. Or, do both: it's easy as the two venues are less than a kilometer (0.6 miles) apart. www.filbergfestival.com

Early August *(Penticton)*
Peach Festival
Five-day spectacle includes fireworks, floats, lumberjack shows, lots of live music, and the Peachfest Square Dance Festival. www.peachfest.com

Mid-to-Late August to early September *(Vancouver)*
Pacific National Exhibition
Features parades, exhibits, a horse show, entertainment, and sandcastle competition, along with the usual 4-H competition for raising the best farm animals. www.pne.ca

Early October *(Okanagan Valley)*
Okanagan Wine Festivals
A festival including vineyard tours, lunches, dinners, and other events focused on wine, food, education, and the arts. There's a festival for every season, but this one coincides with the harvest. www.thewinefestivals.com

Manitoba

February *(St Boniface)*
Festival du Voyageur
The lively francophone community celebrates the early fur traders. www.heho.ca/en

Late June *(Winnipeg)*
Winnipeg International Jazz Festival
For 11 days, downtown Winnipeg rocks to some of the world's best jazz, blues, funk, and urban music, bringing locals downtown in droves. www.jazzwinnipeg.com

Mid-July *(Winnipeg)*
Winnipeg Folk Festival
The internationally acclaimed folk music festival is held over five days in a provincial park 34km (20 miles) outside the city. A 40-plus year tradition, and old-timers advise: bring mosquito repellent along with sunscreen and a hat. www.winnipegfolkfestival.ca

End of July *(Austin)*
Manitoba Threshermen's Reunion and Stampede
Antique tractor races, sheep-tying, and threshing demonstrations. www.threshermensmb.ca

August *(Dauphin)*
Canada's National Ukrainian Festival
Music, fun, tradition, and plenty of food for all. www.cnuf.ca

First week in August *(Gimli)*
The Icelandic Festival of Manitoba
Gimli, the largest Icelandic community outside of Iceland, celebrates its heritage. www.icelandicfestival.com

August *(Winnipeg)*
Folklorama
This two-week, city-wide festival features the food, dancing, crafts, and culture of 40 different ethnic groups. www.folklorama.ca

New Brunswick

Late June to early July *(Shediac)*
Shediac Lobster Festival
Five days of delicious seafood and lively entertainment held since 1949. www.shediaclobsterfestival.ca

Late July to early August *(Edmundston)*
La Foire Brayonne
The most popular festival in this area of New Brunswick, the mythical République du Madawaska. Started in 1985, the local French-speaking population engages in three days of celebrations. Visitors enjoy the local food and the weaving and other crafts. www.foirebrayonne.com

Early August *(Newcastle)*
Miramichi Folk-Song Festival
Held for more than 60 years, this festival offers a fascinating introduction to the exuberant local ballads. www.miramichifolksongfestival.com

First Monday in August
New Brunswick Day
Barbecues, games, and live entertainment.

Early to mid-August *(Caraquet)*
Festival Acadien de Caraquet
A huge two-week celebration of Acadian culture, this festival begins with prayers for the fishing fleet, and is attended by hundreds of Acadian and francophone singers, musicians, actors, dancers, artists, and writers. www.festivalacadien.ca

Early September *(Sussex)*
Atlantic International Balloon Fiesta
Around 180 balloon flights take place over the lush valleys of Kings County. The festival also includes an antique car show, helicopter rides, and amusement rides. www.atlanticballoonfiesta.ca

Mid-September *(Fredericton)*
Harvest Jazz and Blues Festival
Musicians from across Canada turn Fredericton into the New Orleans of the North, playing jazz, blues, and Dixieland. www.harvestjazzandblues.com

Newfoundland and Labrador

June to mid-September *(Trinity)*
Rising Tide Theatre
A festival of plays, dinner theater, concerts, and special events in outdoor venues all around Trinity Bight, bringing the area's colorful and not-so-distant past to life. www.risingtidetheatre.com

Late July *(Twillingate)*
Fish, Fun, and Folk Festival
One of the province's largest folk festivals, on the scenic northeast coast, this family-oriented gathering celebrates Newfoundland's culture and food. www.fishfunfolkfestival.com

End of July to early August *(Gander)*
Festival of Flight
Honoring the area's role in aviation history, this popular festival offers a wide range of events, from a daring demolition derby with car-crashing thrills to the popular Festival of Flight parade and Newfoundland's biggest kitchen party. www.gandercanada.com

End of July to early August *(St John's)*
George Street Festival
Six nights of outdoor entertainment and parties at George Street pubs and taverns. Recent years have seen such acts as Our Lady Peace and the Arkells. www.georgestreetlive.ca

First Wednesday in August *(St John's)*
Royal St John's Regatta
The regatta on Quidi Vidi Lake is the oldest sporting event in North America, but get up early – the rowing's over before breakfast. The city closes down and general festivities continue for the rest of the day. (If it rains, the race – and festivities – will be postponed until the following week.) www.stjohnsregatta.org

Early August *(St John's)*
Newfoundland and Labrador Folk Festival
Folk groups, dancers, and storytellers from around the province gather in Bannerman Park to provide a taste of the traditional Newfoundland lifestyle. www.nlfolk.com

Nova Scotia

May–June *(Annapolis Valley)*
Apple Blossom Festival
Dancing, parades, and entertainment celebrate more than 80 years of the blossoming apple trees. www.appleblossom.com

Early July *(Halifax)*
The Royal Nova Scotia International Tattoo
Held since 1979, this annual extravaganza that presents more than 2,000 of the best military and civilian international and Canadian performers. www.nstattoo.ca

Early July *(Antigonish)*
Antigonish Highland Games
This action-packed Scottish festival features caber tossing (log throwing) and a continuous display of Highland dancing, with hundreds of marching bagpipers. www.antigonishhighlandgames.ca

Early August *(Halifax)*
Halifax International Busker Festival
Street performers from around the world provide several days of music on the waterfront in downtown historic Halifax. www.buskers.ca

Early August *(Lunenburg)*
Lunenburg Folk Harbour Festival
A popular festival featuring acoustic music performed by some of the best of Canadian talent, dances, and workshops in a range of venues, from tents to a Victorian bandstand, an old opera house, and the wharf. www.folkharbour.com

Early October *(across Cape Breton)*
Celtic Colours International Festival
A nine-day, Cape Breton Island-wide celebration of Celtic culture, featuring artists from around the world and across Canada, along with some of Cape Breton's finest singers, players, dancers, and tradition-bearers. www.celtic-colours.com

The Northwest Territories

Late March *(Yellowknife)*
Long John Jamboree
This three-day festival celebrates spring, such as it is, in the North, with Dene hand games, ice-sculpting, music and lots of other entertainment. It coincides with the Annual Canadian Championship Dog Derby, a three-day, 230km (143-mile) dog sled race. www.longjohnjamboree.ca

Mid-July *(Yellowknife)*
Folk on the Rocks
A three-day outdoor music festival held under the slogan "Where the road ends, the music begins" attracting folk performers from the Northwest Territories and the entire country. www.folkontherocks.com

Mid- to late July *(Inuvik)*
Great Northern Arts Festival
Artists celebrate Inuit culture, 10 days of activities including workshops. www.gnaf.org

Nunavut

Mid-April *(Iqaluit)*
Toonik Tyme Festival
A popular festival celebrating the return of the sun with northern games, snowmobile races, and a memorable community feast. www.tooniktyme.com

Ontario

Early–mid-February *(Ottawa)*
Winterlude
Extravagant carnival featuring ice-sculpting, snowshoe races, ice-boating, and other wintertime fun. Celebrating more than 40 years. www.canada.ca/en/canadian-heritage/campaigns/winterlude.html

May *(Ottawa)*
Canadian Tulip Festival
Over 3 million tulips highlight this festival, which has taken place since 1953, which also offers parades, regattas, craft shows, and other diversions. www.tulipfestival.ca

April–October *(Stratford)*
Stratford Festival
The annual **Stratford Festival** (early April–October) draws over half a million theater-goers from around the world to this town on the banks of the Avon river. Three fine theaters perform Shakespearean, classic, and modern dramas.
   Tickets typically go on sale in late February. Write to the Stratford Shakespeare Festival, Box 520, Stratford, ON N5A 6V2, tel: 1-800-567-1600 toll-free from Canada and the US; www.stratfordfestival.ca

May–October *(Niagara-on-the-Lake)*
Shaw Festival
Set in one of the best-preserved 19th-century small towns in Canada, the **Shaw Festival** is devoted to performing the works of George Bernard Shaw and his contemporaries. Expert productions with renowned actors draw large crowds, especially on weekends. Try to make prior arrangements and reservations as early as possible.www.shawfest.com.

Mid-June *(Toronto)*
Luminato
A magnificent 10-day international festival of arts and creativity, held at indoor and outdoor locations citywide. www.luminato.com

June *(Toronto)*
Pride Month
Pride has been declared for the entire month since 2016, and is one of the largest Prides in the world, with celebration of Canada's inclusiveness, including an arts and cultural program. www.pridetoronto.com

July 1 *(Ottawa)*
Canada Day
Countrywide celebrations; the largest takes place in Ottawa with concerts, street entertainment, and fireworks over the Ottawa river.

Early July *(Toronto)*
Toronto Fringe Festival
Toronto's largest theater festival, with over 150 international theater companies performing all over the city. www.fringetoronto.com

Mid-July to early August *(Toronto)*
Peeks Toronto Caribbean Carnival (Caribana)
The city's West Indian community celebrates with singing, dancing, and parades, mostly on Toronto Islands, creating a Mardi Gras atmosphere for more than 50 years. www.torontocarnival.ca

Late July *(Oakville)*
RBC Canadian Open
Glen Abbey Golf Club hosts one of golf's top five tournaments. www.rbccanadianopen.com

Early August *(Maxville)*
Glengarry Highland Games
Held since 1948, this is Canada's second-largest Highland gathering after Antigonish. www.glengarryhighlandgames.com

Early August *(St Catharines)*
Royal Canadian Henley Regatta
The largest rowing regatta in Canada. Started in 1880, it draws competitors and spectators from throughout the continent. www.henleyregatta.ca

Early August *(Manitoulin Island)*
Wikwemikong Annual Cultural Festival and Pow Wow
Well over 50 years old, this Pow Wow initiated the restoration of the traditions of dancing and drumming in Ontario. On the August civic holiday weekend, dancers, drummers, and singers travel to the Wikwemikong Pow Wow from across North America. www.wikwemikong.ca

Mid-August to Labor Day *(Toronto)*
Canadian National Exhibition
The largest and oldest exhibition of its kind in the world, featuring air shows, big-name entertainment, and all sorts of exhibits. All this takes place for three weeks at Exhibition Place on Lake Shore Boulevard. www.theex.com

Early September *(Toronto)*
Toronto International Film Festival
A 10-day showcase of the best in global filmmaking. www.tiff.net

Mid-September *(Guelph)*
Guelph Jazz Festival
Considered to be one of the premier jazz festivals in North America. www.guelphjazzfestival.com

First Saturday in October *(Toronto)*
Nuit Blanche
An extraordinary celebration of contemporary art, in galleries, museums, and countless unexpected places from sunset to sunrise. www.nbto.com

Mid-October *(Kitchener/Waterloo)*
Oktoberfest
This famous Bavarian celebration attracts over half a million festive partygoers to the area's 30-odd beer halls and tents. www.oktoberfest.ca

Prince Edward Island

Late May to mid-October *(Charlottetown)*
Charlottetown Festival
The Confederation Center hosts a very fine series of concerts, theater, and film. www.tourismpei.com/the-charlottetown-festival

Mid-July *(Summerside)*
Summerside Lobster Carnival
Three days of fairs, parades, and lobster suppers. www.summersidelobstercarnival.website

Early August *(Tyne Valley)*
Tyne Valley Oyster Festival
Fiddling, dancing, and oyster-shucking contest. Oysters, presented all sorts of different ways, are featured on the menus of the Oyster Suppers. www.tvoysterfest.ca

Late June *(Charlottetown)*
P.E.I. Jazz and Blues Festival
This is a well-attended three-day event that takes over much of downtown Charlottetown, featuring musicians from across the country and around the world. www.jazzandblues.ca

Québec

Mid-January to early February *(Montréal)*
La Fête des Neiges
Winter carnival, including costume balls, ice sculptures, and outdoor sports events held on the islands in the river. www.fetedesneiges.com

Late January to mid February *(Québec City)*
Carnaval de Québec

Québécois engage in more than two weeks of revelry, heightened somewhat by the ubiquitous "Cariboo," a concoction of whiskey, sweet red wine, and other surprises. There's a parade, ice-sculpture contests, and even a canoe race on the frozen St-Laurent. www.carnaval.qc.ca

Early April *(province-wide)*
Sugaring-off Parties
Festivities accompany the collection of maple tree sap.

Early May to late September *(Montréal)*
Tam Tams
Perhaps the largest spontaneous gathering in the world. Montréalers gather every Sunday around the George-Étienne Cartier Monument in Mount Royal Park to play drums, have picnics, throw frisbees, and enjoy the summer sun.

June–August *(Mont Orford)*
Festival Orford Musique
Performances of the Jeunesses Musicales du Canada draw international talent and are presented throughout the summer in Mont Orford Park's music center. www.orford.mu.en

June 24
Fête Nationale
Provincial holiday. www.fetenationale.qc.ca

Early to mid-July *(Québec City)*
Québec City Summer Festival
Free concerts and lively shows take place throughout the city. www.infofestival.com

Late June to early July *(Montréal)*
Montréal International Jazz Festival
A mammoth jam, with over 300 free shows, besides the ticketed events. www.montrealjazzfest.com

Mid-July *(Montréal)*
Just for Laughs Festival
The world's largest comedy festival. Offers more than 2,000 shows, including 1,300 free events. www.hahaha.com

Mid-July to mid-August *(Val-David)*
1001 Pots
An enormous exhibition of ceramics, showcasing 25,000 original pieces by more than 100 ceramicists. www.1001pots.com

Late July *(Bromont)*
International Bromont
On the site of the 1976 Equestrian Olympics, a World Cup equestrian competition takes place in the Eastern Townships. www.internationalbromont.org

Mid-August *(St-Jean-sur-Richelieu)*
St-Jean-sur-Richelieu International Balloon Festival
A family-oriented summer festival, this is the biggest gathering of hot-air balloons in Canada. www.balloon canada.com

Late August *(Montréal)*
18th century Public Market
A trip back in time, to Montréal's first public market. Rain or shine, festivities take place in Place Royale and in the streets around the Pointe-à-Callière Museum of Archeology and History, as farmers, craftspeople, and entertainers recreate the 18th-century market. www.pacmuseum.qc.ca

Late August/early September *(Montréal)*
Montréal Film Festival
Held since 1977, now over 350,000 people flock to this event every year. www.ffm-montreal.org

September to end October *(Montréal)*
The Magic of Lanterns Festival, Montréal Botanical Gardens
Hundreds of lanterns, in an amazing variety of shapes and colors, light up the Chinese Garden each fall, each one handmade in Shanghai by Chinese craftspeople. www.espace pourlavie.ca

Early October *(Montréal)*
Black and Blue Festival, Montréal
Gay festival featuring a wide variety of shows, artistic displays, sports activities, and a parade. www.bbcm.org

Saskatchewan

February *(Prince Albert)*
Prince Albert Winter Festival
This country festival has something for everyone: dog sled races, a chili cook-off, a contemporary country music concert, and a harmonica and accordion extravaganza. www.princealbertwinterfestival.com

First week of August *(Saskatoon)*
Saskatoon Exhibition
This is a popular, week-long fair of contests, historical displays, horse racing, and livestock exhibitions. www.saskatoonexhibition.ca

Late August to Early September *(Regina)*
Regina Dragonboat Festival
Dragonboat festivals have taken Canada by storm and Regina is no exception. Join the 20,000 spectators who come out to see the prairie version of a 2,000-year-old Chinese tradition. www.reginadragonboat.com

The Yukon

Mid-to-late February *(Whitehorse)*
Yukon Sourdough Rendezvous
Native-born Yukoners call themselves "sourdoughs" after the famous biscuits. Now, to qualify as a sourdough, you must have spent one winter in the Yukon. Their rendezvous is a week-long bash celebrating the Yukon's history. It includes such local traditions as dog sled races, packing sacks of flour, log toss, and axe throw, along with drinking heavily at the nightly cabarets. www.yukonrendezvous.com

Early June *(Whitehorse)*
Kluane Mountain Bluegrass Festival
Bluegrass is performed by both international and local musicians. www.yukonbluegrass.com

Third weekend in August *(Dawson City)*
Discovery Days and Yukon Riverside Arts Festival
Parades, dancing, races, and general merriment to celebrate the anniversary of the discovery of gold near Dawson City. Artists from across the Yukon and Northwest Territories showcase their work in parkland beside the Yukon river. www.dawsoncity.ca

Gay and Lesbian Travelers

Canada is one of the world's more gay-friendly countries, and in July 2005 became the fourth country to recognize gay marriage, after the Netherlands, Belgium, and Spain. Vancouver, Toronto, and Montréal's Pride Weeks draw the biggest crowds, but all of Canada's main cities host an annual Pride Week – and Canadian tourism bureaux are increasingly dedicating sections of their websites to gay and lesbian tourists.

For a comprehensive, all-in-one spot to start research, **Travel Gay Canada** (www.travelgaycanada.com), provides Canada-wide information on hotels, events, and travel packages.

Health and Medical Care

As visitors to Canada are not eligible for healthcare in any of the provinces or territories, it is important to be covered by a health insurance policy for the duration of your trip to Canada. It may also be advisable to ensure the policy covers emergency evacuation with a medical escort to your country of residence. Some Canadian companies offer "Visitors to Canada" travel medical policies that can be purchased online.

If you are entering Canada with prescription drugs and syringes used for medical reasons, be sure to keep the medication in its original and labeled container to avoid problems. Syringes should be accompanied by a medical certificate that shows they are for medical use and should be declared to Canadian Customs officials. You should carry with you an extra prescription from your doctor in the event your medication is lost or stolen and to attest to your need to take such prescriptions.

I

Internet

Many coffee shops routinely offer free wireless internet access; or visit any public library. Note that usually there is a time limit for usage of a library's computer. Most hotels and airports have free room internet access or business centers where you can access emails and the internet. To find free hot-spots across Canada, visit: https://wifispc.com/canada.

M

Media

Newspapers and Magazines

The *National Post* and *The Globe and Mail* are distributed throughout Canada. *La Presse* is the ranking Québec daily. Newsstands sell major American, British, and French newspapers and magazines. Canada's largest news magazine, *Maclean's*, is published weekly.

Radio and Television

The Canadian Broadcasting Company (CBC) operates nationwide television networks (French and English), along with an all-news network. CTV Global broadcasts two others. Regional and provincial networks, along with independent and US broadcasters, account for the rest.

Cable networks enable viewers to see programs produced in all parts of Canada and the US, along with a sampling of programs from the UK, Australia, France, and other countries. The majority of large cities originate at least one multilingual or ethnic channel.

CBC operates a national radio network, both AM and FM, in English and French. There are hundreds of private stations that fill the airwaves with news and music.

Money

The Canadian and US dollars have a different rate of exchange. All dollar prices quoted in this book are in Canadian dollars.

Visitors may bring up to $10,000 into Canada without reporting it. When exchanging money, you may be required to provide your passport or other identification. Canadian banks and foreign exchange bureaux will convert funds, often at very attractive rates. US funds are readily accepted by many department stores and hotels, etc., but they may not offer the most advantageous rate.

Credit Cards, Debit Cards, and Traveler's Checks

Major credit cards are widely accepted in Canada. Car rental companies prefer credit cards to cash.

Traveler's checks are not widely used in Canada, as bank debit and

credit cards are preferred. If you do buy traveler's checks, ask your bank about overseas charges and buy them denominated in Canadian dollars. American Express and Visa traveler's checks are still accepted, but generally at banks rather than retailers.

N

Nightlife

Download your free app for restaurant, bars and clubs throughout Canada.

O

Opening Hours

Standard business hours for stores are 10am–6pm, or 9pm in many large cities. Stores in many parts of the country are open for more limited hours on Sunday.

Drug and convenience stores generally close at 11pm, but some operate for 24 hours. Banking hours vary greatly; the majority of banks now open long hours, which may include Saturday, and also, in some instances, Sunday. Bank machines are readily available.

Banks, schools, government offices, and many beer and liquor stores close on national holidays. Hotels, restaurants, and most retail outlets stay open. See the section on Festivals for further information and listings of provincial holidays and festivals.

Most Canadian museums and art galleries offer extended hours on one or more nights a week, and sometimes free admission at certain times as well. Toronto's **Royal Ontario Museum** charges a nominal fee on Friday nights in July–Sept, 4.30–8.30pm. The **CityPass** covers five attractions, including the Royal Ontario Museum, the CN Tower, and the Ontario Science Centre. For further details, visit www.citypass.com/city/toronto.

In Montréal, the **Montréal Museums Pass** gives free access to 46 Montréal-area museums and attractions, with or without public transit, in a package good for three consecutive days. For details, check at www.museesmontreal.org/en/passes.

Out west, the UBC Museum of Anthropology, UBC Botanical Garden & Nitobe Garden in Vancouver offer a single ticket for all three venues, valid for six months, so no need to rush through everything on one day.

Postal Services

Stamps are readily available at Canada's post offices (open Monday–Friday during business hours) and local convenience and drug stores.

Canada Post and international courier companies provide express services across the country and to foreign destinations. Canada Post, along with numerous stores, can also send faxes. Canada Post locations are listed in the business section of the telephone directory.

Public Holidays

Each province has its own public holidays (check with the local tourist board) in addition to the following national holidays:

January 1 New Year's Day
July 1 Canada Day
First Monday in September Labor Day
Second Monday in October Thanksgiving Day
December 25 Christmas Day
December 26 Boxing Day (except Québec)
Movable statutory holidays:
Good Friday
Monday preceding May 24 (Victoria Day, the Queen's birthday)

Whistler resort in B.C. caters for all tourists' needs.

Shopping

Canada is great for shopping with malls packed with goods to suit every taste and budget. More original souvenirs include locally-made handicrafts such as masks, quilts and bentwood boxes, while the nortnern provinces offer furs, wood and stone carvings made by native peoples. In Newfoundland, look out for Labradorite jewelry, seal-skin products and Grenfell cloth parkas. In the Northwest Territories, shop for Polar Bear diamonds and custom-made jewelry featuring gold nuggets as well as Inuit and Dene-made soapstone sculptures, tapestries and prints. Note that genuine articles will cost more than mass-manufactured copies. Download your free app for more detailed information on shopping in Canada, see inside front cover.

Sport

Download your free app for detailed information on sport in Canada, see inside front cover.

Student Travelers

Students traveling within Canada can take advantage of discounts in many areas. For traveling around, VIA Rail and Greyhound offer student discounts, and in most cities

there are hostels and university residences for the budget traveler. For places not serviced by Greyhound there are a number of new operators springing up to fill in the service gaps.

A good source of online information is provided by the ISIC, the International Student Identity Card, at www.isic.org, which covers places and services across Canada.

Telephones

The telephone system in Canada is similar to that in the US. Payphone costs begin at 50 cents, but they can be hard to find. For collect or other operator-assisted calls, dial "0" then the number you wish to reach. Dial "1" (Ottawa +613, Montréal +514 or +438, Vancouver +604 or +778, Victoria +250, Winnipeg +204, Toronto +416 or 647, Québec City +418) for long-distance calls charged to the originating phone. In most parts of the country, for a

⊙ Time zones

Canada straddles six time zones. Daylight saving time begins the second Sunday in March and ends the first Sunday in November, but is not observed in Saskatchewan.

Pacific Standard Time
(8 hours behind GMT) The Yukon, B.C. (Alaska time is one hour behind the Yukon.)

Mountain Standard Time
(7 hours behind GMT) Alberta, western N.W.T.

Central Standard Time
(6 hours behind GMT) Saskatchewan, Manitoba, central N.W.T., western Nunavut.

Eastern Standard Time
(5 hours behind GMT) Ontario, Québec, eastern N.W.T., eastern Nunavut.

Atlantic Standard Time
(4 hours behind GMT) New Brunswick, P.E.I., Nova Scotia, most of Labrador.

Newfoundland Standard Time
(3.5 hours behind GMT; half an hour ahead of Atlantic Standard Time) Newfoundland (including part of Labrador).

Religious Services

Roman Catholics are the largest religious group in Québec, and a significant proportion of the population across the rest of the country, with Protestants in second place. Muslims, Sikhs, Hindus, Buddhists, and Jews are also represented. Any hotel concierge will direct you to the nearest place of worship.

☉ The provinces

Alberta: (*abbreviated* AB)
Capital: Edmonton
Size: 661,190 sq km
(255,310 sq miles)
Area Code: Calgary and southern Alberta 403 and 587; Edmonton and northern Alberta 780 and 587
Postal Address: AB

British Columbia: (BC)
Capital: Victoria
Size: 947,800 sq km
(365,980 sq miles)
Area Code: Vancouver and southwestern section 604 and 778; remainder, including Vancouver Island 250
Postal Address: BC

Manitoba: (MB)
Capital: Winnipeg
Size: 649,950 sq km
(250,970 sq miles)
Area Code: 204 and 431
Postal Address: MB

New Brunswick: (NB)
Capital: Fredericton
Size: 73,440 sq km
(28,360 sq miles)
Area Code: 506 unless stated
Postal Address: NB

Newfoundland and Labrador: (NL)
Capital: St John's
Size: 405,720 sq km
(156,600 sq miles)
Area Code: 709 unless stated
Postal Address: NL

Northwest Territories: (NT)
Capital: Yellowknife
Size: 1,171,920 sq km
(452,480 sq miles)
Area Code: 867
Postal Address: NT

Nova Scotia: (NS)
Capital: Halifax
Size: 55,490 sq km
(21,430 sq miles)

Area Code: 902 unless stated
Postal Address: NS

Nunavut: (NU)
Capital: Iqaluit
Size: 1,900,000 sq km
(733,600 sq miles)
Area Code: 867
Postal Address: NU

Ontario: (ON)
Capital: Toronto
Size: 1,068,580 sq km
(412,610 sq miles)
Area Code: Toronto 416 or 647, Ottawa 613, plus several others for smaller communities: 807, 705, 226, 519, 905, 289, 705
Postal Address: ON

Prince Edward Island: (PE)
Capital: Charlottetown
Size: 5,660 sq km
(2,190 sq miles)
Area Code: 902 with Nova Scotia
Postal Address: PE

Québec: (QC)
Capital: Québec City
Size: 1,540,680 sq km
(594,900 sq miles)
Area Code: Montréal 514 or 438; Québec City and Eastern Québec 418; Southern Québec 450; rest of Québec 819
Postal Address: QC

Saskatchewan: (SK)
Capital: Regina
Size: 652,330 sq km
(251,880 sq miles)
Area Code: 306
Postal Address: SK

The Yukon: (YT)
Capital: Whitehorse
Size: 483,450 sq km
(186,680 sq miles)
Area Code: 867 with the Northwest Territories and Nunavut
Postal Address: YT

local call, you must also dial the area code, even though the call is not long distance: it's a result of so many new phones over the past 10 years.

The first pages in public phone books explain everything you need to know, including emergency numbers, North American area codes, and long-distance country codes.

Toll-Free Numbers

Any phone numbers beginning with 1-800, 1-855, 1-866, 1-877 or 1-888 are toll-free if dialed within Canada

and, frequently, North America, from a land line. Sometimes, hotels and other businesses have two toll-free lines, one for calling from the US and one for calling from within Canada. If calling from outside North America, it's best to try the local 10-digit numbers.

Tourist Information

One of the smartest things you can do upon arrival in Canada is to go to the nearest tourist information center. Aside from being able to answer questions, they distribute

travel brochures and maps on areas of interest to you. Or, if you are really organized, you can order brochures online and they will be mailed to you. Each province and territory also has a toll-free number for tourist information (see the following list). For general information on traveling in Canada you can contact:

Canadian Tourism Commission Destination Canada
800–1045 Howe Street, Vancouver, British Columbia, V6Z 2A9; www.canada.travel and www.destinationcanada.com

Canadian consulates in foreign countries also provide some travel information. See the Useful Addresses section for further details. Some provinces maintain tourist offices in foreign cities.

Alberta

Travel Alberta publishes accommodations and campground guides. Updated annually, they list approved hotels, motels, campgrounds, and resorts. For this, and more specific information, contact:

Travel Alberta
Tel: 780-427-4321/1-800-ALBERTA; www.travelalberta.com

Tourism Calgary
200–238 11th Ave SE, Calgary, AB T2G 0X8, tel: 403-263-8510/1-800-661-1678; www.visitcalgary.com

For comprehensive information about the provincial capital, contact: **Edmonton Tourism,** West Shaw Building, 9797 Jasper Avenue, Edmonton, AB T5J 0C5, tel: 780-782-8034; www.exploreedsmonton.com.

British Columbia

Traveling in British Columbia is simplified by the numerous free guides offered by the province and individual cities.

Tourism British Columbia
Tel: 250-356-6363/1-800-435-5622; www.hellobc.com

Most communities operate Travel InfoCenters at least during the tourism season. In the major cities they are:

Tourism Vancouver
Plaza Level, 200 Burrard St, Vancouver, BC V6C 3L6, tel: 604-682-2222; www.tourismvancouver.com

Tourism Victoria
812 Wharf St, Victoria, BC V8W 1T3, tel: 1-800-663-3883; www.tourismvictoria.com

Manitoba

A variety of Manitoba travel guides are available online and in the form of brochures from:
Travel Manitoba
21 Forks Market Road, Winnipeg, MB R3C 4T7, tel: 204-927-7800/1-800-665-0040; www.travelmanitoba.com

New Brunswick

For road maps, assistance in choosing accommodations, suggestions for itineraries in New Brunswick or a copy of the New Brunswick Touring Guide and Travel Map contact:
Tourism New Brunswick
Box 6000, Fredericton, NB E3B 5H1, tel: 1-800-561-0123; www.tourismnewbrunswick.ca

Newfoundland and Labrador

For complete information about traveling in Newfoundland write to:
Department of Business, Tourism, Culture and Rural Development
PO Box 8700, St John's, NL A1B 4J6, tel: 709-729-2830/1-800-563-6353; www.newfoundlandlabrador.com

Northwest Territories

This territory distributes a yearly *Explorers' Guide*, a listing of hotels, lodges, restaurants, and activities. This, and more information, is available from:
NWT Tourism
Box 610, Yellowknife, NT X1A 2N5, tel: 867-873-7200/1-800-661-0788; www.spectacularnwt.com

Nova Scotia

For information about Nova Scotia and to download a variety of travel guides:
Tourism Nova Scotia
PO Box 667, 8 Water Street, Windsor, NS B0N 2T0, tel: 902-425-5781/1-800-565-0000; www.novascotia.com

Nunavut

Nunavut produces several comprehensive guides to help with the selection of outfitters and packages, as well as ideas for the independent traveler. Further information is available from:
Nunavut Tourism
Box 1450, Iqaluit, NU X0A 0H0, tel: toll-free: 1-866-686-2888 in Canada; 1-800-491-7910 internationally; www.nunavuttourism.com

Ontario

It takes a comprehensive travel bureau to describe and explain all that this province has to offer, but Ontario Travel fits the bill. To contact them, call toll-free from Canada or the continental US 1-800-668-2746. Write to:
Ontario Tourism Marketing Partnership Corp.
10 Dundas St E, Suite 900, Toronto, ON M7A 2A1; www.ontariotravel.net

Ontario Travel booklets and brochures explain nearly every facet of traveling the province. Among these are:

The road map
Guides featuring all the coolest places to play and stay, including information on winter destinations and experiences.
Individual event guides for spring and summer, with dates, locations, and brief event descriptions.
Individual experience guides for spring and summer, outlining all that the province has to offer at this time of year.

Ontario Travel also operate a number of travel information centers, open year-round; most have currency exchanges. The four listed here are all at border points; there are others at Toronto, St Catharines, Tilbury, Bainsville, and Barrie.
Niagara Falls, 5355 Stanley Ave, Hwy 420, west from Rainbow Bridge
Sarnia, 1455 Venetian Blvd, at the Blue Water Bridge
Sault Ste Marie, 261 Queen St W, at the International Bridge
Windsor Park, 110 Park St E, at the Windsor/Detroit Tunnel
For information on diverse outdoor adventure experiences from canoeing to hiking, biking, snowmobiling, etc., contact Nature and Outdoor Tourism Ontario.
Algoma Kinniwabi Travel Association
334 Bay St, Sault Ste Marie, ON P6A 1X1, tel: 1-800-263-2546; www.algomacountry.com
Georgian Triangle Tourist Association
45 St. Paul Street, Collingwood, ON L9Y 3P1, tel: 705-445-7722/1-888-227-8667; www.visitsouthgeorgianbay.ca
Muskoka Tourism
1342 Hwy 11 North, Kilworthy, ON P0E 1G0, tel: 1-800-267-9700; www.discovermuskoka.ca
Niagara Falls Tourism
6815 Stanley Ave, Niagara Falls, ON L2G 7B6, tel: 905-356-6061/1-800-563-2557; www.niagarafallstourism.com
Niagara Parks Commission
7400 Portage Rd S, Box 150, Niagara Falls, ON L2E 6T2, tel: 1-877 642 7275 www.niagaraparks.com

North of Superior Tourism Association
52 Front St, Nipigon, ON P0T 2J0, tel: 807-887-3188; www.nosta.on.ca
Northwest Ontario's Sunset Country Travel Association
Box 647W, Kenora, ON P9N 3X6, tel: 807-468-5853/1-800-665-7567; www.ontariossunsetcountry.ca
The Online guide to Ontario Tourism: www.realontario.ca
Ottawa Tourism
150 Elgin Street, Suite 1405, Ottawa, ON K2P 1L4 130, tel: 613-237-5150/1-833-864-7839; www.ottawatourism.ca
Tourism Kingston
945 Princess St, Kingston, ON K7L 0E9, tel: 613-548-4415, 1-888-855-4555; www.visitkingston.ca
Tourism Toronto
P.O. Box 126, 207 Queen's Quay West, Toronto, ON M5J 1A7, tel: 416-203-2500/1-800-499-2514; www.seetorontonow.com
Tourism Windsor Essex Pelee Island
333 Riverside Dr. W, Ste 103, Windsor, ON N9A 7C5, tel: 1-800-265-3633; www.visitwindsoressex.com

Prince Edward Island

The **Visitor Information Centers** at Confederation Bridge and Wood Islands ferry terminal are extremely helpful. For advance information on what's on offer on the island you can write to:
Tourism PEI
Box 2000, Charlottetown, PE C1A 7N8, tel: 902-437-8570/1-800-463-4734; www.tourismpei.com

Québec

Québec is divided into 17 regional tourist associations, each of which is eager to offer information and tours to visitors to the region. Contact:
Tourisme Québec
tel: 514-873-2015/1-877-266-5687; www.quebecoriginal.com
For information on Montréal contact:
Tourisme Montréal
1255 Peel St., Suite 100 in the downtown, tel: 514-844 5400/1-877-266-5687; www.mtl.org
Québec City Tourism
12 rue Sainte-Anne, Québec, QC G1R 3X2, tel: 418-641-6290/1-877-783-1608; www.quebecregion.com

Saskatchewan

Tourism Saskatchewan offers two guides, lists accommodations and

Many tour packages feature a cruise along Canada's shores.

provides additional information concerning campgrounds, parks, resorts, and outfitters. For further details contact:
Tourism Saskatchewan
189-1621 Albert St, Regina, SK S4P 2S5, tel: 306-787-9600/1-877-237-2273; www.tourismsaskatchewan.com

The Yukon
Tourism Yukon offers a useful publication, *Yukon Vacation Guide*, listing lodgings, restaurants, service stations, campsites, and outdoor adventure guides and tour operators. Contact: Box 2703, Whitehorse, Yukon, Y1A 2C6, tel: 1-800-661-0494; or order online at www.travelyukon.com

Tour Operators

Canada
With the effectiveness of the internet in marketing, there are many Canadian-based tour operators who serve visitors from all over the world, particularly for specialty adventure packages for the North.
For hiking, biking, and kayaking in Rocky Mountains, Western Canada, Newfoundland, the Arctic:
G Adventures
19 Charlotte St, Toronto, Ontario M5V 2H5, tel: 416-260-0999/1-888-800-4100; www.gadventures.com
Adventure Canada
14 Front St S, Mississauga, Ontario L5H 2C4, tel: 905-271-4000/1-800-363-7566; www.adventurecanada.com Northwest Passage and circumnavigation of Newfoundland, among other Arctic tours.
For kayaking tours or straightforward boat rentals on the east coast of Vancouver Island, try Comox Valley Kayaks & Canoes, 2020 Cliffe Ave, Courtenay, BC V9N 2L3, tel: 1-888-545-5595; www.comoxvalleykayaks.com

USA
There are many Canadian tour packages offered by US tour operators; the United States Tour Operators Association has a comprehensive listing of US tour operators; visit their website at www.ustoa.com, or contact them at 345 Seventh Avenue, Suite 1801, New York, NY 10001.
The following list of tour operators gives a flavor of the destinations and activities that Canada has to offer:
Arctic Odysseys
3409 E Madison, Seattle, WA 98112, tel: 206-325-1977/1-800-574-3021; www.arcticodysseys.com
World on Skis
250 Moonachie Rd, 4th Floor, Moonachie NJ 07074, tel: 201-228-5300/1-866-678-5858; www.worldonskis.com
The following tour operators offer vacations with limited impact on the Canadian environment:

Black Spruce Tours has customized tours to the Maritime Provinces, Québec, Newfoundland, and Labrador. Contact:
Fred Vidito, 58 Woodland Drive, Sag Harbor, New York 11963, tel: 631-725-1493; www.blacksprucetours.com
For hiking, biking, and kayaking in Rocky Mountains, western Canada, Newfoundland, the Arctic:
G Adventures
Tel: 212 228 6655/1-888 800 4100; www.gadventures.com

UK
For further details on UK tour operators, visit Destination Canada's site, http://uk-keepexploring.canada.travel.
For tours to **Canada's North**:
Arctic Experience/Discover the World
8 Bolters Lane, Banstead, Surrey SM7 2AR, tel: 01737-886160; www.discover-the-world.co.uk/en/destinations/canada
For tours to **B.C.** and **Alberta** for 18- to 35-year-olds:
Contiki Holidays
Tel: +41 22 929 9216 from Europe; www.contiki.com
Ski trips to Québec, Ontario, Manitoba, Alberta, B.C., and the Yukon are the focus of:
Frontier Ski/Frontier Adventures
61a High Street, Orpington, Kent BR6 0JF, tel: 020-8776 8709; www.frontier-ski.co.uk
Travelpack
523 High Road, Wembley, Middlesex HA0 2DH, tel: 020-8585 4080; www.travelpack.com

---

⊘ Useful addresses

Travelers who want to plan ahead can do so by writing to the Canadian embassy or consulate in their own country for information. Listed below are the addresses and telephone numbers of a selection of embassies and consulates where tourist information may be available:
Australia Canadian High Commission in Canberra, Commonwealth Avenue, Canberra ACT 2600, tel: +61-2-6270-4000; www.australia.gc.ca
There is a Canadian consulate in Sydney and Perth, see above website for further details.
France Canadian Embassy, 130 Rue du Faubourg Saint-Honore, 75008 Paris, tel: +33-1-44-43-29-00; www.france.gc.ca

UK Canadian High Commission Consular and Passport Section, Canada House, Trafalgar Square, Pall Mall E, London SW1Y 5BJ, tel: +44-20-7004 6000; www.unitedkingdom.gc.ca
US Embassy of Canada, 501 Pennsylvania Ave NW, Washington, DC 20001, tel: 202-682-1740; www.washington.gc.ca
There are Canadian consulates in many major American cities, including:
1251 Avenue of the Americas, New York 10020-1175, tel: 212-596-1628
2 Prudential Plaza, 180 North Stetson Ave, Ste 2400, Chicago, IL, tel: 312-616-1860
1501 4th Ave, Ste 600, Seattle, WA, 98101, tel: 206-443-1777

Offers escorted tours, coach and rail tours, self-drive itineraries, adventure and city packages across the country.

Eco-tours to all parts of the country are offered by:

Windows on the Wild
2 Oxford House, 24 Oxford Rd North, London W4 4DH, tel: 020-8742 1556; www.windowsonthewild.com

Committed **anglers** may want to consider:

Anglers World Holidays
46 Knifesmithgate, Chesterfield, Derbyshire S40 1RQ, tel: 01246 221717; www.anglersworld.tv

Visas and Passports

US citizens traveling by air between the US and Canada must present a current passport or other approved travel document. Amtrak also requires a current passport, if traveling by rail between the US and Canada. For those traveling by land, rules are constantly changing, so it's important to check with both Canadian and American border regulatory agencies (what may be sufficient to enter Canada may not be sufficient to return to the US). Residents of other countries must carry a passport. In some cases a visa is also required. Since March 2016, visa-exempt travelers who plan to enter Canada by air need an eTA, a new electronic document. To obtain it, log onto www.cic.gc.ca/english/visit/eta-start.asp. Prospective visitors who are in any doubt about which documents they will need should check with the nearest Canadian consulate. For more information, call 204-983-3500 (outside Canada), 1-800-461-9999 (within Canada), or visit www.cbsa.gc.ca.

Visitors may be asked to produce return tickets and possibly evidence that they have the funds to support themselves while in Canada.

Non-Canadian visitors going from Canada to the US, however briefly, will require a passport with at least six months' validity. Visitors from some countries may also require a visa. Check this with the nearest US consulate before leaving home.

What to Wear

Visitors to urban and resort areas from Europe or the US should be perfectly comfortable in the clothes they wear at home under similar circumstances. Visitors planning a canoeing or hiking trip should bring suitable layers of clothing, including warm and waterproof garments, as weather conditions change rapidly.

☉ What's On Listings

Besides local newspapers, most cities have publications, usually free, which provide up-to-the-minute information on theater, concerts, clubs, festivals, and anything else of interest to locals and visitors. Some of the main publications, both in print and/or online are:
Where Magazine www.where.ca – distributed through hotels in Halifax, Ottawa, Toronto, Muskoka, Winnipeg, Calgary, Edmonton, Canadian Rockies, Vancouver, Victoria, Whistler, and the Yukon. www.dose.ca covers Halifax, Montréal, Toronto, Ottawa, Winnipeg, Edmonton, Calgary, Vancouver, Victoria, and Whistler. *Now Magazine* is a Toronto-area weekly that provides online coverage as well: www.nowtoronto.com. *The Georgia Straight* is by far the best way to find out what is happening in Vancouver – it is produced every Thursday and found on street corners all over town; it's updated daily online at www.straight.com.
The most well-known Montreal publications have shuttered in recent years but *Cult MTL* offers a daily web site and monthly printed version focused on Montreal culture. It is run by former *Mirror* employees. www.cultmtl.com
The Coast provides coverage on Halifax at www.thecoast.ca.
Winnipeg Free Press, an online source of what's on in Winnipeg, at www.winnipegfreepress.com.
Prairie Dog Magazine, Regina's only news, arts, and entertainment magazine, is distributed free throughout downtown, www.prairiedogmag.com.

☉ Weights and measures

Canada uses the metric system, but many things are still expressed in the imperial system and older people frequently speak of "miles" and "pounds." For example, if you ask directions, someone over 55 will probably tell you how far away something is in miles or, if it is closer, in yards. In grocery stores, as often as not, you will see both the price per pound and the price per kilogram or per 100 grams.
1 centimeter (cm) = 0.394ins
1 kilometer (km) = 0.621 miles
1 liter = 0.22 UK gallon
1 liter = 0.26 US gallon (g)
1 kilogram = 2.2lbs

In winter, wind chill can make it seem much colder than the actual temperature, leading to frostbite. Tourists planning to ski, hike, or take part in any other outdoor activity should wear very warm clothing and be prepared to cover exposed skin. Canadians wear both synthetic and non-synthetic clothing in layers to retain heat.

Women Travelers

Canada is probably one of the safest countries in the world for women to travel alone. With so many women traveling on business, hotels and restaurants are fully accustomed to seeing women on their own and are becoming increasingly sensitive to their concerns. Provided a female traveler follows a common sense-based code of conduct, the chances of running into a problem should be minimal.

Some city hotels have recently introduced "singles" tables in their dining rooms, at which hotel guests can ask to be seated – this is a civilized way to encounter other single travelers in a "safe" environment. The hotel's concierge is also likely to be a reliable source of information on suitable or safe places to go and acceptable routes to get there. There are places where single women at night will feel out of their comfort zone, and personal theft of articles, particularly purses in restaurants, is on the increase. The safest thing to do is place your handbag on your lap while sitting in a restaurant.

LANGUAGE

ENGLISH

Though Canada is officially bilingual, English is the language of choice throughout most of the country outside Québec and some relatively small sections of the Atlantic Provinces, Ontario, and Manitoba. Canadians speak with their own distinct accent, but written Canadian English is very similar to that of Great Britain. Americans will note the British spellings, often in such words as "labour" and "centre," and usage, such as "railway" instead of "railroad."

NEWFOUNDLAND ENGLISH

Newfoundlanders speak a dialect all of their own. The accent is vaguely Irish, but the idioms and expressions are truly unique:
"Go to the law with the devil and hold court in hell" – the odds are against you
"To have a noggin to scrape" – an extremely difficult task
"Pigs may fly but they are very unlikely birds" – a vain hope
"in a hobble" – not worrying
"he is moidering my brains" – he is disturbing me
"Long may your big good jib draw" – good luck

FRENCH

Pronunciation

Even if you speak no French at all it is worth trying to master a few simple phrases. The fact that you have made an effort is likely to get you a better response. Pronunciation is key; they really will not understand if you get it very wrong. Remember to emphasize each syllable, not to pronounce the last consonant of a word as a rule (this includes the plural "s"),

and always to drop your "h"s at the beginning of a word. Whether to use "vous" or "tu" is a vexed question; increasingly the familiar form of "tu" is used by many people, much more frequently than in France. However, it is better to be too formal, and use "vous" if in doubt. It is important to be polite; always address people as Madame or Monsieur, and address them by their surnames until you are confident first names are acceptable.

Learning the pronunciation of the French alphabet is a good idea and, in particular, learn to spell your name.

Montréal claims to be the second-largest French-speaking city in the world, after Paris. Some 52 percent of the city's residents and 68 percent of those in the metropolitan area are French-speakers (francophones), with 17 percent and 12 percent English-speakers (anglophones) respectively.

Unique to Montréal is joual, a patois whose name is derived from French for horse: cheval. The earthy dialect flourishes among the city's working class and in the work of playwright Michel Tremblay.

The French spoken in Québec also differs rather dramatically from any other French spoken in the world. Accents distinguish French in Québec from French in Paris or Marseilles. Québec's francophones form sounds deep in the throat, lisp slightly, voice toward diphthongs, and bend single vowels into exotic shapes. While it has also incorporated some English words, such as "chum," as in mon chum or ma chumme, and blonde, for girlfriend, many of the English words used in France are definitely not used here. For example, "le parking" in France is "le stationnement" and "le weekend" is "la fin de semaine."

Even if you don't speak much French, starting a conversation with "Bonjour," is likely to evoke a positive response. Some shopkeepers hedge, with an all-purpose: "Bonjour-Hi."

French Words and Phrases

How much is it? *C'est combien?*
What is your name? *Comment vous appelez-vous?*
My name is... *Je m'appelle...*
Do you speak English? *Parlez-vous anglais?*
I am English/American *Je suis anglais/américain*
I don't understand *Je ne comprends pas*
Please speak more slowly *Parlez plus lentement, s'il vous plaît*
Can you help me? *Pouvez-vous m'aider?*
I'm looking for... *Je cherche...*
Where is...? *Où est...?*
I'm sorry *Excusez-moi/Pardon*
I don't know *Je ne sais pas*
No problem *Pas de problème*
Have a good day! *Bonne journée!*
That's it *C'est ça*
Here it is *Voici*
There it is *Voilà*
Let's go *On y va/Allons-y*
See you tomorrow *A demain*
See you soon *A bientôt*
Show me the word in the book *Montrez-moi le mot dans le livre*
At what time? *A quelle heure?*
When? *Quand?*
What time is it? *Quelle heure est-il?*
yes *oui*
no *non*
please *s'il vous plaît*
thank you *merci*
(very much) *(beaucoup)*
you're welcome *de rien*
excuse me *excusez-moi*
hello *bonjour*
OK *d'accord*
goodbye *au revoir*
good evening *bonsoir*
here *ici*
there *là*
today *aujourd'hui*
yesterday *hier*
tomorrow *demain*
now *maintenant*
later *plus tard*
right away *tout de suite*

⊘ Emergencies

Help! *Au secours!/A l'aide!*
Stop! *Arrêtez!*
Call a doctor *Appelez un médecin*
Call an ambulance *Appelez une ambulance*
Call the police *Appelez la police*
Call the fire brigade *Appelez les pompiers*
Where is the nearest telephone? *Où est le téléphone le plus proche?*
Where is the nearest hospital? *Où est l'hôpital le plus proche?*
I am sick *Je suis malade*
I have lost my passport/wallet *J'ai perdu mon passeport/porte-monnaie*

this morning *ce matin*
this afternoon *cet après-midi*
this evening *ce soir*

On Arrival

I want to get off at... *Je voudrais descendre à...*
What street is this? *Quel est le nom de cette rue?*
How far is...? *A quelle distance se trouve...?*
airport *l'aéroport*
train station *la gare de train*
bus station *la gare routière*
bus stop *l'arret de bus*
platform *le quai*
ticket *le billet*
return ticket *aller-retour*
toilets *les toilettes*
This is the hotel address *C'est l'adresse de l'hôtel*
bed *le lit*
key *la clé*
air conditioned *air climatisé*

Dining Out

Table d'hôte *set menu at a set price.*
Prix fixe *is a fixed-price menu.*
À la carte *dishes from the menu are charged separately.*
breakfast *le petit déjeuner*
lunch *le déjeuner*
dinner *le dîner*
meal *le repas*
first course *l'entrée/les hors d'œuvre*
main course *le plat principal*
made to order *sur commande*
drink included *boisson comprise*
wine list *la carte des vins*
the bill *l'addition*
fork *la fourchette*
knife *le couteau*
spoon *la cuillère*
plate *l'assiette*

glass *le verre*
napkin *la serviette*
ashtray *le cendrier*

Viande (Meat)

bleu *rare*
à point *medium*
bien cuit *well done*
grillé *grilled*
agneau *lamb*
bifteck *steak*
boudin *sausage*
brochette *kebab*
caille *quail*
canard *duck*
carré d'agneau *rack of lamb*
chateaubriand *thick steak*
entrecôte *beef rib steak*
faux-filet *sirloin*
foie *liver*
foie de veau *calf's liver*
foie gras *goose or duck liver pâté*
grillade *grilled meat*
jambon *ham*
lapin *rabbit*
lardons *cubes of diced bacon*
magret de canard *breast of duck*
oie *goose*
perdrix *partridge*
pintade *guinea fowl*
porc *pork*
poulet *chicken*
poussin *young chicken*
rognons *kidneys*
rôti *roast*
veau *veal*
viande hachée *minced meat*

Poissons (Fish)

anchois *anchovies*
anguille *eel*
bar (or **loup**) *sea bass*
cabillaud *cod*
calmars *squid*
coquillage *shellfish*
coquilles Saint-Jacques *scallops*
crevette *shrimp*
fruits de mer *seafood*
homard *lobster*
huître *oyster*
langoustine *large prawn*
lotte *monkfish*
moule *mussel*
raie *skate*
saumon *salmon*
thon *tuna*
truite *trout*

Légumes (Vegetables)

ail *garlic*
artichaut *artichoke*
asperge *asparagus*
avocat *avocado*
champignon *mushroom*
crudités *raw vegetables*

épinards **spinach**
frites **french fries, chips**
haricots verts **green beans**
lentilles **lentils**
oignon **onion**
poireau **leek**
pois **pea**
poivron **bell pepper**
pomme de terre **potato**
salade verte **green salad**

Dessert

clafoutis **traditional baked custard with cherries**
coulis **purée of fruit or vegetables**
crème anglaise **custard**
crème caramel **caramel custard**
crème Chantilly **whipped cream**
fromage **cheese**
gâteau **cake**
tarte tatin **upside down tart of caramelized apples**

Drinks

drinks *les boissons*
coffee *café*
with milk or cream *au lait* or *crème*
decaffeinated *déca/décaféiné*
black espresso *express/noir*
American filtered coffee *filtre*
tea *thé*
milk *lait*
mineral water *eau minérale*
fizzy *pétillante*
non-fizzy *plate*
fizzy lemonade *limonade*
fresh lemon juice served with sugar *citron pressé*
fresh squeezed orange juice *orange pressée*
fresh or cold *frais, fraîche*
beer *bière*
pre-dinner drink *apéritif*
with ice *avec des glaçons*
sparkling wine *vin pétillant*
house wine *vin de maison*
local wine *vin régional*
after-dinner drink *digestif*
cheers! *santé!*

⊘ The Inuit language

There is little available literature on the Inuktitut Inuit language, but there are more and more resources online to expand the number of people with access to learning tools. The best guide to the language and culture is *The Inuit of Canada*, published by Inuit Tapiriit Kanatami, 75 Alberta St, Ste 1101, Ottawa, Ontario K1P 5E7, tel: 613-238-8181.

Canada has a strong literary tradition. Among the best-known writers are Nobel Prize (2013) and Man Booker prize winner Alice Munro (*Friend of My Youth, Runaway*), Man Booker prize winners Michael Ondaatje (*The English Patient*), Jann Martel (*The Life of Pi*), and Margaret Atwood (*The Handmaid's Tale, The Blind Assassin*). Over the past several decades, the multicultural face of Canada has found its outlet in literature through authors such as Joseph Boyden, Rohinton Mistry, Jane Urquhart, Wayson Choy, Douglas Coupland, M.G. Vassanji, Gabrielle Roy, and Elizabeth Hay. Each writes with a strong sense of place – the geography of Canada is often as much a character as the protagonist.

GENERAL

Through Black Spruce by Joseph Boyden. An unforgettable novel about contemporary aboriginal life, with the contrast of forest and city framing this powerful story.
The Call of the Wild is one of Jack London's best-loved masterpieces, dating back to 1903. It is an adventure story set in the Yukon gold rush, depicting the unquenchable spirit of Buck, a kidnapped dog trying to survive in the harshest of environments. Despite its antiquity, this book remains a classic in the adventure genre.
The Apprenticeship of Duddy Kravitz by Mordecai Richler. Set in Montréal, Richler depicts the sheer determination of a working-class Jew to "make it" in a white Anglo-Saxon world.
Beautiful Losers by Leonard Cohen. Although the world-famous singer/songwriter is best known for his music, the Montréal native started his career as a poet back in the 1960s. He has written well over a dozen books, this one examining the cultural forces that have shaped his city.
I Married the Klondike by Laura Beatrice Berton is a memoir of her life in the mining town of Dawson City in the Yukon, from her arrival as a single, 29-year-old kindergarten teacher in 1907, at the end of the gold rush, to her reluctant departure as a wife and mother in 1934.
Late Nights on Air by Elizabeth Hay. A delightful read, with lovable if sometimes pathetic characters living in the magic of the North. The descriptions of the land and the impact of outside development are interspersed with an appealing dark humor.
Innovation Nation: Canadian Leadership from Java to Jurassic Park by Leonard Brody, Ken Grant, and Matthew Holland. Designed to cut through traditional Canadian modesty, this book looks at how over 30 Canadian innovators have redefined the landscape of business in the global technology sector.
Random Passage by Bernice Morgan. The epic story of an Irishwoman, Mary Brundle, and her perilous odyssey from a harsh English workhouse to the remote Newfoundland outport of Cape Random – a struggling settlement forced to be a community through the sheer will to survive.
Still at the Cottage by Charles Gordon. A funny yet affectionate look at cottage life, one of the enduring elements of the Canadian psyche.
The Colony of Unrequited Love by Wayne Johnston. A gripping novel about Joey Smallwood, the true-life controversial politician who was responsible for bringing Newfoundland into the confederation of Canada in 1949. It helps those "from away" understand better the quandaries faced by the proud and passionate Newfoundlanders.
The Handmaid's Tale by Margaret Atwood. This dystopian novel about a United States that has been overthrown by a totalitarian theonomy, entered the cultural zeitgeist following the 2018 HBO series. Atwood's other books, including *Oryx and Crake* and *The Blind Assassin*, are recommended.
This is my Country, What's Yours? A Literary Atlas of Canada by Noah Richler. Originally a CBC radio documentary, Noah Richler interviewed the who's who of Canadian literature about the places and ideas that are most meaningful to their work, to create a bold cultural portrait of contemporary Canada.
Two Solitudes by Hugh MacLennan. This novel, first published in 1945, has become such a classic that the title has moved into common parlance to describe the linguistic and cultural conflicts between Canada's two founding nations.
Who Has Seen the Wind by W.O. Mitchell. First printed in 1947, this is a classic tale of a boy growing up on the prairies of Saskatchewan during the Depression years. Mitchell presents an evocative glimpse of small-town life and death as seen through a child's eyes.

⊘ Send us your thoughts

We do our best to ensure the information in our books is as accurate and up-to-date as possible. The books are updated on a regular basis using local contacts, who painstakingly add, amend and correct as required. However, some details (such as telephone numbers and opening times) are liable to change, and we are ultimately reliant on our readers to put us in the picture.
We welcome your feedback, especially your experience of using the book "on the road". Maybe you came across a great bar or new attraction we missed.
We will acknowledge all contributions, and we'll offer an Insight Guide to the best letters received.

Please write to us at:
Insight Guides
PO Box 7910
London SE1 1WE

Or email us at:
hello@insightguides.com

HISTORY

A Short History of Canada by Desmond Morton. This readable book succeeds at teaching what history classes in school never did.

Canada: A People's History, Vol. I and II by Don Gillmor, Achille Michaud, and Pierre Turgeon. These richly illustrated books tell the epic story of how Canada came to be the nation we know, from its earliest days.

The Arctic Grail: The Quest for the Northwest Passage and the North Pole, 1818–1909 by Pierre Berton. One of Canada's most popular chroniclers, Berton's wonderful storytelling style and excellent research brings to life the explorers who traveled the Arctic, often with disastrous results.

Passages: Welcome Home to Canada is an anthology of essays by immigrants – now public figures and authors – to Canada. It examines the concept of home and how the experience of being an immigrant is increasingly the binding Canadian experience.

A Flag for Canada: The Illustrated Biography of the Maple Leaf Flag by Rick Archbold. Since its birth in February 1965, the red-and-white Maple Leaf has become one of the world's great flags. This intriguing story reflects the history of the country as seen through the evolution of Canada's national symbol.

A Fair Country: Telling Truths About Canada by John Ralston Saul. Making an argument that the Métis nation and the aboriginal way of thinking had as much impact on the growth of Canada as that of the English and French, Saul writes that Canada's future rests upon the need to recognize and value the First

Nations' original contributions to the country.

LANGUAGE

French Fun: The Real Spoken Language of Quebec by Steve Timmins. Written by an Ontario translator who now lives in Montréal, it takes a humorous look at the colorful idioms in common use.

The Dictionary of Newfoundland English, edited by G.M. Story, W.J. Kirwin, and J.D.A. Widdowson. First published in 1982 to widespread acclaim, this historical dictionary focuses on the varieties of English spoken in Newfoundland over the last four centuries. An entertaining book, it offers a wide view of the island's unique culture.

TRAVEL LITERATURE

Smalltown Canada by Stuart McLean. A well-known author and radio host takes his readers on a cross-country tour of small-town life in seven communities across Canada, presenting a humorous, rich portrait of the people and their history.

Beauty Tips from Moose Jaw by Will Ferguson. A humorous account of the writer's three-year journey around Canada using every mode of transportation – from helicopter to canoe – imaginable.

The Good Life: Up the Yukon Without a Paddle by Dorian Amos. The story of a couple from England who decide to sell up and move to Canada in search of a better life and the people and problems they come across before finding the dream they were looking for.

City of Glass: Douglas Coupland's Vancouver by Douglas Coupland. The cult author turns his pen to his hometown.

Passage to Juneau: A Sea and Its Meaning by Jonathan Raban. Raban documents his 1,000-or-so-mile journey from Seattle up the Inside Passage to Alaska.

Sacré Blues: An Unsentimental Journey Through Québec by Taras Grescoe. A spicy, irreverent examination of a unique part of North America, with nary a mention of a politician. It explores the heart of contemporary Québec and how it relates to its neighbors.

OTHER INSIGHT GUIDES

Insight Guides

The Insight Guides series is the main series in the Insight stable, known for its superb pictures, in-depth background reading, detailed maps, excellent coverage of sights, and comprehensive listings section.

There are a number of **Insight Guides** to North America. Current titles include *Alaska*, and *USA On The Road*.

Insight City Guides

Insight City Guides are written by locally based writers, who show you how to make the most of the city.

There are Insight City Guides to North American cities including *Boston*, *Seattle*, and *Vancouver*.

Insight Fleximaps

There is also a **Insight Fleximap**, with clear cartography, travel information, and a laminated finish, available for *Toronto*.

CREDITS

INSIGHT GUIDE CREDITS

Distribution
UK, Ireland and Europe
Apa Publications (UK) Ltd;
sales@insightguides.com
United States and Canada
Ingram Publisher Services;
ips@ingramcontent.com
Australia and New Zealand
Woodslane; info@woodslane.com.au
Southeast Asia
Apa Publications (SN) Pte;
singaporeoffice@insightguides.com
Worldwide
Apa Publications (UK) Ltd;
sales@insightguides.com
Special Sales, Content Licensing and CoPublishing
Insight Guides can be purchased in bulk quantities at discounted prices. We can create special editions, personalised jackets and corporate imprints tailored to your needs.
sales@insightguides.com
www.insightguides.biz

Printed in China by CTPS

All Rights Reserved
© 2019 Apa Digital (CH) AG and
Apa Publications (UK) Ltd

First Edition 1978

Eleventh Edition 2019

www.insightguides.com

Editor: Tatiana Wilde
Author: Joanna Ebbutt, Gael Arthur
Updater: Magdalena Helsztyńska-Stadnik
Head of DTP and Pre-Press: Rebeka Davies
Managing Editor: Carine Tracanelli
Picture Editor: Tom Smyth
Cartography: original cartography Polyglott Kartographie, updated by Carte

CONTRIBUTORS

This eleventh edition of *Insight Guide Canada* was updated by **Magdalena Helsztyńska-Stadnik** and builds on the work of previous authors, including Toronto-based **Joanna Ebbutt** and Vancouver-based **Gael Arthur** as well as on the original edition, which was produced by **Andrew Eames** and **Hilary Cunningham**.

Contributors to previous editions also include: Michael Algar, Colette Copeland, Charles Foran, Geoff Hancock, Patrick Keyes, Philip Street, Malcolm MacRury, Matthew Parfitt, John Lucas; Anne Matthews, Diane Hall, John Loonam and David Dunbar.

ABOUT INSIGHT GUIDES

Insight Guides have more than 45 years' experience of publishing high-quality, visual travel guides. We produce 400 full-colour titles, in both print and digital form, covering more than 200 destinations across the globe, in a variety of formats to meet your different needs.
  Insight Guides are written by local authors, whose expertise is evident in the extensive historical and cultural background features. Each destination is carefully researched by regional experts to ensure our guides provide the very latest information. All the reviews in **Insight Guides** are independent; we strive to maintain an impartial view. Our reviews are carefully selected to guide you to the best places to eat, go out and shop, so you can be confident that when we say a place is special, we really mean it.

Legend

City maps

	Freeway/Highway/Motorway
	Divided Highway
	Main Roads
	Minor Roads
	Pedestrian Roads
	Steps
	Footpath
	Railway
	Funicular Railway
	Cable Car
	Tunnel
	City Wall
	Important Building
	Built Up Area
	Other Land
	Transport Hub
	Park
	Pedestrian Area
	Bus Station
	Tourist Information
	Main Post Office
	Cathedral/Church
	Mosque
	Synagogue
	Statue/Monument
	Beach
	Airport

Regional maps

	Freeway/Highway/Motorway (with junction)
	Freeway/Highway/Motorway (under construction)
	Divided Highway
	Main Road
	Secondary Road
	Minor Road
	Track
	Footpath
	International Boundary
	State/Province Boundary
	National Park/Reserve
	Marine Park
	Ferry Route
	Marshland/Swamp
	Glacier Salt Lake
	Airport/Airfield
	Ancient Site
	Border Control
	Cable Car
	Castle/Castle Ruins
	Cave
	Chateau/Stately Home
	Church/Church Ruins
	Crater
	Lighthouse
	Mountain Peak
	Place of Interest
	Viewpoint

INDEX

MAIN REFERENCES ARE IN BOLD TYPE

Ottawa

0   500
0   500 yd

Masson →

Rue Bernault

Rue Lambert

Blvd Fournier

Blvd Montclair

50

5

Rue St-Rédempteur

Blvd Sacré-Coeur

PARC
JACQUES-
CARTIER

Rivière des Outaouais

Ottawa

ROCKCLIFFE

Rockc

GATINEAU

Blvd St-Laurent

Rue St-Etienne

Blvd St-Laurent

Rue de Carillon

Rue Charlevoix

Rue Garneau

Rue Papineau

Rue St-Rédempteur

Rue Frontenac

Rue Vaudreuil

Rue Hôtel de

Rue Wright

Rue Wellington

Prom. du Portage

Rue Laval

Rue Kent

Rue Dollard

Rue Champlain

Rue Notre-Dame

Blvd Maisonneuve

Rue Laurier

Rue Laval

Rue Kent

Rue Champlain

Rue Notre-Dame

Ville

Rue Laurier

Pont Macdonald-Cartier Bridge

Québec
Ontario

Pont Alexandra Bridge

Sussex Dr.

Sussex Dr.

Green
Island

Maple
Island

STANLEY
PARK

Rideau

Union St

Crichton St

Mackay St

Minto Bridges

Stanley Ave

Thomas St

Sussex Dr.

Porte
Islan

Musée Canadien
de l'Histoire

Royal Canadian
Mint

Boteler St

Bolton St

Cathcart St

Bruyere St

St Andrew St

Dalhousie

St Patrick St

Old St Patrick St

Cobourg St

MACDONA
GARDE
PA

LOWER TOWN

National
Postal Museum

National Gallery
of Canada

Guigues Ave

St Patrick St

Murray St

Clarence St

York St

King Edward Ave

Nelson St

Cumberland St

George St

Rideau Canal

Canadian War Museum

Pont du Portage Bridge

Victoria
Island

National Library
of Canada

Supreme Court
of Canada

Parliament
Buildings

Chateau Laurier

ByWard
Market

Sussex Dr.

Rideau St

BRONSON
PARK

Wellington St

Sparks St

Confederation
Square

National Arts Centre

Besserer St

Daly Ave

Stewart St

Wilbrod St

Augusta St

Chapel St

Friel St

Queen St

Albert St

Slater St

Kent St

Bank St

O'Connor St

Queen St

Albert St

Slater St

Laurier Ave

Gloucester St

Nepean St

Lisgar St

Cooper St

Somerset St

Laurier Bridge

Laurier Ave

University
of
Ottawa

SANDY HILL

Laurier Ave

Gloucester St

Nepean St

Lisgar St

Cooper St

Somerset St

Elgin St

Queen Elizabeth Drwy

King Edward Ave

Henderson Ave

Nelson St

Sweetland Ave

Russel Ave

Chapel St

Blackburn Ave

Goulburn Ave

Marlborough Ave

Range Rd

Osgoode St

Somerset St

OTTAWA

Gilmour St

Lyon St

James St

Florence St

Gladstone Ave

McLeod St

Flora St

Arlington Ave

Bronson Ave

Percy

N. Cambridge St N.

McLaren St

Gilmour St

Metcalfe St

Cartier St

Prom. Col. By Dr.

Nicolas St

Waverly St

Templeton
St

Mann Ave

Lees Ave

Catherine St

Kent St

Bank St

O'Connor St

Gladstone Ave

McLeod St

Argyle Ave

Canadian Museum
of Nature

Prom. Colonel By Dr.

Nicolas St

Queensway

Chamberlain Ave

Queensway

Imprior

Isabella St

Strathcona Ave

Lees Ave

Hurdman Brid

Renfrew Ave

Powell Ave

Clemov Ave

Glebe Ave

1st Ave

Powell Ave

Clemov Ave

Glebe Ave

1st Ave

Monkland Ave

Linden Terr.

Evelyn Ave

Springhurst Ave

Main St

GLEBE

2nd Ave

3rd Ave

4th Ave

5th Ave

Chrysler St

Percy St S.

Lyon St S.

Bank St

O'Connor St

2nd Ave

3rd Ave

4th Ave

5th Ave

Prom. Queen Elizabeth Drwy

Prom. Col. By Dr.

McGillivray St

Drummond St

Main St

Clegg

Rideau

HURDMAN PARK

Holmwood Ave

Craig St

Ralph St

Monk St

Bank St

Holmwood Ave

Bower St

OTTAWA EAST

Riverside Dr.